I0836670

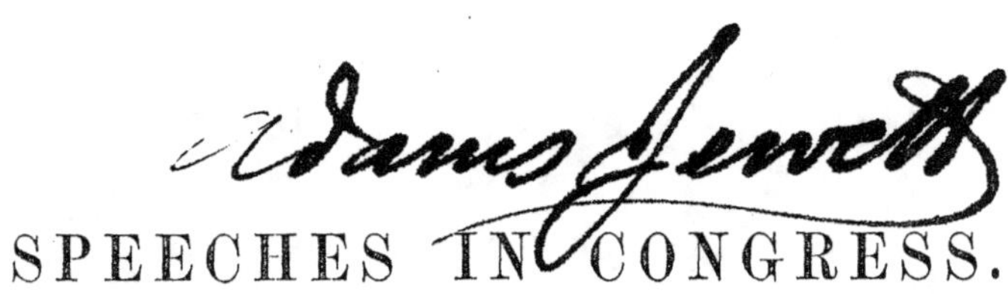

SPEECHES IN CONGRESS.

BY

JOSHUA R. GIDDINGS.

BOSTON:
PUBLISHED BY JOHN P. JEWETT AND COMPANY.
CLEVELAND, OHIO:
JEWETT, PROCTOR AND WORTHINGTON.
LONDON: SAMPSON LOW, SON & CO.
1853.

CAMBRIDGE:
ALLEN AND FARNHAM, PRINTERS.
REMINGTON STREET.

PREFACE.

WHEN, fifteen years since, I entered Congress, the nation was engaged in the Florida War. Our army was actively employed in capturing and returning fugitive slaves to their owners; and I then learned that hostilities had been commenced for that purpose; while the principal expense was expected to be borne by the people of the free States.

Conscious that they were not informed of those facts, I commenced a series of Speeches intended to show the manner in which the freemen of the North were involved in the expense, the crimes, and disgrace of southern slavery; while at the same time I would trace as clearly as possible the constitutional line of demarcation intended by the founders of our government, to separate us from the burdens and responsibilities of that institution.

In compiling this volume, I have selected only those Speeches which have reference to that subject, omitting such portions as relate to other questions, or which constitute a re-argument of some point previously ex-

A *

amined. The work contains my views upon all questions touching slavery which have been presented to the consideration of Congress, since I have been a member of that body.

J. R. GIDDINGS.

Jefferson, Ohio, March 18, 1853.

CONTENTS.

ANNEXATION OF TEXAS.

ANNEXATION OF TEXAS.

JOINT OCCUPATION OF OREGON.

INDIAN TREATIES.

THE MEXICAN WAR.

THE WILMOT PROVISO.

PRIVILEGES OF MEMBERS OF CONGRESS.

MEXICAN WAR.

THE PRESIDENT'S ANNUAL MESSAGE.

PAYMENT FOR SLAVES.

MEXICAN WAR.

RELATION OF THE FEDERAL GOVERNMENT TO SLAVERY.

SPEAKER OF THE HOUSE OF REPRESENTATIVES.

CALIFORNIA.

NEW MEXICO.

ANNUAL MESSAGE OF THE PRESIDENT.

AGITATION OF THE SLAVE QUESTION.

THE COMPROMISE MEASURES.

THE BALTIMORE PLATFORMS.

SPEECHES IN CONGRESS.

THE FLORIDA WAR.*

CAUSES OF ITS COMMENCEMENT AND RENEWAL — ITS CHARACTER AND DESIGNS EXPOSED — THE FREEDOM OF DEBATE VINDICATED.

[The resolutions of the House of Representatives adopted in December, 1838, prohibiting debate on the subject of slavery, created much feeling throughout the free States. The tyranny by which silence was thus imposed upon Northern members was deeply felt by Messrs. Adams, Slade, and Giddings, who held frequent consultations as to the best mode of regaining the freedom of debate. Mr. Giddings proposed to test the extent to which they would be permitted to discuss subjects *collaterally* involving the institution of slavery, and volunteered to make the effort. He selected the Florida war as his subject, and so prepared his remarks as to give them a direct bearing upon the bill under consideration; while his principal object was to expose the manner in which the war had been waged and conducted for the purpose of sustaining slavery. This effort proving successful, others of similar character followed, until the repeal of the "gag-rules," as they were called, took place, and the freedom of debate was regained.]

MR. GIDDINGS said he was pleased to hear that the prospect of terminating this war was so favorable; yet (said he) I am somewhat incredulous as to its immediate termination by the means presented by the gentleman from South Carolina (Mr. Thompson).

In order that our legislation shall conduce to its early close,

---

* Speech upon the bill appropriating one hundred thousand dollars for the removal of certain Seminole chiefs and warriors west of the Mississippi. Delivered in Committee of the whole House on the state of the Union, February 9, 1841.

we must act with reference to the causes which have unfortunately involved us in hostilities. This war has occupied the attention of the Executive for the last five years; our whole military force has been employed to carry it forward; our officers and soldiers have fallen victims to the climate; our funds have been squandered; but the propriety of this vast expenditure of life and treasure have been kept from the public view. It is somewhat extraordinary, that in all the discussions relating to this war, which have occurred in this House and in the Senate, no member has attempted to explain the causes of its commencement, its subsequent renewal after a solemn armistice, or the manner in which it has been conducted.

The speech of the honorable gentleman from Vermont (Mr. Everett), delivered two years since, exposed the manner in which we violated our treaty stipulations with the Indians, while we exacted of them a strict observance of their covenants; but he stopped at that point, omitting all reference to the more immediate cause of hostilities.

Before I proceed to that part of my subject, I wish to correct the impression which prevails, to some extent, that we are endeavoring to remove the Indians for the purpose of occupying their lands. That report is erroneous; the lands are of very trifling importance. General Jessup, who has a perfect knowledge of their quality, in an official communication to the War Department, says:

"These lands would not pay for the medicines used by our troops while employed against the Indians."

By the treaty of Payne's Landing, entered into in May, 1832, the Seminole Indians agreed to emigrate west of the Mississippi upon certain conditions. These conditions were not performed on our part. The Indians were, therefore, under no moral obligations to emigrate, and they declined doing so.

The reasons for this refusal may be found in House Document, 225, 3d Session, 25th Congress, in an official letter of Wiley Thompson, Indian Agent, to William P. Duval, Governor of Florida, dated January 1, 1834, in which he says:

"The principal *causes* which operate to cherish this feeling, hostile to emigration, are, first, the fear that their reunion with the Creeks, which will subject them to the government and control of the Creek national council, will be a surrender of a large *negro property*, now held by those people, to the Creeks, as an antagonist claimant."

Thus, Sir, we have official intelligence that the principal cause of the war was the fear of losing this "negro property." And we are led to inquire into the history of these conflicting claims to the "negro property" between the Creeks and Seminoles.

In the letter above quoted, General Thompson, speaking further on the subject, says:

"The Creek claim to negroes now in the possession of the Seminole Indians, which is supposed to be the first cause of hostility to the emigration of the latter tribe, grows out of the treaty of 1821 between the United States and the former."

We have now arrived at the causes which deterred the Seminoles from emigrating west of the Mississippi. Mr. Thompson, from his long and intimate acquaintance with the Seminole chiefs, and from the confidence they reposed in him, possessed the best possible means of intelligence on this subject; and no one will doubt the accuracy of the information which he has given. Yet, few of the members now present will fully understand his reference to the *reunion* of the Seminoles with the Creek Indians, or "the surrender of a large *negro property*," which was claimed by the latter. I am, therefore, constrained to refer to some historical facts, to elucidate those points.

Formerly, the Seminoles constituted a part of the Creek tribe. They lived together, and were known only as one people. Their "lower towns" were in Florida, while their "upper towns" extended far up into Georgia. The different portions of this tribe were first contradistinguished by the term "Lower Creeks" and "Upper Creeks." Subsequently, circumstances brought upon the "Lower Creeks" the name of "*runaways*," which, in their language, is expressed by the word "*Seminoles*." The term originally had reference to the fugitive slaves of Georgia, who found an asylum in these "lower towns," but in process of time gradually came to be applied to the Indians of those towns as well as the negroes who settled with them.

These slaves left their masters between 1770 and 1790, and fleeing into the Indian country passed on to the "lower Creek towns," where they settled, and many of them intermarried with the Indians and became connected with them in all the relations of domestic life. Their owners could not retake them; but called on the authorities of Georgia, who demanded of the President of the United States the interposition of our national influence to assist in regaining their slaves. The President complied; but where he found the constitutional authority for such a prostitution of our national character, neither he nor any other man has deigned to inform us. But, by his orders, an agreement was entered into by the Creeks, in their treaty with the United States of 1791, to return those fugitives to their masters. When the Creeks came to perform their stipulations in this respect, they found the fugitives connected with the Seminoles in the relations of husband and wife, of parents and children, from which they could not be separated. The performance of their stipulation in this respect was, therefore, indefinitely postponed.

In 1821, by treaty at Indian Spring, they surrendered to the United States a large tract of land, for which we stipulated to pay them four hundred and fifty thousand dollars. Of this sum, two hundred and fifty thousand dollars was retained as a trust fund, from which the President was to pay the slave-holders of Georgia for their slaves who resided in the "lower towns," and were connected with the "Lower Creeks;" while the whole nation were interested in the territory ceded to our government. This created a conflict of interest between the Creeks proper and the "Seminoles."

The President, in pursuance of the treaty, instituted a commission to examine and adjust the claims of the slave-holders; and, by allowing twice the real worth of each slave, as Mr. Wirt, Attorney-General, informs us, their aggregate value was found to be only one hundred and nine thousand dollars, leaving in the hands of this government one hundred and forty-one thousand dollars, which in equity belonged to the Indians. They called on the President and upon Congress to pay it over to them. But the slave-holders also claimed it. They sent their petitions to this body asking for it. These petitions were referred to a select committee, at the head of whom was Mr. Gilmer, a distinguished member from Georgia. That committee, after the most mature deliberation, reported to this body that the money "justly belonged to the owners of those fugitive slaves, as a compensation *for the offspring which they would have borne to their masters, had they remained in servitude.*" And it was paid to them by act of Congress. The "Upper Creeks," thus finding themselves robbed of their lands and money to pay for the slaves who then lived with the "Lower Creeks" or "Seminoles," at once determined to obtain a portion of those people and hold them as *property*. The Seminoles refused to surrender their wives and children to slavery; and the Indians thus became separated, and hostile to each other in feeling and in interest. The Creeks proper emigrated west of the Mississippi; but their agents remained in Florida, demanding possession of those fugitives. Thus we see clearly, that if the Seminoles now emigrate and again unite with the Creeks, they will at once become subject to the Creek authorities, and their wives and children will be taken and held as slaves.*

---

* The history of these fugitives is deeply interesting. About five hundred of them emigrated west with the Seminoles, in 1843. But they were afraid to go into the territory assigned to the Creeks, and with their Seminole friends settled on the "Cherokee lands." The Cherokees regarded them as trespassers. The Creeks were dissatisfied also, as they had hoped to get the slaves. The frontier was kept in constant apprehension of hostilities until December, 1846, when a treaty was entered into between the United States and these three tribes, each acting for themselves. All questions concerning these slaves were to be submitted to the President, and the Seminoles went to live with the Creeks, and were again united with them.

In 1850, the Creeks seized and sold to planters in Louisiana about one hundred of these people. This created great alarm, and some two hundred escaped into Mexico with the Seminole chief "Wild Cat," after a severe battle with the Creeks, in which several were killed on each side. More than one hundred

Under this state of circumstances, the Seminoles refused to emigrate. The government insisted upon such emigration, and ordered the army to Florida for the purpose of compelling them to remove west. Hostilities followed, and this war is the result. These fugitive slaves constituted the "negro property" to which Mr. Thompson, the Indian Agent, referred; and their surrender to the Creeks as slaves would have resulted from their emigration.

Mr. WARREN, of Georgia, called Mr. Giddings to order for irrelevancy.

The CHAIRMAN decided the remarks of Mr. Giddings to be in order.

Mr. GIDDINGS. I regard this interposition of the federal power to sustain slavery as unwarranted by the Constitution. This war is, therefore, unconstitutional, unjust, and an outrage upon the rights of the people of the free States.

Mr. HABERSHAM, of Georgia, called Mr. Giddings to order, urging that Mr. Giddings's remarks were not relevant to the bill.

The CHAIRMAN again decided that remarks upon the causes of the war were in order.

Mr. GIDDINGS. I hold, that, if the slaves of Georgia or of any other State leave their masters and go among the Indians, the federal government has no right, no constitutional power, to employ the army for their recapture, or to expend the national treasure to purchase them from the Indians.* It is a matter solely between the masters and slaves. We have no right to interfere. The slaves of the South are held in bondage by State laws. Slavery itself is a State institution, with which this government cannot rightfully interfere, either to sustain or to abolish it. This position is in such obvious

---

were said to have escaped into Canada; and some few are reported as yet living with the Seminoles. — *Vide "Speech on Indian Treaties."*

* Since the year 1790, the federal government has been in the practice of lending its aid for the recapture of slaves. But this appears to have been done by general consent, no objection having been made until the delivery of this speech.

accordance with the Constitution, that I think no member will deny it. Indeed, this body, in December, 1838, by an almost unanimous vote, adopted a resolution expressive of this doctrine.

The CHAIRMAN informed Mr. Giddings that the discussion of those resolutions would not be in order.

Mr. GIDDINGS. I had no intention to discuss those resolutions. I merely cite one of them as an authority in favor of the doctrine I have laid down. It reads as follows:

"*Resolved*, That this government is a government of limited powers. That, by the Constitution of the United States, it has no power *whatever* over the institution of slavery in the States of this Union."

These, Sir, were the sentiments of one hundred and ninety-eight members of this body; while only *six* voted against this doctrine. Every member from the slave States voted for it. Indeed, Southern statesmen from the first establishment of our government to this day, have, with unanimous voice, declared that Congress has no power over the institution of slavery within the States. Such, Sir, are the doctrines of the Constitution. That instrument has been violated, trampled upon, by these efforts to sustain slavery in Georgia. This war, in all its details, has been commenced, and is now carried on, by usurpations of power unauthorized by the Constitution; it is a violation of the rights of the people, and dishonorable to our nation.

I have now shown the reasons why the Seminoles refused to emigrate west of the Mississippi; and that our army was employed to constrain them to emigrate; and that hostilities arose from such attempts to remove them by force.

Having called attention to the remote, and to some of the more immediate causes of this war, I will now ask attention to other facts and circumstances, which show that this war arose solely from the efforts of government to arrest the fugitive slaves of the South.

On the 21st May, 1836, this House adopted a resolution, calling upon the then President for "information respecting the causes of the Florida war." On the 3d June, the President transmitted to the House sundry papers relating to that subject, among which may be found an address or petition of nearly one hundred gentlemen, said to be among the principal inhabitants of Florida, calling on the President to interpose the power of the general government for the purpose of securing them in the possession of their slaves. These gentlemen, speaking of the Seminole Indians, say:

> "While this indomitable people continue where they now are, the owners of slaves in our territory, and even in the States contiguous, cannot, for a moment, in any thing like security, enjoy this kind of property."

These gentlemen appear to have thought it the duty of the Executive to remove those Indians, in order that they might enjoy their slavery in greater security. The presence of those savages was unfavorable to civilized oppression; and these professed Christians desired the removal of the barbarians, to enable them to commit the crimes of slavery with greater impunity. The President listened respectfully to their request, and indorsed on the petition an order directing the Secretary of War "to inquire into the charges, and, if found true, to direct the Indians to prepare forthwith to remove west of the Mississippi."

The treaty of Payne's Landing, which had lain unnoticed for two years, was hunted up, and sent to the Senate for concurrence. Orders were at once sent to different parts of the country, directing a concentration of the army, in order to compel the Indians at the point of the bayonet to emigrate.

These extraordinary efforts of the President to sustain slavery, will constitute an interesting chapter in our political history. I have no time now to comment upon them. They have been kept from the people, and my present object is to bring them forth to the public gaze. The address referred to, says:

> "There are now believed to be more than five hundred negroes among the Seminoles, three fourths of whom are fugitive slaves." *

---

* More than five hundred of those who fled from Georgia, including their descendants, emigrated with the Indians west of the Mississippi; while an equal number, who were captured by our troops, were claimed by the people of Florida as their property, and delivered over to them as slaves.

On the 20th January, 1834, Governor Duval, in a letter to the Commissioner of Indian Affairs, says:

"The slaves belonging to the Indians have a controlling influence over the minds of their masters, and are entirely opposed to any change of residence. It will be best to adopt at once firm and decided measures; such as will demonstrate to the Indians the determination of government to see the treaty justly and fairly executed. This cannot be done until the bands of outlaws, (fugitive slaves,) mentioned in the agent's report, are arrested and broken up; for, so long as they are permitted to remain, every Indian that is unwilling to emigrate will seek their protection."

No man, perhaps, possessed better knowledge of these facts than Governor Duval, who assures us that the negroes controlled the Indians, and that the Indians sought the protection and support of the fugitive slaves. This same officer, acting executive of the territory of Florida, in a letter dated January 26th, 1834, says:

"The slaves belonging to the Indians, must be made to fear for themselves before they will cease to influence the minds of their masters." "You may be assured that the first step towards the emigration of these Indians, must be the breaking up of the runaway slaves and outlaw Indians."

Thus we are informed, that the war must be first waged against the *fugitive slaves*. And it was waged against those oppressed, friendless outcasts; those unarmed wanderers who had fled from oppression, who had sought an asylum in the swamps and everglades of Florida, who had fled from the oppression of professed Christians, and sought protection of savage barbarians. Against them the warlike energies of this mighty nation were brought to bear, for no other cause than their love of liberty.

Mr. Campbell, of South Carolina, called Mr. Giddings to order for assailing the institution of slavery.

The Chairman said, the gentleman from Ohio, (Mr. Giddings,) had declared his intention to discuss the Florida war; and the Chair had understood his remarks as having reference to that subject.

Mr. Giddings resumed. I will assure the gentleman from South Carolina, (Mr. Campbell,) that I intend alluding to slavery only so far as it stands connected with this war. This officer desired to have the war directed against the slaves, because they advised their masters in favor of liberty. The manner in which this was done, will appear from the official communication of the Indian Agent. On the 28th October, 1834, General Thompson, in a letter addressed to the Commissioner of Indian Affairs, says:

"There are many very likely negroes in this nation (Seminole). Some of the whites in the adjacent settlements manifest a restless desire to obtain them; and I have no doubt that Indian raised negroes are now in possession of the whites."

Thus, Sir, it seems that *kidnapping was not* unknown in that country. This same accredited officer of government, on the 9th January, 1835, advises:

"That an expedition should be set on foot for the double purpose of driving the Indians within their boundary, and capture negroes, many of whom, it is believed, are runaway slaves."

And, Sir, our army was put in motion to *capture negroes and slaves*. Our officers and soldiers became slave-catchers, companions of the most degraded class of human beings who disgrace that slave-cursed region. With the assistance of blood-hounds, they tracked the flying bondman over hill and dale, through swamp and everglade, until his weary limbs could sustain him no longer. Then they seized him, and, for the bounty of *twenty dollars* he was usually delivered over to the first white man who claimed him. Our troops became expert in this business of hunting and enslaving mankind. I doubt whether the Spanish pirates, engaged in the same employment on the African coast, are more perfect masters of their vocation. Nor was our army alone engaged in this war upon human rights. They merely followed the example of a class of land-pirates, who are ever ready to rob or murder when they can do so with impunity. On the 28th July, 1835, John Walker, one of the Appalachicola chiefs, belonging to the Seminole band, wrote General Thompson, Indian Agent, as follows:

"I am," says he, "induced to write you, in consequence of the depredations making, and attempted to be made, upon my property, by a company of *negro stealers*, some of whom are from Columbus, Georgia, and have connected themselves with Brown and Douglass. I should like your advice, how I am to act.

I dislike to make any trouble, or to have any difficulty with any of the white people; but, if they trespass upon my premises and my rights, I must defend myself in the best way I can. If they do make this attempt, and I have no doubt they will, they must bear the consequences. But is there no *civil law* to protect me? Are the *free negroes*, and the negroes belonging in this town, to be stolen away publicly, and, in the face of all law and justice, carried off and sold, to fill the pockets of these *worse than land pirates?* Douglass and his company hired a man who has two large *trained dogs* for the purpose to come down and take Billey. He is from Mobile, and follows for a livelihood catching runaway negroes."

This, Sir, is the language of a savage, addressed to his civilized neighbors. He called in vain for protection. A few days after the date of this letter, he was robbed of all his negroes; so says the report of the United States Attorney, addressed to the Secretary of War, and dated April 21, 1836. But the number of freemen who were enslaved is unknown to us. There was no one to speak for them. That hundreds of freeborn Americans were seized, enslaved, and now pine in bondage, no man can doubt who will carefully examine the official documents connected with this war. I will give one more example of the piratical practice by which these Indians were robbed and the negroes enslaved.

E-con-chattimico was also an Indian chief of the Seminole band, living upon the Appalachicola River, one who signed the treaty at Camp Moultrie, in 1832, by which we solemnly pledged the faith of this nation to protect the Indians in the enjoyment of their lives and property. This chief is said to have owned twenty slaves, valued at fifteen thousand dollars. These "negro stealers" were seen hovering around his plantation, and their object could not be misunderstood. By the advice of the sub-agent, he armed himself and people for the purpose of defending themselves. When the negro stealers learned that E-con-chattimico's people had armed themselves in defence of their *liberty*, (for they considered Indian slavery liberty compared with white slavery,) they raised a report that the Indians had armed themselves for the purpose of murdering the white people. On learning this, E-con-chattimico at once delivered up his arms to the white people, and threw himself upon their protection. Disarmed, and unable to defend his people, they were immediately kidnapped, taken off, and sold into interminable bondage. E-con-chattimico now calls on us to pay him for the loss he has sustained in the violation of our treaty, in which we solemnly covenanted to protect him and his property. Robbed, abused, insulted, and deceived, he emigrated to the West, and now looks to us for a redress of the wrongs he has sustained. I give the substance of his statement as related by him in his petition to Congress, and communicated by General Thompson, Governor Duval, and the District Attorney of East Florida, and sworn to by several witnesses.

These outrages upon the rights of the Indians and of the negroes, drove them to the necessity of protecting their liberties and their lives. They were thus constrained to take up arms in self-defence, and we soon found ourselves involved in this disastrous war.

The men who committed these robberies and kidnapped these negroes were well known; for the acts were committed in open day. Their names and places of residence are distinctly mentioned; but I have yet to learn that any one of them has been punished in any manner for this warfare against the liberty of the blacks and the rights of the Indians. Indeed, it seems to have been an object with some of the officers employed in Florida to induce government itself to enter into the business of *capturing and selling slaves.* J. W. Harris, Disbursing Agent of government, in a letter to the Commissary-General of Subsistence, dated December 30, 1836, says:

> "I would respectfully suggest, that you recommend to the honorable Secretary of War, that the annuity due to the hostile Indians be retained to defray the expenses of this war; and that the slaves who shall be captured, whom I believe to have been generally active instigators to our present troubles, *be sold at public sale, and the proceeds appropriated to the same object.*"

This is the first official proposition that has come to my knowledge for the government to enter into competition with the "*negro stealers*," by capturing and selling slaves. We were engaged in open war with these people, who had sought liberty in the wilds of Florida. If they were captured, they would be *prisoners of war;* and for us to sell them as slaves, would be as much a violation of national honor as it would have been for them to have sold as slaves such of our people as they were able to capture. But the efforts of the more humane officers led to an armistice which, had it been observed in good faith by the citizens of Florida, would have been perpetual.

On the 6th day of March, 1837, General Jessup entered into a conventional arrangement with the Seminole Indians, by which it was agreed that hostilities should immediately cease; that the Indians should emigrate west of the Mississippi; that they should be secure in their lives and property; and "that negroes, their *bonâ fide* property," should accompany them. This arrangement revived the hopes of the friends of peace. They indulged the expectation that blood would cease to flow, and that safety to the Indians and to our own people would again extend over the territory. But these fond hopes were soon dispelled.

Twelve days after this convention was entered into, a solemn remonstrance against it was signed by a number of gentlemen of high standing in Florida, and transmitted to the Secretary of War. These gentlemen totally objected to any pacification that did not provide for the recapture of their fugitive slaves. They objected to the Indians going West, until they should take and return to their owners the slaves who had escaped from their masters in Florida. The remonstrance may be found at 55th page of Executive Document of the House of Representatives, No. 225 of the 3d Session of the 25th Congress. It is an interesting paper, but of too great length for me to read at this time. It shows, in a most palpable light, the views entertained by those gentlemen in regard to the object of this war. Whatever others may have thought upon that subject, it is clear that they supposed the war to have been commenced and carried on for the purpose of aiding them in holding their slaves; and they declare it incompatible with the honor and dignity of the nation to permit the Indians to emigrate, until they shall bring the slaves back to their owners. I have no doubt they felt that they were correct in their views; nor do I believe they entertained a doubt of the justice and

2

propriety of taxing the people of the free States to any extent in supporting a war for slavery. There was, however, a cessation of hostilities, notwithstanding these remonstrances. The Indians ceased for a time to plunder the defenceless families of Florida, to burn their cabins, and murder women and children; but, Sir, the fugitive slaves remained yet hidden in the swamps and everglades of that country. Peace on such terms appears not to have been acceptable to the people of Florida. I will not speak the conclusions of my own mind, however, on this subject, but will avail myself of the statement of a high officer of government who was in command of our troops, and who spoke from positive knowledge. Indeed, Mr. Chairman, the facts connected with this renewal of hostilities are of such an extraordinary character, that I prefer they should rest upon the declaration of accredited officers.

General Jessup, in a letter dated 29th March, 1837, and directed to Colonel John Warren, speaking of the anxiety of the Indians to maintain the peace agreed upon, says:

"There is no disposition on the part of the great body of the Indians to renew hostilities; and they will, I am sure, faithfully fulfil their engagements, if the inhabitants of the territory be prudent. But any attempt to seize their negroes or other property would be followed by an immediate resort to arms."

Thus, we have the authority of General Jessup for saying that the Indians were anxious to maintain peace. That he was at the same time apprehensive that the people would attempt to seize the Indian negroes. What reason General Jessup had to suspect that the people of Florida would be otherwise than *prudent*, or what reason he had to fear that they would *seize the Indian negroes*, I know not. He certainly exhibited fears upon the subject, however. For, on the 5th April, being seven days subsequent to this letter to Colonel Warren, he issued a general order in the following words:

"The Commanding-General has reason to believe that the interference o unprincipled white men with the negro property of the Seminole Indians, if not immediately checked, will prevent their emigration, and lead to a renewal of hostilities.

The order goes on to prohibit any person not connected with the public service from entering upon the territory assigned to the Indians. In this order we have official intelligence that the whites did in fact interfere with the Indian slaves, or, in other words, they began to rob the Indians of their slaves almost as soon as hostilities ceased. As to the outrages committed upon the free blacks, during the suspension of hostilities, we have no information in this order, and are left to infer the course pursued towards them from the evidence I have previously given.

On the 18th April, twelve days after the date of his letter to Colonel Warren, General Jessup wrote to Governor Call, saying:

"If the citizens of the territory be *prudent*, the war may be considered at an end. But any attempt to interfere with the *Indian negroes* would cause an immediate resort to hostilities. The negroes control their masters; and they have heard of the act of your legislative council. Thirty or more of the Indian negro men were at and near my camp on the Withlacoochie late in March. But the arrival of two or three citizens of Florida, said to be in search of negroes, caused them to disperse at once; and I doubt whether they will come in again. At all events, the emigration will be delayed a month, I apprehend, in consequence of the alarm of these negroes."

It is quite evident that the Commanding-General was embarrassed by attempts of the white people to seize upon negroes. Indeed, there appears to have been no difficulty in arranging the terms of peace; but the peace could not be maintained in consequence of the rapacity of these slave-catchers. It is also quite evident that some of the people of Florida were restless under the order of the 5th of April, prohibiting them from entering the Indian country. When intelligence respecting that order reached St. Augustine, a public meeting was called, and a committee appointed to procure its repeal, in order that the white people might enter the Indian country for the purpose of seizing slaves.

This committee, said to be composed of men of high standing, addressed a long letter to General Jessup, in which they say, speaking of the people of Florida:

"While they believe that the accomplishment of a certain pacification must, as it ought, be an object of primary importance in these negotiations, they persuade themselves that the preservation of the negro property, belonging to the inhabitants of this desolated country, must be seen by him to be an object of scarcely less moment."

It is a most undeniable fact, borne out by every part of these official documents, that the people of Florida supposed that the great object of the war was to aid the slave-holders in capturing and recovering their slaves. This same protest goes on to recount facts in regard to their slaves having run away, and finding a place of refuge in the Indian country, and the concluding of an armistice by General Jessup, without getting their slaves back; and then the signers add:

"Against such a course, so destructive of their rights and interests, the citizens of St. Augustine and others, in public meeting assembled, for themselves and on behalf of the inhabitants of East Florida generally, *do most solemnly protest.*"

The people of Florida appear to have regarded slavery as more important than peace or human life. They preferred that war, devastation, and bloodshed should continue, rather than to loose their grasp upon their fellow men. And the flames of war were again lighted up. Our army was again put in motion. The Indians became desperate. The blood of defenceless women and children again flowed, in order that the white people might seize and enslave the negroes associated with the Indians. I am led to believe, from a careful examination of the documents, that General Jessup was unable to protect the negroes connected with the Indians, agreeably to his covenant. The war became, in fact, a war between this nation and the *negroes;* for they controlled the Indians. Being unable to subdue them, General Jessup, finding his troops falling a prey to the unhealthy climate in which he was situated, the citizens being murdered, their habitations burned, and his army discouraged, issued the order No. 160, to which I will now call the attention of the committee. That part to which I particularly refer is in the following words:

"All Indian property captured from this date will belong to the corps or detachment making it."

The sense in which the term *property* was used in this order is fully explained in a letter of General Jessup to Colonel Warren, dated a few days subsequent, in which, speaking of the Seminoles, he says:

"Their *negroes*, cattle, and horses, will belong to the corps by which they are captured."

This order bears date on the 3d of August, 1837, and may be found at page 4 of the Documents communicated to this House by the Secretary of War on the 27th day of February, 1839. I think that history will record this as the first general order issued by the commander of an American army, in which the catching of slaves is held out as an incentive to military duty. I mention this fact, and bring it to the consideration of the committee with feelings of deep mortification. As an American, I feel humbled at this act, which cannot be viewed by the civilized world otherwise than dishonorable to our arms and nation. That this officer, intrusted with the command of our army and the honor of our flag, should appeal to the cupidity, the desire of plunder, and the worst of human passions, in order to stimulate his men to effort, is, I think, to be regretted by men of all parties in all sections of our country. Our national flag, which floated in proud triumph at Saratoga, which was enveloped in a blaze of glory at Monmouth and Yorktown, seems to have been prostituted in Florida to the base purpose of leading on an organized company of "negro-catchers." Sir, no longer is "*our country*" the battle cry of our army in their advance to victory; but *slaves* has become the watchword to inspire them to effort. No longer does the war-worn veteran, amid the battle's rage, think of his country's glory, and nerve his arm in behalf of *freedom;* but with eagle eyes he watches the wavering ranks of the enemy, and as they flee before our advancing columns, he plunges among them to seize the sable foe and make him his future slave.

The natural consequence of this order was the capture of a large number of negroes. They were mostly taken by two battalions of Creek Indians, who were then in the employ of our government, assisting in this most *savage* war.

These colored prisoners had to be guarded to prevent their escape. They must also be supplied with food. Their captors had none; and, from necessity, they were supplied from the public stores. These circumstances greatly embarrassed the movements of the army. It became evident, that our officers and soldiers could not compete with professed slave-catchers unless they could find a market for their victims. Under these circumstances the commanding officer issued the general order No. 175, dated at Tampa Bay, September 6, 1837. It reads as follows:

"1. The Seminole negroes captured by the army will be taken on *account of government, and held subject to the order of the Secretary of War.*

"2. The sum of eight thousand dollars will be paid to the Creek chiefs and warriors by whom they were captured, or who were present at the capture, in full for their claim to them.

"3. To induce the Creek Indians to take alive, and not destroy the negroes of citizens who had been captured by the Seminoles, a reward was promised them for all they should secure. They captured and secured thirty-five, who have been returned to their owners. The owners have paid nothing, but the promise to the Indians must be fulfilled. The sum of twenty dollars will be allowed to them for each from the public funds.

"4. Lieutenant Searle is charged with the execution of this order."

The documents before me show that this order was approved by the honorable Secretary of War on the 7th October following. Thus, Sir, the people of this mighty nation, through the efforts of their accredited officers, became the purchasers of slaves. They paid eight thousand dollars for human flesh; and we became literally a nation of slave-holders.

In this manner we have been led on by slave-holding influences, step by step, until we find our government and nation involved in the crime of holding slaves. The people have been kept ignorant of these facts. No solitary voice has been raised to inform them of these violations of their rights, of the rights of humanity, and of the Constitution; of this stain upon our nation's honor.

It further appears that the people of the United States,—the laborers of Ohio and other free States,—have been compelled to contribute of their hard earnings to pay a bounty of twenty dollars for each negro captured and delivered to the white people as a slave.* Among the negroes thus captured

* It appears, from documents subsequently transmitted to Congress, that more than five hundred negroes were captured and delivered over as slaves to the white people; and more than *ten thousand dollars* were paid from the public treasury as a bounty for these barbarous acts.

and enslaved were doubtless many, perhaps a majority, who were born *free*. Thus have we been made to contribute our money to the purposes of enslaving FREEMEN.

These flagrant outrages upon humanity have been kept from the knowledge of the people. Our public servants have avoided the popular odium, by keeping their acts hidden from the public view.

The Commanding-General appears to have entered into this business of catching slaves with a good degree of spirit. In a letter dated at Tampa Bay, 25th May, 1837, directed to Lieutenant-Colonel Harney, General Jessup says:

> "If you see Powel (Oceola) tell him I shall send out and take all the negroes who belong to the white people; and he must not allow the Indian negroes to mix with them. Tell him I am sending to Cuba for bloodhounds to trail them; and I intend to hang every one of them who does not come in."

If the negroes had quietly suffered themselves to be trailed with bloodhounds, or supinely permitted themselves to be hanged for their love of liberty, they would have deserved the name of slaves.

The expenditure of five thousand dollars for bloodhounds in Cuba was not, as has been supposed, for the purpose of trailing Indians. In this letter we have it officially announced that they were sent for and obtained for the purpose of *catching fugitive slaves*. I desire the people of this nation to understand distinctly that they are taxed for the purpose of maintaining and supporting slavery in the slave States; that their treasure has been appropriated directly and publicly to that purpose; that our army, many of whose officers and soldiers were bred in the free States and in the love of liberty, has been employed, by order of the Commanding-General, in pursuing and capturing fugitive slaves. Nor is that all. The freemen of the North are taxed for the purchase of bloodhounds to act in concert with our army in this disgraceful and disgusting mode of conducting the war.

It appears that all the laws of humanity and of honorable warfare were suspended. Colored men were bribed by the promise of liberty to turn traitors to their race and to their friends. On the 24th of September, 1837, General Jessup wrote the Commissioner of Indian Affairs, saying:

"The Seminole negroes are now all the property of the public. I have promised Abraham the freedom of his family, if he prove faithful to us; and I shall certainly hang him, if he be not faithful."

I understand that Abraham was taken into the service of the army as a pilot to guide them to the negro settlements, in order to capture other colored people. If he proved faithful to our army, and a traitor to his own people and kindred, he and his family were to be free; but, if he obeyed the dictates of humanity, and proved faithful to his God, then he was to be hanged! Such, Sir, have been the instrumentalities for conducting this war. We shrink from contemplating them, while duty constrains us to make them known to the country.

Mr. Chairman, in the remarks I have made, it has been my object to develop the causes which originally involved us in this war, and which occasioned its renewal, as well as to portray to the country the manner in which it has been conducted. In discharging this duty, I have relied entirely upon official documents.

The effect which the publication of these facts are to have upon the character of those who have conducted the war, is not for me to predict. It is due to the truth of history that these facts shall go forth to the people; that the country shall be made acquainted with them. But the verdict which civilized and Christian nations shall pronounce upon them, and the opinions which posterity shall form of this war and the manner of conducting it, must be recorded by the future historian.

REDUCTION OF THE ARMY.*

EXCLUSIVE JURISDICTION OF CONGRESS OVER COMMERCE AND NAVIGATION — SLAVERY LIMITED TO THE JURISDICTION OF THE POWER CREATING IT — NO POWERS VESTED IN THE EXECUTIVE BY WHICH HE CAN INVOLVE THE PEOPLE OF THE FREE STATES IN THE SUPPORT OF THE SLAVE-TRADE — THE RIGHTS OF A REPRESENTATIVE VINDICATED.

[In 1841, the slave-ship "Creole," sailed from Richmond, Virginia, for New Orleans. While at sea, the slaves rose and asserted their liberty. In attempting to reduce them to subjection, *Hewel*, one of the slave-dealers, was killed; the others, together with the crew, surrendered the ship to the negroes, who guided it to Nassau, in the island of New Providence. Landing them on British soil, they at once became free under British laws. The owners of the slaves then called on the President of the United States for payment for the slaves, and that functionary espoused their cause. Mr. Webster, then Secretary of State, sent instructions to our Minister at London, directing him to demand of the British ministry compensation to the owners of the slaves for their losses. This letter of instructions being sent to the Senate, was published by order of that body. Mr. Giddings, seeing the influence of our government thus prostituted to the support of the slave-trade, introduced to the consideration of the House of Representatives a series of resolutions denying the constitutional authority of the President thus to involve the people of the free States, or of the nation, in the support of a commerce in the image of God. For this he was publicly censured by resolution of the House. He immediately resigned his office, and left Congress. His constituents re-elected him, and by resolutions instructed him to maintain the doctrines he had asserted. On his return to Congress, a proposition to reduce the army came up for consideration, and was opposed on the ground that a war might grow out of this transaction. In reply to these objections, Mr. Giddings made the following remarks. Only so much of the speech as had relation to this subject is published in this work. It may be proper to add, that this demand on Great Britain has not been urged by our government since this opposition in 1842.]

---

* Speech upon the bill to reduce the Army. Delivered in Committee of the whole House on the state of the Union, June 4, 1842.

Mr. Chairman, — The gentleman from Massachusetts, (Mr. Cushing,) insists that we have a "question of honor with the British government, growing out of the Creole question;" and therefore objects to the reduction of the army. I entertain a different opinion. I deny that this government either has, or can constitutionally have, any thing to do with that transaction. The Creole was engaged in the atrocious employment of transporting slaves. And we cannot *honorably* lend any encouragement or support to "that execrable commerce in human flesh." Every principle of morality, of national honor, forbids that we should lend any aid or assistance to those engaged in a traffic in the bodies of men, of women, and of children. If we prostitute our influence in behalf of persons thus engaged, we shall dishonor ourselves and the people whom we represent.

Sir, I would not retain a single soldier in service, to maintain this slave-trade; on the contrary, I should rejoice if every slave shipped from our slave-breeding States could regain his liberty, either by the strength of his own arms, or by landing on some British island. Instead of maintaining an army to sustain this traffic, I would pass laws to punish every man who makes merchandise of the image of the Creator. We have already enacted laws to punish those who follow the African slave-trade. We pronounce them pirates, unworthy of human association, and hang them; but they are far less guilty than those who deal in the more enlightened and christianized slaves of this American land. No man believes that the crime of dealing in human flesh depends upon the latitude or the longitude in which it is committed; yet, while we punish with death the man who commits this offence on the African coast, our President and the Secretary of State are exerting the influence of government to aid and encourage those who commit the same offence in more aggravated forms on our own coast. Such inconsistency must affect our character with all Christian, and even with Mohammedan nations.

No one denies that Virginia has the power under the Constitution to hold slaves. It is an institution of her own, with which we have no right to interfere. While these owners kept their slaves within that State, they held them in subjection under her local laws. While there, the owners could scourge them, sell them, or do as they pleased with them. Those laws had disrobed the slaves of their manhood; had taken from them the right of self-defence, and subjected them entirely to the will of their owners. But the operation of those laws was confined to the limits of the State. They could not extend into other States, nor upon the high seas. Virginia, by adopting the federal Constitution, had surrendered, in definite language, all jurisdiction over the subjects of commerce and navigation upon the high seas; and had delegated to Congress the sole power to define and punish felonies committed thereon. It is, therefore, very obvious, that after the adoption of the Constitution, neither Virginia nor any other State held jurisdiction upon the ocean. Congress alone was authorized to enact laws for the government of people on board American ships.

Holding these principles in view, we see that when the ship Creole left the State of Virginia, went beyond the jurisdiction of her laws, and entered upon the Atlantic ocean, these slave-dealers and their victims could no longer be controlled by the local laws of that State. The slave-code had ceased to operate upon them; they were governed by the common law, modified by the laws of Congress respecting "commerce and navigation." Under those laws, no slavery could exist.

These persons had originally been seized in their native land, torn from their friends and country, and forced on board the slave-ship. There, they were held in subjection by means of whips and chains. They were then upon the waters of the Atlantic, within the jurisdiction of Congress, where no slavery existed. They were *free in law*, although made slaves *in fact*, by the superior intellectual and physical power of their oppressors. Had they then risen upon their captors, and thrown them overboard, or carried them back to Africa, we should have rejoiced; and they would have performed a duty which they owed to God and man; nor would they have offended against any laws of the United States, or of any individual State, by such summary administration of justice. As yet they were *free*, and as much entitled to their liberty as when they stood upon their native soil. The piratical action of their captors had no effect upon their natural or their legal rights. These rights were suspended, or rather they were unable to maintain them against the brute force which now surrounded them. Thus they remained until taken within the jurisdiction of the laws of Virginia. There the slave-code threw its penalties around them, and they became slaves in *law* as well as in fact. The moment they entered the limits of that State, they came under the jurisdiction of laws which took from them the right of self-defence; robbed them of the character of *men;* degraded and brutalized them, and rendered them the subjects of sale and purchase, like swine in the market. I do not say that those laws were less criminal than the action of the slave-merchants. Nor do I suppose them to have placed these slaves under the least moral obligation to obey their masters. On the contrary, I suppose that at no moment of time from their first seizure in Africa, until their restoration to freedom, were they under any moral obligation to obey their oppressors, or the laws which held them in degradation; and if they had at any moment possessed the power of releasing themselves from bondage, it would have been just and right and proper for them to do so, at any expense of life and treasure to those who opposed their freedom. This *moral* right was, therefore, never suspended, although the power of exerting it was taken from them for years.

But, Sir, who will deny that these people were reinvested with their legal right to liberty when taken back upon the high seas, beyond the jurisdiction of the slave laws under which they had suffered? Those laws could extend no farther than the limits of that State. They had no force or effect upon the broad ocean. There, I repeat, the laws of Congress alone bear rule. There freedom, and not slavery, prevails; and the moment the ship passed the line which separates the State from the high seas, the chains of these people fell from their limbs; the bars of their prison were broken; they were *free;* they again became *men*, clothed with the attributes with which nature and nature's God "has endowed all men;" they again owned their bodies; they again came into possession of themselves — of their intellects; they again assumed a position among men, and were no longer chattels.

I am aware that the expression of these views is not agreeable to the feelings of those around me; but no member will deny their correctness. They are also in direct conflict with the letter of instructions from the Secretary of State to our minister at London. I entertain the belief, that when that letter was written, the author did not anticipate that it would undergo a public examination in this body. I do not think the principles it maintains were well considered. We have so long been accustomed to submit silently to these encroachments of the Slave-Power, that it is generally expected we shall continue to submit. Indeed, we have recently seen a very distinct expression of that opinion by this body. It has been thought the duty of members here to remain silent when the Executive was prostituting the influence of our nation to encourage this slave-trade, thereby involving the people of the free States in the disgrace of that traffic. I entertain a different view of our obligations. I think it our duty to speak frankly our own sentiments, and the sentiments of our people. Our mission here is to maintain truth, to uphold justice, and support the constitutional rights of each portion of the Union.

It would be a violation of duty for us to sit silently here, and permit the President to involve our constituents in the crimes of these slave-dealers. The people whom I represent, are unwilling to be made parties to this purchase and sale of men. We believe it impossible for us to degrade and brutalize any portion of mankind without experiencing a recoil of the evils we inflict upon others. The misery and suffering imposed upon the slaves of this nation, has in a degree paralyzed the physical energies and the moral sensibilities of a portion of our white population; thereby retarding our progress in the development of our physical and intellectual resources as a people. Feebleness, vice, and pauperism prevail wherever slavery exists. We may as well offend against the laws of our physical nature, as against those of our moral being. We may as well put our hands into the fire, with the expectation that they will not be burned, as to commit crime with the expectation of impunity. The penalty is just as inseparable from the transgression in one case, as it is in the other. The idea that oppression, injustice, and slavery can be perpetrated upon our fellow men, without inflicting their penalty upon the offenders, was entertained by an ignorant, a barbarous age; but it is inconsistent with the philosophy, the ethics of the nineteenth century.

The Secretary, in his letter of instructions, assumes the protection of this commerce in mankind as one of the duties of our federal government. With all due respect to that high officer, I must dissent from that doctrine. I protest against it. No such duty is enjoined upon us by the Constitution. You may search that instrument in vain for such obligation, or for any authority to exert the power or influence of the nation in behalf of the slave-trade. Will any member of this body, or any intelligent elector of the nation, assert that our Constitution was adopted for such a purpose, or that it gives such authority?

Did Franklin, or Madison, or Sherman, or Gerry, or any of those patriots who framed that charter of American liberty, intend, or expect the powers of this nation to be exerted in favor of a commerce in our own species? Such an imputation would be a libel upon their memories.

As I have already shown, these persons, being upon the broad ocean, beyond the jurisdiction of all slave laws, were *free.* They were free in *law* and free in *fact;* entitled to our protection, for they were under the American flag. While in this condition, these slave-dealers attempted to carry them to New Orleans, to re-enslave, degrade, and brutalize them; to sell them like swine in the market. Were they then under moral obligations to fold their arms and supinely surrender themselves victims to their oppressors? They had the same *legal* and the same moral right to carry their former owners to Africa, and sell *them* as slaves, as those owners had to carry them to the barracoons of New Orleans. Quondam owners and quondam slaves stood upon the same level, entitled to the same rights, and subject to the same laws, which deal equal justice to all under their jurisdiction.

When, therefore, the slave-dealers attempted to hold the negroes in subjection, to carry them by force to the slave-markets of Louisiana, they committed an act of *piracy;* they became pirates in law and in fact. And, I ask, why did the President espouse their cause? Why did the Secretary of State consent to act as the agent of these pirates? Why did he demand of Great Britain payment for the bodies of these freemen? Neither the British government, nor the people of England had gained any pecuniary benefit by the freedom of these persons. The negroes secured their liberty, and were the only persons benefited. Why then should this nation demand from the people of England compensation for their liberty? Why was this demand made after the slaves had been voluntarily emancipated by their owners, in taking them without the jurisdiction of slave laws? Was not that demand undignified and wrong, I will not say absurd and ridiculous? Those terms would not be respectful towards the officer who made the demand.

But the error of the gentleman from Massachusetts (Mr. Cushing) consists in supposing it our duty to sustain the claim of these slave-dealers. If we are under obligation to sustain them in their vocation, it follows that we are bound to do it, even at the expense of war; and we should therefore prepare for hostilities; we should increase the army.

I assure gentlemen, that the people I represent have no intention to shed their blood in defence of this slave-trade. They would far rather hang every pirate who deals in human flesh upon our coast, than go to war for their protection! They deny most distinctly and emphatically that they are bound to hazard their lives, or spend their treasure, or stain their moral character, by supporting that commerce in mankind which has long disgraced our nation. They know that the President and Secretary of State have overstepped the limits of their constitutional authority; that the character of the nation has suffered from this unauthorized attempt to extort money from the people of England to compensate these slave-merchants for the loss of their "human chattels;" they discard and repudiate this action of the President and of the Secretary of State; they now, and at all times, insist upon their right to be entirely exempt from the crimes and disgrace of the slave-trade; they believe it our solemn duty to pass laws for the punishment of all who thus offend against the dictates of humanity; they regard the crime of dealing in slaves to be one of the most revolting character, and that it should be punished by the severest penalty known to human laws. And, I have no doubt, that the passage of a bill of that description would be far more acceptable to the popular mind than any action of government in favor of the slave-trade.

But the honorable Secretary of State, speaking of these people in his instructions to our minister at London, refers to them as guilty of "*mutiny and murder.*" Had he made demand of them as murderers or mutineers, the British government would, in all probability, have surrendered them, in order that they might suffer the penalty attached to those crimes under our laws. But he has made no such demand. He merely demands pay in dollars and cents for their blood and bones, their muscles and sinews. His zeal and anxiety is on behalf of the slave-dealers, not of justice. He demands pay, not punishment. And the question very naturally arises, Why did that officer attempt to stigmatize those people as guilty of "mutiny and murder?" If true, it would not strengthen the claims of these pretended owners. Their claim would not be made stronger by the guilt of their victims.

I would not judge harshly of any man; but to me it looks very much as though the honorable Secretary was willing to divert public attention from his position as agent and solicitor for these slave-merchants, by exciting popular indignation against those victims of oppression. He appears to think that the mass of people will draw no distinction between *mutiny* and the refusal of these persons to obey the slave-dealers.

No man better understands the definition of "mutiny" than the honorable Secretary of State. It is said to be "the resistance of legal authority to which the mutineer has voluntarily become subject." Thus, a soldier, having voluntarily entered the army, enlisted, and become subject to the rules and regulations of the service, would be guilty of that offence, if he resist the lawful commands of his officer. But, Sir, if you or I were unlawfully taken by force, against our will, to an encampment, and an officer should attempt to control our movements, or inflict punishment upon us for disobedience to his command, we may lawfully resist such attempt; and such resistance will constitute no crime or offence.

So, also, if a man enter a ship as a sailor, having signed the ship's articles, and submitted voluntarily to the laws and regulations which govern those employed in that capacity, he thereby becomes bound to obey all legal orders of his captain and other officers, and resistance to such orders would be *mutiny*. But, Sir, if the same man were unlawfully and by force taken on board such ship against his will, no person could urge that he was bound to obey the captain, or that resistance to the captain's authority would be *mutiny*. I have stated, and, I think, demonstrated, to the satisfaction of those who heard me, that these men stood upon the deck of the Creole *freemen*, released and fully emancipated from slavery. While in this situation, the captain and former owners were taking them to New Orleans to re-enslave and to sell them. And the question arises, had they a lawful right to resist this attempt of the slave-dealers? Did resistance to those dealers in human flesh constitute "mutiny"? Will the honorable Secretary, will any jurist or lawyer avow such doctrine? I think not. They will, perhaps, speak of it as "mutiny;" refer to it as such; but they will never appear before this or any other public body, and attempt gravely to maintain such doctrine by reason or argument.

Again, the honorable Secretary refers to these persons as "*murderers*." He, Sir, is an eminent lawyer. He understands well the definition of that crime. The first book almost which was put into his hands, as a student of that profession, taught him that, —

"Murder, is the killing of a reasonable being in the public peace, without warrant or excuse, and with malice aforethought."

These persons had suffered the horrors of slavery under the laws of Virginia. While in that State, the whole power of that commonwealth had been arrayed against them, to hold them in bondage. At length their owners carried them beyond the jurisdiction of those slave-laws. They were upon the high seas, subject only to the laws of Congress. These piratical dealers held them in subjection without law, and in violation of justice and the dictates of humanity. In the spirit and dignity of their manhood, they rose and asserted the rights with which the God of nature had endowed them. The slave-dealer (Hewell) thrust himself between them and their freedom, and attempted to disrobe them of the liberty which God had given them, and to subject them to his will. They defended their lives and their liberty. They slew him, for which you and I and all mankind honor them. We applaud their heroism. The whole civilized world will say they did *right.* Not a slave-holder present will say they did wrong. Would the honorable Secretary, in their situation, have done less? Would he, with a craven heart and a dastardly soul, have quietly submitted to be carried to the barracoons of New Orleans, and sold like a beast of burden? If so, he would not have deserved the name of *man.* They possessed no moral right to surrender the liberty of themselves and offspring in all coming time; to doom their descendants to sighs and chains, and tears and suffering.

Yet, the Secretary calls this heroic, this high imperative duty "*murder!*" Epithets are of little importance. We may use language in various ways; but this appears to me as great an abuse of our native English as any I have met. Had these persons no "*warrant,*" no *excuse*, for defending their lives and their liberties? Was Hewell in the observance of the public peace when attempting to slay them for asserting their liberty? Did they exhibit *malice* in thus protecting themselves against the attacks of a man who was pursuing a vocation hated of man and cursed of God?

Sir, I will not pursue the subject farther. The Secretary of

State has mistaken the objects for which this government was instituted. Our patriot fathers, who proclaimed our independence, declared that "governments are instituted among men, to secure to all the enjoyment of life, liberty, and the pursuit of happiness." But the honorable Secretary appears to think its principal design is *to secure slave-dealers in the pursuit of their execrable vocation.*

Sir, the doctrines advanced by the Secretary of State are unworthy of the reputation he sustains, or the position he holds. They are in conflict with the spirit of the age in which we live, and of the religion we profess; they are opposed to the Constitution, and to the humane promptings of our nature; they are hostile to the popular sentiment, and to the interest of the people. The people love freedom; they admire justice; but they hate oppression, and detest crime.

Yet this body is not prepared to oppose the policy, or the doctrines of the Secretary of State. The influence of the Slave Interest and of Executive power is felt here, and members have become accustomed to act in concert with the administration. But our Creator has not left his attributes of truth and justice to depend upon the favor of men in high places. Those attributes of Deity are omnipotent. They will prevail. When the political strifes around us shall cease; when the Secretary of State and ourselves shall sleep in our graves; when our names shall disappear from the records of time, the great, undying truth, "that all men are created equal, that they are endowed by their Creator with the inalienable right to Life and Liberty," will be acknowledged and observed. In the avowal of these views, I have not consulted the feelings or the influences with which I am more immediately surrounded. I could not do so consistently with the obligations I owe to myself and those who shall bear my name in coming time. I could not do so with a due regard to the duties which I owe to my country and to mankind.

The maintenance of truth and justice to the extent of our power, is an imperative duty from which we cannot be excused, although in its discharge, we may be constrained to expose political wickedness in high places.

THE AMERICAN SLAVE-TRADE.*

LEGISLATIVE STRATEGY TO MAINTAIN IT — ITS CHARACTER — FRAUD PRACTISED BY OUR MINISTER AT LONDON — CONGRESSIONAL LEGISLATION TO ENCOURAGE IT — MORAL RESPONSIBILITY OF LEGISLATORS — RIGHT OF THE PEOPLE TO BE EXEMPT FROM ITS CRIMES.

[This bill, as originally presented, was objectionable to the friends of liberty. To secure its passage, a substitute was presented, and passed by unanimous consent. While in the Senate, this substitute, as it passed the House, was struck out, and the original bill, in its objectionable form, was substituted, and passed that body. When it came back to the House, Mr. Stanley, of North Carolina, demanded the previous question, which was sustained, and thus prevented all amendments, and cut off all debate. Mr. Giddings appealed to him to withdraw the demand, that he might state his objections to the bill. Mr. Stanley refused. Mr. Giddings then voted for the bill, in order to obtain the floor to move a reconsideration of the vote, which he did as soon as it was announced. On this motion, he made the following remarks.]

MR. SPEAKER, — I have made the motion to reconsider the vote just taken, more for the purpose of calling attention to the character of the bill under consideration, than with a hope to prevent its passage.

I also desire to absolve myself, and those whom I represent, from all participation in the guilt of legislating for the encouragement of this slave-trade. Should this bill become a law, as I presume it will, I desire that the odium of its enactment may rest upon gentlemen who are willing to sustain and to vote for it; and not on those who are opposed to it.

---

* Speech on the bill to relieve the owners of the slaves lost from on board the ships " Comet and Encomium," delivered in the House of Representatives, February 13, 1843.

The duty which now devolves upon me, has resulted from the action of other gentlemen. I sought to avoid it. I call this House and the Country to witness that I have not, at this time, nor upon any former occasion, thrust this subject upon their consideration. I have at all times acted upon the defensive. Such is most emphatically the case at this time.

The history of this claim is briefly this. Some nine years since, two slave ships, the "Comet," and the "Encomium," sailed for New Orleans; the one from Alexandria, in this District, and the other from Charleston, South Carolina. They were both wrecked near the British island of New Providence, and the slaves being landed on British soil, became free. The slave-dealers applied to the President for payment for their losses, who, through our minister at London, demanded compensation for the loss of those cargoes of human flesh. He obtained twenty-five thousand pounds sterling from the British government. This amount, except about seven thousand dollars, was paid over by the Secretary of State to those who claimed to own the slaves on board those ships.

As President Van Buren was about to retire from office, his Secretary of State, Mr. Forsyth, paid over the money which remained in his hands, to the treasurer of the United States, and took a receipt therefor.

During the past year, other claimants appeared for this balance, and the Treasurer refused to pay them, until authorized by act of Congress. They then applied to this House, and the Committee on Ways and Means, through their chairman, (Mr. Fillmore,) reported a bill authorizing the payment of this money to these claimants. Seeing this bill upon my table, I examined the subject so far as to satisfy myself that the whole proceeding of the Executive, and of our Minister at the Court of St. James, was unauthorized by the Constitution, a violation of moral principle, and derogatory to the character of the United States. I therefore determined to oppose its passage. It came up for consideration twice on those days when no bill can, under our rules, pass, if objection be made. I objected to its consideration. The gentleman who reported it,

(Mr. Fillmore,) personally appealed to me to let it pass. I assured him that my objections were substantial, and that I could never consent to legislate for the benefit of those whose vocation is to traffic in our own species.

The gentleman from North Carolina (Mr. Stanley) came to my seat, requesting me to withdraw my objections, and appeared to think it unkind for me to prevent the passage of the bill. Anxious to satisfy him and all others that I was governed by principles which I deemed important, I told him, that while I would not consent to legislate for the benefit of those who deal in the bodies of mankind, I would cheerfully consent that the money should be returned to the Secretary of State, or to the President, leaving them to pay it out to whomsoever they pleased.

An amendment was thereupon drawn up, simply authorizing the Secretary of State to withdraw the money. This amendment would have prevented any discussion of this slave-dealing transaction, into which I am now unexpectedly drawn without one moment's preparation. The gentleman consulted with his colleagues, and agreed to the amendment, which was adopted by the House; and without further objection the bill passed this body. I supposed him to be acting in good faith, and entertained no suspicion that he was governed by less liberality and candor than I myself exercised. But for his apparent satisfaction, I should have continued my objection, and defeated the bill, at least for the present session; or, had it come up for discussion in committee, I would have had the privilege of expressing my views upon it. It went to the Senate, where it was amended by striking out the whole bill as it passed this body, and inserting the original as reported by the committee of this House, and then sent back to us for concurrence.

It came up this morning, upon the question of agreeing to the amendment of the Senate. The gentleman (Mr. Stanley) being upon the watch, obtained the floor, and after stating that the money belonged to the claimants, and that no member had objections to its passage except myself, who, he said, entertained "peculiar views on the subject," he demanded the "previous question," which cut off debate, and brought the House to a final vote on the bill. It was in vain that I appealed to him to withdraw his demand, and permit me to state my objections. This he refused, and has thereby forfeited all claim to that courtesy which I supposed him to possess. I voted in the affirmative on agreeing to the Senate's amendment, for the purpose of moving a reconsideration of the vote, and thereby have obtained possession of the floor by a sort of legislative stratagem, which I would not have practised under other circumstances. Having now legitimate occupancy of the floor, I will take occasion to say, that the gentleman from North Carolina (Mr. Stanley) was not authorized to express my views, either as *peculiar* to myself, or as common with others. I, Sir, have never constituted him the exponent of my sentiments. I usually speak for myself; and if he intended to say that I am the only member opposed to this bill, he states that which he was not authorized to assert. Other gentlemen were anxious to state their objections; but his adroitness in demanding the previous question, cut them off from this ordinary privilege in legislation.

I mention these facts to justify myself before the country, and to inform the people of the legerdemain, the tricks made use of by slave-holders to prevent exposure of the iniquities which attend their cherished institution. I will now proceed to the examination of the bill.

We are called on to interpose our legislative powers in aid of certain individuals of this city and of South Carolina, who, in 1831, entered into a commercial speculation in the bodies of men, women, and children. Many of them were born here under our laws, and were entitled by every principle of humanity to our protection. Here, Sir, in view of this hall, under the shadow of "the star-spangled banner" which floats over this edifice, consecrated to freedom, to the maintenance of the undying truth "that governments are instituted to secure all men in the enjoyment of life, liberty, and the pursuit of happiness," these hucksterers in human flesh critically examined the bodies and limbs, and judged of the age, the qualities, and marketable value of fathers, mothers, sisters, brothers, and children. I doubt whether any slave-market in Africa was ever attended by more expert dealers in human chattels, than was the market of this city, which profanes the name of Washington. But, Sir, their victims were born and bred under our laws for this very purpose. This city, and the surrounding country, had been familiar to them from their earliest recollection; here were the scenes of their childhood, to which they had become attached; here they had formed their associations; in our churches they had listened to the preaching of the gospel, and there they had been admitted to church fellowship; and there they had partaken of the holy communion, as members of our various Christian denominations. Such were the people whose bodies were made merchandise under our laws. Such were the people purchased by those slave-dealers, who now ask us to aid them in carrying out their speculations in the bodies of Presbyterians, Baptists, Methodists, and Episcopalians.

Who shall attempt a description of the separation of these people, — the tearing asunder of all the ties of domestic life, — the brother taken and the sister left, — the parent forced from her weeping children, — the shrieking wife forced away from her frantic husband and family?

I judge not for others; but I would as soon have united in that speculation, and shared in the crimes of those purchases, and the scenes to which I refer, as I would encourage those iniquities, by legislating for the benefit of those who committed them.

But this coffle of native-born Americans was marched to yonder wharf. There lay the ship "Comet," ready to receive her cargo of humanity. Her manifest was made out and signed by the proper officer. Those people cast a last, long, lingering look, and bade a final farewell to the scenes of their childhood and youth, and to all they held dear in this world. We, Sir, were in our places in this hall, bland and smiling as a summer's morning. The unutterable horror which rested upon those sad hearts did not oppress us. The pangs which tortured their souls did not disturb our enjoyments. But we are now asked to participate in that guilt, by passing this bill; and, methinks, if we will but listen, we may hear the sighs and groans of those victims of oppression.

I am unable to say, with precision, what we were doing when those objects of congressional barbarity bade a lasting farewell to the proud dome which towers above us. Probably, some member was expatiating upon the "*inalienable rights of man*;" upon that "*largest liberty*," of which we hear so much. Or, peradventure, some slave-holding member was demonstrating to this body that Congress possesses no right to interfere with this slave-trade, which is upheld and sustained by laws of our own enactment, and which we are now asked to encourage, by passing the bill before us. Whatever we were engaged in, these people were taken on board the "Comet," at a port in this district, under the exclusive legislation of Congress. The sails were unfurled; and no port upon the savage coast of Africa ever sent forth in one ship more sighing and weeping and human suffering than was borne from yonder wharf in that slave-ship.

Our laws, — the statutes of Congress, — authorized this savage barbarity, this perpetration of crime, from the contemplation of which we shrink with horror. The "Encomium" took her departure from Charleston, South Carolina. Her cargo of human chattels was purchased and collected under the laws of that State, and both ships left the jurisdiction of the local laws which authorized the holding of man as property. They entered upon the "high seas," where no slavery exists on board American vessels. These people, therefore, became free *in law* the instant those ships passed beyond the jurisdiction of South Carolina and Virginia. The "Comet," when passing down the river, entered within the jurisdiction of Virginia, and her slaves were held as such, under Virginia laws, until they passed out upon the Atlantic, beyond the jurisdiction of that State. Then the people collected here and shipped as slaves became *freemen*. On this point I expressed my views fully in June last, in some remarks which I then had the honor of making relative to the slave-dealers, who claimed to own the people on board the "Creole." I will not now repeat that argument. It applies with its full force to this bill. All jurists will agree, that the moment these ships passed beyond the jurisdiction of State laws, and entered upon the "high seas," the shackles fell from their limbs, and they were, in the eye of the law, transformed to freemen, clothed with all the attributes of American liberty.

While thus free in view of the law, they were yet held in subjection by the superior intelligence of their oppressors, who, with the aid of chains and the scourge, held dominion over them, intending to carry them to New Orleans for sale.

While they were thus held in subjection, they were shipwrecked near the British island of New Providence. The wreckers carried both them and their former masters to the port of Nassau, where they became subject to British laws. An overruling Providence had thus conducted them to a British island, where their rights were protected. By landing on British soil, they gained no new right, nor did they thereby become possessed of any legal privilege to which they were not entitled while upon the Atlantic Ocean. But, once on British soil, their legal rights were protected by British authority.

This, Sir, was the misfortune of these piratical slave-merchants. When they had landed on that island, they became subject to *law*. They were no longer able to trample upon the rights of their victims. Chains and whips became useless where the law of human rights was in force. They saw their "locomotive property" move about with an entire indifference to their commands. The British officers would neither seize these emancipated slaves, nor furnish bloodhounds to perform that task; but permitted them to go from place to place at the dictation of their own wills, without heeding the griefs, or listening to the entreaties of their late oppressors. The people who had thus become free greatly rejoiced in their liberty, and devoutly thanked God for their deliverance from the oppression and degradation to which they had been subjected in this land of boasted freedom.

Thus closed the voyages of these slave-ships. The slave-merchants returned to this city, and called on the President for remuneration. They declared, that, inasmuch as the colored people carried from this district and from South Carolina would not go to New Orleans to be sold like swine in the market, therefore the people of England ought to pay for their bodies. And it appears that the President was of the same opinion. But, be that as it may, he consented to act as the agent of these speculators in human flesh; to use our national influence to sustain this traffic in the bodies of native-born Americans.

Here, Sir, was the point where the Executive transcended his constitutional obligations. He had no legitimate nor constitutional right thus to involve our nation in the support of this piracy. He had not been elevated by the people of this great Republic to that high office for the purpose of thus disgracing the nation in the eyes of the Christian world. That prostitution of our national character and influence was unconstitutional, and an outrage upon our character as a nation. I expressed my views on this point, also, in my remarks upon the "Creole case," to which I have heretofore referred.

I submit to the consideration of gentlemen, whether the time has not arrived when the representatives from the free States ought to speak frankly and fearlessly on this subject. Is it not due to the President, as well as to ourselves, that he should hear an expression of the popular feeling on this subject? For, Sir, the people of the North are indignant at being thus involved in the guilt of this infamous traffic. Gentlemen here from the free States are either willing to see their constituents and themselves thus subsidized to the support of this "American piracy," or they are opposed to it. I desire to hear those who favor this slave-trade speak out in plain and definite language, and avow their opinions. Let them point us to that clause of the Constitution which authorizes the President thus to involve the people of the nation in the crimes attendant upon this execrable commerce. Why do members sit here in silence? Why so timid and trembling? Do they distrust the power of truth? Do they tremble before the frown of the slave-holder? Sir, let us be *men*. Let us maintain the dignity of our manhood, the rights of our people, and the Constitution of our country. If gentlemen really feel that our people are bound to maintain this slave-trade, are under constitutional obligations to go to war and shed their blood, that these pirates may pursue their vocation, let them say it. If not, let them speak against it. If the President were acting in pursuance of his constitutional duty, in demanding of Great Britain a compensation to these slave-holders, it is unquestionably our duty to sustain him in that demand, even at the expense of war. But, if we are not under such obligation, then has that officer overstepped the bounds of his constitutional authority. No one would suppose, that the duty of this government is performed, when the President makes a demand in such case, and his demand is refused. If it be his duty to encourage and sustain the slave-trade, by demanding compensation for slaves, who are emancipated in the manner that these were, it would, unquestionably, be our duty to sustain that demand by an appeal to arms, if we should fail to obtain indemnity to the slave-dealers in any other way. This subject is, therefore, important to the people, and to the civilized world.

Gentlemen may differ in their views; but I would as soon see northern men pierced by British bayonets, while defending this slave-trade, as to see them disgraced, by tamely submitting to become the instruments for sustaining it.

But, Sir, the President was not alone in his efforts to involve the nation in the odium of this slave-trade. His Secretary of State, (Mr. Van Buren,) a northern man, bred in the love of liberty, united with the President in this work, gave official instructions to our minister at the Court of St. James, and brought all the resources of his intellect to the aid of these miscreant dealers in the bodies of men, who were greatly their superiors in all that constitutes moral worth. The zealous interest which he took in the maintenance of this slave-trade, is well expressed in his letter to our minister at London, in which he says:

"In the present state of our diplomatic relations with the government of his Britannic Majesty, the most immediately pressing of the matters with which the United States legation at London is now charged, is the claim of certain citizens against Great Britain for a number of slaves, the *cargoes* of the three vessels wrecked in the British islands in the Atlantic."

We then had a controversy with Great Britain, in regard to our north-eastern boundary. In order to protect our interests there, soon after the date of this letter, Congress provided, and placed at the disposal of the President, ten millions of dollars, and gave him power to raise fifty thousand troops. Yet, the vast interests at stake in that quarter and in the North-west, were all matters of minor consideration, when compared with these *cargoes*. Mark the language of a professed democrat, — "*cargoes*" of women, and "*cargoes*" of men. This, Sir, is the language of him who is considered the very paragon of northern democracy; who is destined, by the magic of his influence, to prostrate the political aspirations of the talented favorite of the democrats of the South. Sir, will our democratic friends at the North, those who, with the patriots of '76, hold that "all men are created *equal*," consider this language, this servile truckling to the slave-breeding interests, as a sufficient passport to their favor?

Another gentleman acted somewhat conspicuously in this negotiation. He, Sir, was bred in the "Old Dominion," where, to use the words of one of her most talented sons, "*men are reared for the market like oxen for the shambles.*" It was, therefore, expected that he would bring to the discharge of his duties, as assistant agent, resident in London, all the zeal and devotion which subsequently characterized his efforts to subserve the interests of his employers. I refer to *Andrew Stevenson*, our late minister at the Court of St. James. But, Sir, I speak of him and the others as *agents for these slave-merchants*, for the reason that they acted *as such*. When thus acting, without any constitutional authority, they were to be regarded as acting in their individual characters, and not as public officers. Had they, or either of them, undertaken to act as the commission agent or broker for any other band of pirates than those who avowed themselves such, no one would have regarded their acts

4*

as binding upon this nation or the people of these United States; yet they possessed the same authority to prostitute our character to the support of any other piratical transaction, as they had to involve this nation in a commerce that we ourselves and the whole Christian world denounce as *piracy*.

I crave the attention of the friends of Mr. Stevenson. I hope and trust they will not fail to do all in their power to sustain the accuracy of his official assertions. In his letter to Lord Palmerston of December, 1836, speaking of this claim for slaves, he says:

"The undersigned feels assured, that it will only be necessary to refer Lord Palmerston to the provisions of the Constitution of the United States, and the laws of many of the States, to satisfy him of the existence of slavery, and that slaves are regarded and protected as property; that, by these laws, there is, in fact, no distinction in principle between property in persons and property in things; and that the government have more than once, in the most solemn manner, determined that slaves killed in the service of the United States, even in a state of war, were to be regarded as property, and not as persons, and the government held responsible for their value."

Now, Sir, if there be an instance in which this House has acknowledged slaves to be property, Mr. Stevenson and his friends can show us the record. If this body, or Congress, in any instance, from the formation of the government to this day, has determined "that slaves killed in the public service, in time of war, [or in time of peace,] *were to be regarded as property, and the government held responsible for their value*," the friends of that gentleman, after corresponding with him, and having full time to examine the subject, can refer us to such case; can show us the record of its passage. As chairman of the Committee on Claims, it became my official duty, long since, to examine this subject. I did so carefully and thoroughly; and, I hesitate not to declare, that no such record exists; that the records of this body and of the Treasury Department show this assertion of our minister at London to be *unfounded and untrue*. These records show, that, in every instance where application for such payment was made, the claim has been refused. I, therefore, say to the people of the nation, and to the British ministry, that this assertion of Mr. Stevenson was deceptive and fraudulent; that this money, which we are now called on to pay over to these slave-dealers, was obtained from the people of England by "*fraudulent pretences.*"

The British ministers could not be supposed to understand the action of our government, in regard to the payment for slaves. They had a right to expect the assertions of the American minister to be correct and truthful. Relying upon his statements, they concluded to deal with Americans, as in former times they dealt with Algerines, — to pay an extravagant ransom for those people; and the sum of seventy-five thousand dollars was therefore paid over and transmitted to the honorable Secretary of State. These funds were not placed at the disposal of Congress, neither were they paid into the Treasury of the United States. The whole transaction was managed by the Executive. He received the money, instituted the inquiry as to those who claimed to be the owners of the slaves, and paid to each his portion. In all this, he acted independently of Congress. He made no report of his doings. In truth, the people were ignorant of the whole matter; nor were we, the representatives of the people, consulted. The money was mostly paid over to the claimants; but when Mr. Van Buren and his cabinet were about to retire from office, the Secretary of State had in his possession some seven thousand dollars of the money thus extorted by fraud and misrepresentation from the British government. Mr. Van Buren, not having fully completed the business in which he had been so long engaged as *the representative of slave merchants*, bequeathed to William Selden, treasurer of the United States, the trust of closing the transaction. The money was paid to him, and a receipt taken. This was done without any authority of law whatever; and the treasurer might have paid it to the slave-owners, by virtue of the same authority as that by which he received it. The veriest tyro in law will at once see that it is not in the power of every man who pleases, to charge the government with moneys, by making a deposit with the treasurer, unless it be authorized by law; no such law existed in this case, and the only legal effect was to make the treasurer liable in his individual capacity, as trustee of the persons who possess the real interest in the money. Now, I think it perfectly clear, that no action whatever of Congress was necessary to authorize the withdrawal of this money from the Treasury. In contemplation of law, it had never been there, but was in the private custody of Mr. Selden. Yet, we are called on now to close up this slave-dealing agency by a solemn act of Congress; thereby making ourselves and constituents participants in the fraud, the moral turpitude, and the crime that have characterised this transaction, from the purchase of these cargoes, up to the time of paying the money to Mr. Selden. I can see but one object in pressing this law upon the consideration of this body. Its passage will involve us in the odium which the President, Secretary of State, and our minister to London have brought upon themselves. It will make us share the disgrace with them. To such action I object.

For many years, the people of the free States have endeavored to relieve the nation from the deep odium resting upon it by reason of this slave-trade. For that purpose they have sent to us their petitions, couched in the most respectful language, asking that it may be prohibited, under suitable penalties. And what treatment have these freemen — these supporters of our national character — met in this hall? Why, Sir, they have been assailed with almost every opprobrious epithet which our language could supply. Their petitions have been scouted from our presence without being read, or heard, or even received at the hands of their representatives. I myself have presented the requests of thousands of our most worthy citizens, — of our philanthropists, our divines, our jurists, and statesmen, — invoking the action of this body against this slave-trade, praying that it might be prohibited under the same penalties which are attached to like crimes when committed on the African coast. But, Sir, if I happened to cast my eye upon the petition, or assumed the appearance of reading it, cries of order, *order*, ORDER, would be shouted from the mouths of scores of slave-holders and overseers.

Sir, what magic wand has been waved over us, that we now

sit so quietly deliberating upon this bill to encourage the slave-trade; or rather, why do we now pass this bill without deliberation? Shall we turn round at the bidding of this slave-dealing influence, and quietly submit to do the bidding of our southern masters? Sir, I feel humbled, deeply humbled, when I cast my eyes around this hall, and see representatives of the free States sitting in mute silence, and aiding by their vote the passage of a bill shamelessly bearing on its title the character of a bill for the relief of slave-traders. What power has thus miraculously silenced the voice of northern freedom and northern honor? What spell has now palsied the arms which should defend the rights and interests of the free States? Shall we now submit, and meanly assist in carrying out this attempt to involve ourselves, and our constituents, in the disgrace of the slave-trade? Wherewith shall we humble ourselves before those who claim this control over us? Where shall we find sackcloth with which to cover our bodies, or ashes to cast upon our heads, while, with downcast eyes and trembling voices, we give a response disgraceful to those whom we represent? Sir, the trembling slave, who dares not look up in the presence of his tyrant master, has some excuse for his degradation; but I can find no justification whatever for northern men, — the representatives of freemen, — who thus tamely surrender the rights and the honor of their constituents, and become the willing instruments for carrying on and sustaining this detestable commerce in slaves.

Sir, I have a curiosity to witness the response of members to the question which will soon be propounded, to see how many will now vote in favor of this bill, who, for years, have regularly voted to gag their own constituents upon this identical subject. If I were to suggest a subject for the pencil, it should be the one on which I am now commenting. I would select a northern democrat, holding a gag in the mouth of his constituent with one hand, while the other is employed to examine his pockets for money to pay the expenses of this slave agency; at the same time most solemnly saying to his constituent, "*you have nothing to do with the slave-trade,*" "you have no right to interfere with the matter."

I regret being forced into these remarks. I have made every effort to avoid it which duty and independence would permit; but, notwithstanding my exertions for that purpose, I have been driven to it, and I trust that gentlemen will excuse me if I speak frankly. The subject of slavery, or of the slave-trade, never ought to have been mentioned in this hall. Accursed be the memory of him who first profaned this temple of freedom with the discussion of slavery and the slave-trade. Let the execrations of posterity rest upon those who involved the national government in these subjects, by enacting laws for the support of slavery. But we have become involved in these questions; and it shall be my object now, and at all times, to correct the error into which we have fallen. I will use my utmost exertions to banish it from our deliberations; to erase these laws from our records; to separate the people of the free States and this government from slavery; and to place an impassable gulf between our people of the free States and an institution which we detest. It was this desire which led me to consent to the arrangement by which these persons might have obtained this money, without involving us in their guilt and disgrace.

Yet, Sir, this bill is thrust upon us; not, however, with the intention of discussing it, but for the purpose of forcing us to pass it without discussion, and without investigating its merits. We are asked to sustain it without examination; and if we refuse to do that, it is to be forced upon us by means of the previous question. This want of examination, and consequent ignorance of the bill, is one reason why we ought not to vote for its passage.

Sir, self-respect, a proper regard to consistency, forbids the passage of this bill. We, Sir, by former statutes have declared the slave-trade upon the African coast to be *piracy*, and have affixed to it the highest penalty known to human laws. We hang those who deal in slaves on that coast, as unfit for human association. But, the offence of the persons who now seek our aid is greater than is that of men who deal in African slaves. People born here, in the midst of civilized life, who have attained some knowledge of their rights, who have been taught their own immortality, and feel the dignity of manhood stirring within them, suffer far more keenly under the degradation which the slave-trade subjects them to, than do their more ignorant and stupid brethren of Africa. It is more shocking to the feelings of our people to see Christians buy and sell those who worship the same God, trust in the same Redeemer, rely upon the same salvation as ourselves, than it is to see them deal in the savages of a heathen land. I do not say that the iniquity is really greater, but I insist that it is more abhorrent to the popular feeling. But, Sir, while we hang men for dealing in slaves on the African coast, we are called to aid those who commit the same crimes on the American coast. This is inexcusable. The character of crime is not modified by the longitude in which it is committed. God views this buying and selling of his image with the same detestation, whether practised on the eastern or the western shores of the Atlantic. And, Sir, we ought to deal out justice with an even hand. Those slave-dealers, for whose benefit we are asked to pass this bill, are more deserving the halter at our hands, than they are pecuniary encouragement.

We expend a vast amount of the people's money annually, to suppress the slave-trade in Africa; while we are called on to pass this bill to sustain and encourage the committing of the same crimes here in our midst. Will gentlemen vote to encourage this traffic to-day, and then turn round to-morrow and vote millions from the public treasure to suppress it? Have we not sufficient regard to the reputation of Congress to avoid such tergiversation?

Sir, this bill provides that the treasurer shall pay this money to the *owners of those people!* What is to be the evidence which shall entitle one man to hold another as property? The proposition is of itself an absurdity too palpable to require exposure. What authority has our Creator given these slave-dealers to hold in degrading servitude men who are in every accomplishment which constitutes moral worth, their superiors? The only title which any man ever had to his fellow-man is that of power, of *brute force.* It is the same title which the robber has to your purse; or the pirate to his captured ship, and the victims on board. The people whom I represent, repudiate such claims. I detest them.

But the bill goes further, and directs the treasurer to pay to the owners of each slave "such sum as he is entitled to receive." By this form of expression, I suppose it was intended to give to each the value of the person claimed. How will you estimate the value of a man? Does it depend upon his complexion? for, Sir, there are all grades of color in this market. Or which is deemed the most valuable, — black or white, or a mixture of both? Or shall our officer be governed by the genealogy of the slave in estimating its value? If he have descended in the paternal line from one of the best families in the "Old Dominion," shall he be deemed of greater value than though he were of pure African blood? Does such mixture *improve* or *deteriorate* the value of a man? These, Sir, are, all of them, "*delicate questions*," which I should like to hear answered by some of the friends of this bill. Again: some may desire to know whether intelligence is to fix the value? Is a man who reads and writes, and possesses better information than his master, or than masters generally possess, of more value than one who is stupid, ignorant, and incapable of instructing his owner? And, Sir, others may wish to know what the political faith of a man is, before they fix his value. They will inquire whether he be a whig, or a democrat, or an advocate of freedom? Others will inquire to what religious sect he belongs? and which sells the highest in market, Presbyterians, Methodists, Quakers, Baptists, or Episcopalians? These may be termed "*delicate* questions," but they will, of necessity, come under the consideration of those who are to fix the value of men and women under the provisions of this bill.

But, it is said that we hold this money as trustee of the owners of these slaves. I deny the assertion. I have already shown that the money was placed into the hands of the treasurer without authority of law, and that he now holds in his individual, and not in his official, capacity. That he may now dispose of it without any reference to the action of this House. We, Sir, have never consented to act as trustee of these slave-dealers. They could not constitute us such except by our consent. The Constitution has imposed upon us no such duty. Neither the President, nor his Secretary of State, nor our Minister at London, nor all of them acting together, could impose upon us the duty of acting as the trustee of these outlaws; nor could they impose upon us the constitutional or the moral duty of legislating for the benefit of a commerce hated of men and cursed of God. Those high officers of government can impose upon me no moral obligation to participate in this crime of making merchandise of mankind. No, Sir, they cannot step between God and myself, and absolve me from the allegiance I owe to Him; nor can they release me from the command of Him, who, speaking as never man spake, enjoined upon me to "do unto others as I would that they should do unto me." I would not be willing to suffer at the hands of my fellow man that, brutal degradation which this slave-trade inflicts upon its victims. Nor, Sir, will I by vote, or act, encourage or sustain others in that work, that crime of degrading and brutalizing our fellow men, by selling them like swine in the market.

Sir, I would be as willing to go forth into the city and country, and buy up men, women, and children, and transport them to New Orleans and sell them, as I would to sit in this hall and vote for the bill before us. Sir, it is an acknowledged principle in ethics, that the responsibility of man is measured by his intelligence. If that be true, I submit to gentlemen whether the guilt of numbers here is not even greater than is that of those who, under our laws, buy and sell mankind.

These laws have been enacted by Congress; no man denies or doubts that we have power to repeal them. Every schoolboy is conscious that we possess authority to repeal those laws; yet, Sir, when our constituents from the free States, send their petitions here asking such repeal in respectful language, we treat them with contempt; we refuse to hear them read, and in order to insult those who send them here, we refuse to refer or take any notice of them; they are silently laid upon the table; and those members who would advocate their respectful consideration, are not permitted to speak in their favor.

But, Sir, when these slave-merchants, dealing in human flesh, happen to have made an unfortunate operation, they send us a petition to help them recover their loss; we receive their petition with respect; we treat it with marked attention; we refer it to the most important committee of this body; a bill is immediately reported, and attempts are made to carry it through without discussion.

Thus do numbers here lend their influence and energy to encourage and maintain this slave-trade. We do it with a full knowledge of the pain and intense suffering which it inflicts upon our fellow men. But the slave-dealer is more ignorant; he has been bred to his vocation; his feelings have become callous to human suffering; his sympathies for his fellow beings have been blunted; he knows that Congress, composed of intelligent men, distinguished for their moral character, have authorized this commerce in our own species, and he pursues it with but little compunction of conscience; he sees us scout all efforts to prevent this traffic in the bodies of men and of women, while we lend our efforts to encourage those engaged in it. Our example is respected, and bears an influence throughout the country. His is limited, and few are led to follow his practice.

Now, Sir, who will deny, that the member sitting in this hall, voting for this bill, and to exclude all petitions for the abolition of this slave-trade, incurs even greater guilt than the ignorant dealer in human flesh?

I protest against all participation in such guilt. I will not bathe my hands in the blood of those victims. I will not be made a party to those crimes. I will not insult my constituents by voting for this bill, while their voice is not permitted to be heard in favor of humanity. I will not lend my influence to carry out this speculation in the bodies of women and of children; to aid men who deserve the gallows and halter, instead of legislative encouragement. Patriotism, self-respect, the honor of our race, forbid that we should lend our legislative aid in favor of this slave-trade; our love of virtue, justice, and humanity forbid it; the voice of Christianity, the laws of God, forbid that we should become parties to the crimes of these slave-merchants, or to the frauds and misrepresentations of our minister at London.

Sir, place this subject in whatever attitude you please, throw around it whatever sophistry the human intellect is capable of calling into exercise, yet the disgusting *fact* will stand portrayed to the world in coming time, that, in the year 1843, this American Congress sat gravely legislating in aid of this traffic in human flesh. Let it go upon the record. Let the archives of this body bear to coming generations the proof that two hundred and forty-two American statesmen were on this day engaged in granting relief and encouragement to persons engaged in that execrable commerce, which Mr. Jefferson declared had "*rendered us the scoff of infidel nations.*" But let not my name be found among its advocates. Let not my descendants, in future years, be called to blush for their ancestor, on reading the record of this day's proceeding. Sooner, far sooner, would I have it erased from the records of this House; yea, sooner would I have it blotted from existence, than see it placed on record in favor of the bill before us.

Yet, Sir, I am conscious that the bill will become a law. Gentlemen from the free States, representing constituents who detest the slave-trade, will vote for the bill. The house is committed in favor of its passage, and members are impatient at the delay occasioned by my remarks. Soon as I close, it will be pressed to the final vote, and a deed will be consummated which will excite deep and lasting astonishment in the minds of those, who, in future years, shall read the story of this day's legislation.

RIGHTS OF THE STATES CONCERNING SLAVERY.*

POWER OF THE FEDERAL GOVERNMENT IN TIME OF WAR — JURISDICTION OF CONGRESS IN TIME OF PEACE OVER DISTRICT OF COLUMBIA — DUTY OF MEMBERS TO MEET THE QUESTION OF SLAVERY — RIGHT OF THE PEOPLE TO PETITION CONGRESS RELATING TO SLAVERY.

[As early as the year 1832, the people of the free States sent various petitions to Congress relative to slavery. In 1835, a resolution was introduced by a slave-holder from Virginia, and adopted by the House, for suppressing all action upon such petitions. Similar resolutions were adopted at each Congress, up to 1841, when the principle was incorporated into the rules of that body. All these movements for suppressing the right of petition, were steadily and ably opposed by the Honorable John Quincy Adams and a few others who sympathized with him. At the commencement of the twenty-eighth Congress, the question of continuing this rule came up, and was decided in the negative. This decision was important, as this constitutional right was thereby regained. On this question Mr. Giddings delivered the following speech.]

Mr. Speaker, — If we judge of the importance of the subject under discussion, by the talent and zeal elicited during the debate, we shall surely regard it as a matter of the highest consequence. Indeed, some gentlemen have declared that it involves the permanency of our Federal Union. In this opinion I concur. I do not believe it possible to continue this rule and preserve the Union. Yet, I have been highly gratified in witnessing the candid and dispassionate manner in which the debate has been thus far conducted. Gentlemen have participated in the discussion with that forbearance and kindness

* Speech upon a motion to continue the rule excluding petitions respecting slavery. Delivered in House of Representatives, February 13, 1844.

becoming statesmen engaged in the examination of matters of high interest to their country. The subject of slavrey has been examined in the spirit of candor, and gentlemen have treated each other with the same toleration that is exhibited on other occasions. I rejoice that the time has arrived when we can meet in this hall and compare views and examine the rights of different sections of the country, without excitement, and in a manner becoming those who feel their responsibility to the public.

I am aware that the discussion of any subject relating to slavery is unpleasant to a portion of our fellow members; but, should gentlemen who follow me in this debate forget the decorum which is due to the dignity of this body, it shall not arise from any example of mine. I intend to speak forth my own sentiments freely; but I hope to do so without personal offence.

In the discharge of our legislative duties, we have reached that point at which we unfortunately find ourselves divided in opinions upon an important subject. The adoption or rejection of the former rule of this House, by which the great mass of petitions concerning slavery have been heretofore rejected, is soon to be determined.

These petitions have been characterized by those who have preceded me as *abolition* petitions; but what those gentlemen understand by the term "abolition," we have yet to learn. It is, undoubtedly, understood by some to mean the abolition of slavery in the States; by others, to refer to the abolition of slavery in the District of Columbia; by others, it is understood to refer to the coastwise slave-trade; by others, to the separation of the people of the free States from the support of slavery. Indeed, petitions for the repeal of any of the laws now in force within the District of Columbia, relating to slavery, petitions to prohibit officers of the Federal Government from the capture of fugitive slaves, or against appropriating the national treasure to the support of slavery or the slave-trade, are denominated "*abolition petitions*," and are not suffered to be read, referred, or reported upon. The objections to them are, that they interfere with the rights of the people of the slave-holding States;

yet no gentleman has attempted to set forth or define the rights which he considers as encroached upon by these petitions. Here all our difficulties arise. Let us once clearly determine the rights of the several States, in respect to slavery, and it will then be easy to say, whether such right is sought to be encroached upon by any particular petition. These rights of the States were fixed by the Constitution, and we must resort to that instrument, to the debates in the Convention that framed it, and to contemporaneous history, in order to ascertain precisely their character.

Prior to the formation of our Federal Constitution, each State possessed and exercised supreme and unlimited control over the institution of slavery within its own territory. Virginia, in obedience to the will of her people, upheld and continued it. Massachusetts, in the exercise of her supreme power, emancipated her slaves. In the exercise of this act of her sovereign power, she took counsel from none of her sister States; she acted in obedience to the will of her people, and set an example which was soon after followed by six of the other original States. The example was well calculated to exert an influence upon the institution of slavery throughout the Union. Yet, whatever may have been the effect upon the slaves of other States, they could interpose no objection to this proceeding of their patriotic sister, for the reason that she was as independent of them on this subject, as she was of any foreign power.

When the Convention that framed the Constitution assembled, the delegates brought with them the same diversity of sentiment that exists among us to-day. One portion were hostile to slavery, and another portion were in favor of its continuance. There was, therefore, but one mode of disposing of the question. That was, to leave it precisely as it was, and to let it remain with each of the several States. Each State, therefore, retained its whole and entire power over that institution. They surrendered no portion to the Federal Government. I desire to be understood distinctly on this part of the subject. I wish to ascertain, if possible, the precise point of disagreement between us. I am anxious to develop the exact issue on which we are contending; to let the country know definitely what is claimed by the South, and denied by the North; and what is claimed by the North, and denied by the South.

I, therefore, lay it down as one of the principles on which our Federal Constitution was based, that each of the several States should retain to themselves and their people, the entire power over slavery which they had previously enjoyed. In saying this, it is not my intention to deny the doctrine advanced by the venerable member from Massachusetts, (Mr. Adams,) "that, in case of war, when the existence of our government is threatened, we may then avail ourselves of that right of self-preservation which is based upon the law of nature;" and, if necessary to the public safety, may release any portion or all of the slaves in any or all of the States. It is a power which lies behind all constitutional provisions, and is consequent upon a state of war only, but has no application in time of peace. It is, I believe, well understood by military men; it was practised by General Jackson, General Gaines, and General Jessup, and, I believe, by General Scott, while commanding our armies in the South. They did not hesitate to sever the relation of master and slave, whenever they believed the public good demanded it. In doing that, they merely exercised that power which is always attendant upon a state of war, and which is seldom denied. It therefore forms no exception to the doctrine which I have asserted, that each of the several States now holds and enjoys the same power over slavery, within its own territory, that it enjoyed under the old confederation; that Virginia and each of the slave States now holds her slaves as independently of the other States and of the Federal Government, as she does of Mexico or of other foreign powers; that the Congress of the United States possesses no right to interfere with that institution in Virginia or any other slave State. On this point, I think southern men will agree with me. Indeed, I understand this to be the doctrine entertained by northern men, and that there is an entire concurrence of opinion on this point.

I stated that each of the several States retains its entire power over the institution of slavery which it possessed under the old confederation. It therefore follows, that Massachusetts and the free States have the same supreme and unqualified right to be wholly exempt from the support of slavery that they enjoyed prior to the adoption of the Constitution; and that Congress possesses no more power than does the Parliament of Great Britain, to involve them in the expense, the odium, or the guilt of that institution. That this right of the people of the free States to enjoy their liberty, free from all participation in the support of slavery, is as supreme and unlimited as is the right of the slave States to continue and enjoy it. I wish to call the particular attention of those who follow me in this debate to this right of the free States.

If there be any issue between us, it must be founded on this particular doctrine. I, therefore, most respectfully ask southern gentlemen to meet me upon it. If they admit the correctness of my doctrine, let them say so; if they deny it, let them declare such denial in a plain and direct manner. It is surely time that we should know and understand distinctly the cause of our controversy; that we should bring forth the well defined subject-matter in dispute, and place it conspicuously before the country. In the spirit of kindness, I request them to keep no longer at a distance from the point in issue; that they will no longer deal in vague generalities; that they will lay aside all declamation; that they will cease to denounce *abolition*, and meet the matters in controversy by fair argument and dispassionate reason. It is unbecoming us as statesmen, to occupy our time here contending before the nation for years, without being able to lay our finger upon the precise point in controversy.

Mr. Speaker,—if we do not possess the moral courage to examine minutely and particularly the cause of contention, I feel that it is our duty to retire from this hall, and to give place to those who will not fear to meet these questions upon their true merits. I, Sir, am regarded as an abolitionist. I have no more objection to the term than Washington, or Jefferson, or Franklin had. I care not what name gentlemen attach to me, provided they do not misrepresent my principles. Of these I prefer to be my own exponent; and I repeat, that whatever issue I take with southern gentlemen, is based entirely upon this plain and obvious doctrine of the Federal Constitution, — that this government possesses no power whatever to involve the people of the free States in the support of slavery.

Here, Sir, I take my stand, where I have always stood since I entered this hall. For this doctrine, I shall continue to contend, until convinced that it is erroneous. I am not to be driven from it by the cry of *abolition;* for if it be abolition, then am I an abolitionist. Neither am I to be frightened from this position by the cry of *fanaticism;* for if this doctrine be fanaticism, then am I a fanatic. This is the doctrine which I have maintained in public addresses, and in private conversation, in my writings, and in my oral communications on this floor and among my constituents. I go not beyond it, nor do I stop short of it. In this respect, I believe I may say that the great mass of those called abolitionists agree with me. It is true that they are much misunderstood and much misrepresented; but I know of none who advocate any encroachment upon the constitutional rights of the slave States. It is true that they, and nearly all of our northern people, hold slavery in abhorrence. They will, on all occasions, exert their moral influence against oppression in all its forms. They regard that a duty, and so do I; and whether I am in this hall or elsewhere, I can never cease to exert my moral influence against slavery, wherever that influence may extend. But, Sir, duty teaches me obedience to the Constitution which I am sworn to support; and while that remains unchanged, I cannot either here or elsewhere exert my influence to violate it. Nor do the abolitionists ask or expect such an exercise of the powers intrusted to us. But they and the whigs, and the great mass of those within my district, called democrats, demand and expect of us a firm and decided resistance to all attempts to encroach upon their rights, by involving them in the support of an institution which they hold in execration.

I am, however, aware, that a large portion of our people, both North and South, have been unconscious of the extent to which the people of the free States have been involved in the support of slavery. The discussion of all subjects connected with that institution, has for many years been suppressed, both in this hall, and among the people. During these years of silence, this government has usurped to itself powers never delegated to it by the Constitution. Southern men have pressed the claims of slavery upon Congress, and northern men have quietly and without resistance permitted the government to become the patron of that institution, and the people of the free States to be made the instrument of its support.

For many years, the treaty-making power has been in the habit of embracing, in almost all our treaties with the southern and south-western Indians, a stipulation that they should surrender up, and, in some instances, that they should be vigilant in arresting and delivering up such fugitive slaves as should seek an asylum among them. For these and other stipulations, the money of the nation, drawn from the people of the free States, has been paid. For the purpose of enabling the owners of southern slaves to regain their runaway negroes, we waged a bloody and expensive war with the Indians of Florida.

At the last session of Congress, we sat here at an expense of thousands of dollars per day, legislating for the benefit of slave-traders. We spent our time, and the money of the people, to enable slave-dealers to carry out their speculations in human flesh; thus, Sir, violating the Constitution, and the constitutional rights of our people. They have sent their petitions to us couched in the most respectful language, asking that they may no longer be subjected to these abuses. And what has been our reply? Why, Sir, we have thrown their petitions back into their faces, and denounced their signers as *fanatics*.

Yet, Mr. Speaker, no man has been found willing to come forward and meet the subject upon its merits. No member here of any party, either whig or democrat, from the North or from the South, would hazard his reputation by saying that we possess the power thus to apply the funds of government to these base purposes. Nor has any man been found who would take issue with the petitioners, and say to them, and to the country, that they were bound thus to contribute of their wealth to the support of southern slavery; but we have constantly heard the same answer that is now urged against receiving these petitions. That answer, and the only answer yet adduced, is the cry of "abolition," "fanaticism," "interference with southern rights," "Hartford Convention," and "dissolution of the Union!"

I may be permitted to assure gentlemen, that the people of the North know their rights, and that such answers to their petitions will neither satisfy nor silence them. If there be any better answer, it should be brought forward; and gentlemen do themselves and their cause injustice, by neglecting to meet the question fairly. But if there be no other answer, — if gentlemen who seek the adoption of this rule, and who have preceded me in this debate, and those who shall follow me, are unable to find any other objections to these petitions than such as I have referred to, I then ask them if they do themselves justice on a subject of such grave importance, by opposing these plain and obvious truths by mere declamation.

In 1816, a large number of fugitive slaves had collected within the territory of Florida, then subject to the Spanish crown. They settled upon the Appalachicola river, erected their cabins, planted their grounds, and, with their wives and their little ones, were enjoying that liberty which the people of the North prize so highly. They also erected a fort to protect them. The President issued his orders to General Gaines, to send a force "to break up their settlement, and to return them to their owners." A gun-boat was sent up the river to execute this design. She opened a fire of hot shot upon the fort, by which the magazine was exploded, and two hundred and seventy men, women, and children were instantaneously murdered, for no other crime than a love of that liberty.

This act was committed by our servants, acting in our name, and paid with our funds. Their blood rests on the people of this nation. It was as much the act of the North as of the South. Nor was this all. During the 25th Congress, a law was passed giving more than five thousand dollars to the officers and men who committed this wholesale murder. Our people have petitioned against further acts of this kind, and shall we reject their requests? During the war in Florida, our officers and men were not only engaged in searching out and capturing fugitive slaves, but bloodhounds were procured to aid in that execrable work. Indeed, if the intelligence which we see in the public press be worthy of credit, officers and men employed in our land, naval, and revenue service, have within a few months past put forth their efforts to recapture persons fleeing from southern bondage to a land of liberty.

These facts are regarded by our people of the North, as derogatory to our national character; they hold that our Federal Constitution was formed to perpetuate liberty, and not for the support of slavery. They regard these prostitutions of our national power as involving them in the support of slavery; and they send their petitions here, praying that these abuses may cease. These respectful petitions, addressed to their servants here, are scouted from this hall, and treated with contempt. Yet no man has been found willing to stand before the nation, and boldly assert the right of this government thus to involve the people of the free States in these outrages upon the rights of man, or that we have the constitutional power to involve them in this war against human nature.

When slave-dealers, with their cargoes of human beings, have been shipwrecked near the British islands, in the West Indies, and the slaves have regained their liberty by being accidentally thrown upon free soil, our President has condescended to act as the agent and solicitor of such traders in human flesh, and, in the name of the people of this nation, to demand of the British government a compensation, in dollars and cents, for the liberty thus gained by his fellow men.

Such an interest has our Executive taken in this slave-trade, that when the persons on board the slave-ship Creole, looking forward to the deep degradation that awaited them in a southern slave-market, and inspired with that love of liberty which the God of nature has implanted in the breast of every man, arose upon their oppressors, asserted and maintained the rights to which they were entitled, he demanded of the British crown their value in dollars and cents, as a compensation to men who would have been hanged under our own laws, had they followed the same vocation on the shores of Africa.

All these acts of the government were plain and obvious violations of our Constitution. They were unauthorized by any constitutional provision. They involved the people of the free States in the support of an institution which they abhor. Our people feel themselves dishonored by them, and have, therefore, sent numerous petitions, praying us to separate this government from all farther participation in this unconstitutional support of slavery. These petitions were numerously signed by men of high respectability, of intelligence and moral worth. And what answers have we returned to their reasonable requests? Why, Sir, we have spurned them from us, and have slammed our doors in the face of those from whom we hold our seats, and whose servants we are. But we have not possessed the moral courage to say to them, that we have the constitutional power thus to involve them in the inexpiable guilt of those acts to which I have referred. No, Sir, we dare not attempt to justify ourselves by argument. We shudder at the thought of appealing to reason, for that is hostile to crime. We dare not rest our justification upon the force of truth, for that would condemn us. Discussion would be equivalent to conviction. We have, therefore, refused to speak upon the subject-matter of these petitions. We have shielded ourselves behind this rule, which prohibits their being read to us, and then attempted to justify the rule by denouncing all "*interference with southern property*," and declaiming against "*incendiary petitions*."

It is a most extraordinary fact, that no gentleman who has spoken in favor of this rule, has condescended to enter upon an argument to refute the propriety or duty of granting the prayer of one of the several classes of petitions to which I have referred; and I predict that no one who comes after me, will attempt a task so difficult. They will condemn all these petitions in general terms, but they will not discuss the constitutionality of any one in particular. Such discussion would lead to an examination of *principles*, — a result from which they start back with horror. I repeat, that those gentlemen who denounce abolition so loudly and eloquently, can neither be flattered nor provoked to meet us upon any moral, political, or constitutional question in regard to slavery, embraced in any class of these petitions.

I will now proceed to the consideration of another numerous class of petitions, all of which are sought to be excluded by the adoption of this rule. They all relate to slavery within this district; some of them pray for the modification, and some for the abolition of the slave-trade here; others for the repeal of some one or more of the old laws of Maryland and Virginia, that have been re-enacted by Congress, and which are now in force within the District of Columbia; others for the repeal of all laws now in force here which support slavery, and others for the abolition of slavery generally within this district. If the rule be adopted, all these petitions are to be excluded from being received or read by the House.

We have listened to arguments intended to show that we ought not to receive these petitions. The first which I will notice is that of the gentleman from South Carolina, (Mr. Rhett,) who took it upon himself to say that the petitioners were not seeking the objects prayed for, but sent their petitions here in order to affect slavery *in the States*. I am acquainted with many of the petitioners, and know them to be men of intelligence, and in point of character and respectability not inferior to members of this body. I believe them incapable of saying one thing and meaning another; and I regard the imputation as unfounded and altogether gratuitous. Other members urge that Congress possesses no constitutional power to abolish slavery in this district, and therefore these petitions ought not to be received. If the proposition were correct, that Congress has not the power to abolish slavery within this district, I should nevertheless regard it as our duty to receive their petitions, and to treat them respectfully, and to return civil answers to those who send them to us. They are sincere in their belief, and they approach us in respectful language; and shall we throw back the petitions to them, and insult them by a contemptuous silence? If we differ from them in opinion, it would be more in accordance with my views of propriety to receive the petitions, refer them, and let a respectful report be made, showing the error into which the petitioners have fallen. This government is founded upon the will of the people; and when they become dissatisfied with it, they have the power to change or alter it, or the agents employed to carry it on. It is, therefore, important that every cause of discontent should be removed from the public mind.

Other gentlemen appear to think that the petitioners rest their demands merely upon the reception of their petitions; and that if we receive them and lay them on the table without farther notice, it will satisfy the signers. I will assure gentlemen who adopt these views, that they mistake the sentiments of those who demand our attention. They deal in no technicalities. They regard us as their servants, sent here to do their business, and carry out their wishes; and if we differ from them in respect to our powers, or in our views of policy, they expect us to say so frankly, and in a respectful manner to point out the constitutional principles, or the policy which forbids a compliance with their requests. They are competent to weigh and judge of the reasons which guide our action. They regard Truth as omnipotent, and are willing to bow to its dictates. They feel that Error alone seeks obscurity, and attempts to hide itself behind the silence of mock dignity. If, therefore, we attempt to dispose of these petitions, by laying them silently on the table, and refuse to assign our reasons for the act, it will become their duty to dismiss us, and to send agents here who possess the moral courage to set forth the reasons on which they act.

But, Mr. Speaker, I am desirous of meeting the great and principal issue which gentlemen have tendered us on this part of the subject. If the existence of slavery in this district be constitutional, if it have any legal existence within this ten miles square, it must be by force of our laws. I have no hesitation in saying, that if slavery has a legal existence here, we have the same power over it that we have over the subject of crimes, the collection of debts, or any other municipal regulation.

Slavery is defined by jurists as "the creature of municipal law." Yet it is quite certain that one man may hold another in subjection, may scourge him into obedience, without law, or even against the law under which they live. When slaves were originally imported to Virginia, there was no law authorizing slavery there. Africans were brought there, and sold, and held as property. This was done by the superior physical and intellectual power of the white people. Under the moral code of that day, it was believed to be right and proper to enslave the heathen. But those heathen soon were converted to Christianity, and their religion would not permit them to hold Christians in such degradation. The legislature, therefore, interposed its power and declared that baptism, or conversion, should not be regarded as an emancipation of the slave. This was the first statute in that State which recognized slavery. It did not establish it, but merely recognized the interest of the master in the body of his slave.

The slaves, however, soon evinced a disposition to go from place to place, at the dictation of their own desires. This propensity rendered them useless to their masters. The legislature, therefore, passed a law, authorizing any constable or other person to arrest any slave found away from his master's plantation without a passport, and to return him to his master. This, of itself, did not appear to answer the purpose, and the constable or other person making the arrest, was authorized by another statute to flog the servant, and to pass him over to the nearest constable, who should also flog him, and pass him to the next, until he reached his master, who was bound to pay a certain quantity of tobacco for the arrest, and for whipping the slave. But it was found that the slave would often run from those who attempted to arrest him, and would resist with his physical powers those who laid hands upon him. It therefore became necessary further to curtail the rights of the slave, and a statute law was then passed, authorizing the constable, or other person who should attempt to arrest such slave, to shoot or kill him, if he ran from such officer or other person, or if he resisted them after his arrest.

A subsequent statute forbade the slave to raise his hand in opposition to any white man, even in defence of his life. The natural rights of the slave were thus taken from him, one after another, until he was by *statute law* reduced to his present degraded condition. These laws gave to the master, and those who were not slaves, powers over their servants which were new and unheard of. As I have shown, they authorized the master to whip and scourge and torture the slave, and, under certain circumstances, to shoot and murder him. These powers of the master were based entirely upon statute law, and the disabilities of the slave were established by the same authority.

Now I think few men will deny that the legislature of Virginia or of Maryland had full and ample power to change, modify, or repeal any or all these statutes at the pleasure of their legislature. This point admits of no doubt or argument. It is equally plain that the repeal of any one or more of these acts of the legislature would, to a certain extent, be a modification of slavery, and that the repeal of all these laws would be a total abolition of that institution.

Notwithstanding the apparent correctness of these propositions, some gentlemen deny that the legislature of Virginia possessed the power to abolish slavery in her territory. They will not deny her power to repeal her own laws. This proposition is so plain, that they will shrink from a denial of it. They leave that point untouched, and proceed to say that her legislature cannot abolish slavery within her territory. Now, Sir, all that abolitionists ask, and all that the slaves of that State will ask, is *the repeal of those laws.* Let them be repealed, and we will no longer contend about abstractions, but we will let slavery take care of itself.

But gentlemen urge that the "master has a vested right of property in the slave." I wish some one of those eloquent members who have so often repeated this declaration, had condescended to inform us from whence the master derives his title to his slave. I ask from whence is this "vested right" derived? Biblical history informs us, that "God gave to man dominion over the fish of the sea, and over the fowls of the air, and over the cattle, and over all the earth, and over every creeping thing that creepeth upon the earth."

These are property, and we derive our title from Him who created them. But I have yet to learn that any man holds title to his fellow man from that high source. Where then does he obtain his title? Why, Sir, he holds it entirely from statute law — from the laws that authorize the master to whip and shoot his slave, and which take from the slave his natural rights of self-defence and of locomotion. Repeal those laws, and these *vested* rights would be *divested.* Let the legislature take from the limbs of the slave the cords with which they have bound him, and he will stand forth a freeman. He will then possess as much right of property in his master, as his master will in him; or rather, neither will possess any right to, or power over, the other.

Let us throw as much obscurity as we can around this subject, it will remain perfectly clear to every intelligent mind, that this right of property, and the whole power of the master over his slave, is derived from statute law, which may be repealed at the pleasure of the legislature. The slaves are as much a class of human society as the masters are. The municipal laws have degraded them, and elevated the masters. The same laws have given power to the master, and have forbidden the slave to exercise his natural rights. But these laws are at all times subject to the legislative power, and may be changed, modified, or repealed at pleasure. This was the situation of slavery within the District of Columbia, while it belonged to the States of Virginia and Maryland.

In the year 1788–'9, those States, by their separate deeds of cession, surrendered their powers over the territory now composing this district to the United States. The general government was fully authorized to take possession of it under a particular provision of the Constitution, and in pursuance of that power accepted the grant; and by act of Congress, approved February 27th, 1801, provided for its government. When Congress once spread its jurisdiction over this district, and passed laws for its government, the laws of Maryland and of Virginia ceased of course to have further force or effect here. This proposition is too plain to require illustration. From that instant, the power and laws of Virginia and Maryland ceased, and those of Congress took effect, and from that day to this, have had exclusive force and effect over the district and persons therein. But what may have misled a casual observer is, that the laws then in force within the States were re-enacted by Congress, and thereby made laws of the United States; so that the people within the district, on each side of the river, continued to be governed by the same municipal laws that had previously been in force there.

The same remark applies to all other municipal laws then in force here, — whether they had relation to the punishment of crimes, to the collection of debts, or to any of the relations which men hold to slavery.

I desire to be understood as stating the case most strongly in favor of our opponents. For my own part, I deny the power of Congress to adopt, continue, or to uphold slavery here or anywhere else. The objects of the Constitution were "to secure liberty," and not to promote or sustain slavery. If we had the constitutional power to sustain slavery, we had the power to create it. If we had the power to create it, we possessed power to say what class of people should be slaves, and what class should be masters. Yet I think no man will urge, that we possessed the power to enslave the white people who resided here. But I have no time to argue that point. The most favorable view for our opponents is, to say, that this district then presented a political blank, on which we possessed the power to affix the dark character of slavery, or the more congenial one of liberty.

In pursuance of this power, Congress passed the act approved 27th February, 1801. By that law, all those acts to which I have alluded, became "acts of Congress," and we now possess the same power to alter or repeal any or all of them, that the State of Maryland or Virginia possessed prior to the cession. We may modify slavery, by repealing the act authorizing persons to arrest slaves; or that which authorizes any person to shoot a slave who will not surrender when ordered, or that which forbids him the right of defending himself; or we may repeal all of them, and thereby abolish slavery altogether. If any gentleman will deny this doctrine, I would feel under deep obligations to him, if he would point us to the particular law which we have not power to repeal or amend at pleasure. But no man, I think, will be found willing to attempt that task. Our judiciary committee have lately reported a bill for the repeal of some of those laws adopted by the Act of 1801, and, from the reports, both of the majority and minority, some of whom are slave-holders, it would appear that the power of Congress to repeal any of those laws was not doubted by a single member.

But the repeal of those laws is objected to, on the ground that the abolition of slavery here will be likely to affect that institution in the adjoining States. That objection I regard as a strong argument in favor of its immediate extirpation from the district. I deny that we are under the least conceivable obligation to continue slavery here, in order that it may be prolonged in the States. The Constitution has imposed no such duty upon Congress, or upon the people of the free States. We say to southern gentlemen, take care of your own slaves. The institution belongs not to us. We have no concern in the matter. It was never brought into the political copartnership. We will have nothing to do with it, except to use our constitutional efforts to eradicate it from the face of the earth. We hold it in deep abhorrence, and we deny the right of Congress to involve the people of the free States in its expense, its turpitude, or its odium.

Our motto is, "hands off!" Leave us to enjoy our liberty. We will not be contaminated with slavery to any extent. We will wash our hands of it. We will separate ourselves from it, and make plain the line of demarcation between our people and that institution. We will purify ourselves from its corruptions and its crimes, and leave it where the Constitution left it, confined strictly to the States in which it exists.

Mr. Rayner, of North Carolina, said he desired to interrupt the gentleman from Ohio, in order to propound a question to him.

Mr. Giddings. Certainly.

Mr. Rayner. I wish to inquire, whether the gentleman believes the decalogue to be of Divine origin?

Mr. Giddings. I do; but I would not, if it sanctioned slavery.

Mr. Rayner. The tenth commandment says, "thou shalt not covet thy neighbor's man-servant nor his maid-servant." What does the gentleman understand by that?

Mr. Giddings. I have servants at home, — *hired* servants, not *slaves*. I hope the gentleman does not covet them; and God forbid that I should covet his slaves.

But, Mr. Speaker, I have shown that slavery exists in this district by virtue of the act of Congress, to which I have referred. That law was passed by the aid of northern as well as southern votes. For its existence, and for its continuance, the people of the free States and their representatives are responsible, as well as those of the slave States. It is *our* law that upholds and sustains slavery here. It is *our* law that authorizes the master, within this city, to scourge and torture his fellow man, until he shall become the pliant instrument of his own will. It is *our* law that forbids the slave to raise his hand in self-defence. It is *our* law that authorizes any constable or other person to shoot him, if he attempts to flee from the cruelty and oppression which now surround him. These are *our* laws, and *we*, Sir, the representatives of the free States, boasting of our love of liberty, of our hatred of oppression, of our exalted devotion to the Rights of Man, year after year sit in this hall, and refuse to repeal these barbarous laws of our own enacting, or even to suffer our constituents respectfully to request us to relieve them from this load of moral guilt which Congress has brought upon them. And the question now is,

Shall we continue contemptuously to spurn their petitions from us?

I am aware that gentlemen are constantly menacing us with a dissolution of the Union, if we agitate this subject. I answer, we will not cease to assert our constitutional rights to be exempt from slavery, on account of these threats. Release us from this unconstitutional support of that institution, and of course we shall then have no cause to agitate or discuss slavery in this hall. But, while you take from us our money to support slavery, while you dishonor us by making us the supporters of the coastwise slave-trade, while we are involved in the crime of slavery in this district, we shall not be frightened into a silent submission to these violations of the Constitution, by threats to dissolve the Union.

The Union was formed upon the basis of the Constitution; it can only be preserved by maintaining the Constitution. If, Sir, the rights of the North, under the federal compact, are to be violated and trampled upon; if we are to involve ourselves in the blood-stained guilt of slavery, — to be disgraced before the civilized world, by supporting the slave-trade as the condition, and the only condition on which the Union can be preserved, — then, Sir, we shall not hesitate in our choice. Our southern friends may hold their bondmen in subjection, but they must not enslave the freemen of the North.

If slaves are to be held within this district, they must be held without our aid. If the master here continues to tyrannize over his fellow man; if he continues to hold his brother in subjection by the torture of the whip and scourge; if he shoots him for refusing to surrender at his command, or if he takes his life for defending himself, he must commit these crimes without the aid or sanction of the people whom I represent.

Neither our moral nor political power will be prostituted to the support of such a warfare upon mankind. In saying this, I do not allude to the abolitionists particularly. I refer to the feelings and sentiments of our whigs, our democrats, and our liberty men. I refer to the sentiment of the great mass of northern men, of all parties, denominations, and classes. They generally concur in the wish and determination to separate themselves from the corruption and disgrace of these laws of a darker and comparatively barbarous age.

There is a tide in public sentiment now rolling on, which will inevitably sweep these laws from existence. That tide is going forward with resistless force. Demagogues, politicians, and political partisans are unable to stop or even check it in its course. Its progress is visible to the most careless observer. Each week bears witness to its increasing power. The changes in this hall are such as to silence the most skeptical. Nor can political interests or prejudices drive from our breasts the feelings of humanity and patriotism. The great apostle of southern slavery may thunder forth his bulls of excommunication against his political friends; he may pronounce his political anathemas against those who act in favor of the Constitution and of humanity; but his denunciations will prove as useless as they are harmless. His political friends in this hall will never consent to continue the traffic in mankind, which is now carried on in this district; for, if we may credit the reports of the day, there have been more than five thousand men, women, and children sold and transported from this district to southern slave-markets within the year past; and that, too, by virtue of our laws passed by Congress, and which we refuse to repeal.

Yes, Sir, you may look from those windows, and view the principal slave-prison in the midst of this city of boasted freedom. There, Sir, within its gloomy walls, are now sighing and groaning the victims doomed under *our* law to the slave-markets of the South. Who will estimate the amount of suffering and woe that exists within its hated cells? Count there the mothers torn from their children; the sisters violently separated from their brothers and parents by the execrable dealers in human flesh; the children forcibly taken from their parents, and herded together, waiting for the sailing of the slave-ship to convey them to their gloomy destinies upon the rice, cotton, and sugar plantations of the South, and then say whether we will receive petitions to stop this accursed traffic.

Let me say to every member of this House, whether he come from the North or from the South, that he who refuses to receive these petitions, — he who refuses to discuss this subject, — and he who refuses to repeal these acts of Congress, will be held responsible to the country, to posterity, and to God, for the crimes committed under the protection of these laws.

[Here Mr. Giddings's allotted hour expired.]

THE AMISTAD NEGROES.*

HISTORY OF THEIR IMPORTATION AND ESCAPE — THEIR RIGHTS UNDER THE LAW OF NATIONS — OUR DUTIES TOWARD THEM — OUR TREATY STIPULATIONS — ATTEMPT OF THE SENATE TO MODIFY THE LAW OF NATIONS BY RESOLUTION — TIMIDITY OF SENATORS.

[Mr. Ingersoll, of Pennsylvania, Chairman of the Committee on Foreign Affairs, reported a bill to pay the Spaniards, who claimed to own the negroes on board the Amistad, seventy thousand dollars. The bill was accompanied by an elaborate report in favor of the payment; and the author, Mr. Ingersoll, moved to print ten thousand extra copies. This motion was designed to give influence to the measure; and Mr. Giddings, desiring to meet the subject at the first legitimate stage of the proceedings, brought the whole merits of the bill before the House on this motion, by the subjoined speech. After Mr. Giddings had closed his remarks, a motion was made to lay the proposition to print on the table. This was carried; and neither the bill nor report was ever called up for consideration afterwards.]

Mr. Speaker, — I am opposed to the motion of the gentleman from Pennsylvania, to print ten thousand extra copies of this report. If the motion be sustained, it will imply a favorable consideration of the principles advanced in the report. It, therefore, becomes important that gentlemen should understand its precise character and doctrines before the vote shall be taken.

In 1839, a number of slaves were imported from Africa to the island of Cuba, in violation of the laws of Spain, and contrary to her treaty stipulations. When they reached Havana they were imprisoned in the barracoons until a sale was made

* Speech on motion to print extra copies of the Report of the Committee on Foreign Affairs. Delivered in the House of Representatives, April 18, 1844.

of fifty-two of their number to two Spanish slave-dealers named Montez and Ruiz, who appear to have purchased them of the importers, in order to carry them to "Principe," on the south end of the island. For this purpose, they obtained from the Governor licenses to transport fifty-two "*ladinos*," or legal slaves, to that place. It should be borne in mind, that these passports were granted on application of the slave-dealers, while the people to be thus transported were in the barracoons, shut out from all intercourse with any human being who sympathized with them, or who was disposed to aid them to regain their liberty.

Mr. INGERSOLL. The gentleman from Ohio is stating facts that do not appear upon the record.

Mr. GIDDINGS. I am aware that the record does not go into detail so far as to say, in express language, that these people were not present at the time these licenses were granted; but it shows they were imprisoned from the time they reached Havana until shipped on board the Amistad. Of course they could not have been at the Governor's palace when he granted these permits. The facts I was stating are, therefore, authorized and confirmed by the record. Indeed, all are conscious that, in such cases, the negro is not consulted. The slave-dealer no more thinks of it, than he would of consulting a horse or an ox, when about to sell him.

The passports were made out, and the permits were delivered, granting to these slave-merchants license to take fifty-two "ladinos" from Havana to Principe. The license was not given to the negroes to go there, but the parties to the transaction were Montez and Ruiz on one part, and the Governor-General on the other.

The negroes were shipped on board the Amistad, as other property was shipped, and the vessel took her departure for Principe on the 26th June, 1839, and, after being five days at sea, they rose upon those who held them in durance, and asserted their right to liberty. In the struggle that followed, the captain and cook were slain, and the other persons, forming the crew and passengers, surrendered, and the negroes thus became masters of the vessel. They, however, appear to have been actuated by no other motive than a love of liberty. They shed no more blood than was necessary to obtain their freedom. They placed two of the sailors belonging to the ship on board a boat, in order that they might reach the shore. They retained Montez and Ruiz on board to navigate the ship, and directed them to steer for Africa. These men, being unwilling to go to Africa, ran the vessel for New England, and in August reached the eastern end of Long Island. A portion of the crew went on shore to procure water and provisions. While they were on shore for that purpose, Lieutenant Gedney, of the navy, took charge of the ship and of the persons on board, claiming vessel and people as "derelict property." Some of the inhabitants also arrested the negroes on shore, and, claiming them to be property, insisted upon their right to salvage, as though they had been so many boxes of dry goods. Montez and Ruiz claimed to be owners of the ship and cargo, and of the people on board. The negroes claimed that they were free under the laws of nature, of nations, and of Spain. They denied that they had ever been slaves under the laws of Cuba or any other government. The case was managed by able counsel, and, after the most mature deliberation, the court decided them to be free; and they were, therefore, permitted to enjoy their liberty. They returned to their native country long since; and now, after the lapse of four years, it is urged that the court erred; and the Committee on Foreign Affairs report a bill to take seventy thousand dollars from the people of this nation to pay these slave-holders for their loss of human flesh. Most of this sum must come from the people of the free States, who hold this traffic in detestation.

The proposition goes one degree beyond any other ever made to this body. We have been called on to sustain our own coastwise slave-trade, but never were we asked to support the African slave-trade, until the presentation of the report under consideration. We have been called on, as the House are aware, to legislate for the encouragement of our own slave-merchants, but never, until this report came before us, were we asked to sustain the slave-dealers of Cuba. We have surely entered upon a new era in our national legislation. The people of the free States should certainly understand the burdens we are about to place upon them.

The advocates of oppression are desirous of preparing the public mind to receive the insult about to be tendered the people of the North. Hence the necessity of sending out this extraordinary number of the report, which is, perhaps, the ablest vindication of the foreign slave-trade that has emanated from any legislative body *during the present century. And, it* is hoped, that this argument will have the effect of reconciling our people of the North to the degradation of becoming involved in the guilt of sustaining this commerce.

The author of the report is entitled to much credit for the boldness of his positions. To stand forth upon the records of our nation as the advocate of Spanish slave-merchants; to espouse the cause of foreign slave-dealers, and to denounce those who oppose that "execrable commerce," requires at this day no small portion of moral courage. The report in question, with great gravity, proposes to review and examine the solemn decision of the highest judicial tribunal known to our laws. It goes on to point out the supposed errors, and proposes that we shall correct them.

This, I believe, is the first proposition of the kind ever brought before this body. A new precedent is sought to be established. We are to erect ourselves into a court for the correction of errors committed in the judicial branch of government. How far the precedent is to extend, I know not; nor am I able to say, whether this supervisory power is also to extend over the executive department, or not. We have generally found much more business than we have been able to transact, while we confined ourselves to the legitimate subjects of legislation. But if, to these ordinary duties, we add that of a court for the correction of errors, it will become necessary to have another department formed, whose duty it shall be to *legislate* for the nation. And what, I ask, is the occasion which demands of us thus to assume new duties unknown to the Constitution? Why, Sir, it is nothing less than to pay a sum of money from the public treasury to these slave-traders, in a case where the law will not give it; where respect for ourselves, for our own consistency, and for the character of the nation, forbid it; where justice, humanity, and the Constitution forbid it.

We appropriate a million of dollars annually to suppress the African slave-trade, and to hang our own people who engage in it; and we are now asked to pay a large sum to these Spanish slave-dealers, to encourage them to persevere in their accursed vocation. How many gentlemen who placed their names on record but a few days since in favor of so large an appropriation of money to suppress this African slave-trade, are now willing to record their names in favor of an appropriation of seventy thousand dollars to promote it? How many are prepared to vote for that trade to-day who voted against it yesterday?

But I object entirely to sitting in judgment upon the doings of the Supreme Court. It constitutes no part of our legitimate duties; it is not embraced within our constitutional powers.

As an evidence of the impropriety of entering upon such an undertaking, I need only refer to some points in this report. The first error assigned by the committee, to which I will call the attention of the House, is this, — that the court did not regard the passports or license, given by the Governor of Cuba to Montez and Ruiz, as conclusive evidence against these Africans. The committee speak of these passports as "documentary evidence of a high nature," and appear to regard them as conclusively showing that the negroes were slaves. I have heretofore stated that they were given by the Governor to Montez and Ruiz, while the negroes were not present. It was done without evidence, or even the least inquiry whether these people were "ladinos" or not. The license was merely to take fifty-two "ladinos" from the Havana to Port Principe. But the Governor called no witness to ascertain whether these people were "*ladinos*" or "*bozzals*," legal slaves or colored persons, imported against law, and, therefore, *free*. He made

7 *

no inquiry on that point. He did not in this license refer to *these* people in any respect; that paper refers, in express language, to "*ladinos*," while these people are shown to be "*bozzals;*" and the license, therefore, could not refer to them, but to colored men who were *legal slaves.*

The negroes were not parties to this instrument; had no voice in the transaction; and could not in reason, nor in law, be affected by it to any extent. I need not cite authorities to prove this point. Every farmer and every mechanic will understand that no two men, by any writing or transaction, can affect the legal rights or the interest of a third person, who is absent, and ignorant of their doings. No two men, under Spanish law or American law, can take from a third person a sheep or a swine in that manner; much less can they rob such third person of his liberty.

These passports were doubtless evidence between the parties to them. They bound the Governor who made them, and being official, were evidence to the custom-house officers, showing the authority of Montez and Ruiz to carry fifty-two "ladinos" to Principe. This was the sole, the only purpose for which they were executed. Montez and Ruiz had paid the customary duty, and these licenses were evidence that the Governor had received it. Here their legal effect ended. The idea that he was in any degree affecting the claim of these people to freedom, by executing this license, never entered the mind of the Governor, or of the slave-dealers.

Mr. Ingersoll. The Governor had the bills of sale by which the negroes were transferred to Montez and Ruiz before him, when he granted the passports.

Mr. Giddings. I have no recollection of that fact. But suppose it were true; it does not in any degree affect the position. These bills of sale were made out and signed by the importers, who, under the Spanish treaty and Spanish laws, are pirates. They had brought these people from Africa, and knew they were not "ladinos." They sold them to Montez and Ruiz, who, also, as appears from the record, knew they were not "ladinos," and who were equally pirates. Now I can hardly believe that the honorable chairman of the Committee on Foreign Affairs, (Mr. Ingersoll,) will urge that a bill of sale made by one pirate to another without oath, would be regarded as possessing any validity either here, or in any court of justice.

Suppose the honorable chairman who framed this report was seized, together with fifty other citizens of Philadelphia, by these same pirates; carried to Havana; imprisoned there in the barracoons; and, while thus confined, their captors were to make bills of sale to Montez and Ruiz, who should lay them before the Governor, and obtain permits to take fifty-two "ladinos" to Principe, — would the gentleman admit himself and friends to be thus manufactured into slaves? Does he admit slave-dealers to possess such power? Would the Governor's permit be acknowledged by him as evidence that he is in fact a "ladino," *a legal slave?*

The law would be the same with him and his neighbors, that it is with these Africans. These "bills of sale" would be as valid when offered in evidence against the gentleman, as when offered against Cinquez and his associates. So, too, the Governor's permits. They would prove the honorable chairman to be a slave, to the same extent which they show these Africans, but no farther. Now, Sir, I am not desirous of promulgating the principles contained in this report, among my constituents. We may send this report to the people of my district, but no one there would be likely to sanction the doctrines it sets forth.

The report speaks of these Africans as "*murderers* and *pirates.*" Opprobrious epithets cost but little. The word "murderer," is as easily written as "African," and to those who reflect but little, it carries at least an imputation of guilt; and it may impress such minds with the idea, that a person held in degrading slavery, in violation of law, and of natural right, ought not to assert his freedom, or slay the piratical slave-dealer who oppresses him. The time was, when Africans seized and held Americans in bondage. They had as much *right* and as much *law* to do so, as these Spanish pirates had to seize and enslave these Africans.

In 1803–4, our citizens were held in Algerine slavery, and there is not a reason nor an argument now brought forward by this committee in favor of this claim, which those Algerines might not have urged with greater force, in favor of holding our people as slaves. Yet the whole civilized world pronounced those followers of Mohammed, "pirates and robbers;" while this report refers to Montez and Ruiz as "much-abused Spanish *gentlemen*." We slew the Algerines, and this committee desire us to give these more guilty slave-merchants of Cuba money instead of a halter. If the Algerines deserved death, these Spaniards are more worthy of it. If Decatur, and Caldwell, and Sommers performed generous and noble deeds in butchering the Algerines, Cinquez and his associates performed more gallant acts, and are more worthy of our admiration. Yet this report is a labored attempt to disparage deeds of heroic patriotism. It endeavors to fix odium upon these Africans for defending their liberty, for faithfully performing one of the highest and most sacred duties which ever devolved upon man. I do not wish to impress such dastardly sentiments upon our American youth. I would sooner, far sooner, spend this seventy thousand dollars in erecting a monument to perpetuate the memory of those rude Africans, than to give it to those hucksterers in human flesh.

Another feature of this report is, in my view, derogatory to the character of the American people. I allude to that part of it which attributes the efforts of those who are now endeavoring to maintain the doctrines, and arouse the spirit of freedom among the people, to "British influence." It conveys the idea that our hatred of slavery, our war against oppression, against the crimes of the slave-trade, are called into action by "foreign influences." Sir, the imputation is unworthy of any committee of this body; it is unworthy of this House; it is unworthy of the American character; it is untrue and unjust.

It was this love of freedom, this hatred of oppression, which impelled our pilgrim fathers to leave their native land, to bid adieu to all the ties that bound them to the mother country, and meet dangers upon the trackless deep; to encounter the hardships, privations, and sufferings which awaited them amid the wilderness of this new world. It was this love of freedom which guided the pen of Jefferson and his associates, when with unanimous voice they proclaimed the great, undying truth of man's equality, as the cause of their final separation from Britain, and from "British influence."

And, Sir, are the people of this republic now to be told, that the doctrines uttered by our fathers have been repudiated by their sons? That the high-souled love of liberty, so zealously inculcated by the heroes and patriots of the revolution, has fled from the bosoms of their descendants? That it is only kept alive in this republic by "British influence?" Have we, Sir, yielded those principles for which so much effort was put forth, so much treasure expended, and so much blood was shed in our revolutionary struggle? Do the sons of the pilgrim fathers now bow submissively to the "dark spirit of slavery," unless operated upon by "foreign influences?" If such be the case, let us mourn over our degeneracy; but, in the name of justice, let us not incur the unnecessary expense of publishing such facts to the world, by sending this report to the people.

But, Sir, what shall we say of those who practically deny these doctrines, and uphold wrong, injustice, oppression, and crime, — those who stand forth as the open advocates of this Spanish slave-trade in all its hated deformity, — who would sustain that execrable commerce in human flesh at the expense of our laboring people, — who would appropriate the earnings of our freemen of the North to encourage Spanish slave-dealers in their purchase and sale of fathers and mothers and children? I will not accuse them of being operated upon by slave-trading influence. I leave them, their influences and motives, to the judgment of those to whom we are all accountable; "to their own masters, they must stand or fall."

Another portion of this report speaks of these heroic Africans, as the *property* of their Spanish oppressors. I, Sir, deny "that man can hold property in man." The doctrine that one man may hold another as property, had its origin in an ignorant and a barbarous age, among an ignorant and a barbarous people. It is opposed to the more enlightened views of the present era, and at war with the first principles of civil liberty. It was denied by the enlightened jurists of England, nearly a century since. It was denied by Mr. Madison at the very formation of our Constitution.

Mr. INGERSOLL. I wish to know where the evidence of Mr. Madison's opinions may be found?

Mr. GIDDINGS. They were recorded by himself in "the Madison papers," among the debates on framing the Constitution. He declared "it would be wrong to admit in the Constitution that man can hold property in man." This committee, however, entertain a different opinion. They deny man's equality of natural rights; they take issue with the signers of our Declaration of Independence, that the right to liberty is inalienable; they make war upon the doctrine "that governments are instituted among men to secure the blessings of liberty;" and insist that we shall turn aside from our ordinary subjects of legislation, and exert the influence of this American Congress to secure these Spanish slave-dealers in the commission of crimes which chill the blood of every lover of liberty; and then they ask us to print ten thousand copies of their argument on this subject, and send them out to the people.

Sir, man may be chained and fettered; he may be scourged and tortured until he surrenders his independence, his will, his intellect; until he becomes degraded and brutalized, robbed of his liberty, of his associations, of his hope of happiness; until the only apparent evidence of his manhood shall be his external form, the image of his Maker; but you cannot transform him into a brute, a chattel. Low down in the deepest recesses of the heart, the fire of immortality will continue to burn. It cannot be smothered, nor extinguished; and when he sees an opportunity, he will arise from his stupor, assert his right to freedom, and by the power of his own arm, will vindicate the dignity of his nature.

The case before us is a beautiful illustration of this idea. These Africans, bred amid the ignorance and superstition of their native land, were seized, placed in irons, whipped, imprisoned, sold like brutes. Montez and Ruiz purchased them; took bills of sale, as they would in the purchase of mules or sheep. They thought the love of liberty had been driven from their breasts; that the last lingering desire for freedom had been extinguished. They vainly thought the immortal intellect had been blotted out, and the image of God reduced to a level with swine. They called them property. But when upon the mighty deep, where no aid could be obtained to hold them in that condition, the hidden fire of their natures burst forth into a flame; their chains were cast from them, their fetters were broken, their arms were nerved, they struck for freedom, and those who attempted to restrain their action, were laid low in death. Those who had purchased and claimed them as property, trembled, turned pale, surrendered, and plead for mercy at their hands. They were glad to take the places which had been occupied by these Africans. These "Spanish gentlemen," as the committee term them, became subject to the quondam slaves, and as much the property of Cinquez and his associates, as *they* had been the property of the Spaniards. They were held by plainly the same title, *brute force*. But the Africans stood upon the quarter-deck of the Amistad as its masters; they commanded, and these "Spanish gentlemen" obeyed; they frowned, and these "Spanish gentlemen" trembled before them.

Sir, the day has come when this idea of property in man should be scouted from this hall, and from all Christian nations; no force, no barbarity, no enactment, no human power can transform men into chattels.

These people were at no time slaves under the laws of Cuba. They had been imported in violation of the laws of Spain, and in violation of her treaty obligation, and could not at any time have been recognized as slaves in any court of Cuba, or of Spain; yet for the sake of the argument, I will suppose them to have been imported, prior to the treaty with Great Britain, and in pursuance of the laws of Spain, and to have been held as slaves under the laws of Cuba; and that while thus held, they had made their escape in the manner they did; and to have landed upon our shores, and have sought our hospitality. Would we have delivered them up to their masters? Is there any principle in the law of nature, or the law of nations; in the comity of nations; in our treaty stipulations, requiring us to do so base an act?

Sir, the practice of all civilized nations is opposed to such practice. No monarch of Europe would have suffered them to be surrendered under such circumstances. Every principle of good faith, of hospitality, forbids it. When strangers come to our shores, they are entitled to hospitality, to security. We have recently entered into express treaty stipulations with England, to deliver up criminals who escape from justice there, and come to this country. But we did not surrender malefactors until the law of nations had been thus modified by treaty; and we do it now with no other nation, and no other nation does it with us.

Suppose a serf should escape from Russia and come among us, and his master should follow and demand him. Shall we institute an inquiry into the law of serfdom, — the relation between the noble and his serf, — and then determine that one is *property*, and the other *owner*? This committee should have learned the Law of Nations from the practice, the experience we have had on this identical question.

Those gentlemen cannot have forgotten the fact, that many of our slave-ships have been wrecked on British islands; but, I ask, did British authorities or British law, ever surrender to us, or to our slave-holders, a single slave? Of all that have once set foot on British soil, not one has been given up. The case of the Creole is too recent to be forgotten by any gentleman. There the negroes slew one of their owners, took forcible possession of the ship, and landed on British soil, and were *free*. But did Britain surrender them? Why, Sir, our Secretary of State too well understood the Law of Nations to demand them, even under our treaty. Yet this report seeks to overthrow this law of nations, this universal practice among all civilized governments. It urges that these Africans should have been delivered over to the slave-dealers. I will not sanction these doctrines of the committee, by voting to send them among the people. *I think it would be an unprofitable and disgraceful* expenditure.

The committee, however, feeling a want of confidence in their positions, quote the eighth, ninth, and tenth articles of our treaty with Spain in 1795, to justify their positions. They very carefully avoid specifying *which* of those sections they rely upon. By the article first referred to, this government covenanted to permit Spanish vessels, driven into our ports by stress of weather, by pirates or enemies, to depart with their people. Now what connection there is between the provisions of this section and the case under consideration, I am unable to discover. No Spanish vessel was driven to our ports by stress of weather, or by pirates. We have not refused permission to any such vessel to depart. We have neither detained such vessel, nor the people who belonged to such vessel. Nor do the committee allege that we have. Why this section was quoted to sustain the doctrines of the report, I think is a question which neither the committee nor any other member can answer.

The ninth section provides, that we will deliver to their Spanish owners, all ships and merchandise rescued out of the hands of pirates or robbers. Now, what connection there is between "the ship, and merchandise on board of it," and the paying of these claimants for negroes, is a matter not very apparent to my mind. Neither the bill, nor the report, speaks of any claim to the *ship*, or to the *merchandise* on board. They both refer to these negroes, and propose to pay seventy thousand dollars for *them*, not for the *ship*, nor for her *merchandise ;* and I am not able to see any connection whatever between this section of the treaty and the claim before us.

The last article quoted, refers only to the payment of charges and dues, when vessels of either nation shall be under the necessity of repairing in the ports of the other. This section unquestionably has just as much relation to the subject of paying for negroes, as either of the others. The author of the report appears to have been unwilling to point to either section in particular, as creating any liability applicable to this case ;

but refers to them all collectively, as though the reader might be able to discover some connection which the committee were unable to discern.

But, Sir, the judicial branch of our government has had this whole matter before them, and have made a solemn decision of each question. They were unanimously of opinion that neither section had any reference to this subject, and the committee now appear anxious to reverse that decision. As already stated, I regard such legislation as incompatible with our duty.

There is, however, another point in this report, to which I desire to call the attention of the House. For the purpose of giving color to the claim of these slave-dealers, the committee evidently felt the necessity of establishing some new principle in the law of nations; some doctrine unknown to the *savans* and jurists who have written upon the principles of international law. In order to do this, they quote certain resolutions adopted by the Senate of the United States in 1840. I am bound to speak of that body with respect; yet I am bound to speak of their doings agreeably to the dictates of truth. These resolutions were adopted under circumstances, which must forever excite doubts as to the correctness of their doctrines. The slave-ship "Enterprise," had entered "Port Hamilton," in the British island of Bermuda, in distress. The slaves went on shore, and were free. Our President did not demand the surrender of the slaves, but the price of their bodies. The British authorities refused payment; and a distinguished slaveholding senator (Mr. Calhoun) introduced to the consideration of that body, a series of resolutions professing to declare the law of nations in such cases. I am aware that this code is said to be often modified by treaty between two or more nations; and it is too plain to require illustration, that in similar cases this international code may be modified, so far as those nations who are parties to the treaty are concerned. But I think all will admit it is a novel doctrine that one nation can, by its own act, so change or modify this international code, as to affect the interest, or the rights, of any other nation; yet the

Senate of these United States made the attempt. That body gravely took into consideration and adopted the following resolutions:

"1. That a ship or vessel on the high seas, in time of peace, engaged in a lawful voyage, is, according to the laws of nations, under the exclusive jurisdiction of the State to which her flag belongs — as much so as if constituting a part of its own domains.

"2. That if such a ship or vessel should be forced by stress of weather, or other unavoidable cause, into the port and under the jurisdiction of a friendly power, she and her cargo, and persons on board, with their property, and all the rights belonging to their personal relations, as established by the laws of the State to which they belong, would be placed under the protection which the laws of nations extend to the unfortunate under such circumstances.*

"3. That the brig Enterprise, which was forced unavoidably by stress of weather into Port Hamilton, Bermuda island, while on a lawful voyage on the high seas, from one port of the Union to another, comes within the principles embraced in the foregoing resolutions; and that the seizure and detention of the negroes on board by the local authority of the island, was an act in violation of the laws of nations, and highly unjust to our own citizens to whom they belong."

I am not prepared to adopt these resolutions as an exposition of the law of nations. They are distinctly opposed to the principles of that code, as understood and expounded from the earliest writers upon international law to the present day. No writer ever intimated such principles as having found a place in the law of nations; and when introduced to the Senate, they were novel and unheard of.

Mr. INGERSOLL. They are regarded as law by all civilized nations.

Mr. GIDDINGS. I aver that up to the time of their introduction to the Senate, nor since that time, has any writer upon the law of nations advanced such doctrines; and I defy the

* It may be proper here to say, that Mr. Calhoun's State, (South Carolina,) notwithstanding this resolution, practically disregards its doctrines. The imprisonment of a freeborn British subject, Manuel Pereira, for no crime, who was driven by stress of weather into the port of Charleston in the year 1852, shows that they paid no respect to the laws of England, or to the rights of her subjects. The "local authorities" of South Carolina imprisoned Pereira for the color of his skin; and the recent message of the Governor of that State insists upon the enforcement of this regulation, whatever may be the consequences.

gentleman to produce any author avowing such principles. I speak with great confidence; and if the gentleman can produce such author, I will most cheerfully confess my error before the House and the country.

Mr. INGERSOLL. The Chamber of Deputies in France has very lately recognized the same principles.

Mr. GIDDINGS. I would far rather see the official report, before I lend full credence to the charge of their having so widely departed from the established law of nations. So conscious were a number of senators that these resolutions were in conflict with the recognized principles of international law, that they would not vote for them.

Mr. INGERSOLL. It was an unanimous vote.

Mr. GIDDINGS. I am aware that all of the senators who voted, were in favor of their adoption; yet there were but *thirty-three* votes given, while there were fifty-two members.

Mr. INGERSOLL. They were all present.

Mr. GIDDINGS. I feel humbled under the allusion of the gentleman. If the senators were present, as he states, and silently permitted these resolutions to be adopted by the slaveholding portion of that body, aided by their northern "*allies*," they are responsible to the country, to their constituents, and to posterity. It is not for me to come forward as their accuser. To their own masters they must stand or fall. Yet I cannot but regret that honorable senators from the free States should have permitted such resolutions to find a place on the journal of that body, without opposition. It was unworthy of the American Senate.*

I can very clearly discover good reasons why senators should have refused to vote for the resolutions; but I can discern none whatever for not voting. The first resolution is a truism. It merely states that —

"A ship pursuing a lawful voyage, while on the 'high seas,' is under the exclusive jurisdiction of the State to which her flag belongs."

* But one whig senator from the free States is said to have voted on this occasion. He was from Rhode Island. He and every senator who voted, recorded their names in the affirmative.

The word "State" has reference to the *government* to which her flag belongs; as the States of this Union have no flags, nor have they any jurisdiction upon the "high seas."

I deny that the Amistad was engaged in a "lawful voyage." She had on board fifty-two Africans, imported to Cuba in violation of the laws of Spain and of her treaty obligations. The ship was engaged in completing the original voyage, by which these persons were imported, as much as she would have been had she taken them on board at "Fernando Po." Her voyage was as much piratical as was that of the ship which brought them from Africa; and she was liable to the same penalties and forfeitures. She was not under the jurisdiction of Spain; for she had set at defiance Spanish laws and Spanish treaties. Nor was her voyage *lawful* in any sense of that term. This case, therefore, does not come within the scope of these resolutions.

The Africans were neither slaves in *law*, nor slaves in *fact*. They had been torn from their homes and their friends, in violation of all law, by pirates, who were entitled to no other treatment than that which was due to their crimes. The opportunity was presented for them to regain their liberty. They owed it to themselves, to their country, to their descendants, to free themselves as soon as they had power to do so. No considerations of mercy to their oppressors ought to have detained them one moment from the assertion of their freedom, even at the expense of every white man on board. They rose, asserted their rights, and became masters of the ship. They were thousands of miles from their native land, from which they had been torn by the rapacious slave-dealers. Montez and Ruiz had been aware of all the outrages which had been committed against these people at the time they purchased them. They had thus made themselves parties to the crimes of those who imported them from Africa, and, in all respects, stood in the same situation morally which those importers would have stood in, had they continued on board the Amistad. And can any man doubt the right of Cinquez and his associates to employ the ship, and compel Montez and Ruiz to navigate it back to Africa? In doing this, they obeyed the dictates of nature's law, offended against no principle of the law of nations or of Spain. The Spanish slavers, while bringing them from Africa, and in carrying them to Principe, were "*outlaws*," entitled to no protection from any nation, nor from the laws of any nation. While on shore in Africa, nor while on the "high seas," was there any law to shield them from the vengeance of those they held in chains. Had their victims bravely risen at any time and turned the ship's head toward Africa, and carried their captors there and sold them into slavery and kept the ship for their own use, no law would have been violated thereby.

It would give me pleasure to hear from the author of this report on these positions, and also as to the moral duty of those Africans. Were they bound in conscience to remain in chains, while they had the power to regain their freedom? Or, after they had taken possession of the ship, were they bound to go on to "Principe" and quietly be made slaves? What would the honorable chairman of this committee have done, had he been in their situation? I hope he may give us light on the subject.

And, when that gentleman takes the floor, I beg his attention to another question. If these Africans, while returning to their native land, had found it necessary to call at the island of "Fernando Po" for water, would the people of that island have possessed the right, under the law of nations, to take their ship from them? To me, these questions appear of easy solution. I regard the ship, in this case, to have been as clearly and absolutely the property of Cinquez and his associates as any ship captured by Americans in the late war with Great Britain was the property of the captors.

Slavery itself, in its most legal form, is nothing less than a state of war between masters and servants. It is so defined by our ablest writers. It is guided by no law of nature or of nature's God. It is in conflict with both. The only mode of reducing a man to slavery is by brute force, the only power known in a state of war. These Spaniards, when they went to

Africa, could have been justified by no law of human enactment. Had these persons been imported prior to the treaty between Spain and Great Britain, and according to Spanish law, yet no decree or law of the Spanish Crown could have imposed any moral duty whatever upon them, to submit to their captors. On the contrary, had the whole physical power of Spain been exerted to prevent their return to freedom, they would have been fully justified in asserting their liberty, although it had cost the life of every man of that nation.

We live at a period of time, when the vague superstitions of ignorance and of a barbarous age can no longer mislead the enlightened consciences of men. Slavery is not only a state of *war*, but it is itself a *crime*, which no human enactment can sanction or modify. We may pass such laws as we please, authorizing certain persons to buy and sell the image of God. We may authorize the worst form of piracy known to man, so far as human enactments can authorize them; yet those who commit these crimes are in no degree justified before God or good men. By such enactments, we, who make the law, become participators in the guilt and the crimes which we encourage by such laws.

These considerations lead me to the satisfactory conclusion, that these Africans committed no *moral error* in taking possession of the ship, and in striving to return to their native land. I think no man will deny that, by every principle of international law and of natural justice, the ship and cargo was theirs, for every purpose necessary to carry them back to Africa. For that purpose, they had the perfect right to use the ship and the provisions on board, and the money belonging to Montez and Ruiz, that may have been, with perfect justice and propriety, expended by them, if necessary to carry them back to their native land. And I will go still further, and say they had a perfect right to compel Montez and Ruiz, and the crew of the ship, to labor in working it, so far as necessary to land them on the soil from whence they had been taken.

These Africans had possession of the ship and of her cargo.

They had the power over Montez and Ruiz, — were compelling them to guide the ship; were in every possible way endeavoring to return to the land of their nativity, when they approached our shores. They came to us peaceably and quietly. They wanted a supply of water and provisions. They were entitled to our hospitality, our friendship, and our sympathy. They came within the scope of our laws, and were thus subjected to our jurisdiction. Under these laws, they could not hold the Spaniards in slavery, nor compel them to go further on the voyage; but our laws did not interfere with their right to the ship or to the cargo. The interest which the Africans held in them was not affected by our laws.

Here I meet the doctrine of the second resolution of the Senate. The law of nations has fixed the boundaries of every government at a marine league from shore. All civilized nations understand this rule, and conform to it. All rivers, bays, and harbors, are within the jurisdiction of the government, and to the extent of a marine league into the sea. All writers on international law have fixed this as the rule, and no exceptions were ever made to it, until the adoption of this resolution of the Senate.

When a ship leaves England, she continues to be governed by English laws while upon the high seas. Her captain, crew, and passengers, know no other. They are controlled by no other. They will permit no foreigner to enter on board, unless invited; will exhibit no papers to such foreigner, and hold themselves subject to no other power. But, when they reach our waters, and come within a marine league of our shore, our pilots, our revenue officers, and our health officers, go on board; they examine passports, bills of health, bills of lading, &c. &c. Those on board then submit to our laws entirely. And such has been the case from time immemorial, is now, and will continue to be, these resolutions of the Senate to the contrary notwithstanding.

The attempt of the Slave Power to change that law by senatorial resolution, to my view, appears rather ludicrous than serious, as diminishing the influence of that body, rather than changing or modifying the law of nations. With these principles before them, the Senate resolved that, —

> "A ship, driven by stress of weather within the jurisdiction of a friendly power, carries with her the laws of the government under whose flag she sails; and that the persons on board, and their relations to each other, as established by such laws, are to be protected by the government within whose jurisdiction she seeks safety."

How far this effort of senators will affect the principles of international law, remains to be seen.* At this time, I believe no other nation has recognized this extraordinary doctrine, nor do I believe any other nation, or even this nation, ever will adopt it. I do not believe this House will ever stultify itself by asserting principles so much at war with the common sense of mankind. Yet the Committee on Foreign Affairs appear to have received it as a sound exposition of international law. The report says:

> "Thus, wherever the flag goes, the country is. In whatever distant seas or foreign ports, wherever the national flag floats, there is the nation. Spain, therefore, with all her laws, reigned on board the Amistad as much at sea, and in Connecticut or New York, as at Havana."

Sir, who believes that the Spanish laws of slavery were in force on board the Amistad, while in Connecticut and in New York? By the laws of Cuba, the master may flog his slave, may sell him. Would the authorities of New York look on and see a Spanish slave-holder flog his slaves or commit violence upon them? Would they listen to the shrieks of the slave, in such case, and remain silent? Or, if the master in New York were to sell his slave agreeably to the laws of Cuba, would the transfer be legal? Is New York liable to be converted into a "slave-market" in that way? If the slave resist the violence of the master in Cuba, the master may shoot him down. If he do it at the wharf in New York, would the people there look on with their arms folded, saying, "*it is done under Spanish laws*," or would they say, in the words of this

---

* It is believed that no further effort whatever has been put forth by our Executive to induce any nation to recognize the doctrine of these resolutions.

report, *the act was committed in Spain, for* SPAIN IS AT OUR WHARF?

Agreeably to this doctrine, a Brazilian slave-ship fastens to a wharf in New York. The people of that city go on board, find the decks stowed full of emaciated, starving Africans, suffering all the horrors incident upon that disgusting traffic. Those who appear too far gone to be regarded as profitable stock are thrown overboard while yet in life; those who exhibit signs of discontent, are flogged; and those who resist, are shot down, or murdered with a bowie-knife or cutlass. This is all done at the wharf, in plain view of the people. But the Brazilian flag floats at the mast. Brazil is there, and Brazilian laws are in force, and the people must permit these "much abused slave-dealers" to be guided by their own sense of justice.

Sir, suppose a slave-ship from South Carolina, or any other sister State, were to enter the port of Boston from stress of weather, would the laws of Massachusetts lend their protection to the slave-dealers? If the slaves should rise in a body, and come on shore in pursuit of their freedom, would the officers of that State, or the people of Boston, be bound to pursue such fugitives through the streets of that city? Or, if in pursuit of freedom, they were to seek sanctuary in "Fanueil Hall," that old cradle of liberty, would the good people of that patriotic commonwealth seize them and drag them forth, replace them on board the slave-ships, and deliver them over to the tender mercies of piratical dealers in human flesh? If they were to lend their protection to the personal relations of those on board, as established by the laws of South Carolina, they must do this; yet I cannot believe that any slave-holding senator, who gave his vote in favor of these resolutions, would advocate such doctrine before the country; nor do I believe that any northern senator, who sat in silence when that vote was taken, would now publicly admit the correctness of such doctrines.

It was a most unfortunate attempt of the Senate to change the law of nations. They overstepped the bounds of their power and of their influence. They will regret the vote.

Their descendants, in coming time, will blush, when they read the record of that act.

Sir, the year preceding these transactions on board the Amistad, a Captain Wendall was on board his vessel in the port of Havana. He was an American, commanding an American ship, and the American flag was flying at his mast; and, of course, according to this report, "this nation was there." This captain was charged with having treated his mate with great inhumanity. He was taken from on board his ship, and imprisoned under Spanish laws and by Spanish authority, and was detained in prison for a long time. A full representation was made to Congress, but no member of this House then felt that it was an outrage upon our national rights, nor was the doctrine of these resolutions then thought of. Even the grave senators who adopted these resolutions were then silent. They did not at that time appear to have become conscious of the existence of those great principles which were subsequently called forth in favor of slave-merchants. Their lips were hermetically sealed, when our citizens, in the pursuit of an honorable commerce, were rendered subject to Spanish laws. The idea that our laws were in force at Havana, that our *nation was there,* had not then entered the minds of senators.

These efforts to sustain slavery and the slave-trade, are becoming a reproach to our nation. They are bringing our government into disrepute among Christian nations. This desire of public men to lend governmental influence in support of the slave-trade and of slavery, is rendering us "a hissing and a by-word among enlightened nations." There appears to be no absurdity in favor of oppression that does not find supporters; while the advocates of liberty are timid, faltering, and generally silent.

We have been called to legislate in favor of the slave-dealers of our own land. We have been asked to pay them for slaves lost and for slaves, stolen; but never, until this report was made, has Congress been called on to pay foreigners for their losses while dealing in human flesh. I have felt it my duty to meet this proposition at the threshold, and to oppose it with what energy and influence I possess. I have done so, knowing the feeling arrayed against me; but the country, the people of this wide-spread Republic, now and hereafter, will pronounce judgment upon those attempts to prostitute our powers to the support of a commerce in our own species. For these reasons, I felt unwilling to give a silent vote upon the motion before the House.*

* After the adjournment of Congress in 1844, Hon. John Quincy Adams published the speech he intended to deliver in the House, in case the motion to print extra copies of this report had been insisted on.

ANNEXATION OF TEXAS.*

DESIGNS OF ITS ADVOCATES — PAYMENT OF HER DEBTS — OBJECTIONS TO THAT MEASURE — GUARANTIES OF SLAVERY — RIGHTS OF THE SEVERAL STATES.

[In 1837, the authorities of Texas applied to the Executive of the United States for annexation to our Union. The President, Mr. Van Buren, considering such act unconstitutional, rejected the proposition. In 1843, rumors were circulated that the philanthropists of England were seeking to abolish slavery in Texas. This appears to have aroused President Tyler and his cabinet, who immediately commenced a correspondence with the authorities of Texas, upon the propriety of their uniting with us, and becoming a member of our federal Union. The reasons assigned by the Secretary of State in his letter of instructions was, the apprehension that Texas would abolish slavery through the influence of Great Britain, and that the institution in our Southern States would thereby be endangered. It was further urged that Texas, if annexed to our Union, would furnish an outlet for the surplus slave population of the slave-growing States. A treaty for annexation was soon negotiated, but doubts were entertained as to its ratification by the Senate. In this state of the question, southern members of the House were endeavoring to prepare the public mind for the consummation of their object, by making speeches in favor of the measure, while northern men were silent on the subject. The following remarks were the first uttered against it in the House of Representatives. Mr. Giddings obtained the floor late in the day, with the expectation that the committee would then rise; but they refused, and he proceeded in his remarks without having any notes before him, or even the documents to which he referred.]

Mr. Chairman, — I rise to call the attention of gentlemen to the real questions involved in this issue, now before the country. Texas is a revolted State of the Mexican Republic, carrying on a war against the federal power of which she was

---

* Speech upon the Naval Appropriation Bill. Delivered in Committee of the whole House on the state of the Union, May 21, 1844.

formerly a member. Her revolt was occasioned principally by a law of the Mexican Congress, which abolished the institution of slavery throughout the different States of that confederacy. In order to retain her slavery, she declared herself independent, and it is sought now to annex her to our Union, for the purpose of aiding the people of that State in sustaining slavery, and also for obtaining a market for the surplus slave population of our own States.

This real issue has been formed. It has been placed upon the records of our government, and will go down to coming generations for inspection; it has been published in our newspapers; it is already before the people, who are to try and to determine the question. The President, his Cabinet, and a portion of this House, aver, in substance, that this federal government shall take upon itself the burden of sustaining and perpetuating slavery in Texas; and of the slave-trade between our slave-breeding States and the people of that government. If we comply with their demands, our army and navy are to be employed, and our energies as a nation put forth; our character is to be disgraced for the attainment of this object; we are to violate our faith, pledged to Mexico by treaty stipulation; acknowledge ourselves hypocritical pretenders to freedom; dishonor the memory of our revolutionary sires, and wage an unrelenting war upon human nature.

Against this policy are arrayed the advocates of liberty and of justice. They steadily and firmly oppose these measures, motives, and designs, and every member must take position on one side or the other.

The annexation of Texas is urged upon us as the proposed means of extending and perpetuating slavery therein; but the ulterior and important design, I think, is most obviously to enhance the price of human flesh in our slave-breeding States, by opening up a slave-market in Texas. This object is most clearly apparent in the correspondence between the Secretary of State and our minister at London; between the Secretary of State and our "Charge de Affairs" in Texas; and in the correspondence between that officer and the British minister resident in this city. The same object is avowed by most of the papers south of Mason and Dixon's line. It is also apparent in the public addresses put forth by almost every political meeting in the slave States, called to consider this question. It was fully and frankly avowed by the gentleman from South Carolina, (Mr. Holmes,) who spoke yesterday, and by the gentleman from Virginia, (Mr. Atkinson,) and the gentleman from Alabama, (Mr. Belser,) both of whom spoke to-day. These gentlemen met the issue frankly and fairly. Not so with the gentleman from Indiana, (Mr. Owen.) He is from a free State, and appeared to be embarrassed while advocating the interests of slave-breeders and slave-dealers; but he spoke learnedly of treaties, of governments "*de facto*," and of governments "*de jure*."

There are objections to the annexation of Texas, which meet us at the very threshold of the argument. When it is proposed by the people of Texas to erase the name of that republic from the list of nations; to surrender their existence as a separate, independent people; and to place themselves under the government of the United States; we know there must be an object, an actuating motive, that induces them thus to merge their nationality with the people of these States. These objects are all set forth in the treaty now under discussion in the other end of this capitol. The first of those objects to which I will call the attention of the committee, is *the payment of their debts by the people of this Union.* This is one of the conditions of the treaty, without which the people of Texas would not listen to any proposition for annexation.

To this there are some strong objections. A portion of the representatives in this hall, are desirous that the people of our free States shall contribute of their hard earnings some ten millions of dollars, to satisfy the debts of slave-holding, repudiating Texas. To this proposition the whigs, both North and South, object.* The President, the southern democrats, and

---

* Mr. Brown, a whig of Tennessee, subsequently introduced the resolutions of annexation into the House, and eight southern whigs voted for them. Mr.

the gentleman from Indiana, urge its propriety, and insist that it is the duty of our people to pay the debts of Texas, in order to continue slavery there, and to provide a market for our slave-breeding States.

And now what say our democrats of New England and New York and Ohio? I call upon them to come forth and express their views; I hope they will play the man, meet the issue fairly, and let us have no dodging. We shall soon return to our constituents, and must meet this question before the people. Will the gentleman from Indiana then stand forth frankly and say to the democrats of his district, "you must work hard, and live cheap, and be economical, for we have agreed to pay the debts of Texas, and every laboring man in the nation must contribute a portion of his earnings?" * And then suppose the honest farmer, in the true Yankee style, should inquire for the benefits which this nation are to derive from the payment of this sum to Texas; will that gentleman frankly and boldly declare to him, that, by paying that amount of money, we have established slavery and a first-rate slave-market there? I cannot distrust that gentlemen's sincerity, and yet I think he would rather talk of some other points, and leave these important considerations out of view, as he has done here to-day. I could not wonder at the policy which he manifested; particularly as his State is unable to pay the interest on her own debts, I had no right to expect him to speak of his anxiety to tax his constituents to pay the debts of Texas. How is it with the democrats of the other States, which are unable to meet their engagements? Will they insist upon paying the debts of Texas, and leave their own States to be dishonored by repudiation? Has Pennsylvania more interest

---

Foster, a whig senator from the same State, introduced them into the Senate, and three whig Senators voted for them.

* The advocates for annexing Texas were unwilling to make any express stipulation for paying the debts of Texas in the resolutions of annexation, while the question was pending. But the fraud was consummated by one of the compromise acts of 1850, under pretence of paying Texas for that portion of New Mexico lying east of the Rio Grande. A more stupendous fraud was probably never committed upon the American people.

in maintaining the slave-trade than she has in maintaining her own honor? Will the democrats of that State forget their own indebtedness, and spend their money to perpetuate slavery in Texas, and open up new slave-markets there?

I wish the American people to understand that they are made to pay for suppressing the slave-trade on the African coast, and at the same time they are to be to an indefinite amount taxed to maintain and encourage it on the American coast. I should be pleased to hear the eloquent gentleman from Indiana (Mr. Owen) explain to his constituents the precise line on which this slave-trade changes its character; on the East of which it is the most detestable of crimes, and West of which it becomes a laudable commerce, worthy of our fostering care. It is due to each member who really desires to open this slave-trade between our slave-breeding States and Texas, that they stand forth before this body and before the country, and, like the honorable Secretary of State, frankly avow their object.

I repeat that the object of this annexation on our part is distinctly avowed to be, the perpetuation of slavery in Texas, and the establishment of a market for the surplus slaves of our Southern States. There is no doubt that it will greatly enhance the price of human flesh in this district, and in all the northern slave States.

Texas is also engaged in a war with Mexico, and wants us to fight her battles. The maintenance of that war may also involve us in hostilities with England. It certainly will with Mexico. And our constituents from the free States will be called on to go forth to maintain this slave-trade upon the field of battle. Our people are brave and generous in a good cause. But will this war in favor of oppression and crime, be of such character that we can conscientiously look to heaven for its blessing to rest upon our arms? On the contrary, we are conscious that the "Almighty has no attribute which will permit him to take sides with us in such a contest." These battles must be fought by northern men principally, for southern men will be constrained to remain at home to watch their slaves.

9 *

It is a historical fact, that, in 1780, South Carolina sent a special agent to Congress, to inform that body that their State could furnish no troops for the defence of the nation, "as it had become necessary for their men to remain at home to protect their families from anticipated insurrections of slaves."

It would gratify me to have some advocate of this policy stand forth and describe that love of oppression and of crime, that contempt for his race and of God's law, which would induce him to die upon the battle-field, fighting to establish a more profitable market for the slaves reared in Maryland and Virginia. If a constituent of mine were to fall in such a cause, amid the carnage of battle; his life's blood fast flowing from mortal wounds; his countenance pale and distorted with pain, with no friendly hand to minister to his wants, or wipe the cold sweat of death from his brow, I do not believe he would draw very rich consolation from the reflection that he died fighting to extend the slave-trade, to perpetuate the most revolting crimes which man is capable of committing.

Our sailors, too, will be anxious to have this longitudinal line, which fixes the character of the slave-trade, distinctly drawn. To them it would be important to know the precise point in going East, at which they are to cease fighting *in favor* of this slave-trade, and to commence fighting *against* it. If he falls in battle fighting in favor of it, on our own coast, what consolations are to smoothe his pathway through the dark valley of the shadow of death? But if he dies on the African coast, contending against those pirates who deal in God's image, he will of course be told that he falls in the discharge of duty. We have been taught to regard justice as universally the same in all places. But this new philosophy teaches us that it has become versatile, changing with the longitude in which it is administered. The time has come when *Western* justice is to be regarded as synonymous with slavery and the slave-trade, and *Eastern* justice is to be expressive of liberty and freedom. Ancient philosophy taught us to look upon justice as *eternal;* but these advocates of annexation are about to fix the time, when it is to change, and be viewed as antagonist to its former character. They speak of extending American liberty to Texas, by founding it upon perpetual slavery, and insist that, by establishing the most degrading oppression there, we shall carry to that people the enjoyment of true democratic principles. I was delighted with the eulogium of the gentleman from Indiana, (Mr. Owen,) upon democratic liberty. While urging the duty of annexation, he spoke in thrilling terms of the effulgent glory of our *American institutions*, including slavery and the slave-trade. Those poetic strains may delight the ears of slave-breeders and slave-dealers ; but I have mistaken the character of our northern people, if eloquence itself can lead them to forget the fundamental principles of freedom.

The principal burdens of this war, in case of annexation, must rest upon the people of our present Union. This will surely be very acceptable to the people of Texas. They are willing to buy negroes from our slave-breeding States, provided we will furnish an army to protect them while they remain on their plantations, and scourge their slaves into subjection, according to the true principles of liberty as expounded by the present Secretary of State.* The Executive and his cabinet, and the advocates of annexation, appear to think that this purchase of a slave-market will be highly advantageous. And now I wish to know what our northern democrats think of it? We know that the whigs are opposed to it.† And I ask the democrats whether they are prepared to go to Texas, and stand sentinel there, and defend the fugitive criminals of that country, provided they will condescend to purchase the slaves of Virginia? ‡

What say our democrats of New England, of Maine, of

---

* Mr. Calhoun, Secretary of State, in his instructions to our minister at Paris, avows that the object of our government in seeking the annexation of Texas, is to perpetuate slavery, and thereby establish liberty.

† At the time this speech was delivered, the whigs were professedly opposed to the extension of slavery.

‡ It is well known that many of the early settlers in Texas, were men who fled from the United States to avoid punishment for crimes committed in this Republic.

Massachusetts, Connecticut, Vermont, and New Hampshire? I want them to step out boldly, and let us understand their true positions. If they are to arrange themselves in favor of purchasing this slave-market at such price, I trust they will avow it before the world.

It is well known, Mr. Chairman, that, since the formation of this confederacy, there has been a supposed conflict between the interests of free labor and of slave labor, between the southern and the northern States. I do not say that the conflict is *real;* I only say that in the *minds of the people,* both North and South, and in this hall, such conflict exists. This has given rise to a difference of policy in our national councils. I refer to the tariff in particular, as being a favorite measure of the North, while free trade is advocated more generally by the South. I refer also to our harbor improvements, and the improvement of our river navigation, as other measures in which the North-west and West have felt great interest, and to which the South have been constantly opposed. But so equally balanced has been the political power between these opposing interests, that for five years past our lake commerce has been entirely abandoned; and such were the defects of the tariff, that for many years our revenues were unequal to the support of government.

By the fixed order of nature's law, our population at the North has increased so much faster than it has in the slave States, that under the late census the North and West hold the balance of political power; and at the present session, we have passed through this body a bill for the protection of our lake and river commerce, which awaits the action of the Senate to become a law. But let us admit Texas, and we shall place the balance of power in the hands of the Texans. They, with the southern States, will control the policy and the destiny of this nation; our tariff will then be held at the will of the Texan advocates of free trade. Are our friends of the North prepared to deliver over this policy to the people of Texas? Are the liberty-loving democrats of Pennsylvania ready to give up the tariff? To strike off all protection from the articles of iron and coal and other productions of that State, in order to purchase a slave-market for their neighbors, who, in the words of Thomas Jefferson Randolph, "breed men for the market like oxen for the shambles?" *

I do not argue to the policy of protecting our American manufactures. I only say, that at this time, New England and the free States generally are in favor of it, while the slave States are equally opposed to it. And I ask, are the mechanics and manufacturers of the North prepared to abandon their employments, in order that slave-markets may be established in Texas, and a brisk traffic in the bodies, the flesh and blood of our southern population may be maintained? Are the farmers of the West, of Ohio, Indiana, and Illinois, prepared to give up the sale of their beef, pork, and flour, in order to increase the profits of those who raise children for sale, and deal in the bodies of women? Are the free States prepared to suspend their harbor and river improvements for the purpose of establishing this slave-trade with Texas, and to perpetuate slavery therein? †

But, if Texas be admitted to the Union, it is to be a slaveholding State, out of which several States are hereafter to be admitted, with the advantages over our free States of holding a representation on this floor, and a vote in the election of president and vice-president, and in the administration of the federal government, in proportion to the number of slaves they shall hold in bondage. In other words, their influence on all these subjects is to be proportioned to their contempt of liberty. The Texan, who holds five slaves, is to wield an influence over our national interests, equal to four of our northern freemen. If

---

* The democratic members from Pennsylvania gave their votes for the annexation of Texas; and the members from Texas subsequently gave their casting votes in favor of repealing the duties on iron, which nearly destroyed the iron interests of Pennsylvania.

† It is a historical fact, that when a bill subsequently passed Congress to improve our harbors and our river navigation, President Polk vetoed it, assigning as a reason therefor, that all the pecuniary means of the nation were required to carry on the war between Mexico and the United States, which had been assumed by the annexation of Texas to our Union.

each holds fifty slaves, his influence will be equal to that of *thirty-one* of the independent electors of the free States. I ask the learned gentleman from Indiana, (Mr. Owen,) if he really estimates the political worth of his constituents so low as to require thirty-one of them to form an aggregate of political influence equal to that of the piratical owner of fifty "human chattels" in Texas? Or does he estimate his own political worth at one fourth part of that which he attaches to the holder of five slaves in Texas? I wish gentlemen here would speak out, and let us know the real estimate which they put upon the moral and political worth of northern men? Would to God I were able to speak to every man of every party, north of Mason and Dixon's line. I would demand of them as *men*, as *freemen*, to come forward, and let the country understand whether any one of them is willing thus to degrade himself; or whether any one of them is willing to be thus degraded by his representatives in this hall. This proposition, come from whom it may, from persons high in office, or from those *wishing* to be high in office, is insulting to northern feeling and northern honor. Sir, why not propose at once that our people shall surrender themselves as slaves to the Texan planters? Why not advise the people of our free States at once to leave their homes, to go to Texas, and become the voluntary "hewers of wood and drawers of water" to those fugitive criminals, who, within the last fifteen years, were driven from the United States to avoid punishment for their crimes?

My main objections to the annexation of Texas, however, are confined to the burdens and resulting effects of that policy. If she were to come into the Union upon terms of equality with our free States, — if her annexation were to promote the cause of freedom, most gladly would I have had her as one of the States of this confederacy.

But I must hasten through my subject. I was wholly unprepared to address the committee. I had taken no notes, nor have I before me books or papers of reference; but the committee appeared anxious to proceed, and I was compelled to put to sea, upon the wide ocean of this debate, without chart or compass, and with nothing to guide my course but the glittering star of truth, as it shines in the moral firmament, unobscured by political clouds. Whether I shall again reach the shore, within the brief space allotted me by the rules of the House, is of little consequence. I shall probably be compelled to stop before I can possibly bring my argument to a close.

It is, however, due to myself to say, that I would not have occupied the attention of the House one moment, if any other northern man had exhibited a disposition to address the committee; but as we have now had some six or eight speeches in favor of the annexation of Texas, and not one against it, I began to fear that our people of the North would think we either have nothing to say, or that we are too delicate to speak our sentiments.

I feel constrained to bestow a passing notice upon the positions assumed by the gentleman from South Carolina (Mr. Holmes) yesterday, and to-day by the gentleman from Virginia, (Mr. Atkinson,) and the gentleman from Alabama (Mr. Belser). It is also one of the positions assumed by the late Secretary of State, Mr. Upshur, and by the present Secretary of State, Mr. Calhoun, in their correspondence connected with the treaty lately sent to the other branch of the National Legislature.

The point to which I allude is, — "that the federal government have guaranteed slavery to the southern States of this Union;" and they urge that, in order to carry out such guaranty, it is necessary to annex Texas, lest slavery shall be abolished there; and, in consequence of such abolition in Texas, slavery will become valueless in our southern States.

Now, Mr. Chairman, with all due respect to the legal talents and constitutional learning of those gentlemen, I may be permitted to deny that any guaranty in regard to slavery ever found a place in the Federal Constitution. You, Mr. Chairman, will recollect, that when the gentleman from Alabama (Mr. Belser) put forth this doctrine, I respectfully inquired of him where he found it. He at first answered that he found it in *common sense;* he next said it was found in *common justice;* and, lastly, he asserted it was found in the Constitution. I then inquired, in what part of the Constitution I would find it. To this he replied, that he *had not then time to inform me.* It is true that an hour is a short time for a speech, but, as I now see the gentleman in his seat, I give him notice that I will surrender to him the necessary time out of my own hour, if he will but inform me of the article and section of the Constitution in which such doctrine is to be found. In the mean time, I must take issue upon the gentleman's assertion, that *common sense* furnishes any proof of such guaranty for the continuance of slavery. I deny the assertion. Every principle of common sense is *opposed* to slavery in all its forms; every dictate of common sense is in favor of freedom. I must also emphatically deny the assertion of the gentleman, that a guaranty of slavery is to be found in *common justice.* The principles of common justice are at war with the existence of slavery; "common justice" would strike the shackles from every slave in our country. Does that gentleman understand that "common justice" authorizes him to hold his fellow man subservient to his will? To compel a fellow being, equal in natural rights with himself, to labor for the gratification of his appetite? Sir, "common justice" gives to the slave precisely the same liberty that it gives to the master.

When God "created man free and equal, and endowed him with certain inherent and inalienable rights, among which are the enjoyment of life, liberty, and the pursuit of happiness," he dealt out to man *common justice.* But it appears to me that the mind must be truly disordered that can find in "common justice" any excuse or apology for slavery; but, apparently feeling that this position was not a safe one, the gentleman said the guaranty was to be found in the Constitution. I will now pause, that he may inform this committee as to the section and article in which it exists.

[Mr. GIDDINGS made a pause, but Mr. BELSER sat silent, and Mr. G. proceeded.]

I was fully aware, when I put the question to the gentleman, that he then had not time to find the guaranty of which he spoke. I was also conscious that he would not have time during my hour to find it. And I now say to the gentleman, and to the committee, that his lifetime will be too short to find it; nay, Mr. Chairman, eternity will not disclose it, *for it does not exist.* Yet, Sir, this senseless jargon, — this eternal repetition concerning the "guaranties of slavery," is daily sounding in our ears. It is put forth by men of character, and those high in office. Sir, the idea that the Constitution contains a guaranty of slavery, is an impeachment both of the sincerity and the judgment of the framers of that charter of American liberty; and I take this occasion to repeat my assertion, that no such stipulation exists, or ever did exist in that instrument. And standing here, in the presence of so many learned and able statesmen of the South, many of whom have repeated the unfounded assumption, I call upon any one, or all of them, to refer me to any such covenant or stipulation in the Constitution.

Mr. Brengle, of Maryland, stated, that at the formation of the Constitution, slavery existed in most of the States, and that slaves were regarded as property; and, in that light, were the subject of protection as much as any other property.

Mr. Giddings. Will the gentleman point me to the section in which I may find this *guaranty?*

Mr. Brengle. I don't refer to any section in particular, but to the whole instrument. (A laugh.)

Mr. Giddings. Well, Mr. Chairman, I have finally chased this notable guaranty into the region of southern abstractions; but I declare I never came so near finding it before. (Laughter.)

But the gentleman is in error when he supposes that the convention who framed the Constitution regarded slaves as *property.* That instrument, in every instance in which it refers to slaves, terms them *persons*, and Mr. Madison, the father of the Constitution, declared in convention that "it would be wrong to admit in the Constitution that man can hold property in man;" and not a member of that body appears to have dissented from that view.

Sir, the only instance in which it can be contended that Congress possesses the constitutional power to legislate for the benefit of slavery, is to be found in the clause relating to fugitive slaves. Even there, no grant of power to legislate is given; and its existence is denied by our ablest jurists. But admitting for the sake of the argument, that Congress may legislate for the return of fugitive slaves; the power must of course be confined to that subject, and cannot be extended to any other. That clause has express reference to slavery, and, of course, excludes the presumption of any other powers upon that subject. To sustain this position, I may here cite the opinions of all jurists and statesmen who have written upon constitutional law. But there is not the least possible color of a *guaranty* to be found in that instrument. We may legislate, or refuse to legislate on the subject, as we please. There is no *guaranty* that Congress will ever notice the subject, or act upon it in any way. But least of all is there any *guaranty* that the slave shall not run away from his master, or that he shall be caught, or even that he shall not kill the master who attempts to take him.

But, I ask, where is the power to annex territory to the Union for the purpose of sustaining slavery in a foreign State? To open up new slave-markets? To assume the war of a foreign State? To use the army and navy, and violate our treaties with other governments, for the purpose of perpetuating an institution which we detest? I denounce all these efforts to plunge us into a war, to pour out the treasure and the blood of the nation that slavery and the slave-trade may flourish, as violations of the Constitution, and of the dearest rights of the people.

I discard the idea of interfering with the institution in any of the States. I admit their power to hold slaves, independent of Congress, or of the federal government. Sir, I admit your legal right, under the laws of Virginia, to hold your fellow man in bondage. I cannot interfere with that privilege.

But while I do this, I demand an equal respect for the rights and privileges of the people of my State. Ohio has an indisputable right to be free and exempt from the support of slavery. To the extent of my influence, of my moral and political power, that right shall be maintained. The citizen of Ohio who would involve our people in the turpitude of slavery, is a traitor to our interests, to the interests of humanity, and to the Constitution. I will not degrade my State, by claiming less respect for her rights than I yield to others. Nor will I claim for myself less respect than I award to those around me.

You, Mr. Chairman, have been educated to regard slavery as excusable, perhaps *right;* I have been educated to hate and detest it. You cherish it; I condemn it. You enjoy in your own State, the opinions you entertain; I enjoy the same privilege in my State. Thus we are each secured in the enjoyment of our views. I will not ask this government to compel you or your State to share with us the blessings of liberty. Nor will I silently permit it to constrain Ohio, or myself, to participate with you in the crimes of slavery.

Fortunately, the Constitution has given to the federal power no authority to involve my State in slavery, or yours in its abolition. Suppose the people of the free States should demand of Congress to annex Mexico to this Union, and assume her war against Texas in order to abolish slavery in that State? Would not our southern friends resist and denounce the proposition? Would they not proclaim it unconstitutional, and declare that a dissolution of the Union would inevitably follow such action? I think they would; but with far less cause than the North will have to make the same declaration, if Texas be annexed, and we assume her war to sustain slavery.

I am aware that the present Secretary of State, and his predecessor, both say that the "abolition of slavery in Texas will endanger its existence in the United States." Suppose that position be correct. I reply that slavery is a *State* institution, over which we have no control. If we had, that power certainly ought to be exerted for the *overthrow* of slavery, and not for its continuance. But may not the people of the free States say with more propriety and more justice, the continuance of slavery in Texas will endanger the existence of freedom in our Union; and, therefore, the federal power ought to destroy the institution there? And would it not be a thousand times more honorable for this nation to take up arms for liberty, than to assume the war of Texas to maintain slavery? But to establish this doctrine, that we are bound to sustain slavery, gentlemen say, "if an enemy land upon our shores for the purpose of seizing slaves, this government and the free States are bound to protect the masters against such enemy."

We, Sir, are under obligation to protect the people of each State "against foreign invasion, and against domestic violence." We cannot permit a foreign enemy to invade our soil; we expel such enemy at once; we do not this to protect slavery, or robbery, or any other crime; but to maintain our territory inviolate, and protect our *people.* We protect the slave as much as we do the master; we don't stop to inquire the object of the enemy; we don't ask whether he came to seize the whites or the blacks, the rich or poor, bond or free, masters or slaves? We drive the enemy from our soil, without reference to slavery. We defend the country.

But for the purpose of showing it to be our duty to sustain slavery, it is urged that this government is bound to protect the masters in case of insurrection; and southern men ask, suppose our slaves rise and murder our people, is not the federal government bound to aid us in holding them in subjection? I answer, not at all; we are bound to protect the people of every State "against foreign invasion and internal violence." The class of persons who commit the violence, is a fact into which we cannot stop to inquire. If the violence rise from masters, we suppress it. If it rise from slaves, we do the same. If both masters and slaves are engaged, side by side, in an insurrection, we shoot them down without knowing or inquiring which is master or which is slave. Our business is to suppress the *violence*, but we have no concern with slavery.

I make this explanation, that I may be understood when I

make the declaration that, under our Constitution, the federal government cannot interfere with slavery in the States for any purpose, either to sustain or to abolish it. This was the doctrine avowed and understood by the framers of the Constitution. It has been the *avowed* doctrine of southern men, and of northern men, from the adoption of the Constitution to this day. It is true that the federal government has often interposed its power in aid of slavery, by the common consent of all the States, when no objections were made by any person; but, up to the present session of Congress, no man of any party, or from any portion of the Union, ever dared to stand forth before the nation and avow the doctrine, that this government possessed the constitutional power or right to exert the influence of the nation, to degrade its character, and exhaust its revenues, in support of slavery, or of the slave-trade. On various occasions I have myself, in this hall, called on gentlemen to avow such sentiments if they entertained them. But never, until since the commencement of the present session, was any member of this body found sufficiently callous to his own reputation to avow such principles.

We have passed more than half a century under our present Constitution, and now the President assumes to himself the power of making slavery a *national,* instead of a *State* institution, and of extending the power and influence of the federal government to its support. He has brought our army into the field in hostile attitude to a friendly power, with whom we are on terms of perfect amity, and has sent a fleet to insult and provoke that government to hostilities. He has by his secret orders, without the consent of the people of the nation or their representatives, and without deigning even to consult his constitutional advisers, suddenly plunged us into a war, for the openly avowed object and purpose of extending and perpetuating slavery. These profligate acts, these usurpations of power, these violations of the Constitution, can be characterized by no term of milder signification than TREASON, — *treason* against the rights of the people of this nation, — *treason* against the Constitution, — and *treason* against humanity itself.

I feel it my duty to declare it such in the presence of the House and of the country.

Mr. Chairman, we at this moment appear before the civilized world in the disgraceful attitude of making war upon Mexico, an unoffending nation, in obvious violation of our treaty stipulations, and our national faith solemnly pledged, for the purpose of extending slavery, and perpetuating the slave-trade. And I am exceedingly desirous of knowing whether any political party, or any respectable portion of any political party, intend to support and maintain this policy. What say our democratic friends? Has the gentleman from Indiana (Mr. Owen) spoken the sentiments of his party? Are the democrats of our free States prepared to follow his lead? Will they enter the field with "democracy and slavery, Texas and the slave-trade," inscribed upon their banners? If so, I ask them to come forth boldly, unfurl your banners, not to the *breeze*, but to the whirlwind of popular indignation, which must eventually scatter you to the four winds of heaven.

Sir, the President, in seeking to sustain slavery in Texas, proposes to annex that government to this Union. Those who oppose this policy, deny the constitutional power to associate a foreign people with us in the administration of government. To this the gentleman from Alabama, (Mr. Belser,) replied rather sneeringly, as I thought, that there was a class of public men who deny the constitutional power of the federal government to annex Texas to this Union. He then went on to say that such were the views of the abolitionists, and that their candidate for President (James G. Birney) had started this doctrine. Now I beg leave to differ with that gentleman as to the authorship of this doctrine. It had been put forth long before Mr. Birney's letter was written. It was put forth by a greater abolitionist than Mr. Birney, — by a man whom I have always regarded as a far greater man, and to whose opinions I have, from my youth up, been taught to pay the highest respect. (Cries, "who is it, who is it?") He was the author of the first abolition tract ever published in the United States, and, in my opinion, the best ever put forth. (Cries, "name him, name him.") I borrowed my own abolition sentiments from his writings, and have cherished them, and should continue to do so, from respect to his memory, if from no other motive. His name was *Thomas Jefferson.* (A laugh.) And his abolition tract was called the "*Declaration of Independence.*" (Great laughter.)

Before I quote his sentiments, I will state that when he wrote, and subsequently to that period, so far as this question has been agitated, statesmen and jurists have drawn a marked distinction between the acquisition of mere territory, of acres or square miles of land uninhabited, and the annexing of a foreign people, who, having formed themselves into a government, attempt to unite with those of another nation. The ability to purchase territory without inhabitants, is one thing, but to annex a foreign government, — that is, the people of a foreign nation, with their habits, their moral and political views, — is another and a different subject.

We must bear in mind that Mr. Jefferson was President, and that the territory of Louisiana had been purchased by a treaty negotiated under his administration, which, at the date of his letter to Mr. Breckenridge, awaited the sanction of Congress. The letter was dated on the 12th of August, 1803, and in it he says:

> "The treaty must of course be laid before the two houses of Congress, because both have important functions to exercise respecting it. They, I presume, will see their duty to their country, in ratifying and paying for it, so as to secure a good which would otherwise probably be never again in their power. But I suppose they must then appeal to the nation for an additional article to the Constitution, approving and confirming an act which the nation had not previously authorized."

These were his words. He, Sir, had never conceived the idea that the Constitution had authorized the purchase of foreign territory. He was conscious that the purchase was without any constitutional power, and suggested that an amendment to the Constitution should be proposed in order to sanction the act. But, lest his views might not be fully and explicitly understood, he proceeds to say: "The Constitution has made no provision for our holding foreign territory, *still less* for incorporating foreign nations into our Union." Here, Sir, is the doctrine, from the pen of a man whose opinions upon the Constitution I have always been accustomed to respect. Are we prepared to overthrow this doctrine, and to say that we have power to compel the people of New England to go into political association with Texan slave-holders?

I trust there will be but one voice from Ohio on these questions now forced upon the country. I do not believe you can find an elector of that State, who is willing to degrade himself by associating with the slave-holders of Texas upon such terms of inequality as those to which I have alluded.

Mr. Payne, of Alabama, interrupting Mr. Giddings, requested permission to propound a question.

Mr. Giddings. An hour is a short time to make a speech; but, if the gentleman will occupy but a moment, he may propound his question.

Mr. Payne desired the reporters to note what he said; and stated that, about two years since, a man by the name of Torrey, a negro-stealer, brought a wagon and team to this district. While stealing some negroes, they were arrested, and Torrey made his escape. Subsequently, it was said that a member on this floor claimed the wagon and team, and he now asked the gentleman from Ohio (Mr. Giddings) what interest he had in the property?

Mr. Giddings. I am not at liberty to receive any thing uttered by a member on this floor as an insult. Indeed, nothing coming from a certain quarter *can* insult me.

Mr. Payne. I call upon the gentleman from Ohio to answer my question; and, if he does not, a committee ought to be appointed to inquire into the fact. (Cries of *order, order.*)

Mr. Giddings. I have witnessed too many of these sudden outbursts of passion to be very seriously alarmed by them.

(Mr. Payne interrupting Mr. G.) A man that will deceive his own party cannot be ashamed of any thing (cries of *order,*

order, from various parts of the hall; the Chairman, rapping with his mallet, distinctly called Mr. Payne to order). After order was restored, Mr. Giddings resumed.

Mr. Chairman, — These little innocent outpourings of the heart are perfectly harmless, even from an *overseer*, when deprived of his whip. You may, in such case, look him in the face with safety. To you, and to the members generally, whom I respect, I will say this is the first intimation that I have ever had, that any member was suspected of being connected with the transaction alluded to. Nor had I any intimation, relative to that affair, until I saw it in the newspapers. But I make this statement for the satisfaction of *gentlemen*, and not for that of the member from Alabama. I do not wish this insinuation to rest a moment uncontradicted in the minds of those who understand the common courtesies of life, who know what *good breeding* is; while I would scorn the idea of making any reply whatever to the grovelling malice that prompts this attack.

But to return from this episode. The legislature of Ohio has, by joint resolution, denied this right now advocated by the President; other legislatures have united in sustaining this doctrine of Mr. Jefferson. These legislatures sustain the view of my venerable friend from Massachusetts, (Mr. Adams,) who opposed the passage of any law to control or govern the people of Louisiana, until the Constitution could be so amended as to authorize the annexation of the people of that government to our territory.

But the people of Louisiana and of the United States appear to have unanimously desired the annexation, and it was done by *common consent*. Texas may now be annexed in the same manner. If the whole people of both governments desire, no other people nor government can object.

The old articles of confederation made express provision for the annexation of Canada, whenever the people of that Province should desire it; but this provision was left out of the Constitution, showing that the framers of that instrument intended to give no such authority to Congress. By adopting our Federal Constitution, a union was voluntarily formed of the old thirteen States. This was the act of each State; for each determined for itself upon the propriety of adopting the Constitution. The compact made provisions for admitting by act of Congress new States, to be formed out of the territory included within the boundaries dividing our government from foreign nations. That union, formed by the wisdom of our fathers, and consecrated by the blood and suffering which had marked their recent struggle for independence, we love and cherish. To it we shall adhere in all its stipulations. We regard it as the sanctuary of American liberty. We shall defend it with our treasure and our lives.

But, for one, I entertain no desire to surrender this Union for a new one with slave-holding Texas. Nor have I any desire to enter into a union with Texas, until it can be done upon terms of equality which shall be honorable to our people. Let her emancipate her slaves. Let her avow the doctrines of freedom, the doctrines of Jefferson, of Hancock, and their associates, the doctrines on which our government was based, and I will then be prepared to give a favorable consideration to this question.

A slave-holding government is the most tyrannical that exists. The Emperor of Russia has not the same power over his serfs which the slave-holder of South Carolina possesses over his slaves. Russia has but one tyrant; the United States contain at least an hundred and fifty thousand, each of whom possesses at this time more absolute power over the lives and liberties of those subject to his rule than does the Emperor of Russia.

We are now called on to increase the number of these despots; to extend the most flagrant despotism known to civilized man; to give it power over ourselves and our descendants in coming time. I repudiate the proposition; I will oppose it here and elsewhere; I denounce it as dangerous to the liberties of the people, as establishing a precedent fraught with evil to the country.

ANNEXATION OF TEXAS.*

ITS EFFECT IN RENDERING THE OTHER STATES LIABLE TO PAY HER DEBTS — TO PERFORM HER TREATIES — OBJECTS OF ANNEXATION — EFFECT UPON SLAVERY — TO INCREASE THE EXPENSE OF OUR ARMY — OUR NAVY — OUR POST-OFFICE SYSTEM — OUR LAND SYSTEM — TO CORRUPT OUR MORALITY.

[Our Secretary of State, (Mr. Calhoun,) in his instructions to our ministers at London and at Paris, argued that slavery was a humane institution, equally beneficial to the master and slave, and of pure moral tendency. Copies of these letters of instruction were before the House, when the resolutions for annexing Texas came up for consideration, and Mr. Giddings replied to them in the following speech.]

Mr. Chairman, — In whatever light the subject before us be viewed, it becomes a question of "union between the governments of Texas and the United States." These governments are, at this time, independent powers, — each acting under a written constitution, each passing laws for the government of its own people; entering into treaties with foreign powers; maintaining peace, or making war; and discharging all the functions of an independent, sovereign nation. The people of each have selected that form of government which best accords with their own views; and it is a reflection upon the people of Texas to talk of extending to them the benefits of a free government. The declaration carries with it an imputation that their present government is oppressive.

It is proposed, by the resolutions before us, to unite these two nations into one consolidated government, so that the

* Speech upon resolutions annexing Texas. Delivered in Committee of the whole House on the state of the Union, January 22, 1845.

inhabitants of the two nations shall become one people, enjoying the same national advantages, liable to the same national burdens, and be governed by the same general laws. We shall of course carry with us all the advantages arising from our present power and influence, and those which will result from our treaties with other nations. We shall carry with us into the new political copartnership, our public lands, and our revenues derived from every source; at the same time, we shall carry with us our public debt, and our liabilities to foreign nations, arising from treaty stipulations. By entering into the proposed union, our debt will become the debt of the consolidated government; our treaties, too, will then be the treaties of the new political union, and must be performed by it. Precisely so with Texas. She, too, will bring with her the debts she owes. Her entering into the new union will not affect the rights of her creditors in foreign nations. By uniting with her, we shall become liable with her people for the payment of her debts. It is true that the resolutions before us provide that the new government shall pay only ten millions towards the debts of Texas. That is the contract between her government and ours; and I need not say to gentlemen on this floor, that no compact between Texas and the United States can change or alter the rights of Great Britain, which that government holds under her treaties or compacts with Texas. These compacts and treaties have been solemnly entered into by Texas while a sovereign nation; and, from the obligations which she has thus assumed, she cannot release herself by any act of hers, or by the joint act of herself and this nation. She is now bound for the payment of her whole debt due to foreign nations. The whole property of the nation is bound for the discharge of her debts, and must remain so until relieved by its payment. And, whether she comes into the Union as mere territory, or as a State, we shall be holden; the whole consolidated government will be holden for its final payment.

The reasons are perfectly obvious. When she enters into this new union, either as a State or territory, she comes under the protection of the federal government; and we must defend her people and their property. Her creditors can no longer make reprisals in case she neglects or refuses to pay her debts. If she fails to pay her debts, the new government, in its consolidated form, must either defend her in the disgrace of repudiation, or pay her debts. Now, the Committee on Foreign Affairs has estimated her debts at ten millions of dollars. They are also estimated by a distinguished statesman in the other end of the Capitol, at twenty-five millions, while others have estimated the amount at fifty millions. It is, however, certain that no person knows the amount of debts which Texas owes. Her own government is ignorant on that point, and has lately adopted measures to ascertain its amount.

I wish most respectfully to propound an interrogatory to the chairman of the Committee on Foreign Affairs. Supposing the debt of Texas to amount to fifty millions of dollars, what do the advocates of annexation intend to do with the balance of forty millions which will remain, after paying the sum proposed by the resolutions before us? As the chairman of the Committee on Foreign Affairs is not in his seat, I will respectfully ask any friend of annexation to answer the question.

Mr. Rhett, of South Carolina, said that he proposed to have nothing to do with it.

Mr. Giddings resumed. I had supposed such to be the intention; but who does not see that a refusal on our part to pay the debts, would involve us in all the disgrace of her repudiation? We should then stand between Texas and her creditors; we should not permit them to coerce the payment, nor would we pay the debt ourselves. The attitude which we should occupy, would surely be any thing but satisfactory. Now, Sir, we should be candid with ourselves and with the people; and we ought to say frankly, at the outset, that we intend to share with Texas the payment of her debts, or that we will share with her the disgrace of repudiation.

Again, Sir, we are told, that on the first of November, 1840, Texas entered into a treaty of commerce with Great Britain, by which she agreed to admit the manufactures of Great Britain into her ports at the same rate of duties which Great Britain demands upon the cotton and sugar of Texas. The precise terms of this treaty are unknown to us. Mr. Urquhart, an English writer, says that the British minister informed the public that a treaty of commerce had been entered into upon terms of reciprocity, but that no copy of the treaty had been published or could be produced from the royal stationer at London. The duty, therefore, upon British manufactures, when introduced into Texas, will be comparatively nominal. This is the solemn stipulation of Texas, for which she has received a full consideration, and which she is solemnly bound to fulfil. We have no right to step between her and Great Britain, to relieve her from the performance of her contract. Now, when Texas comes into the Union, I would ask any friend of annexation whether this solemn treaty is to be fulfilled, or is the pledged faith of Texas to be violated? If any friend of the measure will be kind enough to inform me on this point, and to let the country know their intention, I will now yield him the floor for that purpose. If gentlemen will examine this point, they will find that we must continue, after the annexation, to receive British manufactures into Texas according to this treaty, or we must unite with Texas in repudiating her most solemn obligations, and must share with her the disgrace consequent upon such an act of perfidy. But, Sir, our Constitution provides that "duties on imports shall be uniform in all the States." We shall, therefore, be under the necessity of bringing down our tariff to comport with that treaty, or we must violate the treaty or disregard the Constitution. Which horn of this dilemma will gentlemen prefer? These are some of the difficulties which meet us at the threshold of this measure. Many others of equal magnitude exist, and have been urged by gentlemen who have preceded me in this debate.

While addressing the committee on this subject at the last session of Congress, I spoke particularly of the great injustice consequent upon extending the slave representation. I would again call the attention of the committee to its present bearings. New Hampshire has a free population of 284,573; South Carolina has a free population of 267,360, and has seven Representatives in Congress; while New Hampshire is permitted to have but four. Thus South Carolina, as a compensation for holding slaves, is allowed three members of Congress. Ohio has a free population of more than 1,500,000, and sends twenty-one members to this House; while Virginia, South Carolina, Alabama, and Louisiana, with less free population, sends to this body *thirty-nine* members. Thus the slaveholding interests of those States are represented on this floor by *eighteen members*, who sit here with the representatives of freemen, and vote for laws to govern the intelligent supporters of freedom in our northern States. And what is, if possible, more opposed to justice, they are about to vote to bring in a still greater number of the representatives of slaves by annexing Texas. In this way our intelligent people of the North are degraded to the political level of southern slaves. There is no moral or political obligation that makes it our duty to place the slaves of Texas, or of any other foreign government, upon a level with the intelligent supporters of liberty in our northern States. If this plan be consummated, it will be by the aid of *northern* votes. Will any member vote for this insult to northern freemen, and then say that he has maintained northern rights or northern honor?

The President in his message says, that " the annexation of Texas to the United States, will give to Mexico no just cause of offence." We are all conscious that a state of war now exists between Texas and Mexico. By entering into the proposed union with Texas, we shall become obligated to defend her. And when the armies of Mexico invade Texas, we must of course send our army and navy to repel such invasion. This interference will constitute us the aggressors. We shall thus make the war of Texas *our* war; and our sons will be liable to march to that country to fight the battles of Texas, to shed their blood, and leave their bones to whiten upon her plains, in order that slavery may continue, and the slave-trade flourish.

The gentleman from Indiana (Mr. Brown) says that his constituents had rather *fight* than work. I represent no such constituency. The people of Ohio, in the late war, showed themselves ready to do battle for the cause of *freedom ;* they fought valiantly for their liberty, their firesides, their wives and children ; but they are the last people in the world to fight for *slavery.* That, Sir, is an institution which they execrate, and which they would gladly strike from existence, if they possessed the constitutional power to do so. For me to say that *they* were ready to fight for slavery, would be a libel upon their character.

But this question of annexation is merely a collateral consideration. It is sought only as the means of attaining the ulterior objects of sustaining slavery in Texas, the slave-trade between our slave-holding States, and the people of that government; of perpetuating that institution in the southern States of this Union, and giving to those States a preponderance of political power. This fact was fully stated by me in my remarks made during the last Congress, and I now merely refer to the official evidence, which was not then before me.

The official letter of Mr. Upshur, then Secretary of State, to our " Charge de Affairs " in Texas, commences by stating that " a communication had been received from a gentleman of Maryland," (supposed to be General Duff Green,) " informing the department that a plan was on foot among the abolitionists of Great Britain to procure the abolition of slavery *in Texas,*" (not in the United States). This information gave rise to the whole effort on the part of our government to effect the union now sought. The same officer, in a subsequent letter addressed to our " Charge de Affairs in Texas," Mr. Murphy, declared his conviction,

> " That slavery would be abolished in Texas within the next ten years, and probably within half that time, unless that government were annexed to the United States."

Other letters from gentlemen, said by the President to be men of high standing in Texas, (but whose names are withheld from us,) declare,

> " That unless Texas be annexed to the United States, she will not sustain the institution of slavery five years longer."

The declaration of Lord Brougham, in the House of Lords,

"That the abolition of slavery in Texas would cut off the market for slaves now sent from the slave-breeding States of this Union to Texas, and thereby tend to the ultimate abolition of slavery in those States,"

is referred to, and dwelt upon by the honorable Secretary, as a circumstance of an "*alarming character.*" The continuance of this traffic is one of the objects maintained in the official correspondence to which I have referred. During the late political campaign in some of the slave-breeding States, these objects were eloquently urged in the speeches of stump orators, were maintained by the principal slave-merchants of this city, one of whom kept the banner of the "Lone Star," floating for months over the prison of his sighing and weeping stock of human merchandise. The same object of maintaining this slave-trade was avowed in the other end of this capitol by a distinguished Senator, (Mr. McDuffie,) who, after stating the increase of slaves in the southern States, remarked:

"Now if we shall annex Texas, it will operate as a safety-valve to let off this superabundant slave population from among us."

And the same doctrine was advanced on this floor, by gentlemen from the slave States, who boldly avowed, that

"Slavery must be maintained in Texas, or it must cease to exist in the United States."

But, Sir, these declarations and evidences of the motives and objects of annexation have become so overwhelming, that even a reference to them would appear to be a waste of time and of words. Before I proceed farther, I must notice one point in the argument of the gentleman from South Carolina, (Mr. Rhett). He charged the representatives of the North with agitating the question of slavery on this floor, until we had driven the South into this plan of annexation, as a measure of "*self-defence.*" And is it so? Is this assertion true? Is it founded on fact, or does it rest in empty declamation? Sir, who brought on the present discussion, in which slavery, in all its bearings, is the distinct issue? It was a slave-holding President; a slave-holding cabinet. It is now urged by slaveholders, as a "*slave question.*"

But, Sir, I must turn my attention to the official correspondence before us, and the remarks which I intend to make will be directed to three of the prominent features of Mr. Calhoun's letters to Mr. Packenham and to Mr. King. Those three points are, —

First. The economical bearings of slavery upon our nation.

Secondly. The moral bearings of that institution upon the people of the slave-holding States, both slaves and freemen.

Thirdly. The constitutional powers of the federal government over slavery.

Before I enter upon the examination of these points, however, I will detain the committee for a moment, by calling their attention to the peculiar attitude in which we, as a nation, are now placed before the civilized world. England has abolished slavery in her dominions. France is already moving upon that subject, and Denmark has taken the incipient steps for setting her slaves free. So palpable are the turpitude and disgrace of holding slaves, that even semi-barbarous nations are, at this day, lustrating themselves from its moral contagion. The Bey of Tripoli, in his decree prohibiting the slave-trade, which our honorable Secretary of State is so anxious to maintain, declared that he did it *"for the honor of man and the glory of God."* But while the Bey of Tripoli and the Pacha of Egypt are extending the enjoyment of civil liberty, this government is openly engaged in endeavoring to extend the institution of *slavery*. While we ourselves are sending one fleet to suppress the slave-trade on the African coast, we are sending another to support the same traffic upon the American coast.

While we have entered into solemn treaty with England to exert our utmost effort to *suppress* this trade in human flesh, our Secretary of State is calling upon the King of France to assist us, in *extending and maintaining it.* While we, as a nation, are professing to be lovers of *liberty*, our high officers of government are exerting our national influence to increase and extend *slavery.*

Our representatives in 1776 declared the right of man to the enjoyment of his liberty to be self-evident, while our Executive, in 1844, declares the progress of human liberty in a neighboring government to be highly dangerous to our prosperity. Of all the civilized nations of the earth, ours alone now stands as the advocate of negro slavery. The spectacle is humiliating; but so it is, that the Executive of this nation is now remonstrating with European potentates against their efforts to promote human liberty, and using all the skill and intrigue of diplomacy to prevent the extension of human freedom.

I will further remark, that what I have to say upon the economical bearings of slavery will be strictly in answer to the arguments of our honorable Secretary of State, contained in his letters to the British minister, (Mr. Packenham,) and to our minister at Paris, (Mr. King).

He urges upon Mr. King and the French government, that the abolition of slavery "has diminished the exports of the British West India Islands;" and he infers, that it would have the same effect in this country, if our slave States were to follow their example in respect to emancipation. Now, Sir, the argument is not legitimate. It places pecuniary profit in the scale against the natural rights of man, and gives preponderance to the former. Go to the thief, who lives and thrives by his midnight larcenies; remonstrate with him; tell him that the property of his neighbors *of right* belongs to them, and that he ought not feloniously to take it, — he may turn round, and, in the language of our honorable Secretary, say to you, that were he to adopt your ideas of justice, and cease his thefts, "his exports would be diminished." Go to the pirate, who robs the merchant vessel of its rich lading, and, in order to destroy all evidence of his crimes, murders the crew, and sinks the ship. Tell him that his practice is criminal, and that he ought to cease from farther outrages; and he will reply, in the language of American diplomacy, that his "exports would be diminished." Still, we should regard him as a pirate, and hope that justice would overtake him. His excuse would not mitigate his crimes; nay, it would aggravate his guilt. So with our Secretary's argument. If slavery be opposed to the natural rights of men; if it be a self-evident truth, that "man is born free," and has received from his God the right to enjoy his liberty, then it is a wrong; it is a crime for us to rob him of his God-given rights, although it may thereby "increase our exports."

The honorable Secretary argues, that emancipation diminishes the wealth of a nation, from the fact that the exports of the British West India Islands were diminished after the taking effect of her act of emancipation. He does not notice the fact, however, that while slavery existed there, the whole slave population — men, women, and children — were employed in the production of exports. After emancipation the females were withdrawn from field labor, and employed in preparing comfortable food and clothing for their families; the children were taken from the fields, and sent to school; the males, also, appropriated a part of their time in preparing comfortable dwellings for their families, and in cultivating vegetables for family use. Thus more than one half of the time previously employed in the production of exports, was diverted to other purposes more important; and while the exports were undoubtedly reduced, the people were rapidly improving their physical and intellectual condition. And their intellectual wealth, their happiness, the amount of human enjoyment was increased a thousand fold. Should our States emancipate their slaves, they would undoubtedly export less cotton and sugar for some years afterwards. Their colored population would find new wants in their new condition, which must be supplied. They must have comfortable diet and clothing; they would wear hats, and shoes, and bonnets, and decent attire. These demands would open up a new and extensive market for manufacturers; and, as they would find themselves able, they would begin to purchase small lots of ground, which would increase the price of real estate; and in five or ten years, the lands in those States would be worth more than both lands and slaves are at this time. These deductions are warranted from the well established facts that have resulted from emancipation in the West India Islands.

But I desire for a moment to call the attention of the committee to the effects which slavery has upon the physical ability of a nation to defend itself in time of war. Slavery is an element of national weakness; it is a state of unceasing war between the master and slave. The slaves have been reduced to their present condition by physical force; and the master holds them in subjection merely by superior power, — by violence, outrage, and crime. The laws which authorize the master to exercise control over his slaves, were passed without the actual or implied consent of the slaves. To such laws, they have at no time yielded other than compulsory obedience; they are under no moral obligation to obey such laws; they owe no allegiance whatever to our government. They may at the first possible moment rise, and with physical force make slaves of their present masters, without any greater violation of moral principle than is daily practised by their owners in holding them in bondage. They sigh for liberty; they feel deeply the wrongs to which they are subjected, and will have no hesitation in regaining their freedom at any sacrifice to their oppressors, either of property or of life. The slave will feel himself at perfect liberty to use any, and all means in his power to throw off his chains, whenever a reasonable opportunity is presented. If a hostile army should encamp in his neighborhood, he will join them, though he be under the necessity of taking the lives of his master and family in order to effect it. These slaves would be infinitely less dangerous if they were removed beyond our boundaries. We could, in such case, protect ourselves against them with an army of one tenth of their numbers.

But the danger to us in case of war arises from the fact, that they are scattered through all our slave States, located on every plantation, and in almost every house. They are acquainted with the habits of their masters; with the roads and streams, the arsenals and fortifications; in short, with all the circumstances with which they are surrounded. Now, Sir, let an invading army of a hundred thousand men land in our southern States with the *materiel* for two hundred thousand, and let them proclaim freedom to such slaves as will unite with them; and as the slaves reach their encampment, let them be armed, and drilled, and sent out to liberate their wives and children, and those who have been oppressed with them. Could more efficient troops be employed? Stimulated by a recollection of the wrongs which they had suffered, they would become desperate, and the consequences I will not attempt to describe. Sir, in case of invasion the master will not dare to send his servant abroad, or to the field, unless he is watched; if he does, the servant will not be likely to return. At night, too, they must be watched, and the family must be guarded against their domestics. Thus they detract from the ability of a nation to defend it. In 1779, the authorities of South Carolina sent a special messenger to Congress, to inform that body that their State could furnish no troops to repel the invasion then making upon them, as it required all their forces to remain at home, in order to protect their families against their slaves! The free population of that State was then nearly a hundred thousand greater than that of her slaves. It should also be remembered, that the British army during that war dared not proclaim freedom to slaves, or employ them as troops, from apprehension as to the effect of such a measure upon the slaves in their West India Islands. If, under such circumstances, it required three hundred thousand free people to guard two hundred thousand slaves, what number would have been required if the enemy had proclaimed freedom to the slaves, and employed them as troops against their former owners? We have in the United States fifteen millions of free population, and two and a half millions of slaves; but with this population we are less, far less capable of resisting an invading army, than we should be with a population of ten millions, composed entirely of freemen. Indeed, we are far less able to resist an invading foe with our present Union, than the free States would be if they composed a separate government, without any association with the slave States. In other words, in case of serious invasion, South Carolina, Louisiana, and Mississippi and Alabama would be unable to watch their own slaves, and would require all the force which the northern slave States could spare to assist them in that duty, while the defence of the whole nation would substantially fall upon the free States.

I desire that southern gentlemen will understand me, as making these remarks strictly in answer to the doctrine advanced by Mr. Calhoun and others, and not with any desire to call up unpleasant feelings in the mind of any southern man. General Jackson, and others, say that it is necessary that we should have Texas as a means of national defence. I reply, that every addition of slave territory renders us weaker, and places a heavier burden upon the free States. This extending slavery at the expense of our free States, is what the honorable Secretary regards as *economy*. If southern gentlemen regard it in that light, I may be permitted to assure them, that we of the North look upon its economical bearings as altogether unfavorable to our interests. We are bound by the Constitution to defend the southern States in case of invasion, or of domestic violence. That stipulation we will perform to the letter; but there we stop — we go no further. We will not take upon ourselves any obligation to protect the slave-holders of Texas. If that government will abolish slavery, those who are now slaves will gladly constitute an army that will protect the whole people of that government. Let them adopt that mode; but let not the freemen of New England, or of the free States, be subjected to the degradation of defending the slave-holders of Texas.

The protection of southern slaves has constantly entered into the considerations which have heretofore prompted the increase of our navy. The report of the Secretary of the Navy at the 2d Session of the 27th Congress, recommended an increase of our naval armament to one half the force of the British navy; and the principal reason which he urged for such a vast expenditure, was the *support of slavery*. One of the employments of the "home squadron" has been the protection of the coastwise slave-trade; and little doubt now exists that it originated in a desire to uphold that commerce. And this is the "economy" so desired by our Secretary of State. The annexation of Texas would call for an increase of our naval armament, in order that slavery might be protected there, as well as in the present slave States. This will be one of the consequences of annexation.

This proposed union with Texas will require a large increase of our army. Our present army has often been dispersed in different parts of our slave States, in order to intimidate southern slaves to obedience. For that purpose a regiment has been sent to one place, and a company to another, to stand guard, while southern overseers and slave-holders could scourge their fellow men into subjection. This is another of the "*economical*" bearings of slavery. Methinks that southern men should be content with this use of our present army, instead of endeavoring to make them mount guard to protect the Texan slave-holders from the just vengeance of an enslaved people.

If Texas be brought into the Union, we shall be called on to extend around her a circle of fortifications for the purpose of protecting her from invasion. An expenditure, annually, of many millions of dollars, will be required for that purpose. That labor must be performed by slaves, as all such labor is now performed in our slave States; for free labor is not permitted in slave States to come into competition with slave labor. For this slave labor we pay about the same price per day, as I am informed, that is paid to the laboring free men of the North, while I believe it is universally admitted that one freeman will, upon an average, perform as much labor in a given time as two slaves. In this way, the erection of fortifications in our slave States is rendered important to the support of slavery; as all must see, that while we pay one dollar for the actual erection of forts, we pay another to support slavery. It will, therefore, answer for slave-holders to regard slavery as an economical institution, inasmuch as it enables them to draw money from the pockets of northern men to enrich themselves. Why, Sir, I have known members of this House sitting here and advocating heavy appropriations for southern fortifications, while they were receiving of the moneys thus appropriated thirty dollars per day for the labor of their slaves, who were kept in the constant employ of government. To such gentlemen, I have no doubt, the institution appeared to be profitable, however it may appear to northern men who pay the money. Now, Sir, I object to extending this kind of economy into Texas at the expense of the northern States.

Again, Sir, let us look into the Post-Office Department, and see the effects of slavery upon that branch of our national expenditure. Slaves neither take newspapers, nor write letters, nor pay postage. They prevent the accumulation of a dense population; of course the roads are indifferent, and the transportation of the mail in our slave States is expensive. An average of several years past will show, that we have paid for transporting the mail in the slave States, annually, half a million dollars more than we have received from those States by way of postage; while the free States have paid about the same amount in postage more than has been expended in transporting the mail therein. Thus we all see from the official documents before us, that the people of the free States have been for years taxed, at least half a million of dollars annually, to transport the mail in the slave States. This is another illustration of the pecuniary bearings of slavery. And, for one, I object to extending the transportation of the mail into Texas, at the annual expense to the free States of some three hundred thousand dollars. I do not believe its economical bearings favorable to our interests.

Let us for a moment examine the expenditures and receipts arising from our public lands. From the documents on file in the General Land Office, it appears that the public lands in our slave States have cost us forty millions dollars more than we have received in return upon the sales of those lands; while we have realized a profit upon the sale of our public lands in the free States, to the amount of thirty-eight millions dollars. All will see that the whole amount of this thirty-eight millions has been drawn from the people of the free States, and expended in the slave States, in consequence of the pecuniary bearings of slavery. And this is the economy of slavery so vauntingly put forth by our Secretary of State. Sir, from the public lands of Texas may we be delivered! If the proposed union should be formed, I would at once vote for an appropriation of five or ten millions of dollars to be saved from all further expense arising from them. By the time this government shall have settled the extent of the French grants, the Spanish grants, the Mexican grants, and the Texan grants, paid up the deficiencies in those grants, extinguished the Indian titles, surveyed the lands, and defrayed the expenses of the sales, we may expect a net loss of at least twenty millions to the public treasury. Yet we hear it urged that their lands will yield a net surplus sufficient to pay the debts of Texas. I ask, on what data are such arguments based?

The pecuniary bearings of slavery were well illustrated in the Florida war, which was commenced and prosecuted in order to recapture the fugitive slaves who had sought an asylum in that territory. It was carried on for seven years, at an expenditure of forty millions dollars, and some hundreds of lives, in order to capture and return to their owners some five hundred slaves; making *each slave* cost the nation about *eighty thousand dollars*, mostly taken from the pockets of northern freemen. This is the economy of slavery. Sir, I object to placing ourselves in a situation to be called upon to catch the runaway slaves of Texas. If this be economy, may Heaven save us from its extension.

But argument on this point would be useless to gentlemen who have travelled in the free and in the slave States. Let us look to the largest States at the time of forming our Constitution; I refer to Virginia and New York. Let us examine the latter; take notice of her turnpikes, her railroads, her canals, her industrious and thriving population, her commerce and universal prosperity. Then look at Virginia! Mark her miserable highways, her deserted plantations, her dilapidated dwellings, her ragged slaves of almost every shade of complexion, her uncouth implements of husbandry, the indolence and extravagance of her people, her extensive forests, the almost total absence of all evidence of thrift and prosperity; and we shall not be under the necessity of reading the correspondence alluded to, in order to form an opinion of the pecuniary effects of slavery. At the adoption of our Federal Constitution, in 1790, Virginia contained a free population nearly a hundred thousand greater than New York. In 1840, the free population of New York was nearly four times as great as that of Virginia. Within that period, the slaves of New York have been converted into industrious, enterprising, and intelligent citizens; while those of Virginia remain in their chains, ignorant and degraded, the subjects of merchandise. Ten thousand five hundred and ninety-three primary schools were in progress in New York at the taking of the census of 1840; while Virginia could boast of but one thousand five hundred and sixty-one. At those schools in New York, five hundred and two thousand three hundred and sixty-seven scholars were instructed, while Virginia furnished to her primary schools only thirty-five thousand three hundred and sixty-one. Among the free white population of Virginia over twenty years of age, one in every twelve is unable to read or write; while only one in fifty-three of the same description of population in New York is thus deficient in education. But, in order to form a just estimate of the comparative intelligence of the two States, we should bear in mind that more than one third of the population of Virginia are slaves, kept in the most profound ignorance; so that about five twelfths of her whole population, over twenty years of age, can neither read nor write. Such is the moral degradation of "the Old Dominion;" once the home of Washington, of Jefferson, of Madison, and of Monroe; the mother of States and of statesmen. But now "there is none so poor as to do her reverence." It is slavery that sits like an incubus upon her, prostrating her energies, corroding her morals, and degrading her people. In the language of one of her most talented sons, "she has become a vast menagerie, where men are bred for the market like oxen for the shambles."

But what I have said of Virginia is by way of illustration. The same remarks will apply substantially to all of the slave States; for it is to slavery alone that Virginia may impute her want of prosperity. And, if ignorance in the great mass of people be *economy*, then, surely, may our honorable Secretary of State boast of slavery as an *economical* institution. It was well remarked by the gentleman from Illinois, (Mr. Hardin,) that slavery begets a contempt for labor. Such is undoubtedly the case. It is said of John Randolph, that when he desired to express his utmost contempt for a man, he would assert that "he hoès corn with negroes." In our free States we have no idle persons. Our wives, our daughters, and our sons, are bred to industry; but, in the slave States, the great mass of free people not only refuse to labor, but many of them live in habits of great extravagance, while the non-slaveholding class of free people are generally indolent, and miserably poor. Of the aggregate amount of time usually appropriated to labor by the people of the free States, at least one half is spent in idleness by the people of the slave States. It is, therefore, quite plain that vice, ignorance, and poverty must result from the existence of slavery. Yet the honorable Secretary of State regards it as attended with great pecuniary blessings to our nation.

But I desire to look into the moral influences of slavery, which our honorable Secretary regards as so salutary. I am aware that the honorable gentleman from Massachusetts (Mr. Winthrop) intimated the danger of driving southern whigs from us, if we speak against slavery. I do not entertain such fears. The Secretary of State has sent to this House an elaborate argument in favor of the moral influences of slavery. This argument has been published to the world, and is now before us. If we do not reply to it, we shall be regarded as having given our tacit assent to its truth. If Southern whigs desire us to keep silence under these circumstances, I cannot yield to their wishes. Nay, if they would do that, they are *no whigs*. It is, therefore, my intention to speak with the most perfect frankness. I have never before felt disposed to enter upon the discussion of the morality of slavery, while sitting in this hall, for the reason that it was never before forced upon us. But we now have the argument of the honorable Secretary thrust upon us, as well as the arguments of gentlemen in this hall, who have eloquently insisted upon the humane and moral character of slavery. Under these circumstances, we must meet the arguments, or timidly shrink from the contest.

Sir, I deny that slavery is characterized by either humanity or morality. To take from a man his liberty, is the highest injury you can inflict upon him, except to deprive him of life. Indeed, by taking from him his liberty, you deprive him of the power to protect his life; and it is not unfrequently the case, that the life of the slave is sacrificed by withholding from him his liberty. But I shall again refer to this point; at present I will call the attention of the committee to some illustrations of the morality of slave-holding, which meets us on every street of this city. I refer to the infinite shades of complexion that mark the slave population around us; varying from a perfect black to the lightest complexion of the Anglo-Saxon race; indeed, it is not unusual to meet a slave with a lighter complexion than his master. But a few days since, an advertisement appeared in the principal papers of this city, offering a reward of *five hundred dollars* for the arrest of a fugitive slave, described as a young woman sixteen or seventeen years of age, "*white*, with straight dark hair, intelligent countenance, and agreeable manners." The extraordinary bounty offered for her arrest, was doubtless in consequence of her complexion and manners. Sir, I have no doubt that our people of the free States will marvel at seeing advertisements for *white slaves*. But Mr. Jefferson informs us that "some of the best blood of Virginia runs in the veins of her slaves." Perhaps the fair fugitive to whom I have made allusion, descended from some aristocratic family of "the Old Dominion." I am told that it is not unusual for a man to hold his own children in slavery, and even to sell them to those who deal in human flesh. It is said, also, to be a very common thing for a planter to hold in slavery the children of his father, and even *to sell them as merchandise*. These are mild illustrations of the moral bearings of slavery, which our Secretary of State regards as humane and salutary.

Go to that bastile of slavery on Maryland Avenue, which is

12*

so distinctly in view from the windows of this hall; mark its dark, its hated walls; enter its heavy gates; look into its cells; notice the countenances of its inmates; witness the grief, the deep-seated horror and despair manifest in every face; see the heaving bosoms, and the silent tears; listen to the suppressed sighs; see them chained in coffles, and marched on board the slave-ship; view their unutterable agony of soul as they take a last sad look towards the scenes of their childhood; attend them on their voyage to the slave-market in the far South, to their new homes; witness the deep degradation and suffering to which they are subjected, until death relieves them, and closes up the short drama; then say, whether you are convinced of the benign influence and the moral purity of slavery. We are asked to extend and perpetuate these scenes. Will northern men do it? We, as a nation, have declared our abhorrence of the slave-trade. We have declared it *piracy* by our laws, and we punish with death those who shall engage in it upon a *foreign coast;* while, by our legislative enactments, we continue and sustain it, with all its crimes and horrors, in our national metropolis; and a high officer of this government seeks the aid and countenance of a European monarch, to enable us to maintain it in Texas. For that purpose, he enters into a labored argument to show to the civilized world that it is both *moral* and *benevolent*. This essay in favor of slavery and the slave-trade, is urged upon members of this House.

Why, Sir, I became acquainted with its salutary tendency soon after taking a seat in this hall, some eight years since. I have often related the transaction as it was communicated to me by different persons at the time. I believe their relation to be strictly correct; but if any gentleman doubts its entire accuracy, I should be pleased to have a committee, with power to send for persons and papers, and let the whole truth be called forth and published.

A *lady!* one of that sex in whom we look for all the finer sensibilities of our nature, residing in this city, on Pennsylvania Avenue, owned a slave, said to approximate more nearly to the white than to the colored race. He was intelligent and industrious. He had a wife and several children, to whom he was much attached. His owner informed him that she was about selling him to one of those piratical dealers in mankind, always to be found in this city, and at this time advocating the annexation of Texas, and the extension of the slave-trade. The man remonstrated with his owner; told her that he could not survive a separation from his children, his wife, and his friends; and when she showed no disposition to listen to his supplication, he took a knife from his pocket and attempted to cut his throat in her presence. He was seized by his fellow servants, and the knife taken from him, and a surgeon called, who dressed his wound. After this was done, finding himself relieved from the grasp of his fellow servants, he sprang from them, ran to the bridge across the canal, and threw himself into its turbid waters, preferring its muddy bottom for his grave, rather than submit to the torture, the pangs, and sufferings that awaited his separation from his family. His body was taken from the canal the next morning by his fellow slaves, and lay exposed for some time on the bridge located on Seventh street.

As a further illustration, I refer to a transaction less notorious. I am not prepared to vouch its entire accuracy, though I believe it to be literally true; and if any gentleman doubts its correctness, I will unite with him in asking of the House a committee for the purpose of eliciting the whole truth. I believe my venerable friend before me, (Mr. Adams,) has once referred to the same transaction.* A slave mother, with her

* Mr. Adams subsequently informed Mr. Giddings that the case to which he (Mr. Adams) had once made allusion, was the case of a woman who had lived in Washington city. She had been set free by her owner, who was a widow; but no deed of emancipation was executed, although the woman regarded herself free, and was so regarded by her former owner, and all others. She lived in this situation, and became the mother of a family of four children, when her owner died. The heirs of her owner then seized upon her and her children; took them to Alexandria, and sold them to a slave-dealer; while imprisoned there, she murdered her two youngest children, and, while endeavoring to take the life of the next older, he and the other surviving child raised such a cry of distress as to attract the attention of those without, and they were saved by the timely aid of persons near the prison. The dealer in human flesh, who had purchased the woman and children, returned them to their venders, and sued them "for fraud, in selling a *vicious slave.*"

two children, was brought from the country to the city for the purpose of selling them to those who deal in mankind. They were imprisoned in that common receptacle of "*human cattle*" to which I have heretofore referred. While thus confined in the dreary dungeon, with none but the eye of her God and her children upon her, she reflected upon her lowly hovel, her home, her husband, her children, from whom she had been separated, upon her friends, and the scenes of her happier days. Then as she looked forward to the short life and the speedy death that awaited her, and viewed her two children, and the lives of bondage and degradation to which they were to be subjected, her mind was wrought up to desperation; reason tottered, and reeling, fell from its throne; she became a maniac, and seizing her children, tore from them the life which God had given, then severed the thread of her own existence, and rushed unbidden to the presence of her final Judge. This is but another illustration of the humane influence of slavery, so much extolled by our Secretary of State.

My colleague from the Butler district (Mr. Weller) was anxious to extend our "*democratic institutions*" to Texas. It is this particular branch of our "*democratic institutions*" now sought to be extended and perpetuated. These scenes, to which I have referred, took place in this city, under our own laws, enacted by Congress, and which are now kept in force by the action of the very gentlemen who exhibit so much sympathy for the people of Texas, and who become so eloquent in favor "of extending the area of freedom," by establishing and perpetuating the slave-trade, with its horrors and crimes, its outrages and its murders.

Gentlemen here become pathetic upon the sufferings to which the people of Texas have been subjected during their war with Mexico. They speak in melting terms of the predatory warfare heretofore carried on against Texas, and they ask the people of our free States to relieve them from Mexican barbarity. Why, Sir, there is more human suffering in this city, every year, by reason of the slave-trade, than has been endured by the whole people of Texas during their entire revolution of eight years. The consumption of human life attendant, and consequent upon, the slave-trade *in this district*, is greater every year than it has been in Texas during any period of their war with Mexico. It should be borne in mind that this slave-trade is authorized and maintained *by act of Congress*, which the advocates of annexation refuse to repeal. The scenes which I have described, and the sufferings which I have mentioned, are authorized by our laws, *passed by this body*, and which we now keep in force. Gentlemen on this floor, who, by supporting the gag rule, have for years voted to continue those laws, and the scenes to which I have made reference; whose hearts are unmoved by all the suffering of the slave population here, and by all the blood that is annually shed in this district, become eloquent upon the sufferings endured by the people of Texas. They are willing to spend the national treasure, and pour out American blood to protect the Texans, while they will authorize *by law* all those crimes and outrages, and all the violence and bloodshed attendant upon the slave-trade in this district. Indeed, they are striving to extend and perpetuate those crimes in Texas, under the plea of "*extending the area of freedom.*"

Our President, too, in his message, speaks of the "barbarous manner" in which the Mexicans have prosecuted the war against Texas, and appears anxious to relieve the people of that nation from the persecutions to which they are subjected; while in this city, within view of his own window, the slave population are subjected to a thousand times greater suffering, by reason of our own laws. But for them he has no sympathy, no compassion; nay, he lends his influence to extend and perpetuate in Texas those very crimes and outrages to which I have alluded.

The instances to which I have called the attention of the committee, are merely examples of what is daily taking place in the slave States. The amount of human suffering, and the consumption of human life within those States is incalculable. Upon the cotton plantations they purchase none but full grown slaves. The average of the slaves thus purchased, after entering upon the plantations, is only *seven years*. I speak upon the authority of extensive cotton growers, whose long experience and observation enables them to form correct opinions. It is regarded by cotton growers as more profitable to drive their slaves so hard that the intensity of their labor shall produce death in seven years, and then to supply their places by fresh purchases, than it is to treat them more leniently; thus whole gangs of slaves, consisting of many hundreds on each cotton plantation, are consigned to their graves once in seven years. The driver's lash impels them to excessive effort, and really causes their death, as much as the knife, or the pistol of the murderer, causes the death of his victim. They are hastened to premature graves, in order that their owners may enjoy the fruits of their toil, as much as the inoffensive merchant, when captured by the pirate, is compelled to "*walk the plank.*"

We have all seen notices of a convention of slave-holders, held some years since, in South Carolina, to determine upon the length of slave life most profitable to the master. That is, they met for the purpose of determining whether the master would gain greater profits from the labor of his slaves, by working them so hard as to produce death in seven years, or by treating them so humanely as to lengthen their lives to a longer period! Upon full deliberation it was determined, that *seven years* was the period most beneficial to the *master's interest.* The feelings of humanity, or the principles of justice to the slave, did not enter into the computation. They forgot these considerations, as did our honorable Secretary of State, in his letters to Mr. Packenham, and to Mr. King. Now, Sir, the pirate thinks it most profitable for him to sacrifice the lives of his captives within an hour after he takes possession of them. The cotton planter regards it as more conducive to his interest, to hold his slaves under the torture of the overseer's whip for *seven years.* It is certain, that one is as much the cause of his victim's death, as the other; but as to the relative degree of guilt which each incurs, I will express no opinion. I will leave that question for casuists of nicer discrimination than myself, to determine.

Upon sugar plantations, however, the slaves are worked still harder, and the average life of slaves on sugar estates, is computed at *five* years. That is, the planters on those estates regard it more profitable to work their hands so severely as to cause their death in five years, and then to replace them by fresh purchases, than it would be to use them more leniently. The precise number of slaves thus sacrificed annually, cannot be ascertained. We know, however, that there are less restraints upon the increase of slave population, than there is among the free and enlightened portion of community. But the late census shows that the increase of the slaves in the slave States, between 1830 and 1840, was about four hundred thousand less, in proportion to their whole number, than that of the free population. But some of those slaves have fled to Canada, and to the free States; and others have been transported to Texas. Allowing forty thousand as the number of those who have thus left the slave States, and we shall still find a deficit of three hundred and sixty thousand in ten years; thirty-six thousand annually, and three thousand per month, and of one hundred per day, as the number of persons whose lives are thus sacrificed, under the laws of our slave States, and of Congress. This tide of human gore is constantly flowing, and we are called upon to lend our official aid to increase and extend it. In order to effect this object, the honorable Secretary of State has urged upon us to consider the *humane and moral bearings of slavery*. It is, therefore, due to him that we examine them.

Do we believe there is a Power above us, who will visit national sins and crimes with national judgments? that He will visit upon this great people, the just penalty due to us for the suffering we have inflicted, the blood we have shed, and the murders that have been committed under our laws? I am one of those who solemnly believe that transgression and punishment are inseparably connected by the inscrutable wisdom of God's providence. With this impression, I feel as confident that chastisement and tribulation, for the offences which we have committed against the down-trodden sons of

Africa, await this people, as I do that *justice* controls the destinies of nations, or guides the power of Omnipotence. I "hold these truths to be self-evident, that all men are created equal; that they are endowed by their Creator with certain inalienable rights; that among these are life, liberty, and the pursuit of happiness."

If our African brethren received their lives and liberty from God himself, what must be the guilt of those who step between God and their fellow men, and rob them of their God-given rights? Sir, in the language of Mr. Jefferson, "I tremble for my country, when I reflect that God is just!" I would not decide for others. "To his own master," each member on this floor, "must stand or fall." But I most solemnly declare, that I would as soon share in the guilt of the lawless pirate, or bathe my hands in human blood by direct murder, as I would aid in extending slavery and the slave-trade, by voting for the passage of the resolutions under consideration. In our own land, our African brethren now pine in bondage. Congress cannot relieve them. But, in the eloquent language of Jefferson, I would say, "When the measure of their tears shall be full, when their tears shall have involved Heaven itself in darkness, doubtless a God of justice will awaken to their distress," and "by his exterminating thunder, will manifest his attention to things of this world, and that they are not left to the guidance of blind fatuity."

But the honorable Secretary assumes the doctrine, that this government is bound by the Constitution to maintain and uphold slavery and the slave-trade; that we, the people of the free States, are under constitutional obligations to participate in the crimes, and share in the guilt, to which I have made reference. Sir, I take issue with the honorable Secretary. I not only deny that such obligation rests upon our people of the free States, but I deny that the federal government possesses power, under the Constitution, to uphold slavery, or in any way to interfere with it. I have so often given my views on this point, that I feel no disposition to repeat them; particularly after the able argument of my colleague from the Loraine district, (Mr.

Hamlin). I hold to the doctrine which was maintained by southern and by northern men, on this subject, eight years since.

At the last session of the 25th Congress, resolutions in regard to slavery were introduced to this hall, by a gentleman from New Hampshire, now a member of the other branch of our National Legislature, (Mr. Atherton). It was then reported and believed that those resolutions were agreed upon in a caucus of the democratic party; that Mr. Calhoun was a member of that caucus, and that the resolutions were originally framed by him. One of these resolutions was in the following words:

> "*Resolved,* That this government is a government of limited powers; that, by the Constitution of the United States, it has no power *whatever* over the institution of slavery in the several States of this Union."

For this resolution I voted, and so did one hundred and ninety-six members of this body; indeed, there were only six members present who refused to vote for it, and those gentlemen objected rather to the practice of asserting abstract principles, than to the doctrine of the resolution.

During the same session, Mr. Clay, in the Senate, maintained the same position. He declared that, —

> "Under the compromises of the Federal Constitution, no power whatever was granted to the general government over the institution of domestic slavery, except those which relate to taxation, representation, and the power to restore fugitive slaves to their owners." "All other powers (said he) were withheld by the several States, to be exercised exclusively at their own discretion."

I mention Mr. Clay's sentiments, not for the reason that he is a whig, but because he is an eminent statesman, and that his sentiments at that time were universally approved by southern gentlemen, and almost equally so by northern statesmen. In his letter to the editor of the Lexington Observer, dated on the 2d September last, Mr. Clay declares, —

> "That Congress has no power over the institution of slavery; that the existence, the maintenance, and the continuance of that institution depends exclusively upon the power and authority of the States in which it is situated."

These are my sentiments. They are the sentiments of southern men and of northern men. They are the sentiments of our people generally. They were put forth and distinctly maintained by the whigs of Virginia in their address published in September last. But a different doctrine is now held by the Executive and by the advocates of annexation. They now declare that the people of the free States are bound to spend their wealth, and shed their blood, in support of the institution which they hold in such general abhorrence. There are two parties in the United States; one insists that we have power to *sustain* slavery, and the other urges that we have power to *abolish* it. But the great mass of our people, consisting of both the great political parties, hold to what I regard as the very obvious doctrine of the Constitution, that we have not the constitutional power to do either.

Why, Sir, at the formation of the Constitution, an amendment was offered by a member from South Carolina, providing that "fugitive slaves should be arrested and delivered to their owners in the same manner as fugitives from justice." But Mr. Wilson, of Pennsylvania, and Mr. Sherman, of Connecticut, objected that such a provision in the Constitution would implicate the people of the free States in the support of slavery, and the proposition was withdrawn. Does the spirit of Wilson now inspire the sons of my native State? Do they hold that institution in such unmitigated detestation, that they will, in no respect, implicate themselves or their constituents in its support? Will they, like their immortal Franklin, "go to the very verge of the Constitution to suppress and abolish it?" I will not doubt their regard for the inalienable rights of men, and the honor of our nation. Nor will I suspect that the successors of Sherman will prove recreant to the noble sentiments which he maintained in the Convention that framed the Constitution. I cannot distrust any party from the free States. It is impossible for me to believe that any member north of Mason and Dixon's line, can be brought to vote for an extension of the crimes, the wholesale murders, to which I have called the attention of the Committee.

The momentous questions of Liberty and Slavery are now before the people of this nation. They have been forced upon us by the slave-holders of the South. Northern men cannot, will not, shrink from the discussion. They have become the great absorbing topics in this hall, in most of our State legislatures, and by the people of the United States generally. Public indignation at these attempts to involve us in the crimes and disgrace of slavery, is already awakened. It is rolling forward with an irresistible force; which, ere long, will redeem and purify the people of the North from the crimes and the corroding influences of that blood-stained institution. The car of universal liberty is moving; it has acquired a momentum that cannot be stopped; and those who throw themselves before it, in order to obstruct its progress, will be crushed beneath its resistless power.

JOINT OCCUPATION OF OREGON.*

BY ANNEXING TEXAS, WE COMMENCED THE POLICY OF EXTENDING OUR TERRITORY — DUTY TO CONTINUE IT UNTIL THE BALANCE OF POWER BETWEEN THE SLAVE AND FREE STATES BE RESTORED — PROPHECY THAT THE PRESIDENT WILL SURRENDER A PORTION OF OUR TERRITORY IN OREGON.

[President Polk in his inaugural address, and in his first annual message, declared our title to the whole of Oregon to be "*clear and unquestionable;*" the British government showed no disposition to recede from their position. The democratic party declared their intention to maintain our "claim to Texas, and to the *whole* of Oregon." In the Senate, leading members declared "war to be inevitable," and that "the hearts of the people must be prepared for that event." With these indications, a very general apprehension of war spread through the country, and our commercial men were alarmed.

This was the situation of affairs, when the Committee on Foreign Affairs in the House of Representatives reported a resolution to terminate the joint occupancy of that territory, "and to take possession of it;" and the members generally spoke of war as probable.

Mr. Giddings spoke upon this resolution; and in taking the grounds which he assumed in the following speech, and in using the language he did, he was prompted by the conviction that a war with England would destroy southern slavery, and that the leading statesmen of the South were conscious of that fact. It is unnecessary to add that his prophecy on this subject was literally fulfilled.]

MR. SPEAKER, — When this subject was before us at a former session, our government had not adopted the policy of extending its powers by the acquisition of new territory. I then preferred that the Union, which had been formed by our

---

* Speech on the resolution terminating the joint occupation of Oregon, and authorizing the President to take military possession thereof. Delivered in the House of Representatives, January 5, 1846.

fathers of the Revolution, should remain and be perpetuated. I saw, or thought I saw, difficulties and dangers in attempting to bring other governments under our jurisdiction. I had seen in this hall, since the day on which I first entered it, a conflict of interest between different portions of the Union, which threatened the final overthrow of our government, if not confined to its then existing limits. Even then, a spirited contest had been carried on for many years between the southern and northern portions of the Union, in regard to our protective tariff. At one time it had actually arrayed in arms one member of the confederacy against the power of the federal government. That controversy still continues, and is likely to increase in interest.

Another controversy, between the eastern and western portions of the Union, has long been carried on in respect to the disposition of our public lands. That controversy still continues. But, Sir, a conflict of a more absorbing character, between the slave-holding interests of the South, and the advocates of freedom at the North, had been increasing and extending among all classes of society, both in the free and in the slave States. There was then a large balance of political power in favor of the free States; while a liberal and perhaps commendable policy, on the part of the North, had given to the slave-holding territory an equal number of States, and of course an equal representation in the Senate with that of the free States. I then believed, notwithstanding all these sectional conflicts, that our Union might be preserved, if the government were confined to its then existing limits; but I was most solemnly impressed with the opinion, that if our territory were extended, and the interests of different sections thereby rendered more conflicting, the permanency of the Union would be endangered.

These views were based upon the irrevocable laws of nature. The soil and climate and products of Texas, are totally different from the soil and climate and products of New England; but they are not more different than are the real interests of the people in those sections of the country.

It will be as impossible for Congress by any laws of our enactment, to reconcile the interests of Texas and Massachusetts, as it would for us to compel the cotton and sugar of Texas to grow on New England soil, or the manufactures of New England to flourish in Texas. So, too, with Oregon. The principal commerce of that territory must be with the Sandwich Isles and with China; ours with Europe. No law of ours can reverse or reconcile these interests, founded upon the different positions of the Atlantic and Pacific coasts. We may extend our laws over Oregon; we may admit her as a new State to our Union, as we have already admitted Texas; but time will demonstrate to the people of Texas, and of Oregon, that they gain nothing by the association; and our people of the East and the North will find, by future experience, that a union with Oregon and Texas will require of them the sacrifice of a portion of their own interests, without in any degree adding to the happiness of the human family.

When these things shall be fully seen and felt by all portions of the Union, a separation will be inevitable, and such new confederations will then be formed as shall be thought more conducive to the general good. With these views, I preferred the independence of both Texas and Oregon, rather than see them united with us. I was fully aware that the tide of emigration which was setting from our western States to Oregon, would people that territory with those who understand the value of our free institutions, and who are devoted to the cause of civil liberty. Their wisdom and patriotism would soon erect a government there, modelled after our own, while it would be free from the errors to which ours is subjected. Under these circumstances and with these impressions, I felt that the great interests of all would be far better subserved by their becoming independent governments, than they would by their being members of our confederacy. Indeed, I felt that the policy of receiving them as members of our Union, would eventually prove fatal to our confederation. Nor do I now entertain any doubt whatever on that point. I therefore voted against terminating our joint occupation of Oregon, and against all political association with Texas. Yet the policy of territorial aggrandizement *has been adopted.* It has been done without my consent, and against my will. For the resulting consequences, I am not responsible.

But since this subject of Oregon was before us during a former Congress, the policy of the nation has been changed. Indeed, the government itself has been changed in its essential elements; its fundamental principles have been overthrown. The Union, formed by our venerated predecessors, has been dissolved, and a new slave-holding confederacy, with a foreign government, has been formed.

It is true that the action of this body and of the Executive, in regard to the annexation of Texas, has imposed no moral or political obligation upon the people of Ohio, or of any free State, to enter into this new slave-holding confederacy. But, from present indications, they will all submit and become parties to the new Union. This cannot be fully determined until after the senators and representatives of Texas shall take their seats in Congress. Then if Ohio shall elect members of Congress to come here, and act with those of Texas in passing laws to govern our people, we shall thereby become parties to the new compact.

But, Sir, our State will become a party under the expectation that the policy of adding new States shall be continued, until the balance of power shall be restored to the northern section of the Union. It is the annexation of Texas that has rendered the *whole* of Oregon necessary to restore that balance of power. By the annexation of Texas, the slave States now have a majority in the Senate. They will continue to retain that majority, unless we add territory to our northwestern border. By the annexation of Texas, the protection of the free labor of the North has been surrendered to the control of the slave power; our constitutional rights, and the honor of our free States, are delivered over to the keeping of slave-holders.

Indeed, our people of the free States have been politically bound, hand and foot, and surrendered to the rule and government of a slave-holding oligarchy. This has been done by the party in power, under the declared policy of obtaining Texas and retaining the *whole of Oregon*. But having obtained Texas, a portion of the party now propose to give up a part of Oregon. Their plan is, to add territory to the South, and surrender up territory on the North, to *increase* their power, to *decrease* ours; to enlarge the area of slavery, to diminish the area of freedom. But while, by their acts, they are saying these things, they appear to have suddenly conceived a sort of holy horror of sectional views, and of sectional feelings. Last year they openly avowed their anxiety for Texas, in order to increase their political power. They have obtained Texas, and with it an increase of political power, and they have now suddenly become impressed with the impropriety of sectional feeling. But if any thing be well calculated to excite sectional feelings, it is sectional injustice.

We have had abundant demonstrations of southern feelings in regard to northern interests. We know it is vain for us to talk of maintaining the interests of the manufacturers of Pennsylvania, New York, and New England, while the political power of the nation is swayed by those who have always been inexorably opposed to them. No man of reflection can for a moment believe that southern statesmen, who have from time immemorial striven to destroy all protection of northern labor, will now turn around, when they have the power in their hands, and, for the first time, lend their aid to sustain northern industry.

No, Mr. Speaker, it becomes us to act like men; to look our difficulties in the face, and to pursue the best mode of retrieving the advantages which have been thrown away. That can only be done by restoring the balance of power, by adding new States at the west and north-west. To admit new States on that border, we must have the territory out of which such States may be formed. But southern gentlemen, whose voices at the last session were heard, loud and long, in favor of Texas and the *whole of Oregon*, now see "a lion in the way." They were then chivalrous; now they are all for peace. Then they waxed valiant; now they "roar you gently as sucking doves." But a year ago their motto was, *now or never;* at this time, "*a masterly inactivity*" is their maxim. Last year, they spoke in strains of fervid eloquence of the glory of extending the American sway over new territory, and of adding new States to our brilliant constellation; now they call upon their northern friends to stop this mad career of extending the power of our government, and to leave the political control of the nation in their hands for a few years, until Great Britain shall quietly give up her claims to that territory.

The northern portion of the democratic party say, that they stand pledged to maintain our rights to the *whole* of Oregon by their Baltimore resolutions; and they demand of their southern allies to aid in carrying out their solemn pledge. Here, then, is the issue between the southern and northern portions of the democratic party. The North desire to act in good faith, and the South insist upon a violation of their pledge; and the whigs are called upon to decide which shall be done. I have no hesitation whatever in answering for myself. I shall vote to give the notice, and to terminate the joint occupancy of that territory. It is said, that the giving of notice will produce a war. But war, in my opinion, will not necessarily follow the notice; still, it is said that the subsequent taking possession of the whole of Oregon will be followed by a war. I am inclined to that opinion. On this point, I differ from my venerable friend from Massachusetts, (Mr. Adams.) I do so, however, with the greatest diffidence; for I have generally found myself in error when I have differed from him. Yet, being impressed with this opinion, I am bound to look to that as a possible, or rather as a probable result, from taking possession of the *whole* of Oregon.

Under these circumstances, I must choose between a war with England on the one hand, and a supine, inglorious submission to the slave-holding power on the other. I have seen enough of war to form an idea of the suffering it brings upon a nation. I have witnessed its devastating effects upon public morals, and the consequent misery which it inflicts upon those who are doomed to feel its curse. Yet, Sir, with all its horrors, revolting as they are to the feelings of humanity, I prefer meeting it for a few years rather than see the people of the free States sit down in quiet indifference under the control of the slave-holding power.

I am aware that some who have reflected but little upon the subject will disagree with me on this point; but when I reflect upon the manner in which this government has been used as the instrument to uphold the institution of slavery for the last half century; to sustain the slave-trade in this district and on the southern coast; the manner in which our army has been employed in murdering fugitive slaves; and when I reflect that the people of the free States are thus involved in crimes of the deepest guilt, and of the greatest magnitude; when I reflect that the whole people of the nation are involved in the sacrifice of more than thirty thousand human lives annually to the Moloch of slavery; when I look back but a few days to the vote of northern men in this hall to unite in political brotherhood with a State whose constitution provides for eternal slavery; and when I reflect that this heaven-provoking iniquity has scarcely called forth a note of disapprobation from the public press; — when these things rush upon the recollection, I am compelled to say that I prefer war to seeing the people of the free States submit, in supine apathy, to the government of those accustomed to torture their fellow men into subjection, and who deal in human flesh.

I have sons whom I tenderly love; and I declare that I would rather see them fall in battle, contending for freedom, than to see our people of the North ingloriously surrender up the blood-bought privileges, won by the valor of our fathers, to the keeping of men who deny the "self-evident truths" on which our hopes of freedom are founded; dooming those who shall bear my name, in coming time, to the degradation of living and dying the subjects of a slave-holding tyranny.

I am aware that a war with England must be attended with great destruction to the commercial wealth of the North. Their ships will be captured, their ports blockaded, and their commerce for the time being destroyed. I fully appreciate the feelings and motives of the gentleman from Massachusetts, (Mr. Winthrop,) who the other day made so able and so eloquent a speech in favor of peace. He represents the great commercial emporium of New England, and must of course feel deeply anxious on the subject. But it is well known that that gentleman was the first distinguished statesman of New England who publicly avowed his submission to the new slave-holding confederation with Texas. His State, like Ohio, Vermont, Rhode Island, and Connecticut, had declared, in substance, that neither this body nor the federal government could impose any obligation upon the people of her State, to enter into this new union with Texas. The proposition is so obviously correct, that I think few statesmen will deny it. No, Sir; if Ohio shall unite in the proposed confederacy, it will be from the choice of her people, and not in consequence of any obligation which the action of Congress has laid them under to unite with slave-holding Texas.

If our gallant State shall become a party to the new compact, it will not be done because we believe that the exercise of usurped powers by this government can transfer us from the Union formed by our fathers to a new confederation formed with a foreign people upon the principles of eternal slavery. The people of the free States are not yet the subjects of sale and transfer, like oxen in the shambles, or slaves in a southern market. I have at all times desired that the people of Ohio should not enter into the new union. Before Heaven, I think it would be far better for them not to do so; and if my colleagues agreed in opinion with me, no representative of Ohio would retain a seat in this hall beside those of Texas, until the voice of our people should be distinctly known.

But the gentleman from Massachusetts yielded his assent, in advance, of the people of his State. He must have been aware of the position in which they would be placed, by becoming a party to this new compact. He was aware that the dominant party had pledged themselves to maintain our claim to the *whole of Oregon*. If dangers of a war now arise, from carrying out that policy, it will be no more than he had reason to expect. Indeed, I cannot believe that he would now be willing to leave the nation subject to the policy of the slave States. It is very questionable whether the commercial interest of his State would suffer more by a war than the manufacturing interest would, by being subjected to southern rule. I have very serious doubts whether a state of war would prove more destructive to New England commerce, than southern control would prove to New England manufactures. So far as the mere pecuniary interests of the free States are concerned, I think it quite immaterial whether we have war or peace. If Massachusetts shall voluntarily unite in the new confederacy, knowing the policy that controls it, she ought cheerfully to submit to the consequences.

The leading merchants of Boston, distinguished for their statesmanship, are said to have been among the first citizens of Massachusetts who declared "that the time for opposing the political connection with Texas had gone by." Being the first to submit to this gross usurpation of power, they ought to be the last to complain of consequences which must have been clearly foreseen.

A distinguished citizen of Pennsylvania said to me yesterday, that the repeal of the tariff would be worse for the pecuniary interests of that commonwealth than a war with England. And I have no doubt that it would apply to the whole of New England with as much force as it would to Pennsylvania. I verily believe that the laborers of the free States would suffer less, in a pecuniary point of view, by a war with England, than they will by a quiet surrender of their interests to the control of the slave power of the South. I mention the laborers of the free States, including the agricultural interests of the West, as well as the manufacturing interests of New England and Pennsylvania. Indeed, a war with England would create a market for our provisions, and increase the price of our products generally. Let no one charge me with underrating the horrors of war. I am referring to the views and feelings of others; I am referring to their arguments, and not to my own sentiment.

I am aware, however, that I shall be charged with entertaining sectional views and sectional feelings. When, at the last session of Congress, I read the executive correspondence, speaking of southern institutions, southern interests, southern policy, and the extension of southern influence; and when I heard those sentiments reiterated in this hall, by almost every southern speaker, proclaimed by every southern political convention, and heralded forth in every southern newspaper, I began to think it was time for us to speak of northern interests, northern rights, and northern honor.

When I reflect that the Executive has been deeply engaged in efforts, for the last year and a half, to extend and perpetuate slavery, and that Congress has lent its efforts to the same purpose, I really think it time for the lovers of liberty to begin to speak in favor of freedom, of those self-evident truths on which our fathers based their political faith. The slave power has compelled us to think and speak of our rights, and of the rights of man; and if we tamely surrender them to the keeping of those who deny their existence, we may bid a final adieu, not only to our prosperity, but to our honor and to our political privileges.

If war should result from carrying out this measure, as it may, the people of the North possess within themselves the means of defence. There, Sir, all are freemen, and all have an interest in sustaining our institutions and our laws. We have the industry, the energy, the patriotism, which may well defy the world in arms. But, Sir, our greatest difficulty will not consist in defending ourselves, or in taking Canada. No, Sir; our principal burden will be the protection of the South; the weak, helpless, dependent, slave-holding South.

Should a war with England take place, Massachusetts and Ohio, and, indeed, each of the free States will be compelled to contribute double the amount of money and of blood to protect the miserable slave-holders of Texas that they will in defending themselves. The millions, nay, the tens of millions, which we shall be compelled to expend, and the thousands of lives which must be sacrificed in defending the heaven-provoking institution of slavery, and those who sustain it in Texas, will constitute a most striking illustration of the argument urged upon us at the last session of Congress, — "that it was necessary to annex Texas in order to *protect* our south-western frontier." The protection of Texas will require fifty thousand troops, and an expenditure of ten millions of dollars annually.*

But, Sir, we shall not only be compelled to protect Texas, but we shall be under the necessity of furnishing troops from the North to defend every slave State lying upon the Atlantic coast. Each of those States contains a large population, who are not only the most bitter and unrelenting foes to those who scourge and torture and oppress them; but they are equally hostile to the government that lends its aid and power to degrade and to hold them in bondage. In case of war, they will be more dangerous than four times their number of foreign enemies.

We are all aware that, in 1789, South Carolina sent a special delegation to the Continental Congress, informing that body that it required all her troops to protect the people against their slaves, and that that chivalrous State must depend upon her northern sisters to defend her against the common enemy. These scenes will again be acted, if we should engage in another war. In such case, all the slave States, collectively, would be unable to do more than protect themselves against their internal foes, and northern troops must be relied upon to defend the coast, from the Delaware Capes to the Rio del Norte, the Mexican frontier, and the whole western boundary. The expense would be enormous; but, in my opinion, not more destructive to the pecuniary interests of the free States than the free-trade policy of the present administration. I am fully aware that the southern portion of the Union must suffer most in case of

* The expenditure by the United States, at this time, (1853,) is more than two millions dollars annually, merely to protect the people of that State against the Indians on their border.

war. I have noticed the alarm manifested in southern papers, at the distant prospect of war with England. They now anticipate destruction to the cotton-growing interest. Slave labor, they say, will be depreciated, and slave property will become valueless. That is doubtless correct. But this policy of extending our territory is theirs, not mine. It originated with southern statesmen, and was forced upon the nation for the express purpose of perpetuating slavery. If God, in his providence, shall overrule their wicked designs to the subversion of that curse, I shall greatly rejoice.

Last year, our southern friends expressed great anxiety for "Texas and the *whole* of Oregon." They now see difficulties before them; dangers present themselves to the further pursuit of their plan of territorial aggrandizement. They have suddenly called to mind the declaration of British statesmen, that "a war with the United States will be a war of emancipation." They see in prospect the black regiments of the British West India Islands landing among them, and their slaves flocking to the enemy's standard. Servile insurrections torment their imaginations; rapine, blood, and murder dance before their affrighted visions. They are now seen in every part of the hall, calling on whigs and democrats to save them from the dreadful consequences of their own policy. Well, Sir, I reply to them, — this is *your* policy, not ours; *you* have forced us into it against our will and our utmost opposition; you have prepared the poisoned chalice, and we will press it to your lips until you swallow the very dregs.

I would not be understood as desiring a servile insurrection; but I say to southern gentlemen that there are hundreds of thousands of honest and patriotic men who "will laugh at your calamity, and will mock when your fear cometh." If blood and massacre should mark the struggle for liberty, of those who for ages have been oppressed and degraded, my prayer to the God of Heaven shall be, that *justice, stern, unyielding justice,* may be awarded to both master and slave. I desire that every human being may enjoy the rights with which the God of nature has endowed him. If those rights can be regained by the down-trodden sons of Africa in our southern States, by quiet and peaceful means, I hope they will pursue such peaceful measures. But, if they cannot regain their God-given rights by peaceful measures, I nevertheless hope they will regain them; and, if blood be shed, I should certainly hope that it might be the blood of those who stand between them and freedom, and not the blood of those who have long been robbed of their wives and children, and all they hold dear in life.

It is true, that when those scenes shall occur, northern freemen, our sons and neighbors, must march to Texas, and bare their breasts to the shafts of battle, in a soul-degrading defence of slavery. In such a cause, who would not be a coward? Our *fathers* fought for the inalienable rights of man; our *sons* must face the cannon's mouth in defence of slavery. Should the black regiments of the West Indies land upon our southern coast, our freemen of the North will be placed in a position, the contemplation of which is most revolting to the feelings of humanity. For the people of the free North to march to our southern States, and stand between the emancipated slaves of the West Indies and southern slave-holders, and defend them, while they flog their bondmen into submission, will be degradation without a parallel, except it be found in the quiet submission of our people to the political control of those who buy and sell their fellow men, and make merchandise of human flesh.

Should the scenes to which I have alluded take place, one great advantage would result. Perhaps no statesman doubts that a war with England must prove the death of slavery. The British government now have no slaves in their West India Islands, as in the last war, to restrain them from raising the flag of emancipation. The paralyzing effects which that institution exerts upon the physical energies of the nation would be exhibited to the world. Our people of the North would be constrained to look upon the evil as it really is.

The slave power would lose its charm; our citizens of the North would be aroused from the lethargy which, for half a century, has held their sensibilities in a torpid inactivity toward the oppressed of our land. We should then find means to sever the cords which have so long, unconstitutionally, bound us to the putrescent carcass of slavery. Great Britain would not be likely again to pay southern slave-holders *twelve hundred thousand dollars* for human cattle, who shall have strayed from their owners, as was done at the close of the last war.

But another consequence would, in all human probability, result from a war with England. We should obtain the Canadas, Nova Scotia, and New Brunswick, adding at least six new States to the northern portion of the Union, each possessing double the population of Texas. These States would restore to the North that balance of power which was surrendered up by the annexation of Texas. It would be in strict accordance with the policy avowed by the party in power, and which was in part carried into practice by the annexation of Texas.

I therefore say to the members of that party, *carry out your policy!* By adopting it, you have brought us under the power of the slave-holding States. Continue your policy, and you will relieve us from our present position, and restore to us the rights you have taken from us. I will vote to render you every facility for carrying forward your plans; it being understood at all times, that I regard the measure as ultimately fatal to the Union, but not as immediately so as it would be to leave the government where it now is. The responsibility must rest upon those who have avowed and adopted the system. To them belong the honors and the responsibilities of the policy. We claim no portion of one, nor will we share in the other.

But, Mr. Speaker, I am unwilling to resume my seat until I express my perfect conviction that this policy cannot be carried out by the party in power. The northern democrats will soon be deserted by their southern slave-holding allies. They have been betrayed by the slave power. Texas is admitted, and the southern wing of the democratic party will now desert their northern friends, and leave Oregon where it is.

If this resolution be adopted, the Executive will find means to escape from the dilemma into which this southern policy has precipitated him. It is most obvious to my judgment, that he cannot be driven into a war with England. As I have already stated, a war with that nation must prove the total overthrow of slavery. Every reflecting statesman must see this as clearly as any event can be foretold by human perception. I do not think the slave-holding portion of the democratic party were aware, that the carrying out of their Baltimore resolutions would sacrifice that institution. They rather believed that, by obtaining Texas, the price of human flesh would be enhanced, and slavery supported. The consequences of seizing upon "*the whole of Oregon*," were not considered. Mr. Polk, in his inaugural address, and in his annual message, evidently overlooked the momentous effect which his twice-declared policy would produce upon the slave interest, to which he is indissolubly wedded. He, and his cabinet, and his party, have made a fatal blunder. They will soon discover their error, and will recede from their position. With the same degree of confidence that I have in my own existence, I declare that they will, before the nation and the world, recede from their avowed policy, and will surrender up all that portion of Oregon north of the forty-ninth parallel of latitude, or let the subject remain as it now is.

I wish to place this prediction on record for future reference. Nor would I confine my remarks to the democratic party. Those southern slave-holding whigs who voted for Texas will now, if necessary, turn round and vote to give up a part of Oregon. It is a question between the slave States and the free States; and the vote when taken will, with few exceptions, exhibit that character. The great master-spirit of southern policy (Mr. Calhoun) has left his retirement, and taken his position in the other end of the capitol, for the avowed purpose of defeating the identical policy, the promotion of which occupied his whole attention only twelve months since. He is an adept in this political versatility. He will, however, carry the President and the southern statesmen generally with him; and will defeat the measure to which he and his party stand solemnly pledged.

Yes, Sir; should this resolution pass both Houses of Congress, the President will find means to give up a part of Oregon, or even the whole of it, rather than subject the institution of slavery to the sure destruction which a war with England would bring upon it. I again repeat, what I have endeavored to impress upon gentlemen, that this policy is not mine; I wash my hands of it. But by carrying it out, we shall place the northern and southern portions of the Union upon terms approximating to equality. And when, from its broad extent, this Republic, like the Roman Empire, shall fall asunder of its own weight, the free States will redeem and purify themselves from the foul disgrace of supporting an institution which has excited the contempt of infidel nations, and dishonored us in the eyes of the Christian world.

INDIAN TREATIES.*

THAT OF EIGHTEEN HUNDRED AND FORTY-FOUR EXAMINED — EFFORTS TO KEEP ITS CHARACTER FROM THE PUBLIC — NOT SEEN BY MEMBERS OF THE HOUSE — OUR POLICY IN COMPELLING THE INDIANS TO RETURN FUGITIVE SLAVES EXPOSED.

[The stipulations contained in our treaties with the Creek Indians, by which they undertook to return the fugitive slaves of Georgia, was the principal cause of the Florida war, as shown by the speech on that subject in 1841. After the attention of the public had been called to this subject, every possible effort of the Executive appears to have been put forth to keep secret every movement in relation to those fugitives. The fact that dangers of a frontier war existed in 1842, 1843, and 1844, was known; but the cause or the sources from which such dangers arose was not known to the people. All official information relating to it was kept silently in the Department. The treaty alluded to in the following speech, although entered into in 1844, was unknown to the members of the House, when called on to appropriate money to carry out its provisions. While this treaty lay concealed in the archives of the Senate, the author found means to get a copy of it, and in the following speech endeavored to expose its character. He was replied to by the chairman of the Committee of Ways and Means, who reported the bill; but that gentleman made no denial of any thing contained in the speech of Mr. Giddings, thereby confirming all that is expressed in the following remarks.]

Mr. Chairman, — When I came to the House this morning, I had not the most distant idea of addressing the committee; yet there are some points involved in this discussion, which I am unwilling to have passed over in silence. The bill before us provides for the payment of forty thousand dollars, under our treaty with the Creeks and Seminoles of 1845. That treaty has never been published, and gentlemen are not in-

* Speech on the Indian Appropriation Bill. Delivered in Committee of the whole House on the state of the Union, February 18, 1846.

formed of its contents. The treaty itself is not only kept from us, but the circumstances which led to it; the consideration which the United States have received for the sums which we are called on to appropriate, are hidden from our view. Under these circumstances, my friend from New York (Mr. Culver) offers his amendment, forbidding the payment of any portion of the money, in consideration of the capture of fugitive slaves, or as a compensation for fugitive slaves who have been recaptured.

Gentlemen have expressed doubts whether the payment of the money stipulated in the treaty was for slaves, or for the capture of slaves. If their suspicions be correct, the amendment will be harmless. It can do no injury, in any event. It is offered as a precautionary measure, and the mover says he has satisfactory reasons to believe the payments are intended as a compensation for slaves. No man denies his statements, or professes to dispute the facts he has set forth. But members appear willing to vote away the funds, not because they are informed on the subject, but because they are *not* informed; not because they know the appropriation to be proper, but because they are unable to say whether it be right or wrong. It appears to me that we have arrived at a new and extraordinary era in the legislation of our country. The Executive demands this money, and calls on us to grant it; but withholds from us, and from the country, all information concerning the objects, or consideration for which it is to be paid. I say it is *withheld;* for the Executive has possession of the treaty, and of the correspondence which shows the circumstances that led to it, as well as the consideration on which it is founded. Yet they are to the members here a "sealed book." Gentlemen are as ignorant of them as they are of the decrees of the Grand Sultan.

The chairman of the Committee of Ways and Means possesses a copy of the treaty; but I think I may safely say, that he never showed it to any member of this House, until since this debate commenced. I, too, have a copy, which has been examined by my friend who offered this amendment, and a colleague, (Mr. Delano,) now confined to his room by indisposition, but who, if his health had permitted, would have favored us with the views which he entertains of this mysterious transaction. With the exception of the honorable chairman of the Committee of Ways and Means, my friend from New York, (Mr. Culver,) and myself, no member now present ever saw or read this cabalistic treaty, to which I intend hereafter to call the attention of the committee. The manner in which I obtained a copy is of no importance. *I have it.* It bears date on the 4th of January, 1845, at the Creek agency, west of the Mississippi. On the 6th of February, 1845, I informed this body, that a slave-dealing compact, called a treaty, had been entered into between the United States and those Indians. In a speech which I made during the discussions of that day, I pointed out the circumstances, and related the historical incidents which had led to the negotiation of this treaty. I then declared, as I now emphatically assert, that this treaty was negotiated for the sole purpose of arranging difficulties, and satisfying claims arising from the capture of fugitive slaves, and for the purpose of paying for such slaves.

On the 5th of March, the treaty was approved by the Senate. From the time of its approval to this hour, it has been entombed in the Executive archives, and kept from the view of gentlemen who are now called to act officially under it. The Executive organ in this city, to which we look for the publication of such important treaties, has never hinted at its ratification or existence. The announcement which I made more than a year since, that such a treaty had been negotiated for the purpose of closing up an old slave-dealing transaction between our government and those Indians, attracted but little attention, and the country is now unconscious that such a treaty is in being; and until the reading of the bill before us, even the members of this House generally were equally uninformed respecting it. Sir, why this secrecy? Why has the treaty been withheld from us and from the people? Why are the circumstances which led to its negotiation kept from us? Why are we not permitted to know the consideration on which we are to pay so much money? Why are two hundred and nineteen members on this floor kept in profound ignorance on the subject of this treaty?

No blame can attach to gentlemen here for not having seen it. The responsibility rests with those who have had possession of it, and whose duty it was to publish it, but who have kept it concealed. This suppression of the treaty, and the facts connected with it, bespeaks its suspicious character in language not to be misunderstood. Although on two former occasions I have related most of the circumstances which led to the negotiation of the treaty, yet I presume they are recollected by few members now present, and it seems proper that I should repeat them. On the 7th August, 1790, the United States entered into a treaty with the Creek Indians, by which they agreed to deliver up to the officers of the United States such negroes as resided among them. These negroes had during, and subsequent to, the revolutionary war, fled from their masters in Georgia, and by this treaty the federal government attempted to recover and return them to their owners. The Indians failed to deliver up the negroes, and the treaty of Colerain was negotiated in 1796.

At the time of entering into this treaty, the Indians renewed their covenant to deliver up the slaves; and did, at the time of entering into it, deliver such of them as were resident in what were called the "upper towns." But many of the negroes had gone into Florida, and had settled and intermarried with the Seminoles. The Creeks could not, therefore, obtain them, and of course were unable to deliver them to the agents of our government. The planters of Georgia became clamorous for their slaves, and in 1821 the treaty of "Indian Spring" was negotiated, under the supervision of commissioners appointed by the executive of Georgia. By the terms of this treaty, the Indians agreed to pay for the slaves, and left in the hands of our government two hundred and fifty thousand dollars for that purpose; all which was subsequently paid over to the Georgia claimants.

The Creeks having thus paid to our government at least three times the value of these mothers and children and fathers, now claimed them as their property, believing they had obtained a good title to them. But the Seminoles being connected with them in all the relations of domestic life, refused to deliver them up as slaves. The Creeks removed west of the Mississippi; but the Seminoles dared not go, fearing that their people would be seized by the Creeks as slaves. They were at length compelled, by the power of our arms, to abandon their homes in Florida, and submit to be carried to the Indian country in the West. Soon as they crossed the western line of Arkansas, they stopped upon lands owned by the Cherokees, and refused to go to the country assigned to them, as it was under the jurisdiction of the Creeks, knowing they would become subject to Creek laws, if they entered it. The Cherokees were offended in consequence of the intrusion of the Seminoles. And if gentlemen will refer to the National Intelligencer of the 27th January, 1845, they will find that it required all the influence of the Executive to prevent hostilities between those Indians.

These difficulties continued during four or five years next previous to the making of this treaty. The cause of the difficulty was not published through the papers, but may be learned from the correspondence on file in the bureau of Indian Affairs. At times, the excitement was so great as seriously to threaten the peace of the frontier, as is set forth in the preamble to the treaty, which I shall soon read to the committee; and is more abundantly manifested by letters and reports in the War Department. These difficulties arose entirely in consequence of our attempts to return the fugitive slaves of Georgia. These are the circumstances which led to the treaty. The transaction, from beginning to end, in its generals and in its details, was a slave-dealing business, disgraceful to those who managed it, and disreputable to the government which authorized and approved it. These circumstances are briefly referred to in the following portion of the preamble to the treaty, to wit:

"Whereas many of the Seminoles have settled and are now living in the Creek country, while others, constituting a large portion of the tribe, have refused to make their homes in any part thereof, assigning as a reason that they are unwilling to submit to Creek laws and government, and that they are apprehensive of being deprived by the Creek authorities of their property:

"And whereas repeated complaints having been made to the United States government, that those of the Seminoles who refuse to go into the Creek country have, without authority or right, settled upon lands secured to other tribes, and that they have committed numerous and extensive depredations upon the property of those upon whose lands they have intruded."

I desire to call particular attention to that portion of the preamble which recites, that "a large portion of the tribe are apprehensive of being deprived by the Creeks of their property." The jesuitical language made use of is only worthy of the transaction. The term "*property*," instead of "slaves," is calculated to deceive the casual reader. But these people were never held or regarded as slaves by the Seminoles. They had fled to the Seminole country, and had voluntarily settled with them, intermarried with them, and become a part of the tribe, and were no more the *property* of the Indians, than the Indians were the property of the negroes; nor were they at any time claimed as slaves by the Seminoles. I deny that any instance can be shown where the Seminoles expressed any apprehension that the Creeks would take from them either *property or slaves,* other than those negroes who lived among them in perfect freedom, but who were *claimed by the Creeks as property.* It is true that, in some of the documents, they are referred to as "negro property," but generally they are called negroes.

I will now call the attention of gentlemen to that portion of the preamble which sets forth the considerations on which the treaty is based, and the objects for which it was entered into. It is in the following words:

"Now, therefore, in order to reconcile all difficulties respecting location and jurisdiction, to settle all disputed questions which have arisen, or may hereafter arise in regard to rights of property, and especially to preserve the peace of the frontier, seriously endangered by the restless and warlike spirit of the intruding Seminoles, the parties to this treaty have agreed to the following stipulations."

The first consideration moving the government of these United States to enter into this treaty is, to "reconcile all difficulties respecting location and jurisdiction."

In pursuance of this consideration the treaty provides, in the two first articles, as follows:

"ARTICLE I. The Creeks agree that the Seminoles shall be entitled to settle in a body, or separately, as they please, in any part of the Creek country; that they shall make their own town regulations, subject, however, to the general control of the Creek council in which they shall be represented; and, in short, that no distinction shall be made between the two tribes, in any respect, except in the management of their pecuniary affairs, in which neither shall interfere with the other.

"ARTICLE II. The Seminoles agree, that those of their tribe who have not done so before the ratification of this treaty, shall immediately thereafter remove to and permanently settle in the Creek country."

These two articles fully "reconcile all difficulties respecting location," by placing the Seminoles within the Creek territory, to which they agree to remove *immediately*, and to settle *permanently* therein. It reconciles all questions of jurisdiction, by giving the Seminoles power "to make their own town regulations subject to the Creek council." The committee will bear in mind, that the sole reason why the Seminoles did not go to the Creek country, in the first instance, was the dread of placing these people, some of whom were their wives and children, within the jurisdiction of the Creeks. These circumstances arose solely from the fact, that our government had extorted money from the Creeks to pay the slave-holders of Georgia for their negroes.

And now, to correct this slave-dealing error of the government, the bill before us grants twenty-six thousand dollars for the removal of the Seminoles from the Cherokee to the Creek country, and for supporting them six months after their removal.

But, it may be asked, why should our government interfere? Why not let the Indians arrange their own difficulties? I answer, the difficulty was brought about by the interference of our government in behalf of slavery; and, if hostilities had arisen from it, our nation would have been still more disgraced than it now is. To save this slave-mongering administration from further disgrace, our constituents are compelled to pay this item of twenty-six thousand dollars. The second consideration set forth in the preamble is, "To settle all disputed questions which have arisen, or may hereafter arise, in regard to the rights of property." This was the great and principal object of the treaty, and is provided for in the third article, which reads as follows:

"It is mutually agreed by the Creeks and Seminoles, that all contested cases between the two tribes, concerning the right of property, growing out of sales or transactions that may have occurred previous to the ratification of this treaty, shall be subject to the decision of the President of the United States."

If gentlemen will refer to the *National Intelligencer* of the latter part of January, 1845, they will find it stated, on the authority of an officer from the Indian country, that an arrangement of great importance had been made with the Creeks and Seminoles, by which all trials involving the right growing out of sales or transactions which had occurred prior to the arrangement, should be decided by the President. And the writer adds:

"This is an important clause, and covers a *delicate question.* The Seminoles objected heretofore to coming under the Creek government, lest they should be molested in their *negro property*, and were fearful of the administration of Creek laws. All unsettled questions *about the titles to negroes* in possession of Seminoles, previous to the ratification of this treaty, will be settled by the President."

All allusion to the original cause of this difficulty was avoided, but the material facts to which I have adverted are hinted at; and all cavil, as to the use of the word *property*, may be set at rest, by referring to the papers of that date. The President of this great and free Republic is to sit as arbitrator between these savages, and is to decide who shall have the body of this mother, and to whom that child shall belong; that the father shall be this man's slave, and the wife shall be delivered to that master. Sir, the subject is most revolting to the feelings of humanity. But I feel humbled, when I reflect that the people of our free States are to furnish the funds for this slave-dealing transaction; and that northern representatives are, by their votes, to involve our people in this degradation.

By reference to the sixth article of this treaty, it will be seen that we are to pay to the Seminoles ninety thousand four hundred dollars, in addition to the twenty-six thousand for their removal and subsistence. This is the compensation which they are to receive for delivering up such of their people as the President shall direct to be held as slaves by the Creeks. But it was evidently expected that about one half would remain with the Seminoles; and would, therefore, be lost to the Creeks, for the Creeks regard them as their property. For these, too, we are to pay the Creeks one hundred and twenty thousand dollars; making in all two hundred and ten thousand four hundred dollars which we are to pay for these slaves, according to the treaty, but which will be cut off, if we carry out the principles of the proposed amendment.*

And now the question is distinctly before us. Will we thrust our hands into the pockets of our constituents, and take this money, and pass it over to a slave-dealing President, to be expended in paying for the bodies of husbands and wives and children? Are the representatives from the free States prepared to enter into this business of huckstering in human flesh? Shall we involve our constituents in this deep and damning crime of trading in the image of our God? Our votes must answer these questions.

The third consideration mentioned in the preamble of the treaty is, "to preserve the peace of the frontier." But the people will ask, how came the peace of the frontier in danger? I answer, it became endangered by these slave-dealing transactions. These people were living with the Seminoles. Our government, in violation of the Constitution, in defiance of justice and of humanity, put forth its influence to force them back into slavery. Unable to do that, we compelled the Creeks to pay for them; and these barbarous Indians, believing that a title thus derived from a Christian nation must be valid, claimed them as slaves, and determined to have possession of them;

---

* Subsequently to the delivery of this speech, Congress refunded to the Creek Indians one hundred and forty-one thousand dollars which had been improperly paid to the slave-holders, out of the two hundred and fifty thousand retained under the treaty of Indian Spring. Thus were three hundred and fifty-one thousand dollars drawn from the laborers of this nation, to carry out this effort to return the fugitive slaves of Georgia, beside the Seminole war, which cost some forty millions more.

while the Seminoles and negroes were determined to resist the demand. Thus, in the words of the preamble, the peace of the frontier became "seriously endangered." The danger was a necessary consequence of the slave-catching efforts of our government, to which I have alluded. Thus every consideration set forth in the preamble of this treaty is connected with, and forms a part of, the history of these attempts of our government to uphold and sustain the slavery of the South.

Mr. Chairman, I have now done with the facts. If I have, in any respect, failed to state them fairly, as they exist, I will thank the chairman of the Committee of Ways and Means (Mr. McKay) to correct any error into which he may suppose me to have fallen, and for that purpose I will gladly yield to him the floor. [Mr. Giddings, after a short pause, resumed.] I referred to the able gentleman at the head of the financial committee, for the reason that he reported the bill before us, and is bound fully to understand the facts connected with this subject. He is, also, the only member who has had an opportunity of fully examining this treaty; but, as he remains silent under my appeal, I will feel under deep obligations to any other member who will point out any error whatever in the relation I have given. [Mr. Giddings again paused, and then remarked]: If gentlemen will examine the documents to which I have referred, and the correspondence in the Department of War, they will find many other interesting facts, to which I have not time to refer, but which show the untiring efforts of this nation to uphold this institution of slavery, so detested by all civilized and Christian people.

Before I proceed farther on this point, I desire to repeat what I have often asserted, that every attempt of this government to sustain the slavery of the South, either by the recapture of fugitive slaves or otherwise, is a direct violation of our Constitution, an encroachment upon the rights of the free States, an offence against the laws of God, and an outrage upon humanity. I have no time now to go into an extended examination of the subject.

An eminent statesman of our own times (Henry Clay) has declared that —

"The existence, the maintenance, and continuance of domestic slavery depends exclusively upon the power and authority of the States in which it exists."

This, Sir, is the doctrine of the Constitution. It is whig doctrine, and the only true whig doctrine.* Agreeably to it, I say, "the existence of slavery (in Georgia) should have depended entirely upon the power and authority of that State." If her people could not support it, let it cease. They had no right to call on the people of the free States, or upon Congress, to aid them in sustaining it; for, as Mr. Clay most distinctly and emphatically declares, "Congress has no power or authority over the institution of slavery."

To appropriate the moneys proposed in this bill to pay for these slaves, will be as clearly a violation of our federal compact as it would be for us to abolish slavery in Georgia, or establish it in Massachusetts. If this government possesses the power to deal in slaves, we may establish a slave-market in Boston, or in New York, and set up business, on government account, at any other point we please. If we possess the power to tax the people of the free States to the amount of two hundred thousand dollars, to be expended in payment of slaves, as contemplated by this treaty, we may tax them two hundred *millions* for the same purpose. The question before us is one of *principle*, and not of amount.

Had our government entered into a treaty with those Indians, and agreed to pay them two hundred thousand dollars for assisting the slaves of Georgia to escape from bondage, we should all of us have pronounced such a treaty unconstitutional; and I do not believe that a member of this body would have voted to appropriate a single dollar in pursuance of it. Yet the unconstitutionality of such a treaty would have been no

---

* This doctrine of Mr. Clay was, at that time, regarded as the doctrine of the whig party; and it was by professing to maintain those principles, that they retained in their ranks a large body of the anti-slavery men of the free States.

more obvious than is that of the treaty before us. It is a perfectly clear proposition, that, if the government have power to restore slaves, they have the same power to entice them away; and, if they have power to pay out the money of the people for one purpose, they have equal power to pay it out for the other.

When a fugitive slave enters our State, we regard him as a person, and not as property. Under our laws, he may sue, or be sued; he may be rewarded for his virtuous deeds, and be punished for his crimes. Indeed, he enjoys all the rights which others possess, except that he is liable to be seized by his master, and carried back into slavery. We feed, clothe, and lodge him, knowing him to be a slave. We teach him his rights, show him the road to Canada, and furnish him with the means to get there. We furnish him with the means of defending himself, in the same manner that we furnish others with weapons. In short, we treat him in all respects as we do other persons, except defending him against his master, or secreting him.

I repeat, that I am most happy in seeing able lawyers and statesmen from the South now before me. They must feel a deep interest on the subject, and if they deny any position which I have laid down, I call upon them to correct me. This is the place where these grave matters should be discussed. Let it be done before the House, and before the country. Let truth be sent forth to the people of the nation, and let them be correctly informed on a matter so vital to both sections of the Union. I certainly can have no object in the maintenance of error, and hope I may be set right, if any slave-holding member shall believe me to be wrong on these points. I make these remarks in order that they may go forth to assist our people in forming correct opinions of their rights on this subject, so important to humanity. The moral feelings of our people are correct. Were they not restrained by the Constitution, they would be as anxious to hang the man who catches a slave in our free States, as they would be to hang him who goes to Africa and commits the same crime. They believe the turpitude of seizing a slave in Ohio, and taking him back to interminable bondage, to be as great as it is to seize the same man in Africa and bring him into slavery.

Mr. McDowell, of Ohio, inquired of Mr. Giddings, if he, as a lawyer, had not counselled masters in regard to obtaining their fugitive slaves.

Mr. Giddings. Never; no, *never*. Why, Sir, you cannot induce a slave-catcher to come into that civilized and Christian portion of the State where I reside. You might as easily induce a Hottentot to enter a church.

Whilst these are the rights secured to us under the Constitution, we have annually, for the last twenty years, made appropriations from the public treasury, to pay for the capture of fugitive slaves; and representatives from the free States regularly vote for them without objection. Holding the clear and indisputable right of being exempt from the expense of slavery, the people of the free States, within the last ten years, have probably paid more than thirty millions of dollars for its support.

The proposition is plain and definite in its character, admitting of no doubtful construction. It prohibits the payment of any portion of the moneys appropriated by this bill for the recapture of fugitive slaves. Can northern men hesitate, or falter upon such a question? Will any one vote to involve the freemen of Ohio, or of any other free State, in the support, in the crimes, in the disgrace of slavery? The record of our votes will express to coming generations the sentiments which we cherish, and the principles which guide our action.

THE MEXICAN WAR.*

STANDING ARMY — MILITARY CONQUESTS DANGEROUS TO THE CONQUERORS — PRESIDENT'S STATEMENTS ERRONEOUS — REVOLUTION OF OUR GOVERNMENT — LOSS OF HUMAN LIFE FORETOLD — DEVOTION OF MEXICANS TO THEIR GOVERNMENT — WAR COMMENCED BY THE PRESIDENT.

[The Mexican war had been commenced by the President's ordering the army to the Rio Grande, with permission to General Taylor to cross that stream, and commence the conquest of Mexico, if he thought proper. Several battles were fought before any reference had been made to Congress on the subject, and General Taylor was in Mexico with his army long before the President made any communication to Congress respecting the situation of our army.

On the 11th May, 1846, he sent a message to each House of Congress, stating the commencement of hostilities. Resolutions declaring war "to exist by the act of Mexico" were forced through the House of Representatives under the previous question, thereby prohibiting all debate. The opponents of the war felt indignant at being thus constrained to vote on the momentous question of war without any expression of their views.

The next day, the House went into committee to consider the above bill, when Mr. Giddings availed himself of that opportunity to express his views in relation to the war.]

Mr. Chairman, — While holding a seat upon this floor, I have ever opposed all increase of the army and of the navy. During the short period of our national existence, we have in *time of peace* expended nearly four hundred millions of dollars upon the army and navy. This money has been drawn from the laboring portion of our people; for, disguise it as we may,

---

* Speech on the Bill to raise a Company of Sappers, Miners, and Pontoniers. Delivered in Committee of the whole House on the state of the Union, May 12, 1846.

every reflecting mind is aware that all our national burdens are indirectly borne by the productive class of our citizens. And, I ask, what benefit have they received in return for this vast expenditure ? Why, Sir, it has been wasted, thrown away ; nay, *worse* than thrown away. It has supported officers and soldiers in indolence, and very frequently in vice, rendering them incapable of discharging the obligations resting upon the citizens of a free government. The officers have been too much accustomed to command, and the soldiers too much habituated to obey. The former cannot well submit to the restraints of civil life, and the latter cannot be raised to the conscious dignity of free citizens. They have all become so accustomed to receive their support from the public treasury, that they are generally incapable of supporting themselves.

The founders of our government evidently believed that we, as citizens, would possess the inherent power at all times of defending our nation. They had seen the patriotic devotion of our militia exhibited at Bunker Hill, at Saratoga, and on other battle-fields of the revolution, and felt the most perfect confidence that they would at all times be able and willing to repel all invasions from any power whatever. In this opinion, I most heartily concur. Our patriot fathers never dreamed that we should become intoxicated with the love of military life, and invade other nations for the purpose of conquest. They knew the fatal tendency of that policy. All history, both ancient and modern, showed them, as well as us, that the extension of territory by military conquest had proven fatal to the conquerors ; and I now declare my unhesitating belief, that the war into which we are rushing with indecent haste, will, if continued as our settled policy, prove the grave of this republic.

In the message of the President, sent to us yesterday, we were told that "American blood had been shed on American soil." In the documents accompanying that message, we were officially informed that the American soldiers who had first fallen upon the Rio Grande, had been shot by order of a non-commissioned officer, without arrest, without trial, without conviction or sentence. American soldiers, entitled to the protection of our laws, whose lives were regarded as sacred as the lives of the members of this body, both by the laws of the land and by the rules and articles of war, by which the army itself should be governed, were murdered in cold blood by their brethren in arms. They are said to have attempted a desertion from the army; but whether such were the facts or not, we have no legal proof. They were not permitted to show that they were absent from the army by permission of the proper officer. Had they been legally enlisted? Were they of sufficient age in law to enter into a contract of enlistment? Or were they minors? Or had their enlistment been obtained by fraud? Were they induced to drink to intoxication, and then, while laboring under the delirium of drunkenness, were they prevailed upon to enlist into the service of the United States? Who will answer these questions? Their mothers, their wives, their orphan children, may perhaps be informed; but this House and the country are not. Sir, what compensation is our nation to receive for the lives of its citizens? Suppose we obtain the whole country between the Nueces and Del Norte, will it vindicate our violated laws? Will it restore to life our murdered brethren? Will it assuage the grief of those who now mourn their untimely deaths?

I refer to this murder of our citizens by our own army, as one of the horrors of a state of war, into which we are now precipitating the nation. Yet the man who ordered, and those who perpetrated these murders, are guilty of one of the highest crimes known to civilized man.

But, Mr. Chairman, I rose for the purpose of calling the attention of the House and of the country to another striking illustration of the danger of a standing army to the liberties of our people and the free institutions of our country. I allude, Sir, to the invasion of the Mexican territory, and the war into which we now find ourselves thus suddenly precipitated. Sir, I have not time to go into a minute examination of the pretended claims set up by Texas, and now advocated by our Executive, to the country between the Nueces and the Rio

Grande. Every intelligent man is aware that so much of Mexico as lies east of this river, was divided into the States of "New Mexico," Chihuahua, Coahuila, and Tamaulipas; that the Rio Grande, from its source to its mouth, was included within these departments; and that the department of Texas, as originally established, was as distinct and as separate from New Mexico, Chihuahua, and Tamaulipas, as the State of New York is separate from Pennsylvania, New Jersey, or Ohio. It was, however, connected with Coahuila for legislative purposes until 1834, when the line which separated it from the latter State was established. Granting, for the sake of the argument, that Texas actually includes all that part of Coahuila lying east of the Rio Grande, it would not give to her, nor to us, any claim whatever to that portion of Tamaulipas which has been invaded by our army. But, as I was saying, the line of separation between Texas and Coahuila was actually established by a commission duly appointed, and is as clearly laid down, and as definitely described, as the line which divides Maryland and Virginia. Commencing at the mouth of the Aransas, it follows up that stream to its source; thence, in a direct line, to the confluence of the Medina and San Antonio, near Bexar; and, following up the Medina to its source, it runs thence westerly, until it intersects the east line of the State of Chihuahua. This line, thus established, was assented to by both Texas and Coahuila. They were the parties in interest, and their mutual compact must remain binding upon each, until, by mutual consent, it shall be abrogated.

After the separation of Texas from Coahuila, each department enjoyed its privileges, appointed its officers, and was governed by its own laws. As already remarked, New Mexico, Chihuahua, Coahuila, and Tamaulipas, each extended far to the east of the Rio Grande, and each had settlements east of that river. Santa Fé, the capital of New Mexico, and the residence of her governor, is situated some thirty miles east of the Rio Grande.

Taos, another village, is still further east. At this place the custom-house is situated, at which our people, during the last year, paid more than a hundred thousand dollars in duties to the Mexican government on goods exported from Missouri. Many of our merchants are now there, protected by Mexican laws, and paying respect to Mexican authorities, while the President is sending us messages to make the people believe that those villages are within the United States, and that the people, their Governor, and all other Mexican officers, owe allegiance to our government.

At Point Isabel, on the Gulf, is also a village, with its Mexican authorities and its custom-house, at which our own people have for many years paid duties under Mexican laws. I know of no other custom-houses on this side of the Rio Grande; but there are villages east of that river, in each of the four departments mentioned. From the first settlement of these villages and towns, down to the day on which General Taylor reached Point Isabel with his army, they were in the enjoyment of all their rights, under Mexican laws and customs, as loyal subjects of that government. Leaving the Mexican settlements on the "Rio Grande," (which is also called the "Rio del Norte," and the "Rio Bravo,") and travelling east, we enter a barren country, a desert, at least one hundred miles in width, which is destitute of settlements. As we approach the Nueces, we find the Spanish settlements which extend along that stream on both sides of it. These settlements are some forty miles west of the Aransas, which was established as the western line of Texas.

The country, therefore, between the Aransas and the Nueces is clearly within the original boundary of Coahuila. But, being on the border of the two departments, it may perhaps be said to have been about as much under *Texian* as under *Mexican* laws. In truth, I suppose it can scarcely be said to have been under any law, during the war between Texas and Mexico. But, as I intend to assume no doubtful position, I will, for the sake of the argument, admit (contrary to the real fact) that Texas has extended her laws and jurisdiction to the Nueces, and, as it is said that some individuals on the west bank of that river have united with the Texans against the mass of people who adhere to Mexico, I will go as far as the distinguished senator from Missouri (Mr. Benton) did, in 1844, and admit their jurisdiction to extend as far west as any individuals can be found who adhere to Texas. And we will suppose the Texans actually to have conquered the country as far as the desert which divides the settlements on the Nueces from those on the Del Norte. West of this desert, no portion of the people have for a moment faltered in their loyalty to the Mexican Government. Texas has sent four several parties of armed men to conquer those settlements. One party only reached the Rio Grande; but every man of it was killed or made captive, and, I believe, some of them are now in the mines of Mexico; others have been released, and the rest are dead. One of the other parties was captured, and the other two were defeated, and fled back into Texas before they reached the vicinity of the Rio Grande.

These facts, so prominent on the page of history, are passed over by the President in his message, and, as a pretext for sending our army to invade and conquer the country upon the Rio Grande, he says:

"Texas, by its act of December 19, 1836, had declared the Rio del Norte to be the boundary of that Republic."

This mere declaration on paper by the Legislature of Texas could not change or alter the *facts*. *They* were entered upon the page of history, as well as upon the records of eternal truth; and no flagrant falsehood by that body, indorsed by a dignitary of this government, can change or alter them. Texas had agreed upon the Nueces as her boundary. But, admitting that she had violated her solemn compact, and had conquered the country as far as the Nueces, or even to the Great Desert, she had never extended her boundary by compact or by conquest beyond that point. And, I repeat, that neither the unfounded assertion by the Legislature of Texas, that her boundary is the Del Norte, nor the repetition of that untruth by any man, however dignified his office, can change or alter the *fact*, which must remain while the Author of Truth shall exist.

Were Mexico to declare, by a legislative act, that her eastern boundary is the "Hudson River," and, on paper, attach the whole of our States south and west of that stream to her congressional districts, and then, on paper, divide our seaboard into collection districts, without being able to enforce her laws in any way whatever, her President may, at the next meeting of her Congress, adopt this portion of President Polk's message, and urge, with equal propriety, that Pennsylvania and Ohio are Mexican territory. But, if Mexico possessed the power and disposition to enforce such views, we should regard the carrying them out to be an outrage unparalleled among civilized and Christian nations; and were a Mexican army to invade our country, in order to compel us to unite with their government, we should meet them sword in hand, and would only yield our country with our lives.

Yet, Sir, Mexico may claim the territory on which we now are, with as much propriety as we can claim the country on the Rio Grande. I have not time to make quotations from authors, but will rest my argument upon the facts given to the country by a distinguished statesman in the other end of this capitol, (Mr. Benton, of Missouri). He has probably examined the subject more thoroughly than any other member of either House of Congress. He is an ardent friend to the annexation of Texas, and a supporter of the President; nor do I believe any member will deny or even doubt a single fact stated by him. I have already quoted him in regard to the boundary of Texas. He estimates the country east of the Rio Grande, which now is in the actual possession of Mexico, and which has ever been in its possession since it became a nation, at one hundred miles in width and two thousand in length, making two hundred thousand square miles, embracing a portion of New Mexico, Chihuahua, Coahuila, and Tamaulipas, with a population of thirty thousand. He informs us that "one-half of New Mexico, with its capital, 'Santa Fé,' containing a population of four thousand, and Taos, with its custom-house, and a population of three thousand, and Albuquerque, with its six thousand inhabitants, and some scores of other towns and villages, all more or less populous, and surrounded by flocks and fields," are on this side of the Rio Grande, within the territory now said by the President to *belong to the United States.* Those people were born there under Mexican laws; they have lived under that government, and are as much attached to it as we are to ours.

Mr. Benton assures us that "no Texan force has ever been seen near it, without being killed or taken to the last man." They have defended their country as gallantly as our fathers defended ours. It is endeared to them by many interesting associations, and I predict they will not be easily subdued. Situated as Santa Fé is, nearly two thousand miles from the Gulf of Mexico, and nearly as far from any considerable settlement, either in Texas or the United States, which can furnish supplies to any invading army, I regard its conquest as no easy matter. I apprehend that much blood and much treasure will be expended, before the people of New Mexico will be compelled to unite with slave-holding Texas. Those Mexicans love freedom. They have abolished slavery, for which they entertain an unconquerable detestation. If I had time, I should like to inquire of gentlemen from New England and from our free States, what benefit our nation or the world are to receive from a conquest of that country, and the extension of slavery over it?

But I must beg the attention of the committee while I look a little farther into the reasons assigned by the President for ordering the army to the Rio Grande. He says, "The jurisdiction of Texas had been extended and exercised *beyond the Nueces.*" He, however, did not presume to assert that Texas had ever extended or exercised jurisdiction beyond the *desert*, which I have laid down as the farthest point to which her laws had ever been carried. Nor does he pretend that the jurisdiction of Texas was ever extended to the Mexican settlements on the Rio del Norte, or within a hundred miles of those settlements. He most evidently intended the reader should understand the expression "beyond the Nueces," as synonymous with "*to the Del Norte.*" This blood was shed more than a hundred miles west of the farthest point to which Texan laws had even been enforced. This attempted deception and fraud is unworthy of the President, or even of an honest man.

Suppose Texas had, in fact, extended her jurisdiction beyond the Nueces, even as far as the barren desert, does that give to her or to us a right to go a hundred miles further, to invade the Mexican territories, and compel the people of that region to submit to our laws, and to unite with Texas in violation of the allegiance they owe to their own government? Is such the logic of the Executive? Is such shallow sophistry worthy of an American President? But he goes on to say, "The country between that river (the Nueces) and the Rio del Norte had been represented in the Texan Congress, and in the Convention of Texas; had thus taken part in the annexation itself, and is now included in one of our congressional districts." The legislature of Texas had *on paper* attached to one of her congressional districts lying east of the Nueces, the whole Mexican territory on the Rio del Norte, including the capital of New Mexico, and portions of the three other departments heretofore named, together with thirty thousand native Mexicans, inhabiting some scores of towns and villages, spread over a country two thousand miles long, and one hundred broad.

The people living on this side of the Nueces were Texans, and they elected the representative, and he professed *on paper* to represent the Mexicans between the desert and the Rio del Norte. But he did so without any authority from them; for I think no man will dare assert that any one of the thirty thousand Mexicans on this side of the Rio del Norte ever gave a vote for a representative in the Texan Congress, or for any other Texan officer; but, on the contrary, they had killed or taken every Texan who dared to show himself in that region.

But the President says this Mexican country "is now included in one of our congressional districts." These thirty thousand people, who, so soon as the bill which passed this House yesterday shall receive the sanction of the Senate, and shall be approved by the President, will be in a state of war with this nation, are to be represented on this floor because Texas has *on paper* attached them to one of her congressional districts. If this act of the Texan legislature has any binding force whatever, it will render every Mexican who opposes our army, a *traitor against this government*, and will subject him to the punishment of death.

Yes, the men who burnt their dwellings at Point Isabel, and with their wives and little ones fled before our invading army, are to be represented in this body. The men who killed Colonel Cross and Lieutenant Porter and their comrades, are citizens of the United States, and to be represented in this hall! Should their representative, according to the democratic doctrine, carry out the views of his constituents, the President himself may, in an unguarded moment, find a "lasso" about his own neck, and the members of our body be assassinated agreeably to the hearty wishes of the people of that district. But, to cap the climax of this *paper* claim, the President refers to the fact that an act of Congress passed during the present session, includes the country to the Rio del Norte, within one of our revenue districts.

Gentlemen will remember that, one evening as we were about to adjourn, the bill referred to was called up and passed, without discussion or examination, and without being understood by the members. It was an expression on paper which, if we had been the actual occupants of the country, would have been binding upon the people, but which could have no effect whatever upon the people living upon the Del Norte under Mexican laws.

Sir, a law of Congress designating the English coast as a revenue district, would have as binding an effect upon the English people as the law in question has upon the Mexicans on the Rio Grande. There has long been a custom-house at Point Isabel; and, notwithstanding our act of Congress, we are told that our own people continued to pay duties to the Mexican government at that place, until the very day when General Taylor arrived there with his army, and the custom-house was burnt. The authorities at Santa Fé still continue to collect duties, and to pay them over to the Mexican government, as they have ever done since that government was established.

Should we send an army there and conquer that people, and

take possession of the country, we should acquire the actual right to establish custom-houses and collect revenues; but the argument that Texas, by her legislative acts *on paper*, could extend her conquests beyond the power of her armies, or that such acts of the Texan Congress, or of this Congress, could impose any obligation whatever upon the people of Mexico, or could give Texas or the United States any right of jurisdiction over them or their country, would be unworthy of serious refutation, had it not come from a high official source. Its sophistry is too transparent, and its absurdity too evident to obtain respect among an intelligent community.

I regard it as having been put forth to divert public attention from the outrage committed by the President upon our own Constitution, and the exercise of usurped powers, of which he has been guilty in ordering our army to invade a country with which we are at peace, and of provoking and bringing on this war. I am led to this inevitable conclusion from the fact that he dare not rest his justification upon *truth*. A mere glance at the message, notwithstanding the tissue of sophistry and misrepresentation thrown over the facts to which I have alluded, will show that he felt compelled to base the justification of his conduct on misrepresentation. He therefore reminds us of the grievous wrongs perpetrated (as he says) by Mexico upon our people in former years, and alludes to the delay of that government in the payment of debts due our people, and mourns over the loss of our commerce with Mexico; all for the purpose of justifying himself in sending the army to the Rio Grande, and commencing the work of human butchery!

If the country be *ours*, why does he seek to justify the taking possession of it by reference to the fact that Mexico is indebted to some of our people? If it be not ours, and he has taken possession of it in order to compel Mexico to pay those debts, why not say so? The fact that Mexico has not paid the debts due to our citizens, can have no legitimate connection with taking possession of our own soil. But the writer of the message was obviously conscious that this invasion of the Mexican territory could not be justified; and he endeavored to extenuate the act by assuring us that "the movement of the troops to the Del Norte was made under positive instructions to abstain from all aggressive acts towards Mexico or Mexican citizens, unless she should declare war."

What aggressive acts towards a foreign power could our army commit while on our own territory? While the army was within the United States they could not commit violence upon Mexico. The order was also to abstain from all aggressive acts towards "Mexican citizens." It seems that the President expected General Taylor to find Mexican citizens located within the United States. And this sentence evidently alludes to the order of the Secretary of War, bearing date July 20, 1846, in which General Taylor was directed to take possession of the whole country "except that which was in the actual occupation of Mexican troops or Mexican settlements." Here is a distinct admission that this country, claimed by the President as a portion of the United States, was in the actual possession of Mexican troops and Mexican settlements. The idea that our army could *peaceably* surround those military posts occupied by Mexican troops, could be entertained by no reflecting mind. The President must have known, and we all know, that those military posts were established for the sole purpose of protecting the country, and the sending of our army there must have been done with the moral certainty that war would ensue. The truth is most obvious to the casual reader. The President obviously intended to involve us in war with Mexico. No sophistry can disguise that fact. That truth will stand on the page of history in all coming time, to the disgrace of this nation, and of the age in which we live.

In order to show still further the inconsistency of the Executive, and expose the wickedness of this invasion of a country so long in the occupancy of Mexico, I will call the attention of the committee to the fact, that as early as the 15th of June, General Taylor was directed to take a proper military position near the Rio Grande, for the avowed purpose of defending Texas. In answer to this order, on the 4th of October, General Taylor informed the department that he had encamped his army at Corpus Christi, and that—

> "Point Isabel would have fulfilled the conditions of this order better than any other position;" "but," he adds, "we had no artillery, no engineer force or appliances, and but a moderate amount of infantry; and the occupation of Point Isabel under these circumstances, with at least the possibility of resistance from the Mexicans, might have compromised the safety of my command."

It should be borne in mind that at this time General Taylor had about four thousand regular troops under his command; yet he regarded it unsafe to attack Point Isabel with that force while destitute of artillery. Unsafe to take possession of our "*own soil*"—of this *congressional district of Texas*"—without artillery? What contradiction in language! What inconsistency in this Executive message! In January, General Taylor was ordered peremptorily to advance with his army, and to take a position near the Rio Grande; and the Secretary of War, speaking by order of the President, says:

> "From the views heretofore represented to this department, it is presumed Point Isabel will be considered by you an eligible position."

Thus, in July the President directed General Taylor to respect the military posts in the actual possession of Mexican troops. In October, General Taylor informs him that it would be unsafe to attack Point Isabel without artillery; and in January, the President orders him to take possession of it, knowing it to be a military post in the actual possession of the Mexican troops.

Truth is at all times consistent with itself; but falsehood and fraud is opposed to fact; opposed to the whole system of God's moral government; opposed to *itself.*

In order to arrive at the object in raising so large an army, we need only look to the documents furnished by the President. Apparently fearful that the orders communicated to General Taylor, directing him to respect such military posts as were in the possession of Mexican troops and the Mexican settlements, might not produce hostile collision between our army and the Mexicans, General Taylor was directed to regard the crossing of Mexican forces to this side of the Rio Grande, even to strengthen or reinforce those posts, "as the commencement of hostilities." The President seems to have believed it right for our army to take possession of the whole country around those posts, but for Mexico to increase the number of her troops in those places, was to be regarded as war. He was also frequently reminded of his powers to call for such number of troops as he should deem necessary; and was authorized, in case of *war*, declared, or *made manifest by hostile acts*, to cross the Rio Grande at discretion, for the purpose of capturing or dispersing any Mexican army that might collect there, and "to take and hold Matamoras and other places in the country."

Now, Mr. Chairman, the ulterior designs of the Executive are unfolded to us in this letter of instructions. The conquest of Mexico and California is the prize for which this game has been played. This object is more clearly manifested in the letter of instructions, bearing date on the 2d March, 1846, where General Taylor is told, —

"If, in the course of events, you should have occasion to enter Mexico, it would be proper to quiet all apprehensions, so far as it can be done, by a public proclamation that the rights of property, persons, and religion, will be respected. Particular care should be taken not to alarm the religious feelings of the Mexicans."

It would be useless to multiply proofs on these points. The orders for General Taylor to march his army to the Del Norte; to take a position opposite Matamoras; to capture Point Isabel; to regard the crossing of Mexican troops to this side of the Rio Grande as the commencement of hostilities; his authority, not to say orders, to cross his army to the south side of the Rio Grande, to take and hold Matamoras and other places in the country; his directions to quiet the apprehensions of the people, and to conciliate them in order to render the conquest less difficult — all these directions develop the Executive designs so fully, that it would be a waste of time for me longer to occupy the attention of the committee to prove that conquest was the design of sending our army to the Rio Grande.

It is equally evident, that the Mexicans viewed the advance of our army toward the Rio Grande as an invasion of their territory. The civil and military authorities of Mexico, in all their intercourse with General Taylor, characterized it "an invasion." The burning of the custom-house and other buildings at Point Isabel, and the flight of the Mexicans before our advancing army; the cautious and warlike manner in which our army proceeded to that part of the country, and the constant military reconnoissances of the Mexicans, showed the light in which they viewed the transaction.

This, then, is the character of the war now waged against a weak and distracted sister republic. It is a war of aggression and conquest. Its prosecution will be but an increase of our national guilt. The death of every victim who falls during its progress, will add to the already fearful responsibility of those who, from ambitious motives, have brought this curse upon our nation. Gentlemen who voted for the annexation of Texas should call to mind that they were solemnly warned of the amount of blood that would flow, the lives that would be sacrificed, by that outrage upon our Constitution, upon the rights of Mexico, and the rights of humanity. They were constantly told by those who opposed that measure, that war would result from it; that Mexico would not submit to a dismemberment of that portion of her territory which lies east of the Rio Grande.

Sir, we then washed our hands of the guilt of annexation, and of its consequences. But we were then told of the vast pecuniary *advantages* it would bring to the northern States. When we spoke of the blood which would flow in this war, we were referred to the letter of Secretary Walker to prove that it was necessary for us to have Texas in order to *protect our south-western frontier*. Let those who then laughed at our predictions with such supercilious confidence, now stand forth and receive the proper odium due to their folly.

But, Sir, I regard this war as but one scene in the drama now being enacted by this administration. Our government is undergoing a revolution no less marked than was that of

France in 1792. As yet, it has not been characterized by that amount of bloodshed and cruelty which distinguished the change of government in France. When the Executive and Congress openly and avowedly took upon themselves the responsibility of extending and perpetuating slavery by the annexation of Texas, and by the total overthrow and subversion of the Constitution, and that, too, by the aid of northern votes, my confidence in the stability of our institutions was shaken, destroyed. I had hoped that the free States might be aroused in time to save our Union from final overthrow; but that hope has been torn from me.

It is true the several States may yet refuse to become parties to the new confederacy with Texas, formed for the suppression of the liberties of mankind and the support of slavery; but I have very little expectation that any of them will refuse their assent to the outrage. Sir, those who come after us will look back upon the annexation of Texas, and will pronounce it the grâve of our Constitution. It has now become an idle mockery for us to speak of constitutional rights. The great charter of our political liberties has been tamely surrendered by our free States to purchase perpetual slavery for the South. Our Union continues, but our Constitution is gone. The rights of the several States and of the people, now depend upon the arbitrary will of an irresponsible majority, who are themselves controlled by a weak but ambitious Executive.

Am I asked for the evidence of this assertion? I point you to the invasion of Mexico, by order of the Executive, while Congress was in session; to the blockade of Matamoras; to those acts which have involved us in all the evils of actual war, without even deigning to consult Congress on the subject. When all this was effected, the majority of this House placed at his disposal the whole military and naval force of the nation, with ten millions of treasure, for the conquest of Mexico, and then indorsed his flagrant misrepresentation by declaring, "*war exists by the acts of Mexico.*" Thus has Congress surrendered its honor, its independence, and become the mere instrument of the Executive, and made to indorse this presidential *falsehood.* This invasion of a sister republic, this usurpation of imperial powers, this most despotic act of making war, has been sanctioned by this body; and in a manner, too, which fully illustrates the disregard of constitutional restraints entertained by this House.

Sir, on this great and momentous subject of peace and war, involving the lives of thousands of our fellow citizens and the welfare of two mighty nations, we were not permitted to speak, to deliberate, or to compare our views. No member was allowed to express his dissent, or state his objections to an act which is to tell upon the future destiny of civilized man. With indecent haste, with unbecoming levity, under the gag of the previous question, our nation is plunged into a bloody war for the purposes of conquest and the extension slavery.*

This war, I apprehend, will prove no child's play. I entertain but little apprehension from pitched battles. Indeed, I doubt whether such a battle will ever be fought. It will be a kind of guerilla warfare. Our army will seldom see their enemies, who will hang around our camps, and destroy our men in detail, as opportunity shall offer. But the pestilence of the climate is to be our most deadly foe. Send your fifty thousand volunteers to the Rio Grande, and the deadly miasma will assail them, will waste their energies. The yellow fever and its concomitant diseases will do their work of death. Your troops will fall before an unseen power, and their bones will whiten upon those distant prairies, and the heart of many a wife, and many an orphan, will bleed ere Mexico will submit to our arms.

Sir, no man regards this war as *just.* *We know,* the country knows, and the civilized world are conscious, that it has resulted from a desire to extend and sustain an institution on which the curse of the Almighty most visibly rests. Mexico has long since abolished slavery. She has purified herself from its crimes and its guilt. Like the semi-barbarians of

* The declaration of war had been forced through the House of Representatives under the previous question on the day before this speech was delivered.

Egypt and Tunis, they have separated themselves from its foul contagion. That institution is now circumscribed on the south-west by Mexico, where the slaves of Texas find an asylum. A gentleman from Matamoras lately assured me that there were in and about that city at least five hundred fugitives from Texan bondage. Experience has shown that they cannot be held in servitude in the vicinity of a free government. It has therefore become necessary to extend our dominions into Mexico in order to render slavery secure in Texas. Without this, the great objects of annexation will not be attained. We sought to extend and perpetuate slavery in a peaceful manner by the annexation of Texas. Now we are about to effect that object by war and conquest. Can we invoke the blessing of Deity to rest on such motives? Has the Almighty any attribute that will permit Him to take sides with us in this contest?

There are also pecuniary considerations addressing themselves to the people of this nation. It is said that the annexation of Texas has already cost us ten millions of dollars, although we have no official data by which to ascertain the precise amount. The ten millions appropriated by the bill of yesterday, will do little more than to man, equip, and set our navy afloat, and bring our army into the field. An additional ten millions will probably be required by the first of January next. How long the war will continue, is beyond our knowledge. But should it continue five years, hundreds of millions will be swallowed up.* These untold sums will be drawn from the people. And what are they to receive in return? Why, Sir, the parasites of the Executive will make splendid fortunes. Thousands of offices will be created, and filled by as many fawning sycophants, who will fatten upon the lifeblood of the nation. The virtue of our better days will yield and gradually disappear, before the flood of vice and immorality now ready to rush in upon us.

* The whole expense of the war has, since its close, been variously estimated from one to two hundred millions dollars.

I know it is said that a large army and heavy appropriations will make a short war. God grant that the prediction may prove true. I apprehend that Mexico has maturely considered the subject, and enters upon the war with a solemn conviction that her existence as a nation depends upon her resistance to our aggressions. The correspondence before us proves the fact. The devotion of her people at Point Isabel conclusively shows it. Why, Sir, look at General Taylor's report, and you will see a devotion manifested by the officers and peasantry of Mexico, that speaks in thunder tones to those who regard the conquest of that people as a trifling matter. See the females and children, at the approach of our troops, leave their homes, consecrated by all the ties of domestic life, and while they are fleeing to the Mexican army for protection, see their husbands and fathers apply the torch to their own dwellings, and then fly to arms in defence of their institutions. I confess I was struck with deep solemnity when that communication was read at your table; and, in imitation of William Pitt, I was ready to swear that, if I were a Mexican, as I am an American, I would never sheathe my sword while an enemy remained upon my native soil.

What force will be necessary to conquer such a people? Let all history give the answer. How long did it require Bonaparte, with his half million of disciplined troops, to conquer the rude and half civilized people of Russia? How long did it require our army to subdue a few hundred miserable Seminoles in our immediate vicinity?

With these considerations resting upon my mind, I was on yesterday called to vote for a declaration of war against Mexico; or, rather, as introductory to such declaration of war, I was asked to declare to the world that "Mexico had made war upon us." That assertion I knew would be untrue, as I have already shown. I felt most deeply the impotence of this body, in thus attempting to change or alter great and important facts already entered upon the records of eternal truth, where they will remain while a God of truth shall exist. Sir, when we were about to assume upon ourselves the awful responsibility of involving our country in a serious and bloody war, with all its consequences; when about to appeal to a God of justice and of truth for his aid in maintaining our national rights, I dared not do so with an impious falsehood upon my lips.

Had this been the only objection to the bill, I should have regarded it as fatal. But, Sir, I saw no necessity for a declaration of war. Let our army be now withdrawn within our own territory, and not a member of this House would entertain either fears or expectations of further hostilities. No intelligent man would hazard his reputation by arguing that Mexico would invade us. General Taylor informs us that no danger whatever was to be apprehended while our army remained at Corpus Christi. I would have voted for any amount of men and money that might have been regarded as necessary, to withdraw our army from the Mexican territory.

I know the insidious efforts put forth, representing those who opposed this declaration of war as opposing supplies and aid to our army, who are now surrounded by Mexicans. I think gentlemen who make these efforts, have underrated the intelligence of the people. Neither General Taylor nor the army have incurred any responsibility by obeying the orders of the President. They were not permitted to judge of the propriety of those orders. They should, therefore, be relieved and brought back to our soil. But for me to vote for a continuance of hostilities, by declaring war, would be to carry into effect the very objects for which our army was ordered into Mexican territory. I will give no vote to continue that invasion, or to declare an unjust war, because the President has provoked hostilities. I would gladly vote to withdraw our troops from Mexican soil, and to disavow the invasion which has been made without authority. As I have already said, I would appropriate any amount of money, or any military force necessary to bring back our troops in safety. Then, Sir, having placed ourselves in the right, we should find but one heart and one mind among us, and that would be in favor of defending our rights and our country.

But I hear it said that "we must go for our country, right

or wrong." If this maxim be understood to require us to go with our country, or with the majority of our country, to commit a wrong upon other nations or people, either in time of peace or in time of war, I deny its morality; but, if it be understood as imposing upon us, at all times and under all circumstances, the obligation of using all our influence and efforts to set our country in the right when we find her wrong, or to keep her right when we find her in the path of duty, then, Sir, I yield my assent to its correctness. We are not to abandon our country because our government is badly administered; but, in such case, we should use our efforts to correct the evil, and place the government in just and able hands.

Again, it is said, "we must stand by our country." The man who would do otherwise, would be unworthy of any country. He only is a true friend of his country who maintains her virtue and her justice; and he is not a true friend to his country, who will knowingly support her in doing wrong. To-morrow, this nation will probably be in a state of war with Mexico. It will be an aggressive, unholy, and unjust war. It will then be my duty to use my efforts to restore peace at the earliest practicable moment that it can be done on just and honorable principles. But, while the war continues, efforts will probably be made to conquer Mexico, and we shall be called on to appropriate money and raise troops to go there and slay her people, and rob her of territory. But the crime of murdering her inhabitants, and of taking possession of her territory, will be as great to-morrow, after war shall have been declared, as it would have been yesterday.

Justice is as unchangeable as its Author. The line of moral rectitude will never bend to our selfish passions. In the murder of Mexicans upon their own soil, or in robbing them of their country, I can take no part, either now or hereafter. The guilt of these crimes must rest on others; I will not participate in them; but if Mexicans or any other people should dare invade our country, I would meet them with the sword in one hand, and a torch in the other; and, if compelled to retreat, like the Mexicans at Point Isabel, I would lay our dwellings in ashes, rather than see them occupied by a conquering army.

We may always justify ourselves for defending our country, but never for waging a war upon an unoffending people for the purpose of conquest. There is an immutable, an eternal principle of justice pervading the moral universe. No nation, or people, or individual, ever did or ever will violate that law with impunity. Bonaparte suffered its penalty. After the conquest of kingdoms, and subjecting a large portion of Europe by his victorious arms, he was driven an exile from his people and country, and died upon a desolate and barren island. His people having sacrificed untold millions of money and hundreds of thousands of lives to annex other governments to France, as we are now endeavoring to annex Texas and a part of Mexico, suddenly found themselves under the power of the allied army, their *annexed* governments again independent, and themselves doomed to pay the whole expense of a long and bloody war. They had violated this law of right, and they suffered its penalty; nor can it be otherwise, while a God of justice controls the destinies of nations.

But we have a more recent example within our own experience. Some two or three years since, while our nation was in the enjoyment of peace and prosperity, our Executive, in order to render the institution of slavery more permanent, thereby insuring the oppression and degradation of a greater number of the human family, commenced negotiations for the annexation of Texas. The object was most iniquitous, but, by the aid of Congress, it has been effected, and the law of eternal justice violated; and now the penalty is inevitable. Sir, how much money and how many lives have already been sacrificed in this attempt to fasten the chains of servitude upon our fellow men?

And now, suppose we send an army into Mexico, and kill hundreds and thousands of her people, burn her cities, and lay waste her country; do you think we shall escape the dread penalty of retributive justice? I tell you, we shall not. As sure as our destiny is swayed by a righteous God, our troops will fall by the sword and by pestilence; our widows will mourn; and our orphans, rendered such by this unholy war, will be thrown upon our public charity. Vice will increase, and patriotism will be depreciated.*

But it is said that the *people* are in favor of war. I deny the assertion. When the annexation of Texas was agitated, during the campaign of 1844, it was urged that it would involve us in a war, precisely as it has done. I know that, to the extent of my observation, such a war, for the support of slavery, was regarded with horror by all parties; and, to avoid the effect which this argument was designed to have upon the public mind, the friends of annexation, in this House and before the people, denied that war would result from it. The war *has* resulted; and I am unable to discover why it should be more popular *now*, than it was then. Had the friends of Mr. Polk then admitted that war would ensue from the annexation of Texas, he would not probably have received an electoral vote north of Mason and Dixon's line. Has the deception practised upon the people, and the falsehoods by which they have been cajoled into this war, rendered it popular?

But again; it is said that war is always popular. I deny this assertion, also. I believe that nine tenths of our people regarded the Florida war with contempt. Their disgust arose from the fact, that it was unjust and cruel, and arose from an effort to sustain slavery. This war is equally unjust, and arises from the same cause, and must be viewed in the same light by the people. It is impossible, in the nature of things, for it to be otherwise. Our people feel no hostility to those of Mexico. The Mexicans have remained at home, "under their own vines and fig-trees;" they have not molested us or encroached upon our rights. It is true that their population is less intelligent than that of our free States; and it is equally true, that they are more rapidly improving their condition than are those of

* Our ablest writers estimate the number of victims who fell in this war, by pestilence and the sword, at eighty thousand. Of these, thirty thousand were said to be Americans, and fifty thousand Mexicans.

our slave States. They are surely in advance of them in the diffusion of universal liberty among their people. The means of intelligence and enjoyment are open to all.

Indeed, taking the whole population of our slave States and of Mexico into consideration, I think we shall find the Mexicans the best informed, most intelligent, and most virtuous. Our people of the North have sympathized with them in their efforts to render their free government permanent and respectable. Can the lovers of liberty now desire to see a sister Republic wantonly subverted, while just coming into existence, and struggling for the permanent establishment of civil freedom? It cannot be. You may declare war; display your banners, your glittering arms, your blazing uniforms; you may raise the battle-cry, and sound your trumpets; but you cannot induce the intelligent men of the North to march to Mexico for the purpose of bathing their hands in Mexican blood for the extension of slavery. You may for the moment excite the young, the giddy, and thoughtless; but their "sober, second thoughts," will lead them to inquire for the *cause* of the war in which they are asked to engage. The true answer to that inquiry must overwhelm its authors with disgrace.

There is, however, one cheering circumstance in the distant future. All history informs us that for ages, no nation or people, once having adopted the system of universal freedom, was ever afterwards brought to the maintenance of slavery. There are now probably eight or nine millions of people in Mexico, who hate slavery as sincerely as do those of our free States. You may murder or drive from their country that whole population, but you can never force slavery upon them. Now I say to those gentlemen, who are so zealous for this conquest, that our slave States will be the last to consent to the annexation of *free* States to this Union. I know that Southern men are now, and have been, zealous in bringing on this war and for extending our territory; but they will, at no distant day, view the subject in its true light, and will change their position, and will oppose the extension of our territory in any direction, unless slavery be also extended.* They desired to annex Texas, and to extend her bounds as far as possible, because she is a slave-holding country; but the increase of free States, either at the North or at the South, will be strenuously opposed by the advocates of slavery.

This war is waged against an unoffending people, without just or adequate cause, for the purposes of conquest; with the design to extend slavery; in violation of the Constitution, against the dictates of justice, of humanity, the sentiments of the age in which we live, and the precepts of the religion we profess. I will lend it no aid, no support whatever. I will not bathe my hands in the blood of the people of Mexico, nor will I participate in the guilt of those murders which have been, and which will hereafter be committed by our army there. For these reasons I shall vote against the bill under consideration, and all others calculated to support this war.

---

* Mr. Calhoun refused to vote for the declaration of war, which passed the Senate the very day on which this speech was delivered.

THE WILMOT PROVISO.*

ITS ADOPTION ADVOCATED — THREATS OF SOUTHERN MEMBERS — NORTHERN MEN MUST TAKE POSITION — OBJECTS OF CIVIL GOVERNMENT — OUR PAST POLICY.

[The advocates of the Mexican war were anxious to bring it to a close. For that purpose they desired to place a large fund at the disposal of the Executive, to be used as he should think proper. To this, the friends of liberty were willing to accede, provided slavery should be excluded from any territory which might be obtained from Mexico. A proposition was made to amend the bill in that way. On this motion, Mr. Giddings delivered the following speech.]

MR. SPEAKER, — The proposition now before us is one of that plain and distinct character, which enables every member to comprehend it at the first view. We are engaged in a war with Mexico. It is most obviously a war of conquest, intended by the Executive to obtain further territory, over which to extend the curse of slavery; and the proposition before us is to make such territory *free*, by attaching to it what is called the "Wilmot Proviso."

Every person who has heard, or read the debates of this body, during its present session, must be convinced that questions of no ordinary magnitude are pending before us. The fierce conflict of opinion, the criminations and recriminations, the stern defiance, the solemn appeals, the impassioned eloquence, show conclusively that we are approaching a crisis of deep and pervading interest. Indeed, we must soon decide,

* Speech upon the motion to attach the Wilmot Proviso to the Bill granting three millions of dollars, to be used by the Executive for terminating the Mexican war. Delivered in Committee of the whole House, on the state of the Union, February 13, 1847.

so far as this present House of Representatives can determine, whether or not the blood and treasure of this nation shall be poured out on Mexican soil, for the purpose of establishing slavery upon territory hitherto consecrated to freedom. The advocates of oppression from the North, and from the South, will arrange themselves in the affirmative, and the friends of freedom will be found in the negative. A few yet remain apparently undecided. The seductions of Executive favor are held out to entice them to enlist under the black flag of slavery; while the still, small voice of reason and of conscience is beckoning them to the ranks of freedom.

Gentlemen from the South, with deep emotions, have solemnly warned us, that if we persist in our determination, the "*Union will be dissolved.*" I do not doubt their sincerity. But I would rather see this Union rent into a thousand fragments than have my country disgraced, and its moral purity sacrificed, by the prosecution of a war for the extension of human bondage. Nor would I avoid this issue, were it in my power. For many years have I seen the rights of the North, and the vital principles of our Constitution, surrendered to the haughty vaporings of southern members. For many years have I exerted my humble influence to stimulate northern members to the maintenance of our honor and of the Constitution. And now I devoutly thank that God, who has permitted me to witness the union of a portion of northern members of both political parties, upon a question so vital to our interests and honor, as well as to humanity.

I also rejoice that this is a question which admits of no compromise. Slavery and freedom are antagonisms. They must necessarily be at war with each other. There can be no compromise between right and wrong, or between virtue and crime. The conflicting interests of slave and free labor have agitated this government from its foundation, and will continue to agitate it, until truth and justice shall triumph over error and oppression. Should the proposition now before us fail, it will surely succeed at the next session of Congress; for it is very evident that public sentiment in the free States is daily becoming more and more in favor of it. The legislatures in six of those States have instructed their Senators and requested their Representatives to vote for this measure. Few gentlemen on this floor will disregard those resolutions when we come to the vote. Whigs and democrats will then be found acting together. Our party attachments will be disregarded, and the interests of the nation will receive our attention.

Sir, for the first time in my life, I see northern whigs and northern democrats standing shoulder to shoulder in the cause of human rights. Would to God that such might be the case on all questions touching the interests, the honor, and the rights of the free States, and of mankind! There is no good reason why northern Representatives should waste their political power by party divisions among themselves. Let them act irrespective of southern influence, and they will agree upon all the great questions so vitally interesting to our people. It is time that we should discard those counsels which have led to the sacrifice of nearly all our political interests. Before God and my country, I solemnly pledge myself never to place political confidence in any man who lacks the honesty or the firmness to speak and act in favor of freedom and the Constitution.

The objects and ulterior designs of this war have lately been so fully avowed, and are now so generally understood, that it would be a work of supererogation to repeat them.

All, I believe, are aware, and admit, that the extension of slavery over territory now free, and under the jurisdiction of Mexican laws, constitutes the object for which such a vast expenditure of blood and treasure is to be made; and I repeat, that each member who is in favor of that object will, of course, vote against the amendment which will prohibit slavery within such territory as we may acquire, if any; and those in favor of the "self-evident truths" put forth by our fathers in 1776, will vote for the amendment offered. The war in which we are engaged has precipitated this issue upon us; and I rejoice that it is thus presented for our decision. I hope and trust, our determination may be such as to meet the approval of our consciences, and of our God. This acquisition of slave territory, is substantially the same question which was propounded to us when we were called to annex Texas to these States. The subject is more generally understood, and better appreciated at this time than it was then.

You, Mr. Chairman, well recollect that the evening on which the resolutions for annexing Texas passed this body, "the loud-mouthed cannon," from the terrace in front of the Capitol, announced to the friends of that measure its final success. I was pensively wending my way to my lodgings, when my ears were saluted by the roar of those guns, which I then regarded as "minute guns," announcing the final overthrow of the Union which had been formed by our patriot fathers. I clearly saw, or thought I saw, my country involved in a system of territorial aggrandizement; involved in aggressive war; expending the blood and treasure of the nation, for the extension of an institution odious to man, and forbidden by the laws of God. As I then looked forward to the circumstances which now surround us, I was greatly depressed with their contemplation.

Sir, long before this war commenced, I declared, in this hall, that "I would rather see a war with Great Britain, with all its horrors, and its devastation of public morals, than to see the people of the free States quietly submit to the annexation of Texas." I then deeply felt what I said. I felt that our Constitution had ceased to limit the powers of either Congress or the Executive; I saw the union of 1787 broken up and abandoned, for the purpose of bringing into our political association a foreign slave-holding government; I saw that foreigners, as destitute of constitutional qualifications as any other foreigners, were to be placed in this hall, to strike down the interests and to control the rights of my constituents, and of the free States; I saw this war in prospect, with its crimes and guilt; I saw the national debt that has been, and is to be, incurred, the disgrace that is to rest upon our nation, the strife and contention in which we are now engaged among ourselves; and I clearly saw that this career of conquest, if persisted in, must prove the grave of our republic. And I repeat, that unless the friends of the Constitution and of humanity can now stop this policy of acquiring territory, the end of this government draws near.

During our present session, I have received petitions from various States of this Union, numerously signed, praying that our political association with Texas may be dissolved. The petitioners base their requests upon the fact, that the people of the free States have never authorized Congress to place their rights or interests at the disposal of foreigners. They feel that they have been transferred, like southern slaves, to an association with Texians; not by the votes of their own Representatives, but by the votes of members from the slave States, who felt that it would be for the benefit of slavery that the freemen of the North should be controlled by southern votes. Believe you that this feeling is to die away while this war, designed still further to degrade the North, shall be continued? Will our people become satisfied while northern freemen are called upon to go to Mexico, and sacrifice their lives that the slave power may be increased, and the North still further disgraced? I assure you, Sir, that our people are becoming aroused to the dangers which threaten them; and although men of high character and of commanding talents may deem it bad policy to speak forth unwelcome truths, yet, Sir, there are instrumentalities at work which will inform the public mind of the true political condition of the free States; and when the people of those States shall understand fully the manner in which their interests have been silently surrendered, and their constitutional rights subverted, they will take care to place more faithful sentinels upon the watchtowers of liberty.

But, Sir, we have been told here, that "the whig party are in favor of prosecuting this war." Sir, I know not on what authority gentlemen make this assertion. I deny that Representatives from Pennsylvania are authorized to express on this floor the wishes of the whig party of Ohio; or that gentlemen from Philadelphia have authority to declare the views of my constituents. The congressional district which I have the honor to represent, gives the largest whig majority of any in the United States. And I have longer represented my constituents consecutively than any other whig member of this body, except my venerable friend from Massachusetts, (Mr. Adams). I shall, therefore, speak for them as I was commissioned to do. Nor shall I silently allow any other gentleman to represent them as so ignorant of their moral and political duties, or so lost to a just sense of their obligations to mankind, and to God, as to be willing to lend any assistance in that work of human butchery now going on in Mexico.

Why, Sir, when the brigade in which the commercial city of Cleveland is situated, was called on for volunteers to aid this war, only about thirty human beings could be found sunk so low in the depths of moral depravity as to be willing to join in cutting the throats of their fellow men in Mexico. Another brigade in my district, after searching all the haunts of vice and dissipation, was able to furnish only *three* volunteers for this war. It should be borne in mind that not one of the whole number was a whig. When the other brigade was called on, they replied with one voice — "We will fight for liberty, but not for slavery;" and to their honor be it said, not a man of either political party would lend his influence to the prosecution of this nefarious war. Sir, let gentlemen speak for themselves, or for their own districts; but let no man presume to slander my people by representing them as favorable to the prosecution of our conquests in Mexico.

They, Sir, understand what it is to defend their country. They have had too much experience on that subject, to be deceived by the cry that is now raised, for the purpose of obtaining recruits to go to Mexico. When, in 1812, British prowess had captured our army under General Hull, and hordes of Indians were hanging upon our frontiers; when the cabins of our pioneers were lighted up by the savage torch; when our women and children were murdered, and the tomahawk and scalping-knife were doing their work of destruction, the fathers of our present soldiery hastened to the field of honor and of danger. They encountered privations and hardships. Windy speeches, and such overflowing gasconade as we have listened to in this hall, would not answer the purpose of that day. With unflinching hearts and steady nerves, they met the savage foe; they witnessed the horrid scenes of blood and strife in defence of their country. Sir, go talk to them now of their duty to volunteer; to encounter such scenes again, in order to extend slavery, and they will regard it as a direct insult to their intelligence as well as to their patriotism. Their motto is, "*no more slave territory.*" It is the motto of both political parties there; and, I trust, this sentiment will be maintained here. The resolutions lately passed by the almost unanimous voice of the Legislatures of six sovereign States, including the three most powerful of the Union, would seem to indicate a determination to adhere to this maxim.

It is now quite evident that this war will prostrate the present administration, and all who continue to lend their influence to support it. When we next assemble here, the whigs will probably constitute a majority of this body. Will they, by their votes, increase our national debt, by continuing our conquests in Mexico? Will they send more of our fellow-citizens there to be sacrificed to this Moloch of slavery? If so, they, too, will suffer the penalty due to such crimes, and in turn will be driven from power.*

But, while the North possess the power to exclude farther slave territory, our danger consists in our own party divisions, and in the far-reaching policy of southern statesmen. But two days since, a distinguished senator in the other end of the capitol (Mr. Calhoun) brought forward a proposition the most dangerous to northern rights that could be devised under existing circumstances. Foreseeing, as all reflecting men do, that the army must be withdrawn, if the opponents of the war remain firm to their purpose, he proposes to compromise the matter, by bringing back the troops to the Rio Grande; to occupy that river from its mouth to the "Passo del Norte," and from thence, to erect a line of fortifications due west to the

* The democrats were defeated the following year. The whigs took up the war, and carried it on, and were again driven from power, precisely according to this prophecy.

Gulf of California; holding possession of the whole Mexican territory on this side of the line thus indicated, until peace shall be restored.

It should be borne in mind, that the Mexican government and the officers of their army are pledged against all attempts at negotiating a peace with us, while our army occupies any portion of their territory. If, therefore, this plan be adopted, we shall be at the expense of holding military occupation of the country for an indefinite period. The Mexicans will not submit to a despotism wielded by our military officers, and, therefore, will leave the country; and slave-holders, with their human chattels, will occupy their places. Our army will act as a guard to keep the slaves in subjection, while their professed object will be to defend the country against the Mexicans. In this way, a sparse slave-holding population will be scattered over it, and, perhaps at some future time, Mexico, exhausted and disheartened, may consent to cede it to us. If so, there being so many slaves already there, will be urged upon us as a conclusive reason why slavery shall continue throughout that vast extent of country. If, on the other hand, a peace shall be concluded, without obtaining a title to the country, then a revolution, after the example of Texas, will take place, and annexation to this Union, with a vast increase of the slave power in the councils of the nation, will be the result; for it should be borne in mind, that the territory thus proposed to be occupied by us, is of sufficient extent to be divided into fourteen such States as Ohio.

Some northern men appear to regard this proposal with a degree of favor which alarms me. In truth, Mr. Chairman, we have been so long accustomed to surrender our rights to the demands of the South, that some of our friends appear to think it improper for us to take a firm position in support of the honor and the interests of our free States. They seem willing to surrender a portion of our rights to appease slave-holding rapacity. Sir, this policy has already brought us to the verge of political ruin; continue it a little longer, and the people of the free States will themselves be slaves. Let the proposition alluded to be adopted, and the power of the free States will dwindle to insignificance in the other branch of the Legislature. We shall then be regarded as useful to the Union, only as instruments to support slavery. Northern rights and northern honor will be looked upon as among the things that *were*; they will be unknown to the future. I would most solemnly caution every man against consenting to this proposed policy. Its effect will be to extend the boundaries of Texas to the Rio Grande. That was stated by the distinguished Senator to whom I have alluded, to be one of the great objects of the war. That plan, once adopted, must prove fatal to the free States. I repeat, let us stand immovably upon the maxim of having "no more slave territory," "*no more slave States*." Let this be our watchword here and in our State Legislatures, and among the entire people of the free States, including all political parties, and, I assure you, we shall have peace at no distant day.*

Again, some northern men who are opposed to extending slavery, appear willing to obtain further territory, under the impression that it will remain free. I greatly fear, Sir, if we add to the extent of our south-western border, it will prove an extension of slavery. I am, therefore, opposed to obtaining any more territory in that direction. I would confine Texas to the precise limits occupied by her at the time of annexation. Beyond that, I would not extend the power of the slave-holder to recapture his slave. I would leave the whole country beyond the valley of the Nueces *free*. Let it be a place of refuge, unpolluted by the footsteps of the slave-catcher, where the panting fugitive may rest in safety; where no Texian master shall have power to seize or re-enslave him, as he may now do in our free States.

I desire to call attention to the immense sacrifice of human life now making to carry on this war. The official documents

* Mr. Benton, in his history, informs us that so vigorous was the opposition to this war, at one time, that the President directed the recall of the army; and an order was actually made out and signed for that purpose; but the President was induced to reconsider his proposition, and the order was withheld.

before us show that *twenty-three thousand nine hundred and ninety-eight officers and men* entered the service during the first eight months of this war; that fifteen thousand four hundred and eighty-six remained in service at the close of that time; that three hundred and thirty-one had deserted; and that two thousand two hundred and two had been discharged; leaving five thousand nine hundred and nineteen unaccounted for. Thus, in little more than eight months, this war has cost the lives of nearly six thousand American troops, or about one third of the whole number sent to Mexico. A distinguished senator (Mr. Calhoun) estimates our loss at one third of those who go to that country. I presume the Mexican loss to be about one third as great as ours,* and the whole number of human beings sacrificed in this attempt to extend slavery, is now about one thousand per month. Sir, what should be the reflections of those gentlemen who have contributed their votes and their influence to send their neighbors and friends in such numbers to Mexican graves? I regard every regiment that marches for that country as a funeral procession, one third of whom are going to their resting-place in that vast charnel-house beyond the Rio Grande, and another third to return with shattered constitutions, doomed to early graves. How long will the free States continue to furnish victims for this sacrifice?

But I return to the question more particularly under consideration. It has been seriously argued that we have no power to prohibit slavery from such territory as we may acquire. Our feelings, Mr. Chairman, often draw us into arguments of the most extraordinary character. The question has been asked with an air of triumph, "Where does Congress find authority to prohibit slavery in our territories?" I answer, we find it in the common powers of legislation; in the power to prevent assault and battery, outrage, and crime. The law that prevents one man from beating and scourging another, is a total prohibition of slavery. Nor can slavery exist where

* This view was nearly correct as to the *army*; but the loss of Mexican lives, including peasants, women, and children murdered, and who died of pestilence, was far greater than that of the Americans.

such law is enforced. Indeed, while you leave the great first law of nature, "self-defence," unrepealed, you will exclude slavery. Leave to man the right of protecting his person and defending his life, and you cannot enslave him. Now, Sir, should we acquire territory of Mexico, Congress must legislate for its government until it shall be admitted as a State. And who will deny that we may pass laws to punish violence and outrage? Who will stand up here in the presence of the nation, and say that Congress will not possess the power to leave all the inhabitants of that territory in possession of the right to defend their persons, their virtue, and their lives, against the violence and brutality of those who would fain assail them? If any member of this body would meet me on this point, and hazard his reputation by avowing such doctrines, I should be delighted to hear him. On the contrary, I should be obliged to any man who will point me to the power which Congress possesses under the Constitution, to repeal the law of nature and of nature's God, — to take from man his right of self-defence, and make him the property of his fellow man.

If we possess the power to degrade one half or two thirds of the people, and convert them into *property*, and vest the title to them in the other portion of community, we may surely vest in one man, or in a larger number of men, the title to all the others. Sir, is such doctrine to be listened to in an American Congress? We hold "that all men are created free and equal, and are endowed by their Creator with certain inalienable rights, among which are life, liberty, and the pursuit of happiness; that to secure these rights, governments are instituted among men." But it is now said that we have no constitutional power to form a government for such purposes in any territory which we possess, or which we may hereafter acquire. I think such doctrine will be heard with astonishment by the people of this government, as well as by those of other nations. Our revolution was based upon those "self-evident truths" to which I have alluded, and our government was founded on them. But we are now told that we have no right to legislate for freedom; that our legislative functions can only be exerted in extending and increasing the curse of human bondage. God only knows what doctrines we shall next be called to listen to.

Gentlemen from the South have constantly referred to what they term "the guaranties of slavery in the Federal Constitution." I am myself unable to comprehend their meaning, by the use of that language. I have made the inquiry on this floor for the article or section in which such guaranty may be found; but, to this day, I have found no lawyer, statesman, or jurist, who could point me to it. I hesitate not to say, there is no guaranty of slavery in our political compact. Slavery is purely a State institution, over which this government possesses no power, either to establish, sustain, or to abolish. This has ever been the sentiment of the entire South, until within the last three years, when they discovered that it was necessary to have Texas, in order to hold their slaves in bondage. Then a new constitutional theory was started. But, Sir, suppose that every slave in the nation should leave his master to-morrow, and start for Canada or Mexico! Our government has not the power under the Constitution to arrest or send back one of them. Or should a slave escape from Virginia to Ohio soil, and while his master should endeavor to arrest him, the slave, in self-defence, should slay the master; there is no law of the Federal Government, or of our State, that would punish him for it. Yet we hear much said in regard to "*federal guaranties of slavery.*" I repeat that I am unable to comprehend what they mean by this language. If their slaves run away, or kill their masters, or destroy their master's property, or refuse to labor, no master would think of calling on this government for indemnity. Yet they will talk of *guaranties*, without object and without meaning.

During the debate, we have heard it asserted repeatedly, that the slave is the *property* of his master. On what right does the master claim title to his slave as property? It is the same title by which the pirate claims title to the goods of his victim. It is the same by which the highwayman claims title to your purse. It is founded in violence, and maintained by crime. Whenever the slave becomes possessed of physical force sufficient, he may relieve himself from bondage by any means in his power, provided he does not injure innocent persons. He may, without incurring any moral guilt, use such violence as he may deem necessary to effect his release from bondage, even to the taking of his master's life. He is called *property* by southern gentlemen. But suppose the slaves of the South were to rise and overpower their masters, and compel them to labor by aid of chains and scourges; they would then have precisely the same title to their present owners as *property* which their masters now have to them. This, Sir, is the only property which man can hold in man.

We read in Scripture, that "God gave man dominion over the fish of the sea, and over the fowl of the air, and over every living thing that moveth upon the earth." This is the title by which we claim property in the brute creation; but man can claim no such title to his fellow man. We, as a nation, in 1804, gave evidence to the world of the light in which we hold the doctrine that man may be held as the property of his brother man. At that time, Algiers held a number of our American citizens as slaves. They claimed them as *property.* Their title was the same as that by which southern masters hold their slaves. It was by physical force. There was less injustice on the part of the Algerines than there is on the part of southern masters. They had held their victims in bondage but a few years; while our slave-holders have kept theirs in servitude for ages. But how did we treat their claim of title? Why, Sir, we pronounced them "*barbarians;*" declared them unworthy of associating with civilized nations, or even to maintain an existence upon earth. We sent an armed force there, and from the cannon's mouth proclaimed to the world the just and bloody fate of those slave-holders who claim to hold the *image of God as property.*

Decatur, Israel, Caldwell, and Somers, offered up their lives in the conflict which released the grasp of those barbarians upon our people. At the western entrance to this capitol, we pass the beautiful monument reared to their memories. They fell while opposing, by their swords, this doctrine of property in man. Many a slave-holder that day "bit the dust" in attempting to maintain the doctrine now advanced on this floor. Sir, if this theory, now the scoff of infidel nations, is to be adopted in this body; if our fellow-citizens, by thousands, are to march to Mexico and shed their blood for the purpose of maintaining this doctrine, let us tear down that monument, raze it to its foundations, scatter to the four winds of heaven the inscriptions which commemorate the deeds of the mighty dead, blot out our records of the past, and let our nation commence a new career of violence, oppression, and infamy.

But, as though no absurdity could be too great for this body, we are told that "a God of justice has ordained and established slavery;" and "that the Scriptures of Divine Truth have furnished authority for holding men as *property*." I had hoped that our holy religion might have escaped this slave-holding sacrilege. Do gentlemen worship a God of oppression, of licentiousness, and of blood? It is a notorious fact that the average life of slaves, after entering the cotton plantations of the South, is but *seven years;* and on the sugar plantations, but *five years,* — that is, the whole number of slaves on these plantations are driven so hard as to close their existence within those periods. Their places are supplied by new purchases from the slave-breeding States, and these in turn are also sacrificed to the master's cupidity. Is the taking of life in this manner less aggravated murder than it would be to slay them at once? Is there less crime in torturing a man so as to cause his death in five or seven years, than there would be in slaying him outright? Again, Sir: look at yonder slave prison; view its gloomy walls; enter its cells; witness the sighs and groans and tears of its unhappy inmates, doomed to a southern slave market; note the unutterable agony of that mother, who has been torn from her home and family, and all she holds dear. Rumor speaks of one who, thus confined with two of her children, became frantic with her suffering, and, in a transport of horror, murdered her children, and then put a period to her own existence, rather than meet the doom that awaited her. Yet we are told, even by those who minister at slave-holding altars, that these "things are dictated by God himself." To me the doctrine appears impious. I would sooner be an infidel than render homage to such a Deity. I loathe and detest such doctrines, whether they emanate from laymen or professed divines. The mind that can impute the moral corruptions, the reeking crimes of slavery, to a holy, just, and pure God, would, in my opinion, sustain the most horrid rites of Paganism; would worship in temples stained with blood, and minister at altars smoking with human sacrifice, if necessary to sustain the curse of slavery. I regard the devotees of Juggernaut far more consistent than such Christians.

Mr. Chairman, this whole body is now theoretically in committee for the purpose of *considering the state of the Union.* The practice was adopted during the revolution, and is unknown to all other legislative bodies. After the colonies had formed a confederation for the purpose of mutual defence, the maintenance of their Union became a matter of great solicitude, and was regarded as their only hope for establishing our national independence. Congress, therefore, frequently resolved itself into a committee composed of the whole body, in order to consider the state of the Union. If any part of it was in danger; if any portion of it complained, or felt dissatisfied, this committee took the subject into serious consideration, and applied the necessary remedy. It was felt necessary then to maintain a union of feeling among the people, and to cultivate a spirit of the most perfect harmony between all parts of the republic. Sir, in imitation of their example, we, the representatives of this mighty nation, have now resolved ourselves into a committee for the purpose of taking into consideration the "*present state of our Union.*" I, therefore, desire to call the attention of the committee to that subject.

One of the stipulations contained in the Articles of the Confederation of 1778, declared that the then existing Union should be *perpetual*, and that no change or alteration should be made without the consent of each of the several States. But it was soon discovered that radical defects existed in that confederated government; and the statesmen of that day saw clearly that it could not be maintained.

In the short period of nine years, the Union of 1778 was abandoned, contrary to, and in direct violation of, the stipulations of the old Articles of Confederation; and a Constitution was adopted, as was emphatically expressed in the preamble, "*in order to form a more perfect Union.*" The new Union formed in 1787, was limited by well defined boundaries. It embraced certain States, together with the territory north-west of the Ohio river, and east of the Mississippi. Slavery existed in the original States; but our fathers, in order to leave a lasting memorial of their intention to confine it to its then existing boundaries, had excluded it forever from all the territory then in the possession of the government. Less than twenty years, however, elapsed, before it was discovered that certain commercial advantages would be gained by obtaining Louisiana. Mr. Jefferson said distinctly that there was no power in the government to make such an addition to the then existing Union; and that an amendment to the Constitution was necessary, in order to render such an act binding upon the States. I am not aware that any statesman of that day denied the doctrine; but all the States, by common consent, received the territory thus purchased into political fellowship; and it thus became a part of that Union, which from that period existed in its modified form until the purchase of Florida, which was obtained by treaty, and, by consent of each of the several States, it also became a part of this confederation. This vast accession of slave territory was received to the political fellowship of the free States, by their own unanimous consent. I think no statesman of that day, or of this, believed that they were compelled by any provision of the Constitution, to enter into a political union with foreign slave-holders, who inhabited the territory thus brought into association with us. But the time approached when new doctrines and new constitutional principles were necessary, to maintain an institution fast sinking into contempt among civilized nations.

Our Executive was informed that slavery would probably

soon be abolished in Texas, and that civil liberty was likely to extend over that republic. He deprecated such an event, and, under the pretence that it was our duty to prevent the abolition of slavery, and consequent extension of liberty, proposed to annex it to this Union, where he seemed to think that oppression, human degradation, and crime would be protected and maintained. Attempts were made to annex the two governments by *treaty;* but the constitutional power rejected the offer. Recourse was then had to joint resolutions, a mode for effecting that object never dreamed of by any statesman, until it was suggested by the desperation to which the slave power was then reduced. Then, Sir, the representatives of the slave-breeding and of the slave-consuming States in this body declared that the people of New England, the descendants of the Puritan fathers, should be transferred from the union formed in 1787, to a political fellowship with the blacklegs and slave-mongers of Texas, in order to sustain African servitude in that government. Thus, Sir, have our rights been made the sport of slave-holding politicians, and the people of the free States rendered the instruments of oppression to our fellow men. Foreigners, aliens to this republic, have been brought into this hall to pass laws for the government of northern freemen. Men who, fifteen months since, were the sworn supporters of a foreign slave-holding government, founded upon the principles of perpetual slavery, sit here to control the interests, and to determine the rights, of those whose fathers encountered the dangers of many a battle field, that they and their descendants might be free and independent of foreign influences.

When Washington and his compatriots framed our Constitution, and solemnly declared "that no person shall be a representative in Congress until he shall have been seven years a citizen of the United States," and "that no person shall be a Senator until he shall have been nine years a citizen of the United States," they did not dream that these important provisions were to be so soon trampled upon, and this hall, consecrated to American liberty, was to be defiled with the presence of strangers, citizens of a foreign government, who deny the "self-evident truths" on which American liberty is founded, and who buy and sell the image of God. Sir, before Him who knows my inmost soul, I declare that I would rather have seen these beautiful pillars crumbled to dust, and this splendid edifice shaken from its foundations, "so that not one stone should remain upon another," than to have witnessed this humiliation of the free North.

Nor is this all. We have assumed the war which these foreigners had waged against Mexico, to prevent the abolition of slavery in Texas. The expense of that unjust and unnatural conflict, is to rest upon the people of the free States, and upon their descendants. Our officers and soldiers are sent to Mexico to sacrifice their lives, that Texians may hold their grasp upon their fellow men; and commit abuses, outrages, and crimes with impunity. This, Sir, is the state of our union with Texas. It is the union which binds the oppressed to his supercilious lordling. It is the union which a slave feels for his master. It is an unwilling, dishonorable, a *hated* union. Yet, I am aware that many of our public men speak of *maintaining the Constitution;* as though Congress, or the Executive were, in some respect, controlled by an instrument, which has long since become obsolete, which has, in fact, ceased to exist, except in name. I am unwilling to mock the people by any such deception. I believe that ninety-nine out of every hundred, in our free States, would rejoice to see the resolutions annexing Texas to these States repealed, and our modified Union of 1787 restored. Indeed, I believe the President and his cabinet would now rejoice to exchange Texas for a peace with Mexico.

In conclusion, permit me to say to the country, that our political horizon is overcast; "clouds and darkness are round about us;" impenetrable darkness shuts the future from our view. Foreign war and internal strife, animosities and heartburnings, indicate that this nation is doomed to suffer the just penalty incurred by the oppression, outrage, and crime which we have perpetrated upon our fellow men. If God deals out to offending nations retributive justice, we cannot escape his displeasure. Yet, when the just penalty of our transgressions shall have been visited upon us; when thousands more of our brethren shall have fallen victims to this unholy war, and tens of thousands more, widows and orphans, shall weep and mourn under bereavement; when the immorality brought upon our nation, by this war, shall have tortured the hearts of hundreds of thousands of mothers and wives and daughters, and the righteous punishment for our transgressions shall have been meted out to us; our rulers, our legislators, will acknowledge that "*righteousness alone exalteth a nation*," while "*sin is a reproach to any people*."

PRIVILEGES OF MEMBERS OF CONGRESS.*

MISREPRESENTATIONS CORRECTED — THE RESOLUTION DEFINED — RIGHT OF MEMBERS TO VISIT PUBLIC INSTITUTIONS — MOBS — THEIR DESIGNS — ENCOURAGED BY MEMBERS — DEFIANCE — ATTACKS REPELLED.

[The reader will recollect that some seventy or eighty slaves attempted to escape from the District of Columbia on board the schooner Pearl, in April, 1848; that they, together with the captain (Drayton,) and the mate (Sayres,) were captured and imprisoned in the jail at Washington; that Mr. Giddings visited them the next morning; that a mob collected, opened the lower gate of the prison by force, and ascended to the one which opened into the hall where Mr. Giddings was conversing with Captain Drayton, and threatened his life if he did not leave the prison immediately. This he refused to do. The next day, Mr. Palfrey introduced a resolution to inquire into these facts. This called forth a very exciting debate, in which several southern members made Mr. Giddings the object of their bitterest denunciation. On the third day, he replied to these assaults in the following speech. After he closed his remarks, a slave-holding member moved to lay the whole subject on the table, and the motion was sustained.]

MR. SPEAKER, — Before entering upon the subject of the resolution under consideration, I will say that, after so frequently expressing my views in regard to the powers of this government concerning slavery, after so often defining my position on that subject, I could not have believed that any gentleman here would hazard his reputation for candor by imputing to me an intention to interfere with the institution of slavery in the States. I call the attention of the House and

* Speech upon the Resolution to inquire whether Members of Congress had been threatened by a lawless mob. Delivered in the House of Representatives, April 15, 1848.

of the country, both North and South, to the fact, that no member in this hall, no person out of it, has ever heard me, in public or in private, by speech, resolution, or intimation, claim such powers to be vested in this government, nor have they ever heard me desire the exercise of such powers. For three days of excited discussion, in which many southern gentlemen participated, I believe all of them have distinctly or by implication, charged me with such designs. Now, Sir, before the nation, I challenge these gentlemen to the proof of what they have thus asserted. If any man can lay his hand upon any speech of mine, any resolution introduced, or any intimation given by me, claiming such power, or that I desired the exercise of such power, let him now stand forth and avow it.

I assert that these imputations are unfounded, entirely false, and unworthy of gentlemen holding seats in this body; and I now call upon those who have uttered them to stand up here before the nation, and maintain the truth of their assertions. For that purpose, I now offer to yield the floor to any member who dares attempt to justify the imputations thus thrown out. (Mr. Giddings paused for a short time, and no member rising, he proceeded.)

Mr. Speaker, where are those gentlemen who, in their excited moments, have charged me with entertaining and uttering opinions in conflict with the Constitution which I am sworn to support? It is a duty which I owe to myself, and to those whom I represent, to disabuse the public mind of these impressions. I disavow all such opinions, purposes, motives, and designs. The country is aware that I was once driven from this hall for daring to offer resolutions denying that such powers existed in this government.

I will now repeat, perhaps for the hundredth time, that the people of the slave States, in my opinion, hold the institution of slavery at the disposal of their own will, with supreme and unlimited powers to continue or abolish it at their own pleasure; that it is strictly a State institution, over which this body, nor the Federal Government, possess any powers whatever, except the power to legislate for the return of fugitive slaves. And when I say this government has no power to interfere with slavery, I mean just what I say. I intend to be understood as saying that the people of the free States have the same indisputable right to be *free* and *exempt* from the support of slavery, which the slaves States have to *sustain* it; that this government has no constitutional power to involve us of the free States in the turpitude of slavery. We possess the positive, unqualified, and indisputable right to remain exempt from its continuation, unstained with its guilt, and disconnected with its crimes. We will not extend that institution, nor create slave markets, upon soil that is now free, nor will we associate with new slave-holding States.

We hold it a cardinal principle never to increase the slave power in the Senate by admission of slave States; nor shall we consent to any extension of the slave power whatever. Our motto is — "Keep your slavery where it is; manage it in your own way, and according to your own discretion; with it we will have nothing to do." I now speak as a legislator. My duties as a member of Congress are so plain, that the way-faring man, though a fool, could not mistake them. This body, Sir, never had the constitutional power to establish it in this district. It exists here in direct violation of the spirit and of the letter of the Constitution. When, therefore, Congress enacted the law of 1801, by which slavery in this district was established and continued, they not only violated their duty to God and to their fellow men, but they disregarded their constitutional powers, and violated the sacred compact of union between the States. Now, Sir, it is one of my objects, and of those who act with me, to repeal all those unconstitutional laws which connect the people of the free States with slavery, and wholly to separate this government from all support and maintenance of that institution. We will not continue involved in its crimes. I notify gentlemen, that we will purify ourselves from its contagion. These objects and designs we will accomplish, God helping us. No earthly power shall deter us from every honorable and lawful effort to bring a "consummation so devoutly to be wished." Nor will we sustain any man for President, or for any other office, who is willing to involve our people of the free States in the turpitude and disgrace of slavery. We contend for *freedom* — for the *rights of man.*

I have, on but one occasion, permitted myself in this hall to be drawn into discussion upon the subject of slavery *in the States.* When a distinguished southern statesman, then a member of the Executive Cabinet, (Mr. Calhoun,) in his official character, undertook to establish the doctrine that slavery was necessary to the enjoyment of mankind, and that it was a humane, benevolent, and philanthropic institution, I made some comments on his letter when it came before this House, and was legitimately under discussion. But gentlemen cannot expect us to remain silent on the subject of the slave-trade in this district while it is supported by our laws, although such discussion may endanger slavery in every State of the Union. Are we to be told that we shall not speak on the subject of the slave-trade here, lest it affect the institution in the States? Unite with us, repeal the laws that involve us in its guilt, separate this government from all participation in its support, relieve the people of the free States from its burdens and its disgrace; then we will be silent on the subject — not till then.

Again, while southern members bring the subject of slavery in the States before the House, they cannot expect us of the North to feel very particularly delicate in answering them.

Before entering upon the subject more legitimately under consideration, I must be permitted to say farther, that I have no intention to reply to those personal attacks that for three days have been made upon me. They are unbecoming the dignity of a legislative body; they are equally unsuited to the occasion. We are discussing the rights of humanity, — a subject dignified and solemn. The eyes of the nation and of the civilized world are upon us; and, Sir, I cannot demean myself so much as to reply to those personal invectives which have been so liberally heaped upon me.

The subject of slavery, which has now been before us for some days, was not introduced by myself, nor by any Northern man. The resolution of my friend from Massachusetts (Mr. Palfrey) does not allude to it; yet it has been forced upon us by slaveholders, and northern men cannot avoid it. I regard it as inappropriate, but have no alternative but to meet it, or admit my inability to oppose the arguments advanced. I do not regret its introduction. It must be met, discussed, and settled in this hall. It has become the great absorbing topic among the people of the nation. It is discussed in the legislatures of our several States, in our political conventions, in our township meetings, in our newspapers, our literary periodicals, our religious meetings, our sermons, and in our religious essays, and in our prayers. It is the subject of conversation at the fireside and by the wayside. It has occupied most of the time of this body during its present session. It occupies the attention of the President and of his cabinet. Southern statesmen are arguing in its behalf, and our army is fighting for its extension. The toiling millions of our nation are made to contribute a portion of each day's toil to rivet the chains of servitude upon their brethren. It guides the appointment of our foreign ministers, dictates the selection of officers for our army and navy, and controls the election of our Presidents. Sir, it would be useless for us to attempt an evasion of this subject. *It must be discussed.*

I will now ask attention to the subject more immediately before us.

The propositions contained in this resolution are few and simple. It would appear impossible to misapprehend them. It proposes to inquire, — *Firstly.* Whether a lawless mob existed in this district for two nights next preceding the day on which it was offered, setting at defiance the laws and constituted authorities of the United States? And, *Secondly.* Whether members of this House have been menaced by such mob?

The entire object of the resolution is to obtain *official information* on these two definite points, and to place that information on record, that it may be sent forth to the country. If there has been such a mob, it is due to the people of the nation that they should know it; if there has not been such a mob, it is due to the people of this district that they should be disabused of the charge. Let the truth be known. Why should we seek to disguise facts, or to withhold them from the public?

That such a mob existed, up to the time of introducing this resolution, is as well known to every member of this body, as any other fact which has transpired beyond our personal observation. Indeed, I am told that many members of this House witnessed the collection of the mob, and saw some of their lawless depredations. There can be no doubt that, on the evening of Tuesday, the 18th instant, several hundred persons collected on Seventh street, with the avowed intention of destroying one of the newspaper establishments of this city.* Their object was publicly proclaimed. They moved toward the accomplishment of their purpose, and actually commenced the work of violence by throwing stones, breaking windows, and doing damage to the building, and injuring some of the police who interposed to protect the property of the publisher. That the auxiliary guard of the city only saved the building, type, presses, etc., by an exhibition of the most determined resistance, for which the officers and men are entitled to much praise.

The mob, finding themselves strongly opposed, publicly adjourned to meet the next evening. During Wednesday, the 17th, collections of half-grown boys, loafers, and drunken rowdies, attended by ruffian-looking strangers in various parts of the city, left no doubt as to their designs to carry out their intentions during the evening of that day.

At nine o'clock on Wednesday evening, it is said that some thousands were collected in and near Seventh street, in the vicinity of the printing-office alluded to. That their intention to destroy that office was publicly avowed and proclaimed. That further violence took place, and further damage was effected. That during both evenings "abolitionists" were

* The National Era.

denounced, and publicly threatened with violence and death. That members of this body were named, their lodgings inquired for, and propositions made violently to seize their persons, and take their lives. I do not say there was danger of such outrage being committed, but I do know that members of this House, and men who were not members, expressed the opinion that it would be unsafe for certain members of our body to be seen in the vicinity of those meetings. I know that individuals of this body were in good faith advised to arm themselves, and provide for their own protection. I know that friendly letters were received by individuals on this floor, advising them to arm themselves, and others of a threatening character came to them through the post-office.

On Tuesday I visited the prison of this district, and saw the mob collected there; an account of which was read by my friend who moved this resolution.* The mob at the prison, I

---

* This statement was drawn by Mr. Giddings, dated 20th April, and is in the following words:

"I, J. R. Giddings, a member of the House of Representatives, state: That during the forenoon of yesterday I visited the jail of this district. I was not acquainted with the keeper; and when I arrived I announced to him my name, and that I was a member of this body. That I further said to him, that I wished to see the persons confined there on a charge of carrying away slaves from this district. I told him that I wished to say to them that they should have the benefit of counsel and a legal trial, and their rights should be protected, and desired him to be present. He went with me to the passage that leads to the cells.

"While conversing with these men in the presence of the keeper, a mob came to the iron gate at the head of the stairway, and demanded that I should leave forthwith. The keeper informed them that he would not open the gate unless I left the building immediately. That I refused to do. The keeper assured them that he would not open the door until they retired. I was further informed, that the mob had compelled the guard at the lower gate to deliver up the key to them; and in this way they had opened that gate, and by that means obtained access to the passage at the head of the stairs.

"After the mob had left the stairs, and entered the lower passage, the keeper and myself and the Hon. E. S. Hamlin, who had visited the jail as attorney for the prisoners with me, came down to the lower gate, in front of which the mob was assembled. He opened the gate, and I walked out. This morning, I have been informed by a gentleman who is a stranger to me, but who says he

believe to have been composed principally of slave-dealers, from Baltimore, Richmond, Alexandria, Annapolis, and of this city, collected to purchase the persons who were confined there for having fled from slavery. Like the offensive buzzards gathering around disgusting carrion, these cormorants had gathered around the slave-breeders, who claimed to own the children and mothers confined in that slave-market. It was this mass of moral putridity which constituted the mob at the prison.

I am informed that the mob collected on Seventh street on Tuesday and Wednesday evenings, was led on, excited, and encouraged by slave-dealers from the various cities mentioned, and by slave-breeders from the country and cities of this region; while some of the clerks in the departments, and officers of the city, united with them; and that members of this body, in their speeches here, encouraged them. The respectable citizens of this city generally, I have no doubt, were not only opposed to the mob, but deeply regretted its existence.

On Wednesday night, the mob again adjourned to meet the next evening. Up to this time, no movement had been made to put down those riots, either by the President, or by any other officer of the United States, or, so far as our knowledge extended, by any other officer except those of the auxiliary guard. Thus far it had set the laws at defiance. And it was at this opportune period, while every movement gave evidence of a continuance of these riotous depredations, that my friend brought forth the resolution before us, proposing an inquiry into these facts.

Gentlemen for three days have held out to the country, that the resolution represented that members of this body had been in *danger*. Sir, it neither alludes to, nor hints at, such a fact. The preamble recites, that common fame represents that mem-

---

was present and heard the proposition made by individuals to lay violent hands upon me as I came out of the prison, one of whom, he informed me, was a Mr. Slatter, a slave-dealer from Baltimore, whom he states to have been active in instigating others to acts of violence."

bers have been *menaced*, *threatened*, and proposes to ascertain whether it be so. That is the length and breadth and extent of the proposition. Now, Sir, I may be permitted to inquire, whether it would not be more statesmanlike for gentlemen to meet the proposition before us, than it is thus to build up a man of straw, merely for the purpose of tearing it down? Again, gentlemen have represented *me* as introducing this resolution. They seem to have mistaken even the author of the proposition in the phrenzy of excitement. My friend who introduced it, will not thank them for this attempt to transfer the honor of that act from him to my humble self. That gentleman introduced it upon his own responsibility, and at the dictates of his own judgment.

Again, it has been urged that the resolution asks protection for the members referred to. It is to me perfectly incomprehensible how gentlemen should give this construction to a proposition simply *to inquire into facts*. Why, Mr. Speaker, it really would appear that the flight of so many human chattels, called "*slaves*," from this city, has positively demented every slave-holder of this House.

But again, Sir, it is said that I went to the prison, where I had no right to claim the protection of this body. Suppose it were so, still it is no answer to the proposition before us, which is merely to *inquire as to facts*. I cannot, however, pass over this assertion without a more particular notice. That prison was erected, in part, with the money of my people, as much as this capitol. It is as much under the control of *our* officers, as the building in which we are now sitting. It is as much controlled by our laws as this capitol, or the post-office, or the treasury buildings. I had the right to examine how our laws were executed; to understand who was in prison; to know what degree of humanity is exercised there by the servants of the people. My constituents have a right to know how their prison is managed, and for what purpose it is used. They have a right to understand whether it is used to confine weeping mothers, and sighing fathers, and helpless infants, guilty of no other crime than a love of liberty. I will not condescend to argue this question. My constituents know their rights, and if gentlemen here have not learned their own privileges, they had better study them. The rights of myself, and of my people, shall be maintained to the extent of my humble powers. They, Sir, have the right to understand these manifestations of slave-holding violence; and, whether you pass this resolution or not, you cannot, you shall not, keep that information from them.

Gentlemen here have constantly represented me as seeking the protection of this House. Yes, Sir, for three days I sat here, and heard gentlemen representing to the country that I was seeking protection at the hands of the members of this body. The resolution proposes no such thing; the gentleman who offered it represented no such wish; I have intimated no such desire. Why, then, are these misrepresentations put forth? Why is falsehood resorted to? Do gentlemen suppose me incapable of exposing these flagrant violations of truth; or did they believe me so destitute of spirit, that I dared not hold them up to the contempt of an intelligent and virtuous people?

Why, Sir, does not every member of this House know, does not the country know, that the mob extended to this hall; that members of this House were also numbered with the mob; that while slave-dealers and those who breed mankind for market were collected in those spacious galleries, members on this floor denounced me from this forum, — declared themselves "ready to unite with the mob to drive me from this hall and from the district," — declared that I "ought to be hung as high as Haman," — and that they "were prepared to justify the mob to the fullest extent?" Does any person suppose me capable of asking protection from such men? No, Sir; I have too often witnessed the spirit of slave-holding violence on this floor to ask protection of the members of this House. I never did degrade myself by such request; I never shall. If I ever had cause to ask protection from human violence, it was from the violence of members on this floor. Sir, could I so far forget my self-respect as to ask protection at the hands of men, who, in this hall, and before the nation, were endeavoring to excite the rabble to deeds of violence? Never, Sir; never. Let the House purify itself, protect its own honor, and maintain a dignity becoming an American Congress, and I will provide for the protection of my person in my own way.

I again repeat that the object, the whole object of the resolution, is *to send forth facts to the people.* I wish the people of the free States to understand that, when representatives visit the public institutions of this district in their official character, they are beset by slave-dealers, by those who drive women to market. That such beings in human shape attempt to dictate to us where we shall go, and how long we shall stay; that they attempt to tell us that our lives are at their disposal, and that our existence will be hazarded, if we disobey their directions. Sir, I desire that the people should understand that slave-holding members on this floor, in their public speeches, justify these base indignities "to their full extent."

I feel deeply humbled, when I consider that these encouragements of the mob were mostly put forth by members on this side of the House, professing to belong to the same political party with myself. And it is but an act of justice that I should also say, that I am informed, that after my friend had introduced this resolution, and an exciting debate had sprung up, both in the Senate and in this hall, and the attention of the country was being called to these facts, the President tendered to the officers of the city the military forces of the United States, and directed the employees of government to prepare to put down the mob. No man will suspect me of courting the President's favor; but I desire to do him justice, as well as those who, professing to belong to the same political party with myself, yet endeavor to excite the rabble to violence. And now, Sir, I will take my leave of the resolution; I have stated the object which brought it forth; that object was to place facts before the country. As to its adoption, I feel entirely indifferent. The facts will go forth; the object of the mover has already been attained. The information intended to be elicited has already spread far and wide. The freemen of the

North will arouse from their silent stupor, and soon we shall hear their indignation expressed in language not to be misunderstood.

When the pending resolution was brought forward, proposing a simple inquiry as to facts, it was instantly seized upon by southern members as the basis of an exciting debate concerning slavery. They insisted upon going back, and inquiring into the circumstances out of which this mob and the threatened violence arose. This was done upon that principle of slave-holding ethics, which teaches that if the captain and crew of the schooner "Pearl" had assisted slaves to escape from this district, it would be just and proper for slave-holders to destroy the newspaper press of this city, and threaten violence to members of this body. It should be distinctly borne in mind, that this subject of slavery was brought forward exclusively, and the discussion has been confined almost entirely, to *southern men.*

Well, Sir, what are the facts at which almost the whole slave-holding fraternity of this body has been thrown into such a ferment? Why, Sir, it is said that some seventy-six men, women, and children, living in this district, possessing the same natural right to the enjoyment of life and liberty as gentlemen in this hall; feeling the galling chains of slavery chafing and festering into their flesh; themselves shut out from the social and intellectual enjoyments for which they were designed by their Creator; bowed down in abject servitude, surrounded by moral darkness, robbed of their labor, and shut out even from the hope of immortality under the laws which we have enacted, and which we still refuse to modify or repeal; inspired with an ardent desire to enjoy the rights with which God has endowed our race, went on board a schooner lying at one of the wharves of this city, and set sail for a "land of liberty." When they reached the mouth of the river, adverse winds compelled them to cast anchor. Thus detained, we may imagine the anxiety that must have filled their minds. How that slave-mother pressed her tender babe more closely to her breast, as she sent up to the God of the oppressed her silent supplication for deliverance from the men-stealers who were on their track; for those bloodhounds in human shape were in hot pursuit, clothed with the authority of the laws enacted by Congress, and now kept in force by this body, and they seized upon those wretched fugitives, and brought them back to this city, and thrust them into yonder prison, erected by the treasure of this nation. There they remained until Friday, the 21st instant, when nearly fifty of them having been purchased by the infamous "Hope H. Slatter," who headed the mob at the jail on Tuesday, were taken in daylight from the prison to the railroad depôt, and from thence to Baltimore, destined for sale in the far South, there to drag out a miserable existence upon the cotton and sugar plantations of that slave-consuming region.

The scene at the depôt is represented as one which would have disgraced the city of Algiers or Tunis. Wives bidding adieu to their husbands; mothers in an agony of despair, unable to bid farewell to their daughters; little boys and girls weeping amid the general distress, scarcely knowing the cause of their grief. Sighs and groans and tears and unutterable agony characterized a scene at which the heart sickens, and from which humanity shrinks with horror. Over such a scene, that fiend in human shape, Slatter, presided, assisted by some three or four associates in depravity, each armed with pistols, bowie-knife, and club. Yes, Sir, by virtue of *our* laws, he held these mothers and children, these sisters and brothers, subject to his power, and tore them from all the ties which bind mankind to life, and carried them south, and doomed them to cruel and lingering deaths.

Sir, do you believe that these members of our body, who stubbornly refuse to repeal those laws, are less guilty in the sight of a just and holy God than Slatter himself? We, Sir, enable him to pursue his accursed vocation, and can we be innocent of those crimes? * How long will members of this

* While Mr. Giddings was speaking, a letter was laid upon the table before him, from which the following extract is taken:

"Among the unfortunate slaves who were lately recaptured, was a brother and three sisters, mulattoes, all very moral and religious. The girls, one in

House continue thus to outrage humanity? How long will the people themselves remain partakers in this enormous wickedness, by sending to this hall men who can here speak of their association with these Heaven-daring crimes in the language of ribald jesting? If other members sanction and approve such torture, far worse than ordinary murder, *I will not.* It is unbecoming a Christian people; it is unsuited to the age in which we live. Why, Sir, what a spectacle do we present to the civilized world? Yesterday, we assembled with the citizens of the district, in front of this capitol, to rejoice and sing in honor of the people of France, many of whom offered up their lives to attain the liberty which we ourselves enjoy. While we were thus collected together, and singing the soul-stirring Marseilles hymn, and shouting praises to our brethren who, on the other side of the Atlantic, have achieved their freedom, and driven their monarch from his throne and country, a different scene was witnessed on the avenue before us, where some fifty slaves, destined for the southern market, were marched to the railroad depôt. The clanking of their chains, their sighs and groans, mingling with our songs and shouts of praise *in favor of liberty*, ascended to heaven, and entered the ear of the God of the oppressed. Yes, Sir, while we were thus professing our admiration of freedom, we, who now sit in this hall, were, at that moment, sustaining a slave market in this city, far more shocking to the feelings of humanity than can be found in any other part of the civilized world. And, Sir, gentlemen in their zeal to uphold the slave-trade in this district, propose to strike down the freedom of debate in this hall, consecrated to free discussion, and even to hang members who dare speak in favor of liberty. I refer to the remarks of the gentleman from Ten-

---

particular, is very fair and pretty. The brother was hired by Mr. ———, as a coachman, and it is said his employer offered a large sum for the purpose of preventing them from being sacrificed to the basest of purposes; but it was in vain; for the fiends were too avaricious, and they were carried away by night to Baltimore. It is said that a *gentleman* offered a thousand dollars for one of the girls." (There is no doubt of the perfect accuracy of this statement.)

nessee, (Mr. Haskell,) who is reported to have said in his speech, on Wednesday, as follows:

"Now a strange state of things was presented here. Members of this body, as he believed, and felt ready to charge, had been engaged, by the course of conduct they pursued on this floor and out of this hall, in the deliberate attempt to scatter the seeds of insurrection and insubordination, if not rebellion, among the slaves in this district. Men on this floor, under the garb of philanthropy and love of human liberty, had been endeavoring to perpetrate felonies, for which they ought to swing as high as Haman. He spoke the plain truth. He was willing to have his words measured, and he held himself responsible for the language he used. An attempt had been made on this floor to abolish slavery in the District of Columbia in the form of law, if they could, and in violation of the Constitution; and, baffled and foiled in that, these mock philanthropists were now, as he believed before God, attempting to abolish slavery in this district, by inciting the negroes to leave their masters.

"Mr. Haskell (continuing) charged that the conduct of these men, their language on this floor and out of this House, had been such as to produce this state of things, — a disposition to insurrection and rebellion among the slaves in this district. He held in his hand a resolution which he intended to move, and which he should move, by way of amendment, when this House entertained the resolution of the gentleman from Massachusetts, having for its object an inquiry into the conduct of these members, and, if they were found guilty, their expulsion from this body, as unworthy to hold seats on this floor."

The gentleman charges me with uttering sentiments on this floor, and out of this House, which have tended "to excite the slaves to rebellion, and to produce *this state of things*," by which I suppose he means their attempt to escape from slavery. For doing this, he thinks I "ought to hang as high as Haman;" and that the House ought to expel me for thus daring to give utterance to the honest sentiments of my heart.

Mr. Speaker, I will inform that gentleman, with all sincerity, that it is too late in the day to attempt to seal the lips of northern representatives in regard to the slave-trade, or on any other subject which comes before this body. I give notice to that gentleman, and to all others, that I shall speak just what I think on any and on every subject which comes before us. It is my intention to call things by their right names, and to speak, so far as I am able, in such direct, plain, and simple language, as to be understood.

It is true that the freedom of speech has been put down in this hall; it was for years trampled under foot by the slave power. I sat here during several sessions of Congress in degrading silence, and often listened to the supercilious tirades of southern members against myself, and against the advocates of liberty, while I was not permitted to reply. The slave power then reigned triumphant in this body. Sir, it is well known that, for asserting in this House some of the plainest principles of constitutional law, I was censured and driven from my seat here. But, thank God, after years of toil and effort, we have regained the freedom of debate. And now, I say to the slave-holders present, *we shall never again surrender it.* When members here shall cease to enjoy the privilege of speaking their minds, and representing the views and wishes of their constituents, my people will send some other man to Congress, or they will cease to be represented in this body.

Why, Sir, does the gentleman from Tennessee expect that I am to ask him or any other member *what* I shall say, *when* I shall speak, and *how* I shall say it? Do southern gentlemen suppose they can bring into this body the practices which they pursue on their plantations? Sir, they forget the theatre on which they are acting. They forget that they are among *freemen.* They surely think themselves among slaves, accustomed to crouch and tremble at their frowns. This hall is not the place for the display of supercilious dictation. Such traits of character are but poorly suited to the dignity of legislation. They will not be submitted to by gentlemen who know their rights, and have the spirit to maintain them. What, Sir, are we to sit here and listen to such language? I would advise the gentleman from Tennessee to read the Constitution of the United States; to study the spirit and genius of the government of which he is a member; to learn the privileges and duties, and endeavor to catch the spirit and inspiration of an American statesman. His thoughts will then be free as the winds of heaven, and he will look with ineffable contempt upon all efforts to restrain the freedom of debate. When this proposition to restrain the freedom of debate shall be published in my district, the school-boys will laugh at its absurdity.

But the gentleman thinks that my language in this hall has excited a love of liberty among the slaves. As to that I have made no inquiry. If it has imparted to them information, or inspired them with a desire to regain the rights which God has given them, I shall rejoice at it. I would not desist from speaking truth in this hall, if all the slaves in the universe were listening to me. No, Sir; if I had the power I would, from this forum, give to every slave south of Mason and Dixon's line a perfect knowledge of his rights. I would explain to their understanding the oppression that weighs down their intellects and shuts out truth from their comprehension. I would explain to them the outrage which has robbed them of their humanity, reduced them to the level of chattels, and subjects them to sale like brutes in the market. Could my voice be heard by them from this hall, I would teach them that they came from the hand of the same Creator as ourselves, and were endowed by Him with the same inalienable rights as those who now lord it over them. I would inform them that they are our brethren, and candidates for the same immortality with us.

Mr. GAYLE, of Alabama, desired to inquire of the gentleman from Ohio, (Mr. Giddings,) if these sentiments were not now uttered in the hearing of slaves?

Mr. GIDDINGS replied, that the gentleman from Alabama perhaps could answer that question more accurately than himself. I (said he) know not whether such persons be present. I hope there may be some to hear me; and if the utterance of such truths can teach them how to release themselves from bondage, God knows their redemption draws nigh. No, Sir; I would say to gentlemen, "go tell your slaves how choleric you are, and bid your bondmen tremble," but come not here and threaten to expel and to hang the representatives of freedom for giving utterance to the sentiments which they entertain. Gentlemen may play the tyrant on their plantations, hold their fellow men in subjection, may cause his lacerated flesh to quiver with the lash, but they shall not impose silence upon northern men, nor dictate the language we shall use on this floor.

Mr. GAYLE inquired if the gentleman alluded to him when he spoke of the flesh being made to quiver by the lash? He never used the lash on his slaves. They would not accompany him here, because they were afraid the abolitionists would skin them.

Mr. GIDDINGS resumed. The gentleman's statement shows to what depths of degradation slavery can reduce the immortal mind. He has been so far successful as to teach his slaves to hug their chains, and to shudder at the thought of being free. He has driven from their minds their instinctive love of liberty. These facts show the most horrid characteristic of that institution. It blots out the intellect, and reduces man, created in the image of his God, to the level of brutes. That gentleman dare not teach his slaves to read the Word of God. It would subject him to punishment in the penitentiary of his State were he to do it. Nor need we go to Alabama to find such laws. If, Sir, you pass over the river (Potomac) lying before our windows, and on its southern bank attempt to kindle in the dormant intellect of a slave the hope of a future life, by teaching him to read the Holy Scriptures, you will be liable to an incarceration in the penitentiary of that Old Dominion, of which we hear so often and so much in this House. Yes, Sir, it is regarded as a *crime* to teach a slave to read the Word of God in this Christian land — this land of sabbaths, and ministers, and bibles, and slaves.

But the gentleman from Tennessee is not the only member here who has assailed my right to speak in this hall the dictates of my own judgment. A gentleman from North Carolina (Mr. Venable) complains that I stated in this hall that the laws of Ohio allowed every person to defend his natural right to life and liberty; and that if a slave on Ohio soil should, in defending himself, slay his master, we would not hang him to gratify the slave-holders of the South; and that I declared "I would call him a gallant fellow." Now, Sir, in slave States they have a statute law depriving the slave of the right of self-defence. Not so with us. Ohio has no such law, and never will have. The defence of those rights to life and liberty with which our Creator has endowed us, I regard as a solemn duty, and look upon every man who complies with this obligation as worthy of my respect. In discussing the legal rights of the slave, I felt it my duty to inform the masters of this principle. But the gentleman seems to think that the slaves will learn what I said, will know their rights, and being once informed of their duty to defend their liberty when they get on to free soil, he apprehends they will do it. Now, I shall certainly regard myself as fortunate if my poor remarks shall have enlightened both master and the slave. And I now repeat, that we would not hang a slave for such an act were it to please all the slave-holders in Christendom. I wish, however, to appeal to the conscience of that gentleman. I understand that he belongs to the Methodist church. Now, the great and good founder of that denomination (John Wesley) has declared slavery to be "the sum of all villanies."

Mr. VENABLE said the gentleman was mistaken, that he was a *Presbyterian.*

Mr. GIDDINGS resumed. Can it be that the gentleman is a Presbyterian, and yet holds slaves, and regards slavery a blessing? Would he sit down on the Sabbath with his slave, who is also a brother in Christ, of the Presbyterian faith, at the sacramental board, commemorative of the Lord's supper and sacrificial death; partake with him of the bread and the wine, of the body and the blood of a crucified Redeemer; and on Monday sell that brother, bearing the image of his God, for paltry lucre, and yet claim to be a Presbyterian? No, Sir, I feel constrained to deny such an absurdity. It cannot be so. No man can be a true Presbyterian who barters his fellow men for gold, or who transforms man into chattels, and shuts out the Scriptures of truth from his brother in the church.

Why, Sir, I can scarcely realize that I live in the nineteenth century, or that I am in a Christian land. Do we exist in an age when even our holy religion is thus perverted to the support of slavery? Are we to be told that religion and slavery walk hand in hand; that virtue and vice have commingled; that purity and crime have blended together?

Mr. VENABLE begged to say to the gentleman from Ohio, as he had alluded to the subject of religion, that he was no Methodist, though he highly respected that sect. He was a Presbyterian; but he would refer the gentleman to the Epistle of Paul to Philemon, from which that gentleman would learn that Paul did not tell servants to run away from their masters, but to return back to them. When the gentleman from Ohio could bring evidence to show that he was better, wiser, and holier than Paul, he would listen to his counsels, and not till then.

Mr. GIDDINGS resumed. I think the gentleman is too much excited for a Presbyterian. By what authority does he pronounce Onesimus a *slave?* Was he not a hired servant, such as we of the North employ and pay for their labor? Did Paul direct that he should return to slavery? No; he commanded that he should be received as a *brother*. But the gentleman from North Carolina has attempted to press St. Paul into a justification of slavery. What is slavery, and what are its effects? Why, Sir, a gentleman, (Mr. Clay,) once a member in the other end of the capitol, and a slave-holder, of accurate information, some years since stated that the average life of slaves, after entering upon the sugar plantations, was only five years, and upon the cotton plantations only seven years. That is to say, they are driven so hard at labor as to destroy the lives of the whole of them every five and seven years, upon an average. Now, Sir, is it not as much murder to destroy the life of our fellow man, by a torture of five or seven years, as it would be to strike him down at a blow? Yea, is not this prolonged torture a refinement in cruelty? I have no time to refer to the licentiousness, or indeed to the almost total obliteration of moral sentiment, to be found not only among slaves, but among all slave-holding communities.

Why, Sir, it is said, and I believe with perfect truth, to be no unusual thing for slave-holders to sell their own children as slaves. Brothers are said to traffic in the bodies of their fathers, sons, and daughters. Such crimes have no names. Yet the gentleman from North Carolina represents St. Paul as approving, and even enjoining slavery, with all its concomitant iniquities. Well might the great and good Wesley denounce slavery as the "sum of all villanies," for it is so in fact. It is not merely *murder*, for it takes life by a slow and regular process of torture. It is not ordinary *theft*, for it steals not only the property and the treasure of men, but it takes from them their intellectual enjoyments. It is not merely *robbery*, for it robs man of himself. The essential elements of all these crimes, in their most aggravated form, are comprehended in the term SLAVERY. And Scripture is quoted to justify such appalling wickedness. Sir, if I entertained such sentiments, I would abjure my religion, and turn Pagan. These arguments are put forth by *Presbyterians*. The general assembly of that church, some thirty years since, declared slavery to be "inherently sinful;" and, of course, it must be offensive to God, and to all good men.

But to return to those gentlemen who have threatened to expel me, to drive me from this district, to hang me for speaking of slavery as I regard it. I wish to inform them distinctly that, before I conclude what I have to say, I intend to give utterance to the solemn convictions of my judgment in regard to that institution; and, if they do not wish to listen to me, they will of course *be at perfect liberty to leave the hall.*

And now I wish to address a few words to gentlemen in regard to the slave-trade of this district. We all know the fate of slaves taken from this country to the slave-consuming regions, the Golgotha of this nation.

We are all conscious that the fifty persons taken by Hope H. Slatter from this city last Friday, are doomed to cruelty, torture, and premature graves. They have gone to painful and lingering deaths; and the momentous question comes home to each of our consciences, on whom rests "the deep damnation of their taking off?" There is but one answer. All who have aided or lent their influence to sustain the law of Congress which authorizes such infernal deeds. Nor is that all;

those of us who have failed to exert our powers to repeal these disgraceful laws are guilty for our neglect. I dare not claim to be exempt myself. We are all involved in the dread responsibility. History will record the fact, and transmit it to unborn ages, that *we*, the members of this House, at this age of light and knowledge, and of civil liberty, maintain and keep in force a law for selling fathers and children, mothers and tender babes, to torture and to legalize murder. In the day of retribution, will not the blood of those victims stain our garments?

Our guilt is daily increasing. Every victim of this barbarous law enhances our responsibility. The gentleman from North Carolina exults that his State was not concerned in the importation of slaves, and connects the "horrors of the middle passage" with New England cupidity. But does that in any way relieve the gentleman from his own responsibility in supporting the slave-trade in this district? He, Sir, has constantly opposed the abolition of this infamous traffic, carried on here before our own eyes, and attended with greater mental suffering than was the African slave-trade in the last century. He must answer for his own sins.

I admit that a fearful responsibility rested upon those of our New England fathers who encouraged or engaged in that "execrable commerce." I justify them not. I condemn them for it. There is but one excuse for them. They lived in a darker age than the present. The force of truth, the rights of man, and the claims of God, were not brought to bear upon the people of that age in the concentrated rays with which they have since pierced the intellectual darkness which then locked up the sensibilities of our race. New England has long since, not only abandoned the slave-trade, but she has discarded the institution of slavery, and proclaimed her hostility to all oppression. The sin of our fathers ought not to be visited upon their children. But, Sir, would that gentleman extenuate the guilt of the present age, by showing that even greater crimes were committed by those who have gone before us? They must answer for the sins which they committed. *We are responsible for our own acts.* And when that gentleman boasts that North Carolina did not engage in the African slave-trade, he should bear in mind that his is a slave-breeding State; that one portion of her people get their wealth by raising and selling their fellow men; that the slaves thus reared in this Christian land must, of necessity, be far more intelligent than those of Africa, and capable of far greater suffering; that the slave-trade now carried on in that State, actually inflicts more distress and heart-rending anguish, in proportion to the number of its victims, than did the foreign slave-trade. Therefore I would advise the gentleman not to boast of the moral purity of his people. They are *now,* at this time, engaged in crimes that would have shocked the humanity of the African slave-dealers of the last century.

We have been assured repeatedly, during this debate, that if we continue thus to express our detestation of slavery, that the southern States will secede from the Union. Now I would advise gentlemen to spare us from those threats. During half a century, the slave-power has controlled this government; holding northern rights and northern interests subject to the burdens of slavery, which has constantly sat like an incubus upon the whole nation, paralyzing our energies, and retarding our prosperity.

The Union of our fathers has long since been abandoned, discarded, and trampled upon by this slave-power. Texas has been forced upon us, in violation and in total subversion of the Constitution. In direct and palpable conflict with its most obvious provisions, slave-holding foreigners from Texas now sit in both Houses of Congress, and vote in the enactment of laws to govern the rights and control the interest of northern freemen. A war has been waged, two hundred millions of dollars expended, and eighty thousand lives have been sacrificed, for the purpose of extending slavery, to confirm the slave power in its control of the government; and now we are threatened with a separation of the slave States from our Union. Of such an event, *I have neither hopes nor fears.* Dependent on us for protection, for support, indeed for the very existence of slavery, I have no expectation nor apprehension that they will abandon us to our best interests, and throw themselves upon the tender mercies of their slave population, who for ages have received nothing at their hand but oppression and outrage. No, Sir; when I shall see a condemned criminal upon the gallows, with the rope about his neck, and fastened to the beam above, become impatient, and, in order to "dissolve the Union" between himself and this world, jump from the scaffold before the drop is permitted to fall, then, Sir, and not till then, will I believe that the slave States may hasten the terrible judgments that await them by seceding from the Union. Not till then will I believe that they can be driven from us.

The gentleman from Virginia, (Mr. Bayley,) as he has often done before, has attempted to show that what he calls the "abolition movement" originated in England, and is now kept up by British emissaries, both in this Hall and through the country. The gentleman has not the merit of originating the charge. It was made many years since by a member from his State, (Mr. Wise). I suppose there can be no misunderstanding as to the terms he uses. When he speaks of the "abolition movement," I presume he refers to the efforts now making to extend human liberty, to restore to mankind their natural rights, to strike off the chains of slavery from the limbs of its victims, to stop the accursed traffic in human flesh to which I have already alluded. That is what we all understand by his language. It is difficult to trace out the origin of these movements in favor of liberty. Some trace them back to the time when the "sturdy barons of England" extorted from King John the great charter of English liberty. Others, to the revolution under Cromwell; and others date it from the commencement of our own revolution of 1776. If the gentleman, however, refers particularly to philanthropic efforts in behalf of the oppressed colored people, I deny the correctness of his history. The first effort in favor of the equal rights of the colored man, put forth in England, so far as my knowledge extends, was by Granville Sharpe, in 1757, for the release of

"Jonathan Strong," a slave to David Lisle. The slave was liberated on habeas corpus, and the owner, in the true slave-holding spirit, challenged Sharpe to mortal combat for thus daring to maintain the rights of humanity. Sharpe continued his efforts until joined by Wilberforce and other distinguished philanthropists, whose labors did not cease until their final triumph.

But long previous to that time, — indeed, as early as 1646, — the good people of Massachusetts, in general court, had taken measures to restore certain colored persons brought from Africa to this country as slaves, and actually sent them back to their homes. If, therefore, the gentleman refers to efforts in behalf of colored men, Massachusetts is entitled to the honor of first moving on the subject of abolition. The legislature of that State was the first on this continent to give universal and equal liberty to all her people. Her abolition act, I believe, dates as far back as 1780. The people of the other New England States, and of New York, New Jersey, and Pennsylvania, soon became abolitionists, and repealed their slave laws, and gradually restored liberty to their slaves. All this, and much more, was done in this country during the last century; while the gentleman dates the movement in England subsequent to 1824, and in this country as late as 1832.

But I wish to call the attention of the gentleman to a very powerful anti-slavery paper, drawn up by one Thomas Jefferson, in 1776, in which he asserts it to be a "self-evident truth" that "men are created equal, and are endowed by their Creator with certain inalienable rights, among which are life and liberty." Now I desire to know whether he charges Mr. Jefferson with being operated upon by British influence? Was John Hancock, and the other members of that Congress, acting under British influence when they signed the Declaration of Independence? At that period, Virginia's noblest sons were the boldest advocates of freedom. "Give me liberty or give me death," was the soul-stirring sentiment of her eloquent Henry, and the watchword of her gallant sons who bled at Yorktown. Were they excited by British influence? At the close of the war, James Madison, when he penned the address of the Congress of the Confederation, asserted that "it had ever been the pride and boast of America, that the rights for which she contended, *were the rights of human nature.*" Sir, if it be true that the spirits of those great men, from the regions of exalted intelligence, are observers of our discussions in this hall, what sensations must they have felt while that member stood here, in the presence of the nation, advocating oppression, degradation, and slavery? If capable of mortification and chagrin, methinks they must have turned from the scene with loathing and abhorrence. But, Sir, the gentleman says it is "British influence" that encourages this spirit of liberty. Yes, Sir, he would charge Benjamin Franklin with being under British influence, when he acted as president of the first abolition society in the United States, and signed the first abolition petition ever presented to Congress. And the eccentric Randolph was under British influence when, in this hall, with scathing eloquence, he denounced the "inhuman traffic in slaves" then carried on in this district, and which has produced the present discussion.

But, Mr. Speaker, those great men of Virginia have passed away, and with them the glory and the moral power of the "Old Dominion" has departed. Then she stood first among the States of this Union. Now she has fallen, and "there is none so poor as to do her reverence." In the words of Thomas J. Randolph, she "has become a vast menagerie, where men are reared for market, like oxen for the shambles."

The gentleman, however, dates the commencement of what he calls the abolition excitement in the year 1832. Why he has fixed that as the time, he has failed to explain, and I am wholly unable to conjecture. At that period, the slave power controlled this government, and directed its energies almost exclusively to the building up of the slave interests of the South. Its influence was even prostituted to the support of the coastwise slave-trade. Soon after this, our army was employed, in company with bloodhounds, to arrest fugitive slaves in Florida, and deliver them to their masters. The treasure of our people was appropriated to these disgraceful purposes. No member of this body then sounded the alarm, or called the attention of the people to the fact that the Constitution was outraged, their rights held in contempt, and the nation disgraced for the benefit of slavery. The political horizon was overcast, and all was dark and dreary.

It was at such a time that Massachusetts sent to this hall a man who had mingled with the heroes and patriots of the Revolution, who had drank deep at the fountains of learning, and had caught the inspiration of the better days of our Republic. His talents, his experience, his reputation were equal to the task which lay before him. With a spirit of self-sacrifice, with ceaseless vigilance, with unrivalled powers, he entered upon the work of reformation. A portion of the representatives of Virginia arrayed themselves against him, and advocated the cause of oppression and slavery, in opposition to the doctrines of Jefferson, of Madison, of Washington, and of Henry. The right of petition had been stricken down; the freedom of debate had been scouted from this hall; and when that world-honored champion of freedom, venerable for his age, his learning, and his virtues, stood forth in this body, and maintained the right of the people to ask for the abolition of slavery and the accursed slave-trade in this district, a representative from Virginia assailed him and those who advocated the rights of man, and charged them with acting under "British influence." The gentleman from Virginia now merely repeats the charge, and calls it *his own* thunder. Let him use it, if it amuses him; I am sure it will be harmless to others.

The gentleman has spoken of the deception of the British government, in regard to philanthropy. Upon that subject I neither attack nor defend the government of England. My duties are with my own government, — to correct its abuses, to improve its administration, to raise its character, and to maintain its honor and integrity. Nor am I able to discover how the hypocrisy practised by British statesmen can diminish the responsibility under which we are placed. If, in the abolition of slavery they acted hypocritically, it can in no degree extenuate our guilt in maintaining the slave-trade here. The breeding of slaves, and the traffic in human flesh, carried on in the gentleman's district, is no less offensive to God, or hateful to good men, because British statesmen may have acted deceitfully. They must answer for their acts; we for ours.

The tone and manner of the gentleman was not unexpected to me. Excessive vanity and supercilious vaporing seem to constitute a part of the slave-holding character; it grows out of the intercourse between master and slave. On this point, Mr. Jefferson, in his "Notes on Virginia," says:

"The whole commerce between master and slave is a perpetual exercise of the most boisterous passions, the most unremitting despotism on the one part, and degrading submission on the other.

"The man must be a prodigy who can retain his manners and morals undepraved by such circumstances."

All who were present to hear his speech on Friday last, will admit that the gentleman from Virginia is *no prodigy.*

The gentleman has seen fit to eulogize the institutions of his State. In reply, I will only say that, could the liberties and oppression of the people of Virginia be brought into common stock, and then each were to draw out his aliquot proportion of slavery and of liberty, it would be pronounced at once the most barbarous and oppressive government upon earth. Suppose that gentleman, by such equitable apportionment, were to receive, at the hands of an inhuman overseer or master, a scourging, until his lacerated flesh should hang in quivering shreds, or to see his daughter torn from his embrace, and sold at public auction for nameless purposes, should we, in such case, hear him extol the humanity of his native State? Were he to receive his share of the oppression and misery and torture inflicted upon the slaves of that State, he would, methinks, be the last man hereafter to advocate a system which has been discarded by the Mohammedan barbarians of Algiers and of Tunis. I would not have referred to Virginia or her institutions, had not the gentleman dragged them before the House, and forced them into debate.

The gentleman, however, says that abolitionists look to the

insurrection of the slaves. Sir, who does not look to that inevitable result, unless the slave States remove the heavy burdens which now rest upon the down-trodden and degraded people whom they oppress? Is there a slave-holder who can shut his eyes to this sure *finale* of slavery? And why should we not expect it? Were we thus oppressed, outraged, and abused, would we not use all the means which God and nature have placed within our power, to remove such evils? Would not duty to ourselves, to our offspring, to God, and to humanity, demand, that we should rise with one accord, and hurl our oppressors from us? Can we justify our fathers of the revolution in their patriotic struggle for political freedom, and then turn round and condemn the slaves of the South for breaking the chains which hold them in physical bondage, and in intellectual degradation? No, Sir; no lover of justice, no unbiassed mind, could blame them for asserting and maintaining their inalienable rights. When that time comes, as come it must, we shall say with Jefferson, "the Almighty has no attribute that will permit him to take side with the slave-holder." Thus spoke the sage of Monticello; and I will merely add, that with him "I tremble for my country when I reflect that God is just, and that his justice cannot sleep forever."

MEXICAN WAR.*

DUTY OF STATESMEN TO FORETELL POLITICAL EVENTS — PROPHECY FULFILLED — EXECUTIVE FAITH VIOLATED IN THE SURRENDER OF OREGON — CONTROL OF THE GOVERNMENT BY THE SLAVE POWER — THE EFFECT OF ANNEXING FOREIGN TERRITORY.

[The author had taken strong grounds upon the resolution to terminate the joint occupation of Oregon, having asserted that the Executive would surrender all north of the forty-ninth parallel of latitude, and that the Executive could not be driven into a war with England. For these assertions he was violently assailed by the press of both parties. Having witnessed the fulfilment of his prophecy, he embraced the opportunity to vindicate his positions in the following speech.]

Mr. CHAIRMAN, — I am now called on to vote for this bill, authorizing the Secretary of the Treasury to issue notes to the amount of five millions dollars to carry on the war against Mexico, in which we are unfortunately engaged. That war was commenced without my vote, and against the dictates of my judgment, and of every feeling of my heart. I believed it wrong, unjust, and criminal, and I am now unwilling to make myself a party to it, or in any degree to participate in its guilt. I shall at all times be glad to vote for any appropriation to withdraw the army from Mexico, and to stop the work of bloodshed. But I shall vote against this bill and every other intended to aid in carrying forward the work of devastation in Mexico.

---

* Speech on the Bill to authorize the issuing of Treasury Notes to supply the present wants of the Government. Delivered in Committee of the whole House on the state of the Union, July 14, 1846.

But I rise at this time for the purpose more particularly of vindicating myself from all responsibility for the present state of our public affairs; and to expose the errors and the policy which has involved our nation in this unholy war.

I regard it the duty of statesmen to forewarn the people of approaching danger. Nor is it difficult, generally, to foretell great political events with almost perfect accuracy. I was somewhat surprised to hear my colleagues on the opposite side of the House complain of the Executive for having surrendered to Great Britain so large a portion of our territory in Oregon. Indeed, I think those gentlemen have disregarded the instruction which they might have drawn from the past history of our government. Had they referred to it, they would have found that it has been for half a century controlled by the slave power. They and I have seen the slave-holding influence plunge the nation into the Florida war. We have seen the leading policy of the nation changed as often as the views of southern men have altered. At the bidding of the slave power we have fostered banks; and, at the dictation of the same influence, we have discarded and opposed them. When bidden by the potent voice of the South, we have imposed heavy duties upon imported manufactures, in order to encourage domestic labor; and then again, under the same guidance, has our policy been changed so as to approximate towards free trade. In short, Sir, for fifty years, we have constantly changed and shifted our sails upon the ship of state, in order to catch the changing southern breeze.

From these important facts, statesmen are bound to draw instruction. From them, my colleagues and other western gentlemen might have easily foretold the result of the Oregon controversy. For my own part, I have never, for a moment, regarded it as doubtful. On the 5th of January last, while the resolutions authorizing the President to give notice to the British Government for terminating the joint occupation of Oregon were under discussion, I felt it my duty to assure the House and the country that there was no possible danger of a war with England, in consequence of conflicting claims to that territory.

I was aware that the President, in his inaugural address, had declared our title to the whole of Oregon to be "clear and unquestionable;" that he had repeated the same declaration in his annual message. Yet, Sir, I felt confident that no danger to our peace need be apprehended. With this conviction resting upon my mind, I expressed my views in the following paragraph, taken from my remarks on that occasion. Speaking of the Executive, I said:

"The consequences of seizing upon 'the whole of Oregon' were not considered. Mr. Polk, in his inaugural address, and in his annual message, evidently overlooked the momentous effect which his twice-declared policy would produce upon the slave interest, to which he is indissolubly wedded. He and his cabinet and his party have made a fatal blunder. They will soon discover their error, and will recede from their position. With the same degree of confidence that I have in my own existence, I declare that they will, before the nation and the world, back out from their avowed policy, and will surrender up all that portion of Oregon north of the forty-ninth parallel of latitude."

Now, Sir, I refer to this extract, to show my colleagues and the House that any man who has studied the operations of the slave interest upon this government, may foretell its action whenever the interests of the "peculiar institution" are concerned. I was fully conscious that a war with England must prove the overthrow of slavery; and, although the Baltimore Convention and Mr. Polk had overlooked that most important consideration, I well knew that a distinguished senator, now in the other end of this capitol (Mr. Calhoun) would never be guilty of such a blunder. I was fully convinced that southern statesmen had at that time discovered the error into which the Executive had fallen, and that the whole force of their influence would be brought to bear in favor of peace with England at any sacrifice. And the subject being within the control of the President, I then assured the House and the country that he would give up such portion of Oregon as was necessary to secure peace, rather than subject the slavery of the South to the dangers of a war.

Now, Sir, I think, with these warnings from me, and with the experience of the past, western gentlemen should have foreseen the surrender of our territory by the Executive, which has recently taken place. Why, Sir, so clearly did I foresee it myself, that I designated the identical line which now divides our territory from that of England. I declared that the "President and his party would surrender all that part of Oregon lying north of the forty-ninth parallel of latitude." In saying this, I claim for *myself no uncommon* powers of perception. Conscious that the President would accept the first offer of a compromise which the British government should make, I had only to determine what that offer would be. I concluded that the selfishness of Great Britain would not prompt her to claim farther than to that parallel. In this, however, I was somewhat mistaken. It seems that she demanded the whole of Vancouver's Island. My error was in the estimate I placed upon the selfishness of England, and not as to the anxiety of Mr. Polk to arrange the controversy. For, as I have just remarked, I was sure he would accept the first offer, whatever it should be. The result has shown the perfect accuracy of my opinion. I will not pretend to say that it was not Mr. Polk's intention originally, to involve the country in a war with England. Far from it. I have no idea that the President or his Cabinet at that time had considered the effect which a war with England would have upon slavery; and, at the commencement of the present session, I believe he fully intended to bring the nation into conflict with that country, and would have done so, except for the advice of southern statesmen. We are, therefore, indebted to southern apprehensions for our peace with Great Britain, as well as to southern influence for our war with Mexico.

But our democratic friends were not alone deceived by this executive error and management. Many whig members of this body, and in the other end of the capitol, were apprehensive of a war, in consequence of the Oregon controversy. Our whig editors became alarmed at the indications of war, and represented to their readers that we were in danger of hostilities with Great Britain. I was determined to put such statements on the record as should show to the House and the country that I fully understood the management then going forward. I told our democratic friends, in explicit language, that they had been betrayed, and that Mr. Polk could not be kicked into a war for Oregon.* I stated my reasons for these assertions. I declared that a war with England would not only destroy slavery, but would ruin the Atlantic slave States; that Mr. Polk was a slave-holder, acting under the influence of the slave power, and would do no act by which the institution would be endangered. I further stated, "he would find means to give up a part, or even the whole, of Oregon, rather than subject slavery to the sure destruction which a war with England would bring upon it."

The perfect accuracy of my prediction is now manifest. I call attention to it for the purpose of impressing upon those who hear me, or who may read my remarks, the important fact that this government has been, and now is, controlled by the slave-holding power of the South. I therefore say to my democratic colleagues who have complained of the Executive for deceiving them in regard to Oregon, if you wish to understand what the action of Congress or the Executive will be on any given subject, go and consult the interests of the slave-holding South! learn the policy which southern statesmen think will best subserve their interests, and then rest assured that that course will be pursued. The eccentric Randolph never uttered a more obvious truth than that bitter reflection upon northern men, in which he declared that the South could always govern the North, "*not* (said he) *by our black slaves*, but by your *white slaves*."

And while on the subject of vindicating myself, I will refer to another important event which lately occurred in this hall. I refer to the repeal of the tariff of 1842. While speaking upon the annexation of Texas, on the 21st May, 1844, I said:

* This expression was actually used by Mr. Giddings in his speech upon Oregon; but he struck it out of the report as being too harsh to go before the public.

"Let us admit Texas, and we shall place the balance of power in the hands of the Texians themselves. They, with the southern States, will control the policy and the destiny of this nation. Our tariff will then be held at the will of Texian advocates of free trade. Are our friends prepared to deliver over this great national policy to the control of Texian representatives? Are the liberty-loving democrats of Pennsylvania ready to give up our tariff? To strike off all protection from iron and coal, and other productions of that State, in order to purchase a slave market for their neighbors, who, in the words of Thomas Jefferson Randolph, 'breed men for market like oxen for the shambles?'"

Sir, I said much more at that time on this subject, feeling, as I then felt, that the vote on Texas was to determine the annexation question of protection to northern labor. Some of my personal friends desired me to speak upon the tariff while it was lately under discussion in this House; but I felt that the time for that had gone by. I had endeavored to caution our friends against this disastrous result at a time when the vote of Pennsylvania might have saved the tariff of 1842, protected her interest in iron and coal, and saved many of her people from that distress and ruin which now awaits them.

It is now more than two years since I declared to this House and the country, that if Texas were admitted, "our tariff would be held at the will of Texian advocates of free trade." This declaration was fully verified on the second day of the present month. The fate of the bill to repeal the tariff of 1842 was admitted on all sides to depend on the degree of protection extended to the article of salt. It was well known, that unless the importation of that necessary of life should be subjected to a pretty fair duty, the representatives from New York would vote against the bill, and that their vote would defeat it. The friends of free trade, therefore, rallied their whole force in favor of protecting salt. With the aid of the two representatives from Texas they succeeded by only *one vote*. That vote secured the passage of the bill in this House, and fully verified my prediction made in May, 1844.

But the bill was carried through the Senate by a majority of only one vote, while both senators from Texas voted for it. Thus was my prediction most amply fulfilled. As I have already remarked, I then felt that the annexation of Texas was to determine the fate of northern industry. I regarded that as the time for the friends of free labor to rally in behalf of northern interests. But, Sir, opposition to that measure proved unavailing. The resolutions annexing Texas were passed. Her representatives took their seats on this floor; and the first important vote given by them was to strike down the most vital interests of Pennsylvania, of New Jersey, New York, and New England, as well as of the northwestern States; for I regarded the interest of those States as much involved as I do those of New England. I do not, in these remarks, charge southern men with inconsistency. I have no doubt that the cotton-growing interest, separately considered, may be benefited by free trade. It is opposed to all the other great interests of the country. In order to strike down the industry of the North, they must have the numerical force. To obtain this, they must extend the slave-holding territory. These objects were foreseen, and, indeed, they were openly avowed. The leading democratic organ in our State acknowledged these to be the objects of annexation as early as May, 1844. The Ohio Statesman, of that date, in an editorial article, declared that "the real objects of annexation were the perpetuation of slavery, and the political power of the slave States. Sir, their political power was extended, and we now see the consequences. The people of the free States will soon feel its weight, and will realize the loss they have sustained by their inactivity.

I would not impugn the motives or the judgment of northern whigs, who hold out to their constituents the hope that they may by their political efforts regain the ascendency, and restore the lost rights of the free States. I may, however, be permitted to say, that when they shall have watched the operations of the slave power as long and as carefully as I have; when they shall have made themselves as familiar with its influences, its designs, and the agencies used to effect its ulterior objects, they will change their views. I may be wholly wrong in my opinions. God grant that time may show my error. But I should fail to express the solemn convictions of my heart if I were not to say, in the most emphatic terms, that the rights and the interests of the free States have been sacrificed; and will not be regained until the North shall be awakened to its interests, its honor, and to its political duties.

I will now turn my attention more directly to the bill before us.

In calling upon the people to contribute a portion of their substance to carry on this war, it is proper that they should understand its objects and designs. We hear this demand coming up to us through the public press from every part of the nation. The people desire to understand the benefits which they are to derive from the expenditure of this immense amount of treasure. What good is to come of it? In what manner is the happiness of this nation or of Mexico to be increased?

Our army is to be enlarged by the appointment of some four or five major-generals, and towards a score of brigadier-generals, and an indefinite number of staff officers, and some thirty or fifty thousand rank and file. They are sent to Mexico, not to defend our own territory, nor to conquer that part of Mexico which lies east of the Rio Grande. General Taylor, with only three thousand troops, had driven the miserable apology for an army there marshalled under the Mexican flag beyond the Rio Grande, before we passed the law for raising any additional troops. He soon after crossed that stream with his forces, and took possession of Matamoras and other Mexican towns, and is now extending his conquest far into Mexico by direction of the President. Still the question recurs, What benefit are the people of the nation to derive from this conquest? What are the objects and designs of this war?

Sir, I was greatly rejoiced the other day on reading the report of the proceedings in the other end of the capitol, to find that a distinguished senator had, in a very emphatic manner, demanded "What were the objects of this war?" In my soul I regretted that this question had not been asked before war was declared. In this hall we did not enjoy the poor privilege of asking the question; we were literally *gagged* into the measure. On the day following the passage of the bill, I availed myself of an opportunity to declare the objects of the war, so far as they were then developed. I distinctly stated the object to be *conquest:* not merely conquest of the Mexican territory on this side of the Rio Grande, but conquest beyond that river! It is true that we are yet without official information as to the definite extent of the conquest intended. From certain anonymous publications in the government paper, and from official whisperings, however, we are led to judge that the intention of the President is, to obtain all that part of Mexico lying north of a line to be drawn from the Gulf of Mexico west to the Pacific Ocean, near the twenty-second degree of north latitude. This will give us the port of Tampico on the Gulf, and Mazatlan on the Pacific. It will add to our territory nearly twenty degrees of latitude, including a greater extent of country than that which now composes the twenty-four States lying east of the Mississippi, and will leave the Mexican government in possession of less territory than that which now composes three of those twenty-four States.

In short, Sir, if this object be accomplished, it will be regarded as the conquest of Mexico; for no gentleman who has read the history of our race will suppose that, having dismembered her of five sixths of her territory, we shall then desist from farther aggressions. That these are the real designs of the Executive no one will doubt, who has carefully consulted the signs of the times. It is true that this object may possibly be defeated by the united efforts of those who really desire to perpetuate the form of a free government; but, when I look at the apathy of the North upon the admission of the foreign slave State of Texas, by which our rights and our influence were torn from us, I can entertain but little hope. The slave power has thus far found means to accomplish all its ends; and I can scarcely hope that, with all the power of the government in its hands, it will be less successful in future. I know that the power in the North is great, and if properly directed, might overcome all the difficulties which tame submission to the slave influence has brought upon us. But at the moment when our rapidly increasing population is flowing into Oregon and California, — when free States are growing up in the former, and the latter gives promise of preparation for annexation, as a counterpart to Texas, — this vast southern country is grasped by this executive power, for the purpose of perpetuating our subserviency.

It is expected that the Mexican people will recede before the progress of our slave-holding population, so that slave States may be formed as fast as may be necessary to retain political influence in the southern hands.

This magnificent scheme of extending the slave-holding power, will doubtless succeed in part, at least, if not fully; and the free States, although possessing vastly greater population, will be in a minority in the Senate; and the free North will become the mere stakes for which southern gamblers will play their political games.

Here, Sir, a most important question is propounded to northern members: "What are our constituents, — what are the free States to gain by the state of things to which I have just alluded?" We are called on to vote the money of our people, to continue this policy of conquest, rapine, and bloodshed, which is to subvert their rights and their interests, disgrace our nation, and subject millions of our race to degradation and slavery. Yet, Sir, it is merely carrying out the designs of annexing Texas. The object of that act was the same as that of our present war. Territorial aggrandizement was the toy held up for the North to play with, while the slave-power was fastening its coils around us by extending and perpetuating the slave-holding interest. Indeed, such was the avowed object of those who conceived and urged forward that plan so fatal to the honor of our nation.

That eminent statesman, Henry Clay, foretold the war in which we are now engaged with perfect accuracy. He said, in his Raleigh letter, that "*annexation and war with Mexico are identical.*" He further described the effect, in the manner proposed, as "*fatal to the Union.*" A distinguished Senator in the other end of the capitol, (Mr. Benton,) was so deeply convinced of that result, that he declared the dissolution of the Union to have been the object of attempting to annex that part of Mexico which lies east and north of the Rio Grande, and between that river and Texas proper.

In March, A. D. 1843, an address to the people of the free States, in regard to the annexation of Texas, was published throughout the northern portion of the Union. It was signed by twenty members of this body, one of whom had been President of the United States, and four others have since been elected Governors of their respective States. They belonged to Maine, Massachusetts, Connecticut, New York, Ohio, and Michigan. Speaking of the prospect of annexing Texas, they say:

"We hold that there is not only no political necessity for it, no advantages to be derived from it, but that there is no constitutional power delegated to any department of the national government to authorize it. That no act of Congress or treaty for annexation can impose the least obligation upon the several States of this Union to submit to such an unwarrantable act, or to receive into their family and fraternity such misbegotten and illegitimate progeny. We hesitate not to say that annexation, effected by any act or proceeding of the Federal Government, or any of its departments, will be identified with dissolution. We not only assert that the people of the free States *ought* not to submit to it, but we say with confidence, they *will* not submit to it."

The signers of that address regarded the annexation of Texas merely as the commencement of a system of territorial aggrandizement for the extension of slavery, which was designed to swallow up and subvert the entire influence of the free States. The same idea was expressed in the letter of Mr. Clay, to which I have alluded, and has been often repeated on this floor. The fact has now become evident. The period is near when the people of the northern States will be compelled to make an open, undisguised resistance to this system of national robbery and extension of slavery, or to surrender all pretensions to equal rights with the slave States. There can be no evasion of this alternative.

We may withdraw our army from Mexico, cease to slay and murder her people, and desist from the purpose of robbing her of her territory; and yet preserve our country from the effects which this policy of extending the slave power must, if pursued, bring upon us. But our decision must soon be made. The representatives of the free States must surrender the interests of freedom to the control of those who have recently been, or now are, citizens of foreign governments, or they must make an open, frank, and manly resistance to this policy, which threatens the overthrow of our liberties.

The Union formed by our fathers, to which we are all attached, has ceased. It no longer protects our interests, our rights, or our honor. In saying this, I do but repeat the declaration of the legislature of my own State, and those of four others; I merely reiterate the sentiments of those twenty members of Congress, whose address I have just alluded to. I reiterate the opinions of Henry Clay, of Thomas Jefferson, and of many advocates of annexation, who admit there is no constitutional power to transfer the people of the free States to an association with those of Texas and of Mexico. But it is unnecessary to cite these authorities. The Constitution forbids the admission of any member on this floor, until he shall have been seven years a citizen of the United States. Here are members now present, who, six months since, were citizens of a foreign nation, — sworn to support a foreign government. They are admitted here by the terms of annexation, in most palpable violation of our compact of Union. Nor does it require the learning of the jurist, or the study of the statesman, to discover that this change of the law-making power is an overthrow of the Constitution in its most vital part. It having been done without authority, constitutes it a *revolution*. What I mean by revolution is, an unauthorized change of the essential elements of government, — whether such change be effected by violence and bloodshed, or by peaceful measures. The revolution in France consisted in the change of government from a monarchy to that of a republic. The anarchy and bloodshed with which it was attended, resulted from the change of government, or from the efforts put forth to effect that change; but they constituted no inherent part of the revolution itself. Had there been no resistance, no bloodshed; had the change been quietly submitted to, the revolution would have been the same; the monarchy would have been overthrown, and the republic would have been established. So in this revolution. If the people of the several States submit quietly to the overthrow of the old Union of 1787, and silently come into the new Union, with Texas and other new slave States, the change of the Constitution and of the Union will be the same as though it were attended with violence and bloodshed. And such change of the government, and of the parties to our Union, will be as really a *revolution* as it would be if the people of the States were forced into it by the murder of one half of their number. I therefore characterize this change of government a *revolution*. By what authority has this change been effected?

The great and leading maxim in all monarchies is, that *the monarch is the source of all power*. The fundamental maxim in our government is, that "the people are the source and fountain of all political power." Our State constitutions have been formed by the *people* of the several States. They have either adopted their State constitution by their own direct vote, or by the vote of their agents appointed for that express purpose. In most of those constitutions they have declared that "all powers not delegated by such constitution remain with the people." In the amendments to our Federal Constitution it is declared, that "all powers not thereby delegated are reserved to the States respectively, or to the people." Hence the emphatic language by which it was proclaimed, that "we the people of the United States do ordain and establish this Constitution," etc.

Now, Sir, it is surely unnecessary to show by argument that the Constitution, thus adopted by the people of the several States, cannot be changed in its fundamental principles by us, who were sent here merely to legislate under its existing provisions. We were not elected for that purpose; no powers were delegated to us thus to change the fundamental law; the exercise of such powers will be a usurpation of authority. The constables or sheriffs of the several States possess as much right, and as much constitutional power to meet and admit foreign nations to our Union, as we do. Their acts on this subject would be as binding upon the people of the several States as ours. On this point, I think there is a very general coincidence of opinion among reflecting men.

All, or nearly all, believe that the resolutions annexing Texas imposed no obligations upon the people of any State to unite with her. I believe the sentiments expressed by the members of this House, in the address to which I have referred, met with very general approbation among both political parties at the North. I then regarded the views expressed in it as correct, and I still think so. Those gentlemen looked upon the annexation of Texas as itself a dissolution of the Union. They regarded the subjecting the people of the several States to the legislation of foreigners, a total change or overthrow of one of the fundamental elements of the government. It is true that the passing of the resolutions of annexation was of itself void. They had no legal or constitutional effect whatever. They neither rendered the admission of the Texan representatives into this body legal or illegal, constitutional or unconstitutional. Those resolutions might have remained upon our statute book forever inoperative, and no one would have had just cause of complaint. It is the uniting of, at least, a portion of the States with Texas in the exercise of that most important act of sovereignty, *legislation*, and other governmental powers, which constitutes the real overthrow of the Constitution. Sir, if Congress could thus place a portion of its sovereign power in the hands of Texas, it could have placed the whole legislation of the nation at their disposal. It is a question of principle, and not of degree.

But it is said that by continuing to elect members of Congress to serve in this hall, with those from Texas, and by uniting with her in the election of President, the several States will give their tacit consent to the change of the Constitution, and to the change of parties to the Union, and will lose their right to dissent. I believe this doctrine to be correct. It is the only ground on which Louisiana can now claim to be a party to the Union.

This, Sir, is the situation into which this policy has brought us. It has thus broken up the Union of our fathers. It has left each State at liberty to continue its association with the others who belonged to our Union, or to refuse farther political connection with them. I will not predict the future action of the several States. They will probably continue as they now are; but the prestige of our Union has departed. We have abandoned the policy of peace, the encouragement of industry, the development of our resources, that adherence to public, to national morality, which alone can secure the respect of ourselves or of the Christian world. We have entered upon a career of conquest, of military force, which has proven the grave of all those republics that have gone before us. If we continue in this course, their fate will be ours. The same God who measured out their retributive justice still rules and reigns. His arm is not shortened, nor his laws changed. The penalty which He visited upon them must fall upon us, if we continue the policy in which we are now engaged.

THE PRESIDENT'S ANNUAL MESSAGE.*

ITS SOPHISTRY — ITS MISREPRESENTATIONS — ITS CONTRADICTIONS — NATIONAL PROSPERITY CHANGED TO A STATE OF WAR — CHARACTER OF THE WAR — OPPOSITION TO IT VINDICATED — WITHDRAWAL OF THE ARMY AND TENDER OF PEACE ADVOCATED.

[War had been declared in May, and its advocates, including the President, had used all their influence to induce a belief among the people that it was *just*, and a war of defence. The following speech was intended to show its real character, and to expose the devices of the President in attempting to disguise its real character.]

Mr. Chairman, — When we met in this hall, in December, 1844, our country was at peace with the whole world. Our agricultural, our manufacturing, and our commercial interests were in a state of unusual prosperity. The circulating medium of the nation was actively employed in the legitimate business of the country. Industry, in all its departments, yielded to the laborer a satisfactory compensation; and prosperity and contentment prevailed throughout the land. Unfortunately, an inordinate desire for territorial aggrandizement had seized upon one of our great political parties. It was opposed by the other with much zeal and ability. They foretold this war as a consequence of the annexation of Texas, and pointed out the present circumstances of our country, with almost as much precision as the pen of the historian can now record them. These predictions, however, were disregarded; and, in the short

---

* Speech on the resolutions to refer the President's Message. Delivered in Committee of the Whole House on the state of the Union, December 15, 1846.

space of two years, we find ourselves involved in a bloody and expensive war, with a large national debt already accumulated, and by the message before us proposed to be increased more than twenty millions of dollars at the present session. That debt is to rest like an incubus upon us and upon our children in coming years.

Sir, we have been hurried from a state of peace and prosperity to our present condition by that policy which through all past time has proven fatal to every popular government that has adopted it. No man who consults the past history of our race, and calmly views our present condition, can doubt that this policy of territorial aggrandizement must, if continued, result in the overthrow of this government. Had we remained satisfied with our territory as it was two years since, this war, with its vast debt, its thousands of human victims, its bloodshed, its crimes, and its disgrace would have been avoided. Let the President fill his annual messages with arguments endeavoring to cast the odium of this war on Mexico; let him and his cabinet do all in their power to excuse themselves, or to extenuate their own conduct; still every intelligent man in the nation must be fully conscious that the annexation of Texas has involved us in this war; and the country, and the civilized world, will hold the advocates of that measure responsible for all the crimes, the misery, and suffering which have, or which shall hereafter result from it. This war has become the subject of inquiry and discussion throughout the country. It is the absorbing topic in our social circles, in stage coaches, in railroad cars, and in steamboats; in our pulpits and religious meetings; in our political conventions, our State legislatures; in Congress, and in the Executive cabinet. It is discussed in the United States, in Mexico, and in Europe.

The people of the nation are demanding of the Executive a statement of the objects of this war. What are the ulterior designs of the government in its prosecution? Why are the people to be taxed to an indefinite amount for the support of an army occupied in carrying bloodshed and suffering to the heart of a sister Republic? What good are we, or the country, or posterity, to derive from this vast expenditure of blood and treasure on Mexican soil? What great and transcendant advantage is the human family to receive from the slaughter of our Mexican brethren, or from the death of our sons, our brothers, and friends, who fall by the sword or by disease in that pestilential climate? The public mind demands categorigal answers to these interrogatories, but the Executive has evaded them all. He returns for answer, in substance, that those who speak their honest sentiments in regard to this war, "lend aid and comfort to the enemy," and are, therefore, guilty of moral treason.

This undignified attack upon the freedom of speech must call forth an indignant rebuke from every friend of popular rights. It is at war with the first principles of a free government. It is unprecedented in the history of this nation. It can find no sanction, except in the despotisms of a darker age. It will meet with encouragement only from tyrants or usurpers, and will be quietly submitted to by none but the miserable sycophants of licentious power.

On looking over the message, the reader is at once struck with its *defensive* character. No person can read it without being conscious that the author felt the pressure of public sentiment, and was endeavoring to avoid public disapprobation. Indeed, had he been arraigned before the Senate on articles of impeachment, I think his defence would have embraced the leading features of this message. I should have expected the same sophistry and misrepresentation which characterize the communication now before us. It is mortifying to me, as an American citizen, to be compelled to use such language in reference to the message of the Chief Magistrate of our nation. But milder terms would not do justice to its contradictions or its perversions of truth. And the attempt on the part of the President to stifle debate in this hall, by declaring all to be traitors who oppose this war, demands of us an unrestrained expression of our honest sentiments.

I wish, however, at this time, to call the attention of the House and of the country to that paragraph in which he says:

"The existing war with Mexico was neither desired nor provoked by the United States. On the contrary, all honorable means were resorted to to avert it. After years of endurance of aggravated and unredressed wrongs on our part, Mexico, in violation of solemn treaty stipulations, and of every principle of justice recognized by civilized nations, commenced hostilities; and thus, by her own act, forced the war upon us."

This is an important assertion; and, if founded on truth, shows us engaged in a *defensive* war; we should, therefore, compare it with established facts, and ascertain if it be correct. We all are satisfied that no hostilities had taken place up to the time that our army left Corpus Christi and advanced to the Rio Grande. General Taylor, in his reports to the War Department, mentions no act of hostility on the part of Mexico until the 23d April last. He had, before that time, taken possession of "Brasos Santiago," where the Mexicans had established and long maintained a custom-house, at which our citizens had paid duties on all merchandise landed there, up to the very day that our troops took possession of it, and drove the Mexicans from it. With his army, General Taylor entered a country settled by Mexicans, where none but Mexican laws had ever been observed, and whose people had ever lived under the protection of the Mexican Government, to which they had always yielded a willing and patriotic support. They fled with their families at the approach of our army, who took possession of their fields and occupied their dwellings. General Taylor erected a battery, and mounted his cannon in such a position as to command the city of Matamoras. On the 6th of April, 1846, he wrote the Adjutant-General as follows:

"On our side, a battery for four eighteen-pounders will be completed, and the guns placed in battery to-day. These guns bear directly upon the public square of Matamoras, and within good range for demolishing the town."

Yet the President assures us that the "war was not *provoked*" by the United States.

On the 15th April, General Taylor informed the Department by letter, that "no hostile movement had then been made by the Mexicans." In the same letter he says:

"I considered the letter of General Ampudia sufficient to warrant me in blocking up the Rio Grande, and stopping all supplies for Matamoras."

Now, Sir, I have no hesitation in saying, there is not a civilized nation upon earth that would not have regarded these acts of our army, if done towards them, not merely as *provoking* war, but as *actual war*.

The next letter of General Taylor bears date 23d April, 1846, in which he says:

> "With a view to check the depredations of small parties of Mexicans on this side of the river, Lieutenants Dobbin, third infantry, and Porter, of the fourth infantry, were authorized by me, a few days since, to scour the country for some miles, with a select party of men, and *capture* or *destroy* any such parties as they might meet. It appears that they separated, and that Lieutenant Porter, at the head of his own detachment, surprised a Mexican camp, drove away the men, and took possession of their horses."

This was, I believe, the first hostile meeting of the military forces of the two governments.

The President says, Mexico "commenced hostilities;" General Taylor says that, by his order, "Lieutenant Porter surprised a Mexican camp, drove away the men, and took possession of their horses." I think no man will doubt that these acts of our troops were *hostile acts*. Yet we have, in this same letter of General Taylor, the official declaration that, "notwithstanding the alternative of war, presented by General Ampudia, no hostile movement had yet been made by his force." Now does General Taylor tell truth? If so, the President's assertion must be untrue, and those who confide in its accuracy will be deceived.

On the 26th April, General Taylor again writes:

> "I regret to report, that a party of dragoons, sent out by me on the 24th instant, to watch the course of the river above on this bank, became engaged with a very large force of the enemy, and, after a short affair, in which some sixteen were killed and wounded, appear to have been surrounded, and compelled to surrender."

He further adds: "Hostilities may now be considered as commenced." For thus attacking a superior force of Mexicans without orders, we are informed that Captain Thornton, who commanded the dragoons, was arrested, and tried by a court-martial; and the record of that proceeding may now be found in the War Department. Thus it appears, most conclusively, that the assertions of the President that "the war was not provoked by the United States," and that "Mexico commenced hostilities," are unfounded and untrue. Sir, I feel that the duty of exposing these misrepresentations of the Executive is unpleasant, but it is nevertheless imperative.

In order to sustain his important assertions, the Executive enters upon a most extraordinary argument to show that the "*Rio Grande" is the true* western boundary of Texas. But, before I proceed to expose the sophistry of that argument, and the further misrepresentation of facts connected with it, I will call the attention of the House to the geographical situation of the country, and to the location of the settlements "between the Nueces and the Rio Grande." At Corpus Christi, being on the west side of the mouth of the Nueces, is a settlement and a Texian custom-house. As you ascend that river, you find within its immediate valley occasional settlements; and, although the original line between Texas and Coahuila was established upon the river Aransas, being some forty miles east of this valley, yet the people on the Nueces united in the Texian revolt, and were associated with those of Texas in forming their government. It may therefore be said, that Texas extended her conquests so far as to include these settlements on the Nueces.

Proceeding west of this valley, you enter a barren desert of at least a hundred miles in width, on which there is no human habitation. Leaving this desert, and descending into the valley of the Rio Grande, you come to the Mexican settlements. Immediately on the coast, and some miles east of the mouth of the Rio Grande is the post of "Brasos Santiago," at which there was a Mexican custom-house and settlement; and, as you ascend the river for two thousand miles, you find plantations, towns, villages, and cities, composed of persons born under Mexican laws, and who have always lent a willing and unfaltering support to that government. These settlements compose a part of four Mexican States. Tamaulipas lies upon the Gulf, and formerly extended across the Nueces to the Aransas; but, as before stated, the settlements in the valley of the Nueces united with Texas, and, therefore, her present eastern boundary may be said to be on the desert heretofore described. Ascending the Rio Grande, you pass from Tamaulipas into Coahuila, then Chihuahua, and then into New Mexico. "Santa Fé," the capital of the last named State, being situated some thirty miles east of the Rio Grande, which the President represents as the western boundary of Texas.

I must pass over some of the arguments of the President, used to establish the Rio Grande as the boundary of Texas. They have been so often refuted, that I should trespass too far upon the patience of the House, were I to occupy time in exposing their fallacy; still the President seems to think that repetition will give them the force of truth. The pretence set up that we had title to the whole country east of the Rio Grande, prior to our treaty with Spain in 1819, by which we released all claim to it, can have no possible bearing upon the boundaries of Texas, which were defined by legislative act in 1834. By the treaty with Spain, we surrendered to her all claim to the territory west of the Sabine; and she released all claim to her territory east of that river, including Florida. Now, if that treaty be valid, then we have no possible claim to any portion of the country west of the Sabine. If it be void, then Spain has a just title to Florida. The argument is too absurd for serious refutation, yet it is brought forward for some purpose.

But the President, speaking of the Rio Grande, says:

"The Republic of Texas always claimed this river as her western boundary, and, in her treaty made with Santa Anna, in May, 1836, he recognized it as such."

Gentlemen should understand that the *republic* of Texas did not exist until she declared her independence; prior to that time, it was the *department* of Texas. When, therefore, the President says, "the Republic of Texas *always* claimed this river as her western boundary," he means merely that it has been so claimed since the *republic* of Texas has existed, that is, since 1836. I will not charge him with an intention to deceive by the use of such language.

As to the *treaty* with Santa Anna, I only wish to say, that any agreement or compact may be called a treaty, whether made between individuals or governments. It is in this view of language that the President speaks of the agreement with Santa Anna as a *treaty*. It was merely a personal undertaking of his own. He did not profess to act for the Mexican people, or for the government of Mexico. In consideration that he should be liberated and sent to Mexico in a government ship, he undertook to use his influence with his government to obtain an acknowledgment of the independence of Texas, with the Rio Grande as its boundary. The compact was never observed by Texas herself. General Lamar, her President, declared it *void*, and no individual of either of those governments, so far as I am informed, ever regarded it, as in any respect, binding upon Mexico. But it is now seized upon by the President, and by a course of sophistical reasoning, used to give color to the claim of Texas over the country east of the Rio Grande.

It is clear to the view of every man, that Texas must have acquired her title, if she had any to the territory in the valley of the Rio Grande, either by *treaty* or by *conquest*. She had no other mode of obtaining it. Neither the President nor his friends dare come to the point and assert, that Texas ever held it, or even claimed it by treaty or by conquest. Yet the President, in this message, attempts to show, by circumlocution and sophistry, what he dare not assert in direct terms.

Thus he goes on to say:

> "By the Constitution which Texas adopted in March, 1836, senatorial and representative districts were organized extending west of the Nueces."

True, her senatorial and representative districts did extend "west of the Nueces," so far as to include the settlements situated on its banks and in the valley of that stream. But did he intend to have the American people understand that they extended across the desert to the Rio Grande? If so, he must have intended to deceive them by making them believe what he dare not assert. He says further:

"The Congress of Texas, on the 19th of December, 1836, passed 'an act to define the boundaries of the republic of Texas,' in which they declared the Rio Grande, from its mouth to its source, to be their boundary, and by the said act, they extended their 'civil and political jurisdiction' over the country up to that boundary."

Yes, they declared "the Rio Grande from its *mouth to its source* their boundary;" the Mexican post and custom-house at Brazos Santiago, and all the Mexican settlements, towns, and villages, on the east side of that river, with the city of "Santa Fé," all, *on paper*, were declared to be within the republic of Texas. And the President adds, "and by said act" they extended their civil and political jurisdiction over the country up to that boundary. It was done "by said act," and not otherwise. It was not done by treaty, nor by force of arms. It was *printed on paper*, and that was the only mode in which Texas ever extended her jurisdiction over the Mexicans in the valley of the Rio Grande. She never sent an officer west of the desert to serve process, or to collect taxes, or to execute Texian laws. When she sent her troops there for the purposes of conquest, every man was killed or captured, or driven back across the desert. Yet the Executive evidently intended that the people should understand from this sophistry, that the Rio Grande was really the western boundary of Texas, and that she had asserted and actually maintained her jurisdiction over the people living in the valley of that stream. He dared not make such an assertion in plain and direct language. No friend of his on this floor has ever dared, or ever will dare, to make such an assertion. It would ruin the character of any man for veracity who should hazard such a declaration. Yet we see such undignified sophistication sent forth to the people by the Executive of the nation to induce them to believe what he dare not declare. But we have still more argument of the same character. He says:

"During a period of more than nine years, which intervened between the adoption of her Constitution and her annexation as one of the States of our Union, Texas asserted and exercised many acts of sovereignty and jurisdiction over the territory and inhabitants west of the Nueces."

Yes, she served process and collected taxes on the west bank of the Nueces. Perhaps she punished crimes committed there by people who acknowledged her jurisdiction. But no such act was done within a hundred miles of the Mexicans in the valley of the Rio Grande.

Among them property was protected, crimes punished, and the people governed by Mexican laws; and such had been the case, not merely for *nine years*, but from the first existence of the Mexican government without interruption. But the President continues:

> "She organized and defined the limits of counties extending to the Rio Grande. She established courts of justice, and extended her judicial system over the territory."

It is true, that *on paper*, she defined the Rio Grande as the limits of her counties. But did she ever maintain her jurisdiction? Did she enforce her laws in the valley of that river? Did she indict, arraign, or punish those who shot down her troops when sent there? Did any Mexican ever take the oath of allegiance to Texas? Did any Texian officer ever venture to arrest a man in that valley, or even to go there? Her judicial system was extended over that territory *on paper*, but not by Texian arms. He adds:

> "She established a custom-house, and collected duties, and also post offices and post roads in it."

I remarked some time since that Texas had established a custom-house at "Corpus Christi," on the west bank of the Nueces. That is conclusive evidence that she held actual possession of that part of the country. And so is the maintenance of a custom-house by the Mexicans at "Point Isabel," and another at Taos, east of Santa Fé, conclusive evidence that Mexico held possession of those parts of the country. And if Mexico in a time of peace had sent troops and taken possession of the custom-house at Corpus Christi, it would have been a hostile act. It would have been an act of *war*. So, on the other hand, for the President to send a military force to take possession of the custom-house at "Point Isabel" was a hostile act. It constituted *actual* war.

The President goes on, with the same specious misrepresentation of facts, to say, that "Texas made grants of land west of the Nueces;" that "a senator and representative in the Texian Congress resided west of the Nueces," etc. To all which I will only answer, that so far as they represent the jurisdiction of Texas to have extended over the people in the valley of the Nueces, and east of the desert, they may be true. But, if understood as saying that Texas ever exercised actual jurisdiction over any portion of the people west of the desert, in the valley of the Rio Grande, then are they unfounded and untrue. Sir, I repeat, that Texas could have obtained title to the country in the valley of the Rio Grande only by *treaty* or by *conquest.* It being occupied by Mexican settlements, there never was, and never will be, any other mode in which Texas or the United States can obtain title to it. No man pretends that Texas ever held or claimed it by *treaty.*

It therefore follows, that she must have held it by conquest, or she had no title to it whatever. The President dared not say, in definite language, that Texas had conquered it. The historical information of the country would instantly have declared such an assertion untrue. No friend of the President in this hall will dare hazard his reputation for truth by putting forth such a declaration. They will rely upon sophistry, upon specious circumlocution, and misrepresentation. They cannot be brought to any definite point. They will rely upon the popular credulity, and not upon the intelligence of the people. Time must demonstrate the success or failure of the experiment. It is an old saying, that "Truth is always consistent with itself." And we may, with equal propriety, say, that falsehood is always opposed to truth. So with this message; its important points are in direct conflict. We are all aware that "Fanta Fé," the capital of New Mexico, is some thirty miles east of the Rio Grande. Now, if the pretences of the President be true, that Texas is bounded on that river, "from its mouth to its source," the city of "Santa Fé" is within the jurisdiction of Texas, governed and controlled by Texian laws. But the President, in the latter part of the message, while speaking of the army, and desiring to blazon forth the glory of our conquests, says:

> " The privations of long marches through the enemy's country, and through a wilderness, have been borne without a murmur. By rapid movements the province of New Mexico, with Santa Fe, its capital, has been captured without bloodshed."

Thus, after a long and tedious argument to convince us that Texas is, in truth, bounded by the Rio Grande; that she had extended her jurisdiction to that river; that her laws were in force over the whole territory east of it, he comes out, and distinctly admits that the department of "New Mexico" extends far on this side of that river; that "Santa Fé," situated thirty miles east of it, is, in truth, the capital of one of the Mexican States; and, of course, that it is not, and never was, included within the bounds of Texas. Instead of submitting to Texian laws, he declares it to have been "conquered by our army." And he informs us, that the commander of our army there has established a civil government over the people of that State. Now these two portions of the message are in direct conflict with each other. They cannot both be true. One of them must, of necessity, be entirely unfounded. And I would solemnly ask, which are the people to receive as true, and which are they to discard as untrue? For the purpose of justifying himself in sending our troops to the "Rio Grande," and commencing hostilities there, he declares "Santa Fé" to be *in Texas*. But, in order to show the conquests of our army, he declares it to be the capital of one of the departments of Mexico. Now a contradiction so palpable, and at the same time so important, would have done no credit to the merest tyro of a county court. Still here it is, in the presidental message, sent forth to the people, and to the world.

My colleague (Mr. Schenck) the other day extorted from a distinguished friend of the President on this floor the admission, that *he* never believed that Texas included "Santa Fé." The admission concedes the fallacy of the whole argument of the President in regard to the boundary of Texas.

Mr. PILLSBURY, of Texas, said he had made no such admission.

Mr. GIDDINGS replied: I did not allude to the member from Texas. I referred to the gentleman on his right from Tennessee, (Mr. Stanton). But I will now inquire of the member from Texas, whether "Santa Fé," be in truth the capital of "New Mexico," as asserted in the latter part of the message? or is it within the boundaries of Texas, as asserted in the fore part of that document? Sir, on which horn of the dilemma will the gentleman place the President? If the gentleman from Texas refuses to answer my interrogatory, I call on any personal or political friend of the Executive to answer this plain and simple question. If any member will do me and the country the favor to answer it, I will gladly yield the floor for that purpose; and I now pause for a reply.

[Here Mr. G. having paused for some time, and no member rising, resumed]:

Mr. Chairman, — The President has many able and warm friends on this floor; but no one steps forth to extricate him from this attitude in which he has placed himself. Sir, "*out of his own mouth is he condemned.*" He has himself placed the evidence of his misrepresentation on the records of the nation. It will go into the archives of the government, and will descend to posterity a perpetual proof of the weakness and wickedness of this administration. It is a humiliating duty thus to expose the uncandid arguments and assertions of the Executive; but a due regard to the cause of truth, devotion to the principles of immutable justice, demand a faithful examination of this very extraordinary document; and I only regret that the duty has not fallen upon one more able to do it justice.

Before I leave this part of the subject I wish to say, that this admission of the President, that "New Mexico" extends this side of the Rio Grande according to its former limits, is a surrender of the whole argument that Texas is bounded by that river. The President defines the boundary to be "the Rio Grande *from its mouth to its source.*" But by admitting that "New Mexico" still includes "Santa Fé," he admits that the line of Texas extends no farther west than she has carried her conquests, and maintained and enforced her laws. That is the correct rule of international law, and it applies to Tamaulipas as well as to New Mexico; to "Brazos Santiago" as well as to "Santa Fé."

The President admits, indeed he says expressly, that our army has *conquered* "Santa Fé." He says so, for the reason that Mexican laws ever had been and continued to be in force there, and Mexican officers commanded them up to the time that our troops arrived and took control of the country. Such was precisely the state of facts in relation to "Brasos Santiago," at "Fort Brown," and through the whole valley of the "Rio Grande." The custom-house at "Point Isabel," was in the care and under the control of Mexican officers, and had been from the day of its establishment; and the people there were governed by Mexican laws, and yielded obedience to the Mexican government, up to the time of General Taylor's arrival, precisely as they did at "Santa Fé," up to the arrival of General Kearney. "Point Isabel," and that portion of the State of Tamaulipas which lies between the Rio Grande and the desert, was *captured* by General Taylor, precisely as New Mexico and "Santa Fé" were captured by General Kearney. The only distinction in the two cases is, that one was invaded and captured in a time of *peace*, and the other in a time of war.

Another feature of this message, is the general representation that this *war is defensive on our part*. But here again the President has recourse to vague sophistry. He does not inform us what portion of our territory was invaded or threatened with invasion. Who, Sir, of all the people of these United States, ever dreamed themselves in danger of Mexican violence?

Why, Sir, in a time of profound peace, our army, by order of the President, left Corpus Christi, and crossing the desert, proceeded more than a hundred miles beyond the farthest limits of Texas and of Texian laws, and entering upon territory which had ever been in the possession of Mexico, they seized upon the custom-house at "Point Isabel," blockaded the Rio Grande, erected a fortification, and mounted cannon, so as to command Matamoras, surprised a military encampment of Mexicans, drove away the men, and took possession of their horses; and, finally, our dragoons charged upon their infantry, before the Mexicans fired a gun. And now the Executive represents this as a *defensive* war!

Our army has crossed the Rio Grande, taken Matamoras, Camargo, Monterey, Saltillo, Tobasco, Tampico, Sante Fé, and the whole of California. We have penetrated to the very heart of Mexico. We have stormed their strong fortresses, bombarded their cities, and involved defenceless women, helpless children, and decrepid age, in scenes of human butchery, and now profess that we are acting in defence of our own people. What estimate must the author of this message have placed upon the intelligence of this body, and of the nation, when he penned these statements? Such absurdities defy argument.

But the President complains that Mexico long since seized the property of our citizens, for which they failed to make compensation, agreeably to treaty stipulations. Much of the message is occupied in calling the attention of the country to these wrongs. It is undoubtedly true, that some of our citizens, residing in Mexico during their revolution, were unlawfully deprived of their property. But it is equally true, that those difficulties were subsequently adjusted by treaty, and Mexico agreed to pay us the amount of loss sustained.

The three first instalments were paid according to stipulation; but, like our repudiating States, she was unable to meet all of her pecuniary engagements. Now all we have to complain of is, her failure to pay over the money as she had agreed. The wrongs and injuries committed upon our people had been arranged. They were merged in the treaty of amity and friendship, by which all past injuries were mutually forgiven. Had Mexico observed the treaty, we could not have complained; having broken it, our complaint, and only legitimate complaint, is on account of such breach. That breach consists in not paying the money at the time stipulated. For that we have no more cause of war than England had against Pennsylvania, or Illinois, or Arkansas, or Mississippi, for not paying their debts. But I deny that the failure of a government to meet its pecuniary obligations is good cause for shooting her soldiers and butchering her people. Surely, we should be the last nation in the world to put forth this doctrine of the President. But Mexico was exerting herself to meet her engagements up to the very time of our commencing hostilities. Not so with some of our repudiating States. They deny all moral obligations to pay. There is, therefore, more cause for murdering the people of those States, than we have to destroy those of Mexico.

But, Sir, what is the amount of money thus due to our people, for the recovery of which the President represents this war to have been commenced and carried on? I believe it is less than three millions of dollars. We have already expended more than thirty millions in this war; and, by this message, we are asked to appropriate twenty millions more. This vast expenditure is said to have been made with a view to extort *three* millions from Mexico. But this fifty millions is but a part of the pecuniary loss which the nation must suffer. The time of every man engaged in this war is lost, yea, worse than lost. The amount of injury to our commerce, and to the business of the country, by diverting the circulating medium from its legitimate channels, cannot be estimated. But the whole pecuniary damage constitutes but a small portion of our real loss. The effect which this war is destined to exert upon the morals of our people is far more to be deplored than its effect upon property.

Again: How can we estimate the anguish and suffering of our sick and wounded and dying soldiers? How shall we compute their agony and despair. Go, count the graves of those whose lives have been sacrificed to recover this three million dollars. Then number the widows and the orphans, and ascertain their griefs, their poverty, their disappointed hopes and blighted expectations. Add these to the whole loss and suffering which this war has brought upon our land. Then proceed to Mexico; form a catalogue of the crimes committed there by our troops, and ascertain the amount of pecuniary, physical, and mental suffering inflicted upon her people. Find the sum total, and compare it with the three millions of dollars for which we are contending; strike the balance, and then judge of the *policy* and *humanity* of this war, and of those who sustain it.

Sir, the Executive never assigned the non-payment of this money as a cause of war, until after hostilities were commenced. Our troops had invaded Mexico. The battles of "Palo Alto" and "Resaca de la Palma" had been fought, before this reason for commencing the war appears to have been discovered. It did not, therefore, operate to bring on the war. It was an after-thought, subsequently brought forth to justify it. But here, again, the different parts of the message do not sustain each other. In the forepart of that document the author says, "*Mexico commenced hostilities*," and, in the latter part, he goes into a long argument to show that we had good cause for commencing the war, and tacitly admits that *we did, in fact*, commence it. But I have only time to touch upon some of the interesting points, these inconsistencies, these contradictions of the message. I have no opportunity, under this hour rule, to go into detail.

I have stated the amount of moneys already expended, and now asked for carrying on this war. The President avows his intention to hold the territory which we have conquered, until Mexico shall repay us this expenditure. We have waged an unnecessary and unjust war upon a weak and defenceless republic. We have squandered untold millions in its prosecution; and now the President expresses his intention to rob Mexico of her territory, unless she repays the money we have so profusely spent. This we all know she can never do. The avowal, therefore, amounts to a declaration of the President's intention to render it a war of conquest. Indeed, we have abundant evidence of such intention.

During the darker ages, and among savage nations, such a

war might have been tolerated; but it will surely be condemned by all Christian nations of the nineteenth century. Such a war is opposed to the sentiment of the age in which we live. Sir, I would as soon lend my vote to commence a system of national robbery or piracy, as I would to support a war commenced for the evident purpose of wresting from a neighboring government a portion of her territory. But how much Mexican territory does the President think it will require to indemnify us for our expenditure? How much land will he demand for the thousands of American citizens whose lives have been sacrificed in this war?

Again, Sir, is the President and his friends conscious that the public lands in the slave States have never paid the expenses of surveying and selling them? They have cost us forty millions of dollars more than we have been able to sell them for. Every acre has been an expense to us. Nearly the entire profits arising from the sale of lands in the free States, has been expended to supply the expense of those in the slave States. Such will be the case with those acquired in Mexico. The more territory we get there, the greater will be the loss. A standing army must be maintained, to hold the people in subjection to our laws. With the expenses of the lands and maintenance of an army, burdens will be incurred that are to sit heavily upon the nation for coming generations. And the more territory we get, the greater will be the expense. Under these circumstances, I leave it for the supporters of this war to determine upon the amount of territory it will require to satisfy us for the money we have paid out for its support.*

But, Sir, this is an *Executive war*. It was commenced by his orders. He directed our army to leave "Corpus Christi," to enter the Mexican settlements, and to take a position upon the "Rio Grande," without advising with Congress. It was under his orders that the battles of "Palo Alto" and "Resaca de la Palma" were fought. The lamented Ringgold, and those

* Such was the expense of maintaining the government in New Mexico, that, in 1852, the Secretary of the Interior recommended giving it up and withdrawing our army therefrom.

who fell with him in those sanguinary conflicts, together with those who bled at Fort Brown, were victims to his unhallowed ambition. For their loss, he is responsible at the bar of public opinion. Before the people of this nation, I charge him with their murder. The imprecations of those who were there rendered widows, and of those made orphans, and of those who were there rendered childless, must in coming time rest on him; and, in the day of final retribution, the blood of our slaughtered countrymen will be required at his hands. In that dread responsibility, I will take no share. Against this war, in all its forms, I ever have, and ever shall, put forth my humble, but my earnest protest.

A few days since, a political friend of the President in debate on this floor, complained that the religious sentiment of the nation had been invoked against this war. Sir, every principle of our holy religion comes in conflict with this war. What, will you talk to Christians about sending an army to invade a neighboring nation; to shoot down our brethren of Mexico upon their own soil; to storm their fortifications, to cannonade their cities, to involve whole families, consisting of all ages, and of both sexes, in those revolting scenes of blood and slaughter which were witnessed at Monterey and at Tobasco? Can we expect Christians to remain silent, while reading the dark list of damning crimes which have been committed upon a weak and distracted people, by those armed ruffians and murderers who have been commissioned by this government to make war upon our fellow beings on the other side of the Rio Grande?

If we credit the intelligence we receive from the army, defenceless females are violated, and unarmed peasants are shot down like brutes. Whose blood does not curdle in his veins, when reading such accounts as have lately been sent forth from our army? We have probably all noticed the account lately published where the females of a family were insulted and abused by those belonging to the army. During the night, one of the offenders, a Texian officer, was assassinated, and in the morning his body was discovered. The "Texan Rangers" were said to have gone forth, and to have shot and murdered from eighty to one hundred unarmed and innocent peasants, in revenge for the death of their guilty comrade. These murderers, these worse than murderers, are paid by the freemen of this nation. They are sent there by our President under pretence of maintaining our national honor, while they thus disgrace humanity. Is it expected that the religious sensibilities of our people will slumber in silence, while our nation thus "reeks with crimes which smell to heaven?" Will the President and his supporters smother the religious feelings of the nation? Will they silence the voice of those whose vocation is to proclaim "*peace on earth and good will to men?*" It appears to me that moral darkness has spread over our land, or these things would not have passed by so silently. I regret to say that the clergy have not spoken on this subject as becomes the "*ministers of the gospel of peace.*"

The history of the world shows that national crimes have ever been followed by national judgments. This government has hurried to premature graves, without any just cause, at least four thousand human beings, who had committed no crime; neither had they offended us, or our government. Many thousands in this government, and in Mexico, have been clad in mourning, and afflicted with the loss of husbands, brothers, and sons. And can we hope to escape the penalty so manifestly due for our national crimes? Do we expect that the immutable law of justice will be suspended or repealed, in order that our nation may pass unpunished? Sir, I would earnestly invoke every preacher of the gospel, every professor of our holy religion, every lover of his country, to put forth his utmost influence to stop this tide of crime, of physical and moral death, now rolling over Mexico.

But a most interesting question is soon to be presented to the members of this body. We shall in a few days be called on to provide the means for carrying on this war. To authorize the sending of more troops to that Mexican golgotha, and to appropriate the money of our people, to continue the crimes and murders now committed there. Sir, I speak for myself, and for my constituents, when I say that no earthly power will induce me to vote away the life of a single soldier to carry on this attempt to subjugate Mexico, by butchering her people. No, Sir; were I to do it, my people would, in my opinion, immediately call on me to resign my seat here, that it may be filled by one who would use his efforts to lustrate them from the guilt of this unholy war.

Our army having conquered one city after another, and one State after another, is now in the interior of Mexico, holding possession of her towns and States. We know that it is a war of conquest, commenced and carried on for the purpose of dismembering Mexico. Now, with all these facts before me, were I to vote for the appropriation of men and money to continue this wicked and murderous war, and to carry out these designs, I feel before Heaven that I should make myself a party to it. I feel that I should become involved in the crimes and bloodshed of those we send there. That act must be done by others, if done at all. I dare not participate in it. I am aware that some who view the war as I do, urge that as the nation is now engaged in it, we ought to help carry it forward by voting supplies of men and money. I do not see the force of the argument. If it be in fact a wicked and unjust war, it follows that the longer it is carried on, the greater will be the wickedness and the injustice of those who continue it. But it is said that to press the war with vigor, will be the shortest mode of obtaining a just and honorable peace. If the war be unjust and dishonorable, I am wholly unable to discover how a vigorous prosecution of it, and a consequent increase of injustice and wrong, can, in the nature of things, be right or proper.

On the contrary, every pang we inflict, every life we sacrifice in this miserable war, must increase our guilt, and consequently our disgrace. There is but one way for the friends of our country and of humanity to do. That is, to use our efforts to stop the war, to withdraw our army from Mexican territory, and to tender to her honorable terms of peace. If then she rejects our offer, and assails us, there will be but one voice and one mind on the subject of defending our country. I am aware that it is said by some that war is popular. I know that to be an error, so far as concerns northern Ohio, and such portions of other States as I have travelled in since this war has existed. Its advocates are few, and they are daily diminishing. The people can find no possible reason why their moral purity should be sacrificed by its crimes, or their pecuniary interests to its support. They can see no good cause why a debt should be contracted, that shall rest upon their children, and perhaps upon their children's children. That this feeling has taken deep hold of the public mind, is shown by the result of the late elections. That feeling is destined to extend and spread, until those who brought this war upon us shall be driven from the high places of the nation. But it is said that we must press the war, or surrender up the conquests we have made. I reply, those conquests are robberies, and the sooner they are given up, the better for our country. When, in 1776, such an argument was advanced in the House of Commons, in regard to the war then waged against our Colonies by Great Britain, Mr. Fox said:

> "The noble lord who moved the amendment said, that we were in the dilemma of conquering or abandoning America. If we are reduced to that, I am for abandoning America."

I, Sir, am for abandoning Mexico at once. Let our troops be withdrawn immediately, and let peace be made. But the President informs the nation, that the war will be pressed until Mexico shall yield to our demands! Mr. Burke, in answer to a similar remark respecting the war against us in 1776, in the House of Commons, said:

> "That it is unbecoming the wisdom and prudence of Parliament to proceed any further in the support of this fruitless, expensive, and destructive war; more especially without any specific terms of accommodation declared."

Sir, these were the sentiments of the illustrious patriots of that age. *They* were under a monarchy — we happily live in a republic. But they certainly spoke more fearlessly than we do. They looked to the great principles of truth and justice, and acted under their dictates. They felt no apprehensions of popular disapprobation for acting in favor of humanity. Upon this question of making appropriations to carry on the war against the colonies, Mr. Fox, in the House of Commons, April 24th, 1776, said:

"To the resolutions he should give a flat negative, and that not because of any particular objection to the taxes proposed, (although it might be a sufficient ground for urging many,) but because he could not conscientiously agree to grant any money for so destructive, so ignoble a purpose, as the carrying on a war commenced unjustly, and supported with no other view than to the extirpation of freedom, and the violation of every social comfort. This he conceived to be the strict line of conduct to be observed by a member of Parliament."

"Col. Barre followed, and adopted the phrase of Mr. Fox, giving his flat negative to the resolutions, as they were calculated to tax the subject for an unjust purpose."

These were the sentiments of the most distinguished members of the British Parliament — of men whom we delight to honor. They, Sir, were "*whigs*,"* and, by rigidly adhering to the dic-

* In the Lords, February 16, 1778, the Marquis of Rockingham said:

"He was determined to serve his country by making peace at any rate."

In the Lords, March 23, 1778, the Duke of Richmond brought forward a motion for the withdrawing the forces from America.

In the Commons, November 27, 1780, on a motion to thank General Clinton and others for their military services in America, Mr. Wilkes said:

"I think it my duty to oppose this motion, because in my idea every part of it conveys an approbation of the American war — a war unfounded in principle, and fatal in its consequences to this country. * * * Sir, I will not thank for victories which only tend to protract a destructive war. * * * As I reprobate the want of principle in the origin of the American war, I the more lament all the spirited exertions of valor and the wisdom of conduct which in a good cause I warmly applaud. Thinking as I do, I see more matter of grief than of triumph, of bewailing than thanksgiving, in this civil contest, and the deluge of blood which has overflowed America. * * * I deeply lament that the lustre of such splendid victories is obscured and darkened by the want of a good cause, without which no war, in the eye of truth and reason, before God or man, can be justified."

Mr. Fox said:

"He allowed the merits of the officers now in question, but he made a dis tinction between thanks and praise. He might admire their valor, but he could not separate the intention from the action; they were united in his mind."

In the House of Lords, October 31st, the Duke of Grafton said:

"He pledged himself to the House and to the public that, while he had a leg to stand on, he would come down day after day to express the most marked abhorrence of the measures hitherto pursued, and meant to be adhered to in respect to America."

tates of justice, by their uniform opposition to the war, which they believed wrong and unjust, they secured the popular approbation, compelled the tories, the advocates of that unjust war, to make peace with the colonies, and finally drove them from power, and themselves assumed the control of the government. The people ever have been, and ever will be, in favor of justice; and, although an humble member of this body, I will respectfully suggest, that were the whigs of '46 to follow the example of those in the British Parliament of '76, a like result would follow. Indeed, I could as soon doubt of my own existence, as I could doubt my duty in regard to this war. Those who oppose it, will stand justified and approved by the sentiment of this and of coming ages. It is impossible that a Christian people — a people who worship a God of justice — can uphold a rapacious war of conquest like this, and spend their money in spreading distress, devastation, and death among a neighboring people. It is impossible that a Christian people shall lend their sanction, their encouragement, to a war waged with the openly avowed purpose of extending slavery, of perpetuating oppression, of opening up new slave-markets for the sale of mankind. These sophistries, these misrepresentations, these self-contradictions of the President, will not deceive the people. They are conscious that this vast expenditure of treasure and of blood, is made to sustain the most revolting system of oppression that has ever cursed the human family.

PAYMENT FOR SLAVES.*

MAN CANNOT BE MADE PROPERTY — VIEW OF THOSE WHO FRAMED THE CONSTITUTION — MILITARY POWER TO IMPRESS SLAVES — MAY SET THEM FREE — NO CONSTITUTIONAL POWER TO PAY THE PUBLIC MONEYS FOR SLAVES — RIGHTS OF THE FREE STATES — HISTORY OF CONGRESSIONAL LEGISLATION ON THIS SUBJECT.

[Since 1816, a portion of the members of Congress from the South, have endeavored to induce that body to regard slaves as *property*, and to pay for them when lost in the public service. The whole history of Congressional legislation on that subject, is given in the following speech. The bill had passed through the Committee of the Whole, and been ordered to its engrossment by a handsome majority. Mr. Giddings moved to reconsider the vote ordering it to be engrossed, and on that motion made the following remarks. He then withdrew his motion; and on the question of its third reading, it was defeated. This vote was subsequently reconsidered, and the bill passed the House, but was never brought up in the Senate.]

Mr. Speaker, — I had not intended to participate in this debate. I did not believe the bill before us could find favor in this body; and I had so often occupied the floor on questions connected with slavery, that I permitted the bill to pass through the Committee of the Whole, and to its engrossment, without any expression of my views. But from the favor with which gentlemen regard it, I apprehend they have not carefully considered the principles involved in its passage. There are certain great and fundamental doctrines which lie at the foundation of our government. We profess to "hold these truths to be self-evident, that all men are created equal;" yet the bill

* Speech on the bill to pay the heirs of Antonia Pacheco for a slave. Delivered in the House of Representatives, December 28, 1848.

before us admits one man to be the property of another; that one man may rightfully hold another subject to his will, may scourge him into obedience, and compel him to labor for the benefit of his master. We profess to believe that all men "are endowed by their Creator with the inalienable right to the enjoyment of life, liberty, and the pursuit of happiness;" yet the bill before us admits the claimant to have rightfully held the liberty and happiness of his fellow man at his entire disposal.

Now if we pass this bill, our professions will be in direct contradiction to our practice. If we really hold to these doctrines, it is certain that we must oppose this bill; and it is equally certain that if we pass this bill, we shall, by such act, deny these truths. We each of us either *deny* these doctrines, or we *hold* to them. We cannot do both. To say that we hold to them, and at the same time support this bill, would be placing our *professions* in direct contradiction to our *actions*. The inconsistency would be too obvious to deceive any one. Tell me not that you hold to the undying truths contained in our Declaration of Independence, and at the same time sit here to estimate the value, in dollars and cents, of the body and mind of your fellow man.

Those who founded our government declared their ulterior object. That object was to "secure all men (residing within our jurisdiction) in the enjoyment of life, liberty, and the pursuit of happiness." Are we to-day carrying out these objects? Here, Sir, are two hundred and thirty American statesmen legislating for the benefit of *slavery*. There is no evading this plain and obvious fact. No subterfuge can hide it from the people. The powers of government were instituted by our patriotic fathers for the express purpose of securing to all for whom we legislate the blessings of liberty. We are now sitting here to compensate the oppressor of his fellow man for his inability to continue his power over the victim of his barbarous cupidity. The members who vote for this bill, will give unmistakable evidence of their approbation of slavery, and their willingness to sustain it.

Before I proceed further, I will give a synopsis of the facts involved in the case. The claimant, in 1835, residing in Florida, professed to own a negro man named Lewis. This man is said to have been very intelligent, speaking four languages, which he read and wrote with facility. The master hired him to an officer of the United States, to act as a guide to the troops under the command of Major Dade, for which he was to receive twenty-five dollars per month. The duties were dangerous, and the price was proportioned to the danger. At the time these troops were massacred, this slave, Lewis, deserted to the enemy, or was captured by them. He remained with the Indians, acting with them in their depredations against the white people, until 1837, when General Jessup says *he was captured by a detachment of troops under his command.* An Indian chief, named Jumper, surrendered with Lewis, whom he claimed as a slave, having, as he said, captured him at the time of Dade's defeat. General Jessup declares, that he regarded him as a dangerous man; that he was supposed to have kept up a correspondence with the enemy from the time he joined Major Dade until the defeat of that officer; that to insure the public safety, he ordered him sent west with the Indians; believing that, if left in the country, he would be employed against our troops. He was sent west; and the claimant now asks that we shall pay him a thousand dollars as the value of this man's body.

The Committee on Military Affairs were unable to unite in a report upon the case. Five *slave-holders*, representing slave property on this floor, and constituting a majority of the committee, have reported a bill for the payment of this amount to the claimant. Four northern members, representing *freemen only*, have made a minority report against the bill. This report of the minority, I think, is sustained by irrefutable arguments.

The majority of the committee assume the position that slaves are regarded by the Federal Constitution as *property*, and that this government and the people of the free States are bound to regard them as such, and to pay for them as we would for so many mules or oxen taken into the public service. The minority deny this doctrine. They insist that the Federal Constitution treats them as *persons* only, and that this government cannot constitutionally involve the people of the free States in the guilt of sustaining slavery; that we have no constitutional powers to legislate upon the relation of master and slave.

There are several other points on which the committee differ, some of which I intend to notice; but I propose first to examine for a few moments that of the constitutional power. It is due to myself and to the country that I should call public attention distinctly to the fact, that these questions are forced upon us by southern gentlemen, against the wishes and remonstrance of every member of the committee from the free States. Involving as it does the great fundamental principles of our government, a distinguished member from the North, (Mr. Rockwell of Connecticut,) introduced a resolution to close the debate in *one hour* from the time we went into committee. I thought it unbecoming northern members to attempt thus to stifle debate on so important a matter, forced upon us by the South. I therefore called for the ayes and noes on that resolution, and now hold the floor by a sort of legislative fraud, having voted *for* the engrossment of the bill, with the sole object of obtaining the floor.

Sir, at the formation of the Constitution, slavery was condemned in the severest language by the delegates who framed that instrument. It is true they had been regarded in England as property. In 1749, Lord Hardwicke had decided that trover lay for a slave in the British courts. That was the *last* decision of the kind made in England, or in civilized Europe. One hundred years have elapsed since that decision. Its doctrines have been a thousand times discarded, contemned, and overthrown by the statesmen and jurists of that nation; but here, in an American Congress, we now hear this barbarous doctrine revived.

In 1772, Lord Mansfield boldly assailed the doctrine laid down in this hall to-day, and exhibited its absurdity in one of the ablest opinions to be found on record. From that period, this doctrine of property in man has found no supporters under the government of England. With all our refinement as a nation, with all our boasted adherence to liberty, on this subject we are three quarters of a century behind our mother country.

When Sir Warren Hastings was on trial in the House of Peers, in 1787, Mr. Sheridan, speaking on this subject, in his own peculiar and fervid eloquence, declared that—

"Allegiance to that power which gives us the *forms* of men, commands us to maintain the *rights* of men; and never yet was this truth dismissed from the human heart; never in any time, in any age; never in any clime where rude man ever had any social feelings; never was this unextinguishable truth destroyed from the heart of man, placed as it is in the core and centre of it by his Maker, *that man was not made the property of man.*"

This was the language of British statesmen sixty-two years since. To-day, we have before this branch of the American Congress the report of a committee, avowing that, under this Federal Government, in the middle of the nineteenth century, "man is the property of his fellow mortal."

These sentiments of the British statesmen and jurists, inspired the hearts of our American patriots in 1776, when they declared it to be a "self-evident truth that all men are created equal." When they framed our Constitution, they declared their object was "to establish justice, and to secure to themselves and their posterity the blessings of liberty." This subject of holding property in *men* did not escape their attention, nor have they left us ignorant of their views in regard to it. Mr. Madison, the father of the Constitution, has left to us a clear and explicit account of their intentions. He informs us, that on

"Wednesday, August 22, the Convention proceeded to consider the report of the Committee of Detail, in relation to duties on exports, a capitation tax, and a navigation act. The fourth section reported was as follows:

"'No tax or duty shall be laid by the Legislature on articles exported from any State, nor on the migration nor importation of such persons as the several States shall think proper to admit; nor shall such migration nor importation be prohibited.'

"Mr. Gerry thought we had nothing to do with the conduct of the States as to slavery, *but we ought to be careful not to give it any sanction.*"

Our people think, with Mr. Gerry, that "we have nothing

to do with slavery in the States." We are determined that we will not be involved in its guilt. With Mr. Gerry, we intend "to be careful to give it no sanction." No, Sir; we will not sanction your slavery by paying our money for the bodies of slaves. This is the doctrine which we hold, and which we expect to maintain; yet the members of this body are now engaged in legislating upon the price of human flesh. If we pass this bill, we shall give our most solemn sanction to that institution which Gerry and his compatriots detested. Will the members from Pennsylvania, the successors of Franklin and Wilson, lend their sanction to slavery, by voting the moneys of the people to pay for slaves?

But Mr. Madison tells us that "Mr. Sherman (of Connecticut) was opposed to any tax on slaves, as making the matter worse, *because it implied they were property.*"

I understand that *some* gentlemen from the North admit that slaves are *property.* Mr. Sherman, and the framers of the Constitution, would do no act by which it could be *implied* that they were property.

Mr. Madison also participated in the discussion himself; and, as he informs us, "*declared that he thought it wrong to admit that there could be property in men.*" And the report of the committee was so amended as to exclude that idea.

In that assemblage of illustrious statesmen, no man expressed his dissent from these doctrines of Gerry, of Sherman, and of Madison. These doctrines are: 1. That we "should have nothing to do with slavery, but ought to be careful not to give it any sanction." 2. That "we should do no act by which it can be implied that there can be property in men." 3. "That it would be *wrong for us to admit that there can be property in men.*" Such were the views of those who framed the Constitution. Will this House stand by them?

The gentleman from South Carolina (Mr. Burt) declared that he would leave us no room to escape this issue; "no loophole at which to get out;" that we must say by our votes, either that there *is* property in men under the Federal Constitution, or that there is *not.* I am most happy to meet the gentleman on that point, and am prepared to submit the question to those who framed that instrument, to Mr. Madison. His decision is left on record. The only question is, — Have the representatives of the people here the firmness and the independence to maintain the Constitution? There stands the record of their intentions. "He who runs may read." No man can fail to understand the intentions of those who framed our political compact. Those intentions constitute the very spirit of the Constitution, which we are sworn to support. The people of the free States are aware of the objects and intentions of those patriots. They know their rights under the Constitution; they hold the indisputable right to be free, and entirely exempt from the corroding stain of slavery. So perfectly were these principles understood in the early days of the republic, that after the war of the Revolution no man asked pay for his slaves that were taken from him, or killed in the public service.

In the year 1830, the Register of the Treasury declared that no instance of the payment for slaves, during the Revolution, was to be found on record. No, Sir; Madison and Jefferson and their contemporaries were then living. They well understood the principles on which the Union had been formed. They respected the rights of the *free* as well as of the slave States, and no man then attempted to involve the people of the North in the support of slavery. I believe the first attempt to make this government pay for slaves was in 1816. This was twenty-six years after the adoption of the Constitution, and forty-two years after the Declaration of American Independence. It is an important historical fact, that shows clearly the opinions then entertained on this subject.

After the close of the late war with England, a bill was pending in this House, providing for the payment of property lost or destroyed during that war. When the section providing for the payment of horses, carts, etc., which were *impressed* into public service and destroyed, Mr. Maryant, from South Carolina, moved to amend the bill so as to embrace *slaves*. The motion was opposed by Mr. Yancy and Mr. Robertson, and was negatived by a large majority.* That was a motion so to amend the bill as to pay for slaves, if killed in the public service, when they had been *impressed.* I have heard northern members express the opinion, pending this bill, that we ought to pay for slaves, if lost, when they were *impressed* into the service. Sir, such was not the case thirty-five years since. Our predecessors then spurned the proposition. Where now is the feeling, the spirit, which animated them? We have no record of the speeches, but every member will see that the case proposed was the strongest case that could be imagined. It was where a slave was taken against the will of the master, and *pressed* into the service, and killed by the enemy. Yet they rejected the proposition by a large majority. The claim before us is of incomparably less force. Here the master hired the slave, at a high price, to go with the troops as a guide, and of course took upon himself all risks.

The next case was that of D'Auterive. He had claims against the United States for wood and other necessaries furnished the army, and for the loss of time and expense of nursing a slave, who was wounded in the service of government at New Orleans. This case is more interesting from the fact, that there was at that time an attempt, as on the present occasion, to break down that well-known principle in our Constitution, that "slaves are *persons*, and not *property*."

The Committee on Claims at that time (1828) was composed of four northern and three southern men. At its head was an honorable southern man, (Lewis Williams of North Carolina,) who served his country longer in this body than any other that ever sat in this hall. For more than a quarter of a century, he was a distinguished member of this House. There are few, very few, now present, who had the pleasure of serving with him; but his contemporaries can attest to his great abilities and deserved influence. That committee reported in favor of allowing compensation for the articles furnished to the army, but said, expressly, that "slaves not being property, they could

* See National Intelligencer, December 28, 1816.

not allow the master any compensation for his loss." This was the unanimous report — Mr. Williams of North Carolina, Mr. McCoy of Virginia, and Mr. Owen of Alabama, uniting in the report. Mr. Williams had been contemporaneous with Madison and Jefferson, and he did not hesitate to avow the doctrines of the Constitution, and to maintain them. Here is the record of his opinion, and of the views of his associates. When the bill came up in Committee of the Whole, certain southern gentlemen suddenly became excited, worked themselves into a passion, threatened a dissolution of the Union, and all that sort of thing. In short, they manifested that spirit of dictation and intimidation which we have so often witnessed on more recent occasions. They made a strenuous effort to reverse the decision of the Committee on Claims; but, after some two weeks' discussion, gave it up, laid the subject on the table, and there the matter ended.

This discussion was thirty-nine years subsequent to the adoption of the Constitution, and more than fifty from the Declaration of Independence. The principle that slaves were *persons*, and *not* property, was reaffirmed, upon full discussion, without the light which we possess on the subject. The Madison Papers were not then published. The views of Gerry and Sherman and Madison, in the Convention, and the action of that body in relation to this matter, were unknown to them. Should we now reverse that decision, and overturn the practice, we shall sin against greater light than they possessed.

The next, and only remaining instance in which the question of appropriating the treasure of the nation to pay for slaves, was in 1843. "A bill for the relief the people of West Florida," intended to provide for the payment of slaves taken by the army of General Jackson from the inhabitants of that Territory, in 1814, came up for discussion. The slaves had been taken, against the consent of their owners, by the military power of the nation. I think there were about ninety, taken from different individuals. The proposition was distinct in its character. The object of the bill was to pay for human flesh. I myself opened the debate, and stated, as the principal grounds of my opposition to it, that slaves were not regarded as property under the Federal Constitution. My venerable and lamented friend, now no more, (John Quincy Adams,) sustained my positions. Several southern gentlemen spoke in favor of the bill. The Journal is now before me, and shows the bill to have been rejected, by a vote of one hundred and thirteen to thirty-six. This was done by a *whig* Congress. Not one of that party from the free States voted for the bill.

I have now given a history of our legislation on this subject. There was a bill passed this body, "*sub silentio*," on one of those days when there is, by the rules of the House, no discussion, by which payment was made for a slave. My friend from Pennsylvania (Mr. Dickey) has stated the facts in regard to it. I knew that such a bill was pending, and so did Mr. Adams; and we had mutually agreed to oppose its passage; but it slipped through unnoticed, and, therefore, constitutes no precedent.

In 1843, a bill passed this body to pay over moneys obtained by the government from Great Britain, and held in trust by us, to be paid to the owners of slaves lost on board the "Comet and Encomium." This bill also passed the Senate, and became a law. At the last session we passed two bills to pay over moneys held in trust for the same purpose. These cases were not to take the treasure of the people of the free States to pay for slaves, but to pay over money that did not belong to us, but which we held for the use of those who claimed it. But, from the dawn of the Revolution to this day, being more than seventy years, this House has expressed but one opinion on this subject. They have at all times refused to tax the people of the North to pay for the slaves of the South. We have never regarded them as property.

But an attempt is now making to change the essential elements of our government. Statesmen, now, in the high councils of the nation, deny that "all men are created equal;" that "they are endowed by their Creator with the inalienable right to their lives and their liberties; or, that "governments are instituted among men to secure the enjoyment of those rights."

It is now urged that this government was instituted for the purpose of robbing men of those rights; of disrobing a portion of our race of their humanity, and reducing them to the state of brutes, and making them the property of others. Will northern members assist to commit this outrage upon the honor of the nation and the constitutional rights of the northern States? Is there a member from the free States who will vote to tax his constituents to pay for southern slaves? If so, let such members place their names on record in favor of this bill, and let that record descend to coming generations, as a lasting memento of the principles which guide them.

I have now referred to the history of our legislation on this subject. The action of our committees was well commented upon by my friend from New Hampshire, (Mr. Wilson). I wish, however, to add a few words on this point. I am not aware that any committee of this House ever reported in favor of paying for slaves, until the First Session of 27th Congress — being more than sixty-five years from the formation of the government.

In 1830, my predecessor, the Hon. E. Whittlesey, reported upon the case of Francis Larche. This was the case alluded to by the gentleman from South Carolina, (Mr. Burt). I understood him to say that the slave of Larche was *not impressed.*

Mr. Burt. The gentleman is mistaken. The statement which I made was this: that no case could be adduced in which a refusal to pay for a slave had been made, on the ground that he is not property. The gentleman is totally mistaken.

Mr. Giddings. I certainly understand the gentleman now, and I refer particularly to the case of D'Auterive, which was rejected on this identical point. The committee say, in express language, that "slaves have never been placed on the footing of property." And they rejected the claim distinctly *on that point.*

But to return to the case of Larche. The Committee on Claims of the Senate (vide Rep. H. R., 401, 1st Session, 21st Congress) say, in distinct language, that—

"The cart, horse, and negro man Antoine, belonging to the petitioner, were impressed, and sent to the lines of the American army, on the 1st day of January, 1815, where the negro man was killed by a cannon ball from the British batteries."

The gentleman from South Carolina (Mr. Burt) assures us that he was *not* impressed. I can hardly suppose that he was authorized thus distinctly to deny the accuracy of that report, in a matter of fact. However that may be, it is certain that the committee understood that the man *was impressed.* They therefore acted upon that hypothesis; and with that belief, the committee unanimously reported against the bill. No stronger case can be imagined. The horse, cart, and negro were *impressed*, as the committee reported and believed. The petitioner was paid for the *property*, — that is, the horse and cart, — but the claim for the slave was *rejected.* Yet, Sir, they had not the advantages of knowing the sentiments of the framers of the Constitution which we possess. They were unconscious that the members of the Convention declared, that "*they ought to be careful to give no sanction to slavery*;" that they should do nothing by which "it could be implied that slaves were property;" "that it was wrong to admit that there could be property in man." I repeat, that to the best of my knowledge, (and I have bestowed much labor upon the subject,) no report was made in favor of paying for slaves from the public treasury during the first half century which this government existed under the present Constitution.

If wrong on any of these points, I ask gentlemen to correct me here, before the country. Let them expose my errors in the presence of this House, where I can meet them; where, with *truth* on my side, I stand prepared to defend my positions. Let gentlemen stand forth in this hall and meet my facts and arguments like men, like statesmen, and not shrink away in silence, and then set their letter-writers to assail me, — to pour forth their miserable abuse upon my humble self. Why, Sir, suppose they destroy *me*, they will leave my doctrines, my principles, untouched. *They* will remain while eternity shall last.

But to resume the history of this subject. In the 27th Congress, the claim of James Watson, for slaves, was committed to the Committee of Claims, of which I was myself chairman. The friends of the claim, by some means, learned that that committee had always reported against the payment for slaves. They therefore obtained the transfer of that case to the Committee on Indian Affairs, who reported a bill to pay for the slaves claimed by Watson. That report, made seven years since, was the first in favor of paying for slaves, so far as my knowledge extends, ever made to this body. During the same session, a report from the Committee on Territories was made of the "bill for the relief of the people of West Florida," to which I have already alluded, and which was rejected by the House.

Mr. BURT. Will the gentleman allow me the floor a moment?

Mr. GIDDINGS. With pleasure.

Mr. BURT. I stated in committee the other day, in reply to the interrogatory of the gentleman from Ohio, that Mr. Whittlesey, in his report on Larche's case, quoted the report of the Senate. I stated further, that Mr. Williams, to whom the gentleman from Ohio alluded, made a report in the Senate, on this case of Larche, saying that there was no evidence that the slave had been impressed at all. I stated further, that I had examined the Senate files in that case; and there is no evidence there, except the depositions of one or two men, (in the absence of any order,) that he was impressed at all.

Mr. GIDDINGS. Here is the historical record, the documentary proof, on which we are bound to act. I ask the gentleman from South Carolina if he intends to overthrow it by his sidebar testimony?

Mr. BURT. What is it?

Mr. GIDDINGS. That this man was impressed.

Mr. BURT. I do, Sir. There is no evidence of the fact.

Mr. GIDDINGS. Then I leave the gentleman to take issue with the history. The documentary evidence is, that this slave was *impressed;* that he was taken to the American lines, and was there "killed by a cannon shot from the enemy's batteries."

At the period to which I refer, I had been placed at the head of the Committee on Claims, by the then Speaker of this House, (Hon. John White of Kentucky,) of whom, though a slave-holder, I can never speak except with respect. There were at that time many claims for slaves before that committee. It was our settled policy to make no reports on those cases, lest we should stir up *agitation* on this *delicate* question.

In this hall, before the House, I was interrogated by a slave-holder (Mr. Wise of Virginia) on this subject. I was asked distinctly whether our committee *would report in favor of paying for slaves?* I answered, that we would follow the established practice on that subject. He replied, that my answer was evasive, but that the established practice was *not* to pay for slaves. It so happened, that on the 21st March, 1842, I introduced certain resolutions declaring the rights of the people of the free States to be exempt from the support of the slave-trade. For this I was censured and driven from my seat. Another member was added to the Committee on Claims; and then, Sir, during my absence, just eight days after I left the committee, this case was urged upon the members, who were most of them inexperienced in their duties, and unacquainted with the precedents. I left this hall on the 22d of March, and, on the 1st day of April following, a bill was reported by a slave-holding member of that committee, to pay for this man Lewis. This was the first case of the kind that ever received a favorable report from that particular committee; and that report was obtained in the manner just stated. It was in the sixty-seventh year of American Independence, and the fifty-third of our Constitution. This is the history of this bill. It was reported seven years since by a whig committee. We are yet to see whether this House can be induced to pass it.

Sir, we have the power to overturn the practice of this body from its first formation; we may overthrow its established and time-honored principles; we may defeat the objects of those who framed the Constitution; we may subvert the essential elements of that sacred compact which we are sworn to support; we may attempt to change the law of our existence, — to deface the work of God, and declare his image to be *property;* we may do all this at the bidding of the slave power; we may humble ourselves in the presence of those who hold the rod of terror over us; but there is a superior power that will hold us to a strict account of our stewardship. Sir, the eyes of the people are upon us; they are watching our actions. The concentrated rays of intelligence now brought to bear upon all our doings, render it impossible for us to deceive them. No evasion, no subterfuge will screen those who would render *northern freemen* subsidiary to the support of *southern slavery.*

To this day there has been in this hall sufficient independence and patriotism to reject all propositions of this humiliating character. As I have said, we are now driven to legislate by southern slave-holders, under the lash.

Mr. Burt. I hope the gentleman from Ohio will allow me this opportunity to disclaim utterly and indignantly any such imputation.

Mr. Giddings. Withdraw it, then.

Mr. Burt. I venture to appeal to this whole committee, who heard my remarks.

Mr. Giddings. I thought, when the gentleman said he would hold northern gentlemen to this point, whether a slave was property, — "*that he would leave no loophole for us to escape,*" — I thought it looked somewhat like the language of intimidation; it smacked somewhat of the plantation, of the crack of the whip. And I took it unkind in the gentleman from Connecticut, that, under such circumstances, he should attempt to stifle debate, to seal the lips of northern men.

This bill is pressed upon us at this particular time, when southern men are holding conventions, and manufacturing their usual amount of mock thunder for dissolving the Union, in consequence of *our* agitation. We hear it rolling along the heavens. It affords amusement to our school-boys, who crack their jokes and sing ditties in regard to it.

Sir, when I reflect that I am now constrained to sit in this hall to legislate upon the price of human flesh as *property*, I feel humbled. Before the nation, before heaven, I protest against this degradation. By what rule shall I arrive at the *value* of this *man?* He is said to be very intelligent and learned, reading and writing four languages. In this respect, he has probably few equals in this hall. I mean no offence by this comparison, either to gentlemen now present, or to the negro who is absent. I regard the moral qualities of a man as the proper criterion by which to graduate my respect. In this light, I know not whether the comparison be unjust to him or to those who estimate *his value at precisely a thousand dollars.* I would be as willing to enter into an inquiry as to the value of the body of the honorable member reporting this bill, as I am to estimate the value of a man who, as a linguist, probably has not a dozen equals in this body. If we are to judge of him by the report of the committee, if placed in this body, he might have reflected honor upon our country and our race. The splendor of his genius might have soared far above the grovelling intellects now engaged in figuring up his value in dollars and cents. His name might have been placed in future history beside that of Wirt, of Henry, of Burke, and of Sheridan; or, perhaps, his philanthropy might have placed him on the roll of fame with Adams and Wilberforce. And yet we are now sitting here to inquire as to the value of this immortal mind, to estimate its price in "glittering dust." My soul shrinks from the impious sacrilege with loathing and disgust. But this ethereal, immortal intellect, was bound in the chains of bondage, shut out from that sphere of usefulness and of action in which God designed it to move; and we are now asked to compensate this claimant for committing this wrong to mankind, this crime against God. I am anxious to see how northern members estimate their fellow men. What price do they put upon their constituents? Let their votes give the answer.

On a former occasion, I cited the opinion of an eminent jurist (Judge McLean) on this subject. In the case of Groves *v.* Slaughter and others, (15 Peters's Reports, 449,) this question came distinctly before the Supreme Court of the United States.

In deciding the law, Judge McLean said:

"By the laws of certain States, slaves are treated as property; and the Constitution of Mississippi prohibits their being brought into that State by citizens of other States, for sale or as merchandise. Merchandise is a comprehensive term, and may include every article of traffic, whether foreign or domestic, which is properly embraced by a commercial regulation. But if slaves are considered in some of the States as merchandise, that cannot divest them of the leading and controlling quality of persons, by which they are designated in the Constitution. The character of the property is given them by the local law. This law is respected, and all rights under it are protected by the federal authorities; but the Constitution acts upon slaves as persons, and not as property."

But one member of that Court dissented from these views. It may, therefore, be regarded as an authority, so far as the Judiciary are concerned.

If the doctrine contended for by the friends of this bill be correct, if slaves be property, slave markets may be opened in Boston, and Massachusetts will have no power to prohibit there the revolting scenes which are witnessed in this city. If the doctrine contended for by southern men be correct, no State can exclude slave markets from its territory, or consecrate its soil to freedom. It well becomes southern gentlemen to examine this subject, before they base themselves upon the principle that slaves are property. Let that be established, and Congress will have power to prohibit the internal slave-trade at its pleasure.

I now proceed to another branch of the case. With great propriety, the gentleman from New Hampshire inquired at what *time* the liability of government to pay for this slave commenced? The question has not been answered, nor do I think it can be answered. The undertaking was hazardous in the highest degree. The troops were all killed but two or three by the enemy, and those were supposed to be dead. This man alone escaped unhurt. This danger was foreseen, and the master put a price upon the services to compare with the risk. Did this contract bind the government to pay for the master's loss, admitting the slave to have been *property*? Was it any part of the compact that the government should insure the property? It strikes me that no lawyer would answer in the affirmative. The law of bailment is surely understood by every tyro in the profession. The bailee for hire is bound to exercise the same degree of care over the property that careful men ordinarily take of their own property. If, then, the property be lost, the owner sustains such loss. Now, conceding this man to be property, the government would not have been liable, had he run away, or been killed by accident, or died of sickness.

Yet, Sir, when property is lost or destroyed by the act of God, or the common enemies of the country, no bailee is ever holden responsible; not even common carriers, and that is the highest species of bailment. Had this officer, acting on his own responsibility, agreed to take this negro through the country for hire, (admitting the man to have been property, and governed by the same rules of law as though he had been a mule or an ass,) and he had been captured by the enemy, no law would have held such bailee liable. But, Sir, an entirely different rule of law prevails, where the owner of a chattel lets it to a bailee for wages. Had this man been a mule or an ass, and the officer had hired him of the owner for wages, to ride through that country, or to work in a team, or in any other manner, and he had been captured by the enemy, the bailee would not have been liable, upon any rule of law or of justice; nor would he have been liable, if lost in any manner, except by neglect of the bailee.

The gentleman from South Carolina (Mr. Burt) said he would place this case upon *strictly legal principles*. Sir, I meet the gentleman on that proposition. I, too, for the sake of the argument, am willing to submit it on principles of law; and I believe that no jurist, or even justice of the peace, would hesitate to reject the claim on those grounds. All must admit that the liability of the government, concerning this man, ceased, when he was captured by the enemy; up to this point, the government was not liable. I understood the author of this bill (Mr. Burt) to argue, however, that we became liable under the contract of bailment. That contract was ended, when the man was captured. The claimant then failed to perform his part of it.

The stipulation on the part of the master was, that the negro should pilot the troops from Fort Brooke to Fort King, the place of their destination, at the rate of twenty-five dollars per month. He was captured when only half the distance was accomplished. Here the master ceased to perform his compact; it was beyond his power to do so. The contract then ceased to exist; and, from that time forth, the claimant had no demand on us, either in equity or in law.

I now enter upon another view of this case. It is shown, by the testimony of General Jessup, that this man was supposed to have kept up an understanding with the enemy, from the time he united with Dade's command, until the massacre of that unfortunate battalion; that, while he was with the enemy, which was more than two years, he united in committing depredations upon the frontier settlements; in short, that he was one of the enemy. Our army was sent there to protect this claimant, and his wife and children and neighbors, against this very man, who, in company with others, murdered the people of Florida, and destroyed their property. This expenditure of blood and treasure by the United States was occasioned in part by this very negro, for whom the master now claims compensation. With his extraordinary intelligence, with a knowledge of the wrongs which he and his people had suffered at the hands of those who claimed them as *property*, he must have thirsted for vengeance. He could have felt no attachment, no respect, for a people at whose hands he had received nothing but abuse and degradation. It was natural that he should have sought revenge; and it was natural that his master should become his victim, if within his power.

But our army was sent there to protect the people against their slaves who were with the Indians, and their effective allies. It was under these circumstances that Lewis was captured, with other enemies. General Jessup says that he would have tried and hanged him, if he could have found time.

This, under martial law, he might undoubtedly have done. And the gentleman who reported this bill admitted that in such case this claim would never have been presented. Suppose he had been slain in battle; I think we should never have heard of this claim. But why had General Jessup a *right* to hang him? Because he was an *enemy, dangerous to the people and to the government.* But who will for a moment hesitate to say, that he had the same power, yea, greater power, to send him out of the neighborhood, than he had to slay him in battle, or to hang him. Humanity surely would dictate that he should be sent out of the neighborhood, rather than his life should be sacrificed. Has the claimant's loss been greater than it would have been had the negro been slain or hanged? Not at all. He had been taken in arms, had committed depredations upon the people; he had occasioned much loss of blood and treasure to the nation. Could General Jessup have left him in Florida, consistently with his duty? I think not.

Here another important question arises. Had the claimant any right to keep an enemy so dangerous within any civilized community? Is there a member of this body who will rise in his place and assert that any master possesses the right to retain such a foe on his plantation? Has any man the right to keep a rabid dog, or other animal, and suffer him to go at large in the community? I am now arguing the legal question. I am considering this man as property, the same as though he were an ass or a mule. And I lay it down as clear and indisputable law, that, had such mule or ass killed the people, and destroyed their property, as this man had done, any member of the community might either have shot him, or chased him out of the neighborhood with impunity.

I therefore meet the gentleman who reported this bill on every point involved in this case, legal, equitable, or constitutional, and I can find no merits in it.

But, Sir, as I am for the moment engaged in a *legal* examination of the case, I desire to follow it a little farther. This man was guilty of treason against the United States, or he was an enemy to our government. I think it doubtful whether slaves can commit treason, as they owe no allegiance to our government. But if he was not a traitor, he was surely an enemy to the country. Now, Sir, whether traitor or enemy, and the master, knowing the fact, "had harbored him," "adhered to him," or "given him aid and comfort," would not the master have been guilty of the crime of misprision of treason against the United States, and punishment under our laws? Of this I think there is no doubt. And yet we are called upon to pay him a thousand dollars for taking away a man thus dangerous to himself, who, if he had remained with him, would probably have subjected him to the gallows. Let gentlemen reflect, and vote as men, as intelligent statesmen.

Another question arises in this case, which, to me, is equally fatal to the claim. A state of war existed. General Jessup was the commanding officer in Florida. He was the agent of the government; and whatever the government might do to insure the safety of the people, their agent for the time being could accomplish under the martial law. By the term "martial law," I mean the *war power*, which is the most dangerous, the most indefinite, the most unlimited, exercised among nations.

I do not refer to the rules and articles of war, but to that vague, indefinite, undefinable power which knows no limits. It is that power which, in time of war, may do any thing in the power of man to accomplish; may command any sacrifice of the people, or of any portion of them, in order to secure the safety of the government, and of the subjects generally. It is that power which authorizes the military commander, in short, to do whatever he deems necessary for the security of the public; by which, suspected men were arrested and imprisoned in Connecticut and New York during the Revolution; by which, others were ordered to leave the country; and by which, others were shot down, their dwellings burned, and their estates confiscated.

It is the power exercised in South Carolina, during the Revolution, by Sumter, and by Marion, and their compatriots. It was by virtue of this power that Jackson, at New Orleans, suspended the writ of *habeas corpus* — adjourned the Legislature of Louisiana — ordered old men and boys, not legally liable to do military duty by law, on to the lines, to defend the city — *sent all foreigners out of the city*, as he regarded them dangerous, as this man was supposed to be — suffered no communication between the city and country — ordered a portion of the slaves also into service, and sent the others back into the interior. Many of those slaves were killed, but we have at all times refused to pay for them. But does any one deny these unlimited powers? Not at all. If General Jackson had the right to send freemen and slaves away from the scene of danger, had not General Jessup the same power? Most assuredly he had.

But the best illustration of this tremendous power is said to have occurred at Fort Erie, at the time the British attacked it in 1814. A lieutenant commanded a *picket guard* at the west of the fort, perhaps a mile distant. A beautiful plain extends in that direction some half or three-fourths of a mile, bounded by a dense forest. He was posted in this forest. As the British column advanced, the brave lieutenant, with his little band, retreated in front of them, keeping up his fire in gallant style, in order to retard their progress, and give notice to our men in the fort, and time for them to prepare to receive the enemy. An officer had command of a heavy park of artillery on that wing of the fort, and as the British column emerged from the forest, he saw its force, and opened a tremendous fire upon it. Our little guard, and their brave commander, were directly between the fort and the advancing column of the British army. They, of course, fell beneath the same fire that cut down the hostile column. As the story is related, General Brown was informed of the fact, and sent peremptory orders to the officer to cease his fire. To this order he paid no attention, but kept up such a shower of grape and canister, that the British column was broken and scattered before they reached the fort, so that not a man scaled its walls. But the whole of our picket guard, with their commander, were sacrificed; not a man survived.

For this conduct the officer was arrested, and, on trial,

showed conclusively that the sacrifice of our own guard of thirty men was *necessary to save the fort,* and those in it. They, Sir, were freemen. Their lives were surrendered for the safety of the army. These five southern gentlemen who reported this bill, now insist that the widows and orphan children of those men shall contribute a portion of their substance to pay for a southern slave, who, for the safety of his own master, as well as others, was sent out of the neighborhood. If there be a northern man in this body willing to lend his vote to consummate such an insult to the honor of the free States, let him stand forth and avow it.

But, Sir, to come more immediately to the precise case before us, I refer gentlemen to the Southampton riots in 1832. The newspapers of that day informed us that slaves, and, indeed, colored freemen, were shot down in the streets, others sent to prison, and others sent out of the neighborhood. Shall northern men be taxed to pay for them? Certainly, if you pass this bill, we must expect to open the treasury to the slave-holders in all these and in ten thousand other cases. By virtue of this same power exercised at Southampton, General Jessup, in order to secure the safety of the people of Florida, sent this man Lewis, with the Indians, west of the Mississippi; and now the master, instead of paying the expense of arresting this man, — instead of refunding to this government and to the people of Florida the losses he has occasioned by bringing this slave among them, — instead of paying for the property this man destroyed, — he comes here, and demands that we should pay him a thousand dollars for preventing Lewis from *killing more people and destroying more property.*

I have now stated my own views in regard to the powers of General Jessup to send this man out of the neighborhood. If he possessed power to deal with him as with any other enemy, no man will urge that we are in law or justice bound to pay for him. Admitting, however, for the sake of the argument, that General Jessup had no right to deal with him as an enemy, but that he was bound, under the order of the War Department, to deliver him over as a slave; that he disobeyed this order, and sent him west upon his own responsibility, and in violation of his duty; in such case, I ask, is there a member on this floor, who, for a moment, would suppose the people bound to pay for a slave taken by General Jessup, in violation of his duty, and of positive orders from the War Department?

Every member must be aware that the rules which control a public agent are the same as those which govern in private life. Suppose I employ a man to act as my agent. While he confines himself to the business on which he is authorized to act, I am bound in law and in justice by his contract. Suppose I employ my friend on my right to go and purchase a horse for me. He makes a contract for the horse in my name; I am bound by it, and must perform it. But suppose he purchase a *farm* in my name; no man would suppose me obligated to take it.

Military officers are the agents of government, to do all things pertaining to their office, and which come within the line of their duties. General Jessup was an agent to send out of Florida all enemies of the country; but he was not our agent to send the friends of government west of the Mississippi. If he has done so, the act is his, not ours. It was unauthorized, and he alone is liable. Now I understand the gentleman from South Carolina (Mr. Burt) to urge that he was an enemy, and dangerous to the country. I admit the fact, and say that he should be *treated* as an enemy. But if he were not an enemy, then there is no claim on the government.

But the committee are not content with urging that he was an enemy to the country, and dangerous. They suddenly change the argument, and say that he was taken for *public use*. An *enemy to the nation* is taken for *public use!* Well, Sir, the argument is ingenious. It never found a place in the mind of Grotius or Puffendorf, or of any writer upon the law of nations or the rights of government. But the point was adopted by the argument of the gentleman from South Carolina, and perhaps I ought to notice it. For *what* use was he taken? *To* what use was he applied? The gentleman admits the right to shoot or to hang him. Would not that have been as much a "taking for public use" as it was to banish him? The *use* of sending him out of the country was the preservation of the *lives and property of the people. That would have been* equally attained by shooting or hanging the negro. But the reply to this is, that he was *property.* Well, I repeat, suppose he had been a rabid dog, or a vicious mule, killing people and destroying their property, and General Jessup had shot or chased him out of the country, to prevent him from killing his master or others, would the government have been liable?

Again; it is said that, by the act of hiring, we admitted the slave to be property, and that the government is now *estopped* from denying that fact. We are bound to treat all arguments on this floor with respect. But to suppose that this obscure lieutenant, who, perhaps, never read a commentary on the Constitution, and who, I dare say, never dreamed that he was affecting, or doing any thing to affect, our rights or our duties; I say, to suppose that his acts would *estop* Congress from maintaining the Constitution, or that such acts would have any weight whatever with this body, is a proposition which I will not detain the House to examine. He was our agent for the purposes of doing his military duty; but we never authorized him to legislate for us, or to give construction to our constitutional rights. Why, Sir, I may hire out my son or apprentice, or my hired servant; but would that be an admission that they were my *property?* Or, suppose I agree that the gentleman from South Carolina (Mr. Burt) shall attend the speaker to a given place; does that imply that I hold him as property? No, Sir; the only fact implied is, that I have a right to receive the wages when the labor or duty is performed, according to my contract. In this case, the claimant agreed that Lewis should accompany the troops, and the officer agreed to pay the master twenty-five dollars per month. The claimant might have made the same arrangement in regard to any freeman as he did in regard to Lewis; and when the labor was performed, he would have the same right to the money. But, in such case, would the government be obligated to pay him for such freeman? No doubt the obligations would rest upon the hirer that now rest on the government, and no more.

But the gentleman from South Carolina (Mr. Burt) says that the act of 1815, levying direct taxes, recognizes slavery as property. That law provides "that such tax shall constitute a lien upon the real estate, and upon all slaves of individuals upon whom said taxes shall be assessed." My presumption is, that this bill was drawn by some southern man, who did not reflect that slaves were less property under the Federal Constitution than they were under the laws of the slave States. The gentleman does not pretend that, at the passage of that law, the question whether slaves were persons or property, was raised, or discussed, or thought of. I need not say that a bill passed *sub silentio* constitutes no precedent. In our courts of justice, the judge takes no notice of questions not made by the parties, nor do the proceedings of a court form any authority on points not raised nor discussed by counsel, nor examined by the court.

The case of Depeyster, to which I referred, was a stronger case than that of the law of 1815. My friend from Pennsylvania, (Mr. Dickey,) as well as myself, stated that that case passed when no one knew it. I knew that my lamented friend (Mr. Adams) and myself both intended to oppose its passage, and we were both watching it; but it got through when we were unconscious of it. Does any man, I will not say lawyer, suppose that its passage constitutes any precedent showing that slaves are *property?* Yet this law of 1815, so far as we know, received no more attention (or at least that part of it relating to slaves) than did the act for the relief of Depeyster. It can, therefore, constitute no precedent.

The force of a precedent consists in the respect which we pay to the *judgment* of a former Congress. It is therefore necessary, to give a precedent any force whatever, that the *judgment* of the tribunal should have been exercised upon the question, whether it be a judicial or legislative precedent. Thus, in each case that I have cited as precedents, either in this House or in committees, the questions now under consideration were discussed, and deliberation had, and a *judgment* given upon the point before us.

Now, Sir, let me say, with all due respect to southern gentlemen, that I challenge them to produce an instance in which this House, or the Supreme Court of the United States, or any respectable court of any free State, has decided *slaves to be property under the Federal Constitution*, in any case where that question has been raised, discussed, or examined. I desire to see gentlemen come to a definite issue on this subject. I wish to meet them fairly and distinctly. They must admit that the framers of the Constitution intended to exclude from that instrument the idea that there could be property in man. To that point I intend to hold them. And I call upon them to meet the record of Mr. Madison, to which I have referred. Let them deny that record, or carry out the intentions of the framers of that instrument.

The gentleman from South Carolina (Mr. Burt) says he "should like to know what was contemplated by that clause in the Constitution which stipulates for the surrender of fugitive slaves, unless it be that their owners hold property in them?" I answer, that clause *means just what it says*. It gives to the holder of slaves the right to pursue and recapture them in a free State, precisely as it gives me the right to pursue and retake my apprentice, or my son, in any State to which he may escape. It no more admits the slave to be *property*, than it admits the apprentice or the minor to be property. I am tired of hearing this clause of the Constitution quoted to prove almost every doctrine advanced by southern men. Its provisions are of the most plain and obvious character. It merely provides for the recapture and return of slaves, and nothing more.

But my hour has nearly expired. My constituents hold slavery to be a crime of the deepest dye. The robbing a man of his money or property, or the seizing of his ship upon the high seas, we regard as grievous offences, which should exclude the perpetrator from human associations for the time being. But we look upon those crimes as of small importance, when compared with that of robbing a man of his labor, his liberty, his social, his intellectual enjoyments; to disrobe him of his humanity, to degrade and brutalize him. On this account we protest solemnly against being involved in the wickedness and in the crimes of that institution. To-day we are asked to pay our money for the liberty of our fellow man. We hold that he was endowed with that liberty by his Creator; that it is impious, and in the highest degree criminal, for a man, or for a government, to rob any portion of our race of their God-given rights.

As the representative of a Christian and a moral constituency, I deny the right of Congress to involve them or me in the support of such crimes. By our compact of Union, no such power is delegated to Congress. By the passage of this bill, we shall become slave-dealers ourselves, — traders in humanity. The people of our State shrink from the foul contagion. With Mr. Gerry, we hold that "we have nothing to do with slavery in the States, but we will be careful not to give it any sanction;" with Mr. Madison, we hold that "it would be wrong to admit that there can be property in man;" and with the signers of the Declaration of American Independence, we hold that it is a "self-evident truth, that all men are created equal."

We believe our rights to enjoy these doctrines unmolested by this government are as clear and indisputable as are the rights of the slave States to *deny* them in theory and in practice. We claim no superiority of privileges under the compact. We admit them, under the Constitution, to enjoy their slavery unmolested by Congress or by the free States. Its blessings and its curses, its horrors and its disgrace, are theirs. We neither claim the one, nor will we share in the other. We will have no participation in its guilt. "It is the object of our perfect hate." Southern gentlemen may continue to misrepresent us, by saying that we seek to interfere with that institution in the States; but, thank God, we have obtained access to the public ear. The people of the free States now understand that all our efforts, politically, are based upon the constitutional right of being exempt from its support.

I am aware of the efforts now making by northern presses, letter-writers from this city, and editors who pander to the spirit of servility, to misrepresent my views, and assail my motives. Sir, let me say to those men, before Heaven, if they will come up to the work, unite their influence, and separate this government from the support of slavery and the slave-trade, and leave that institution where the Constitution placed it, — with the States in which it exists, — with gratitude to God, and with love and good-will to all my fellow men, I will retire from these halls to the obscurity of private life.

Sir, I may, on the present occasion, deny the imputation that I wish to embarrass the friends of the incoming Administration. Those who have done me the honor to observe my course in this hall for the last ten years, must do me the justice to say, that my efforts here have been against existing evils. I desire to see every member of every party lend his influence to support the Constitution of my country, and the rights of humanity. I war upon no party. I wish to see the people of the free States purified from the support, the crimes, the contagion of slavery. I would oppose any member, or any party, who seeks to uphold the slave-trade or slavery by Congressional laws, or lends his influence to continue within this district, or on the high seas, a commerce in human flesh. I know that the sympathies, the consciences, and the judgment of the people are with me. Recent events have demonstrated the power of truth. Its omnipotence is irresistible. It is rolling onward. No political paltering, no party evasions, no deceptions, no dodging of responsibility, will satisfy the people. No; gentlemen must come up to the work; they must take their position upon the line of the Constitution, and maintain the rights of the *free* as well as of the slave States, or they will be overwhelmed by the indignation of a free and virtuous people.

General Taylor and his friends will have an opportunity of gaining immortal honors, and of deserving and receiving the gratitude of the American people. Let them at once abolish

27 *

slavery and the slave-trade in this district, and upon the high seas; let this government cease to oppress and degrade our race; let us cease to legislate for slavery; let the powers and influence of government be exerted to promote human liberty, to elevate mankind in his moral and physical being; and the honors of men, and the blessings of Heaven, and the gratitude of this and of coming generations shall be theirs. But if their influence be exerted to maintain slavery, — to continue this commerce in human flesh now carried on in this district, and upon the high seas, — to involve the people of the North in these transcendent crimes, — then the opposition of good men, the curse of Heaven, and the execrations of posterity, will be their reward!

MEXICAN WAR.*

ITS EXPENSE — POSITION OF THE WHIG PARTY — THEIR POSITION OF 1844 — THEIR CHANGE — THEIR CANDIDATE — HIS POSITION — UNION OF THE WHIGS AND DEMOCRATS.

[In 1844 the whig party took strong ground against the Mexican war, and the extension of slavery. In 1846, they changed their position and voted for the war; and in 1847, having a majority in the House of Representatives, they voted to supply men and money to carry on the war. In 1848, they nominated General Taylor for President, without any declaration of principles. This led to a separation of a portion of that party from those who adhered to the policy of exerting the power of government to support slavery. The following speech was the first declaration in Congress that a portion of the whig party would not support General Taylor; and that a new party was forming, which would take its position in favor of a total separation of the Federal Government from all support of slavery.]

Mr. Chairman, — I am not surprised at the amount of deficiency in the appropriations of last year. This war has proved more expensive than its friends expected. Twelve millions of dollars ought to defray the whole annual expense of our government. But it now only covers the deficit of one year. Efforts are made to place the responsibility upon the "whig party;" for the reason, as it is said, that they have a majority in this body. I have long been an humble member of that party, and think I understand its principles. In 1844, the whigs were unanimously opposed to this war. They exe-

---

* Speech on the bill to supply deficiency of appropriations for 1847. Delivered in Committee of the whole House on the State of the Union, June 30, 1848.

crated it. Now a majority of this House sustain and approve the war.

At that time the party opposed the extension of slavery; now a majority of this House are evidently in favor of that measure. The issues were made up on these questions, and the extension and perpetuation of slavery became the absorbing subject, which, like Aaron's rod, swallowed up all others. Our position was well defined. We then laid the foundation of our political faith upon the rock of the Constitution. When it was asserted in this hall that the Federal Government was bound to protect and uphold the slavery of the South, the whigs denied the doctrine. Such, too, was the case in the other end of the capitol. During the recess of Congress, Mr. Clay, the leader of the whigs, in a letter to the "Lexington Observer," declared "that Congress possessed no powers whatever over the institution of slavery; that its existence, maintenance, and continuance, depended exclusively upon the power and authority of the several States in which it is situated." Thus was the position of our party, as well as that of our opponents, rendered distinct and obvious. A portion of the whig party will adhere to that position, let what may betide us. No seductions will entice us from it; and no array of influence will induce an abandonment of it. I now hazard the declaration, that on this principle of opposing all attempts of the Federal Government to extend and uphold that institution, against all interference or connection with slavery beyond that which is provided for in the Constitution, is now based a party, or the germ of a party, that will at no distant day become dominant in this nation.

That party, call it what you may, will oppose all propagandism of slavery, and all attempts to throw its burdens, its disgrace, or its guilt upon the people of the free States. The old issues between the parties are lost sight of; they are in fact forgotten. Who now speaks of a protective tariff? Who, in this hall, attempts to illustrate its benefits to the free labor of the North? Or who complains of its burdens upon the slave labor of the South? Who now occupies time on the subject of harbor or river improvements? We have no funds for such purposes. They are absorbed in a war waged for the extension of slavery, and the President has indicated his intention to veto any bill for that purpose. No one alludes to a Bank of the United States; and no one complains of the sub-treasury; and the division of the funds arising from the sale of public lands is not spoken of. These issues are laid aside, and we are now altogether absorbed in the great question of extending and upholding slavery, and maintaining the war which has resulted from that policy. The old organizations are in a degree broken up; the old lines of demarcation have become obscure and uncertain, whenever this subject is presented; some who have been called whigs leave us, and some who have been called democrats now vote with us. New political associations are gradually forming. The trammels of party are breaking; and no power can again unite either whig or democratic parties in any measure to extend slavery, or to uphold it. When this subject comes up, each party for the time being is disbanded.

Where now is the democratic party in the State of New York? It is most effectually disbanded; such will soon be the case in all of the free States; the attempts to lead them to the support of slavery, to extend it upon territory now free, has alarmed the honest and humane members of it; they refuse longer to be made the dupes of the slave power. Like honest men, they have cast off their servile leaders; they have thrown the old party issues to the four winds of heaven; and, like true patriots, they are adopting the high and holy principles of "man's inalienable rights" as the basis of their political action. I know it is usual for whigs to distrust and cast suspicion upon the political movements of those who have heretofore acted with the democratic party. I do not participate in that feeling. In the last Congress there were good men and true belonging to the other side of this hall, and I trust there is a still greater number of them in this body now than at any former period. I cannot approve of their support of this war. I am compelled to judge them by the same rules by which I judge those who call themselves whigs. Believing the war unjust and barbarous, it follows, in my judgment, that all who support it must be wrong, whether they be called whigs or democrats ; but, on the question of extending slavery, I regard a portion of the democratic party in all the free States as unalterably pledged against it; and I think they will adhere to that position.

The war in which we are engaged, is but a consequence of our efforts to extend slavery by the annexation of Texas. It was foretold by all who examined the subject. Mr. Clay declared annexation and war to be identical. The whigs did not cease to condemn it, from the first agitation of the subject of annexing Texas, up to the 11th May, 1845, that ill-fated day, when most of our party, in the moments of excitement, voted to recognize this miserable war, brought on as it had been by the President. I mean no disrespect to those friends; they were as sincere and as patriotic as those who differed from them. But they will permit me to say, that I regarded that vote as a surrender of our moral power. They felt constrained to vote for that most obnoxious measure. And, subsequently, most of the whigs voted to give the President men and money to carry on this work of devastation and death.

I would cast no reflections upon my political friends, but I must say, that I have ever regarded it as wholly inconsistent for whigs to condemn the war, and at the same time to lend their votes and influence to carry it on. The idea that gentlemen here are *constrained to do wrong* is, in my humble apprehension, absurd and ridiculous.

I fully concur in what was well said by my colleague, (Mr. Schenck,) that we are following in the footsteps of our opponents. At the last session, they appropriated money, in their estimation sufficient to continue the work of bloodshed in Mexico up to the 31st June next. But the elections have changed the character of the House since that time. And the whigs nominally now control the business of this body. Has there been any change of *policy* by placing the power in whig hands? Not any. The bill before us appropriates twelve millions dollars for continuing the war. Now, Sir, if we pass this bill, where is the distinction between their measures and ours? If we adopt their policy, ought we not also to adopt their name? If there be no difference between them and us, why should we profess to constitute a different party? "A rose would smell as sweet by any other name." If we look back to 1844, and say as we then said, that no whigs can support this iniquitous war, we must say that the whig party is dissolved.

Mr. Chairman, it is due to myself to say, that I never have, and I think I never shall, vote a dollar to carry on this war. I have too long and too ardently denounced it as unjust and wicked, to turn round now and support it. I am constrained to say that, so far as this war is concerned, it has become a matter of some difficulty with me to discriminate between whigs and democrats. Standing now as I did in 1844, unqualifiedly opposed to the war, in all its phases, in its generals and in its details, I have seen a portion of this body, who stood with me at that time, leave the policy which then guided us, and go over to the support of measures which we then condemned. I repeat, that I impute to them no motives other than of patriotism; but I may be permitted to say, that I have yet seen no cause for changing my position on this subject. If other gentlemen feel it their duty to sustain the war, they will of course do so. "To our own masters, we must each stand or fall."

The Committee of Ways and Means have reported bills appropriating all the treasure demanded by the President for carrying on the war. They act as our agent; and the whig party now stands before the country in the attitude of sustaining and continuing the war which they have so much denounced. I regard this as a false position. I do not think the whig party of the nation desire to take upon themselves the guilt and odium attached to the devastation of Mexico. I think a large majority of the whig members of this house would have been pleased to see bills reported appropriating all the means necessary to bring our army back to our own territory in safety. In that event, if enough of our party had felt disposed to unite with the democrats to change such bills, so as to grant the men and money necessary to continue the work of conquest, they could have done so. The responsibility would then have rested where it should rest — on those who intentionally sustain the war. But, as the facts now exist, the whig party have relieved the President and his party of their responsibility, and have taken it upon themselves.

This state of things I had greatly desired to avoid. I foretold its existence in December last, prior to the organization of this House; and to my whig colleagues I expressed my determination to have no share in producing it. I was then conscious that the honorable gentleman who now fills the office of Speaker, if elected, would so constitute the Committee of Ways and Means, as to secure the reports of bills appropriating the necessary means to continue the work of rapine and murder in Mexico. I mention these things with perfect respect for the honorable Speaker, and the members composing the committee to which I have alluded. I presume their motives to be pure, but I could not bring my mind to agree to this policy. Every sentiment of my heart was opposed to it. I was therefore compelled to vote against the election of the honorable gentleman who now fills that office. I had denounced the President for involving us in a war which I deemed barbarous and criminal. Nor could I discover any good reason to believe that the work of cutting Mexican throats had become sanctified in the sight of Heaven by its continuance. With such feelings, I could not lend my vote to assist in electing any man to office who I believed would exert his official influence in favor of continuing this war. I then felt, and I now feel, that, had I voted for the election of any man, knowing that his official influence would be thus exerted, I should have involved myself in the guilt attached to the wholesale murders carried on in Mexico. I refused to vote for the gentleman nominated, for the reason that I believed he would arrange the Committee of Ways and Means precisely as he has done; and that the policy of the administration in regard to this war, would be sustained by the whig party, which would be thus made to assume its odium.

Sir, I would not participate in such responsibility. I intended to lustrate myself, and the people whom I represent, from the guilt attached to the murder of our fellow beings in Mexico. When Pilate, a pagan governor, saw that the people were determined on shedding innocent blood, he took water and washed his hands, declaring himself exempt from the crime they were about to commit; and shall I, a professing Christian, and representing a Christian people, hesitate to wash my hands of the crimes of this war? No, Sir, *never*.

In saying this, I speak for no other person than those whom I represent. I regard every life sacrificed in this war a murder, attended with all the moral guilt attached to that crime. That guilt, in my view, must rest upon all who aid in carrying on hostilities in Mexico; and I wish it to be distinctly understood, that no party ties, nor party policy, can induce me to participate in such guilt. I would not leave the position which our whole party maintained in 1844, to unite with our opponents to sustain a war which we then so loudly condemned. If we were right in opposing it then, we must be wrong in supporting it now. "Men often change; principles never."

The whig party is also placed in a false position on another subject. We have ever held, as a party, that the Federal Government has no power over the institution of domestic slavery. As before stated, Mr. Clay, in 1844, denied that Congress possessed any powers in regard to slavery. I believed Mr. Clay to be correct in that position. Indeed, the whole whig party declared the doctrine true. I still adhere to that position as firmly as in 1844. But, Sir, look at your Committee on the District of Columbia, and that upon the Judiciary. They are the organs of the whig party. To those committees we have sent vast numbers of petitions praying us to withdraw all support of the slave-trade, and to cease all support of slavery in this district. But no response is made to those petitions. They are held in silence. The slave-trade is carried on here, as it were, under the very folds of our national flag. We see our servants seized in our very presence, ironed, gagged, and hurried to the slave market; yet those committees remain silent. No outrage upon humanity can extort from them a report, either in favor of this traffic or against it. I intend doing these gentlemen no injustice. But, Sir, we know, from the votes of this body given on different occasions, that the whig party has not been in favor of supporting this traffic in human flesh. A large majority of it, I believe, are opposed to it; yet, before the country, we stand in the attitude of protecting that commerce which has so long disgraced the nation. Of this heaven-defying outrage upon the rights of a portion of our race, I am also exempt. It is due to myself and those whom I represent that I should say, I do not share in the responsibility of sustaining it. I was perfectly conscious that this state of things would follow the election of our present Speaker. I shall do that gentleman no injustice when I say, that I told my friends, before his nomination, that, if elected, he would so constitute those committees as to protect and sustain this infamous traffic. I do not impute to him any improper motive or design. He doubtless regards it as a duty; but I was unwilling to vote for any man who would use his official powers for such purposes, either from principle or from policy. On this subject, we find whigs sustaining the slave-trade, and democrats voting against it. Party lines have become obscure on this question also. A portion of both parties desire to see the government separated from the support of such crimes.

Sir, I believe the great body of the people of both parties in the free States abhor the slave-trade. They desire to be free from its crimes; they detest its abominations, and will hold responsible those who prostitute the powers of the government to sustain it.

Another important point has not escaped the notice of the public. While the whigs, as a party, have manifested the most determined hostility to the war, denouncing it as wicked, unjust, and barbarous, as an accumulation of crime beyond conception, they have been called on here to express their profound gratitude to those who have voluntarily engaged in this work of slaughtering our race. I am aware of the fine-drawn casuistry which teaches us to denounce the crime, while we praise those who commit it; to execrate the slaughter of women and children at Monterey and at Vera Cruz, while we tender a nation's gratitude to those who voluntarily guided and directed the butchery. I have been unable to discover the force of such reasoning. Probably I have not appreciated the argument; certainly I cannot agree to the doctrine. One of the officers, to whom the thanks of Congress were thus tendered, was my personal and political friend; one who had done much to save the nation from the horrors of war in 1839, when hostilities hovered over our north-eastern frontier. That was an elevated and noble example of philanthropy and patriotism; one for which I would gladly have united in a vote of thanks. But when those officers went to Mexico to engage in devastating that country, in cannonading their cities, and in the slaughter of their people, they did so *voluntarily;* there was no compulsion in the business. I think that a Roman firmness and unbending integrity should then have characterized their conduct. They should instantly have resigned their offices, refused to enter upon the work of butchering a foreign people, and retired to their homes, and received the approval of their consciences, the gratitude of all good men, and the smiles of Heaven.

But, Sir, these officers went to Mexico, took charge of our armies, and became the instruments of carrying out the designs of ambitious rulers, and of executing deeds at the contemplation of which my soul shrinks back with horror. For those acts I felt no pulsation of gratitude. Had I voted for the resolutions, I should have belied my conscience, and done violence to truth. I had at first thought I would remain silent when the vote should be taken, but further consideration convinced me that it was my duty to vote against the resolutions. I was unwilling, by my silence, to encourage the thirst for military éclat which they were calculated to inspire. On this subject both parties fully united; all party distinctions were lost sight of, and I found myself in the very extraordinary position of voting alone in this body. Even though my vote stands solitary upon the record, I feel willing that it should pass the test of an enlightened people. I have witnessed the baleful effects of a standing army. It has brought us into this war. Had we been destitute of an army, the President would have been unable to involve us in hostilities with Mexico. The nation is now sustaining an army in that country at an expense of one hundred and twenty-five thousand dollars per day. This sum is drawn from the hard earnings of our laboring people; and what do they get in return? Why, they subject the people of Mexico to our will. We who have declared that all men are created equal, "that to secure our natural rights, governments are formed amongst men, deriving their just powers from the consent of the governed," now squander untold millions to give evidence of our want of sincerity in the professions we have made. We see the officers of the army on every street of this city, living at their ease, and at the expense of those who toil for their daily bread. These things are inconsistent with republican institutions. Rather than vote for resolutions lauding our military officers for shedding the blood of our fellow men, I would vote to bring back the fifty thousand troops from Mexico, and disband them. I would have them return to civil life; I would have each earn his own support, and by his labor contribute something to the general wealth of the nation. The army is a cancer upon the body politic. It is striking its fibres into the vital parts of society, and extending its virus into the veins and arteries of the government; and, if continued, must sooner or later dissolve our institutions.

On the 4th July last, at an encampment far in the interior of Mexico, at a meeting of the officers of our army, one of their number was nominated for the highest office in the gift of the American people. Thus early in the history of this nation has an attempt been made by the army to dictate to the people a President, — to send us from the camp a man to guide our ship of state, — one whose hands are dripping with human gore, — so that when he shall lay his fingers upon the book to take the oath of office, they will leave the sacred volume polluted with the blood of innocence. Are such things becoming a moral, a Christian people?

Yet both political parties vote resolutions which in their tendency serve to encourage our citizens to leave the peaceful vocations of civil life, and enter the army. I regard the policy wrong, and its influence deleterious. All such votes of our party paralyzes our moral power, and takes from us the ability to do that good for our country which we might otherwise effect. I think our legislation should be placed upon moral grounds; that we should here, in our official acts, adhere to the same morality that we practise in private life. I do not know that it is more criminal in the sight of Heaven for a man in private life to lend his counsel and influence to shed innocent blood, than it is for him in this hall to vote to sacrifice the lives of hundreds and thousands of innocent people. If a man in private life lends his counsel or his influence to shed the blood of his fellow man, he is hanged as unworthy of longer associating with human beings; but if he voluntarily enters the army, and goes to Mexico, and there aids in slaying hundreds of men, women, and children, who never injured us or our nation, why, Sir, we tender him the thanks of Congress; we express to him our nation's gratitude.

Mr. Chairman, this morality will not stand the test of conscientious scrutiny. Our political morality is certainly of doubtful character. No man dares practise in private life upon the principles which guide our votes in this hall. I am aware, Sir, that it is said that the public mind is not prepared to adopt the same morality in our legislation which we practise at home. I answer, that fact depends upon *us who act for the public*. Let us but rigidly adhere to the dictates of a pure morality here, and I entertain no hesitation that the people will justify us. I do not believe that those who sent us here, intended that we should leave our morality at home, or that we should forget our moral responsibility while engaged in the work of legislation.

In what I say against war, I allude only to *foreign* wars, —

to wars of conquest and aggression. I make no allusion to wars of defence; I believe them justifiable and proper. Self-defence is the first law of nature; and were I a Mexican as I am an American, I would meet your army at the frontier with a sword in one hand and a torch in the other, and by every means which God has given me, I would defend my country.

When, in March 1843, I, together with twenty other whig members of this body, including the venerable member whose shrouded seat reminds us of the bereavement which our country has recently sustained,* by a public manifesto, called the attention of the people to the annexation of Texas as the commencement of a system of conquest, which must in time prove fatal to our institutions, *we meant what we said.* It is true that our efforts to arouse the public mind to the evils which we clearly foresaw, proved useless. Our warnings, like those of Cassandra, were not credited; they fell dead upon the ears of the people. But we now see our predictions fully verified. Sir, I must have read the history of our race in vain, if this fostering of a military spirit does not bring upon our nation consequences of the most dangerous character. I am aware that it is said, these resolutions of thanks were nothing more than a scheme of President-making, which is regularly manifested in this hall once in every four years. And I think their presentation was evidently designed to carry out the nomination made in Mexico, to which I have alluded.

From an early period of the session, we have heard gentlemen, in their speeches, lending aid and giving influence to this plan of foisting upon the people, a President whose only recommendation is his military fame. If military service qualifies a man for the highest office of government, it is easy to see that our minor offices will be filled with the same class; and the day is near when our government must become a "military republic." When I have heard gentlemen speaking of the popularity of the distinguished officer to whom I have

* After the death of Hon. John Quincy Adams, the House ordered his seat and desk to be covered with crape during that session.

alluded, and of that political millennium when all parties are to unite in his support, I have desired to inquire what are the principles on which he will, if elected, administer the government?

The most ultra supporters of free trade, and the most determined adherents of a protective tariff, are to unite in support of this distinguished military officer for President. Each knows that he or his allies, must find themselves deceived after the election. But each is hoping it will not be himself, and each rejoicing in the thought that it will be those acting with him. Neither of them has any evidence of General Taylor's real views; but each is willing to bring his political principles into common stock, and hazard the chance of drawing out those of his former opponent. They are willing to stake their whole political fortunes upon the opinions of General Taylor, each thinking he is to overreach the other, and rejoicing in the expectation of success; confident that if he succeeds in electing his man, he will surely gain a *President*, if he lose his *principles*.

Meetings are called in Philadelphia and New York and other cities for the purpose of directing the popular attention to him as a candidate. While here, before the country, no friend of his can inform us what his views are. This is a most extraordinary state of the political parties. Both whigs and democrats are in favor of General Taylor, not because they know his political sentiments to be *right*, but because they do not know whether they are right or *wrong*. They support him, not because they *know* his views, but because they *do not* know them. Yet, Sir, under this state of things, it is said that he is a *whig*. I deny it, and call for the evidence. Where is the proof? What evidence have you of the fact? What public act in his whole life has demonstrated him to be a whig? When or where did he give a whig vote, or advocate whig doctrines? When or where did he ever explain his sentiments, and show them to be such as are held by the whig party? I presume General Taylor to be an honest and an honorable man; but we have had some experience on this subject.

John Tyler called himself a whig. Men in this hall called "whigs," voted for the annexation of Texas. So, too, in the other end of the capitol. Men calling themselves whigs vote to sustain this war, and are in favor of extending our territory, and of carrying slavery upon soil now free. Is General Taylor such a whig? If not, what sort of a whig is he? Let us know something about him. We do not wish to be led blindfolded to his support. We will take no leap in the dark. I am aware that reports are constantly circulated that he is *going to declare his whig principles hereafter.* Very well; let us know his principles, and then ask our support for him. But do not insult us by asking us to vote for him, and leave us afterwards to learn his sentiments. Again; it is said that certain highly respectable whigs assert that General Taylor is a *whig.* If he be such, he surely is not afraid to explain his doctrines. These general averments mean nothing. They explain nothing. On this subject he says, he "*will not be the exponent of the principles of any party.*" Of course he will not be the exponent of whig doctrines. If not, then I cannot support him. I shall adhere to my whig sentiments, until I become satisfied that they are erroneous; then I will abandon them. But, while I remain a whig, I will vote for no man who refuses to pledge himself in favor of freedom, and against extending slavery. That, Sir, has been a fundamental doctrine of our party, and I will not surrender it.

Mr. Chairman, it is not given us to know the future; that is wisely hidden from our view; but I think I speak the sentiments of those whom I represent, when I say to this House and to the country, *we shall not be misled in our votes for President.* Let others do as they please. We shall not abandon our position so long maintained against the annexation of territory; against extending slavery; against conquest; against aggression; against war. Against all these we shall interpose our utmost influence.

RELATION OF THE FEDERAL GOVERNMENT TO SLAVERY.*

POSITION OF SOUTHERN STATESMEN — OBJECTS FOR WHICH THIS GOVERNMENT WAS FORMED — ADDRESS OF SOUTHERN MEMBERS EXAMINED — ITS DOCTRINES EXPOSED — RIGHTS OF THE PEOPLE OF THE FREE STATES — THEIR DUTIES IN REGARD TO FUGITIVE SLAVES — THE DOMESTIC SLAVE-TRADE — COURSE OF THE SPEAKER OF THE HOUSE OF REPRESENTATIVES, AND DECEPTIONS OF THE WHIG PARTY EXPOSED — OBJECTS OF THE FREE DEMOCRACY STATED — THEIR COURSE VINDICATED — PROGRESS OF THE CAUSE OF LIBERTY.

[The question whether the powers of the Federal Government should be exerted to sustain liberty, or prostituted to the support of slavery, had been pressed for some years, until, in 1848, the vote of the free democracy appeared to have alarmed the slave power. In the session of Congress which followed the presidential election of that year, some twenty southern members of Congress published an address to the people of the South, complaining that their slaves were permitted to escape; that the people of the North discussed the institution of slavery and the slave-trade; that they were endeavoring to abolish both in the District of Columbia, and to prohibit the latter as it was carried on upon our southern coast. Efforts were made to get an address answering it, signed by an equal number of northern members. This failed, however, and Mr. Giddings expressed his own views in the following speech.]

Mr. Chairman, — A treaty of peace has been entered into between this government and Mexico; and we are called on to grant the necessary means to carry it into effect. For that purpose, the bill under consideration has been presented. The subject is one of a comprehensive character, and opens up a wide field of debate. Gentlemen who have preceded me have

* Speech on the bill making appropriations to carry into effect our Treaty with Mexico. Delivered in Committee of the whole House, February 17, 1849.

availed themselves of this latitude of remark. But some of them have refused to be corrected on matters of fact and of law, when other members believed them in error. I regard speeches made in this body profitable, only so far as they elicit truth; and will thank any gentleman to correct me upon matters of fact or of law, as I pass along in my remarks. If I labor under error, I desire to be set right at the earliest moment, before I impress that error upon any other human being.

The bill before us has presented to us the important question of the relation which this government holds to the institution of slavery. The exclusion of that institution from our new territories, sustaining it in this district, and the maintenance of the slave-trade here, have all been ably and eloquently debated. I have no hope of bringing any new views before the committee, although I may perhaps present those already advanced in a connection different from those who have gone before me.

On that ill-fated day, when this House adopted the war which had been commenced by the Executive, I saw, or thought I clearly saw, the present difficulties into which we have been precipitated. These difficulties I pointed out in an humble speech which I had the honor of delivering to this body on the day following. During the whole period of hostilities, we were conscious that it was the design of the Executive to acquire territory, principally for the purpose of spreading the curse of human bondage over it. Gentlemen of the two great political parties then united in sustaining and continuing the war, with our present position in full view before them. During the progress of the war, we constantly cautioned our southern friends, we assured them that, if territory were obtained, we should not consent to abolish freedom therein. They now speak of the amount of southern blood shed in that war. It was their own folly. They knew that our army was fighting for the purpose of bringing these questions before us for decision. They now talk of its dangers. Sir, they should have reflected on that before the declaration of war; they should have listened to our advice, and avoided the dangers which we so distinctly pointed out. If our maintenance of liberty be dangerous, that danger has now become unavoidable. We hope to meet it in a manner as becomes freemen.

In the arguments of southern gentlemen, there seems to be a fundamental error common to them all. They assume that this government was founded for the support of slavery. They insist that southern oppression is as much entitled to the encouragement and fostering care of the National Government as are the liberties of the people for whom we legislate. They seem to have overlooked the great object which the founders of our institutions had in view. That design stands recorded on every page of our history; they left perpetual monuments on every battle field of the Revolution, proclaiming, in unmistakable language, their hostility to oppression, and their devotion to freedom. No class of men, at any period of the world, were more inveterately opposed to slavery than were the founders of this government. In setting forth the reasons which induced them to separate from the mother country, and to found an independent sovereignty, they declared that the objects of government were to secure the *lives* and *liberties* of the people. It was hostility to slavery of every description which impelled them to action.

Every argument, therefore, based on the assumption that we are, to any extent or in any manner, to shape our legislation for the encouragement or maintenance of slavery, must of course be erroneous. If we carry out in good faith the intentions of those who framed our institutions, we shall devote our energies to the support and encouragement of freedom, limiting our efforts in this respect by the Constitution, so as not to interfere with slavery within the States. But to encourage its existence even there, would be a violation of every principle which controlled the action of those who achieved our independence, as well as of those who framed our Constitution.

Here, then, is the precise point on which the advocates of slavery and the supporters of liberty differ. We demand that our whole legislation shall be in favor of freedom, of justice and humanity; they insist that we are to place slavery, injustice, and crime upon the same level, and to bestow upon each the same attention and encouragement. Differing thus as to the essential elements of our compact, it were impossible for us to arrive at the same conclusions in our arguments. The controversy is therefore radical. It involves the most vital principles of our association.

Of all the erroneous sayings common to our country, none is more unfounded than the very common assertion that "slavery is guaranteed by the Federal Constitution." We hear it repeated in this hall, and we read it in official documents, and gentlemen appear to regard it as an established maxim, by which we are to guide our legislation. I have often requested those who repeat this assertion, to point me to the article, section, or clause of the Constitution, which *guarantees slavery.* I most respectfully made the inquiry, in the presence of the House, of the gentleman from Virginia (Mr. Meade) who sits opposite; but he failed to name the clause, or section, or article.

Now, Sir, I desire to elict truth, and to expose error. I am surrounded by the ablest statesmen of the South, by men who insist that slavery is thus guaranteed to them. I therefore respectfully desire any one of them now to inform this body and the country on what clause of the Constitution they rely to sustain the assertion to which I have alluded. To enable any one to do that, I now proffer to him the floor.

[Mr. Giddings here paused for some moments, and then resumed.]

Mr. Chairman, here is a most important error, either on my part, or on the part of those who assert that the Constitution guarantees slavery. If wrong, I desire to be corrected now, before this body, and before the American people. I call on gentlemen, in respectful terms, to show the grounds of their faith on this point. They sit in silence. No one is willing to hazard his reputation by attempting it. Sir, there is no such guaranty. The pretence is entirely without foundation. I therefore repeat, that the proper constitutional attitude of this government is in favor of liberty, and opposed to every form of oppression.

The doctrine, that we are bound to encourage and perpetuate slavery, is of recent origin. It was never asserted until 1843. Prior to that period, the doctrine which I have laid down was admitted by statesmen from all portions of the Union. An attempt was then made to change the fundamental principles of our government, and to transform it into a slave-holding, a slave-sustaining confederacy. The great apostle of southern slavery stood forth as the advocate of this new theory. He went out of his way to argue the humane character of slavery in his official correspondence, and to point out the dangers of freedom to the colored race. He went farther, and endeavored to show that it was the duty of this government to uphold, extend, and perpetuate an institution abhorred by nearly all civilized nations. He, Sir, is a bold and honest statesman. He speaks his thoughts, and leaves no doubts as to his position. For this, I honor him. He was born and educated in a land of slavery. His interest has at all times been identified with that institution. His prejudices are in favor of it. It is interwoven as it were with his very existence. This is his misfortune; for that I will not reproach him. This new doctrine was carried into practice by the annexation of Texas. The war and conquest which followed, and the present efforts to appropriate our Mexican territory to the blighting curse of slavery, has precipitated upon us the important questions now pending. These circumstances have aroused the northern people to examine their rights. Southern aggressions have accomplished a work which northern philanthropy attempted in vain. A portion of our northern people have taken their position distinctly in favor of separating this government from all interference with slavery in the States, and of hostility to it in all places where we have the power to legislate upon the subject.

This position of northern men has called forth a convention of southern statesmen. They have issued an address to the people of the South. Upon that address I propose to bestow a few remarks. I wish to approach it with no feelings other than a desire to ascertain truth. Those gentlemen evidently think their rights are invaded. They are dissatisfied, and have sent forth an address stating their grievances. As a member of this body, as a lover of justice, it becomes my duty to inquire into the cause of discontent, if it exists among any portion of the people, either North or South; and if any just cause of dissatisfaction is found, we ought at once to remove it. This is a government *of* and *for* the people. It should be ministered to the satisfaction of all, so far as may be compatible with justice and the Constitution.

With these feelings, I cannot but regret the attempts which are made to array unmeaning prejudices against those southern members who constitute the Convention alluded to. It has been called a "Disunion Convention," a "Hartford Convention," and other terms of reproach have been applied to it. We ought to use only the arguments of truth and justice. Those gentlemen not only possessed the right to meet and compare views and deliberate, but if they felt that the rights of their people were invaded, it was their duty to take such constitutional course as they deemed best calculated to obtain justice for their constituents. I have no doubt they were prompted by these desires.

The imputation of improper motives constitutes no answer to the charges they make. To say that the rights of the *North* have been trampled upon, will constitute no legitimate reason for withholding justice from the *South*. Suppose that, under merely imaginary wrongs, they have contemplated a dissolution of the American Union, we should, nevertheless, treat them kindly, and by the force of reason and the presentation of truth, endeavor to set them right. We should bear in mind that oppression, a disregard of our rights, caused our fathers to dissolve the union between Great Britain and these United States; indeed, we all hold "that whenever any form of government becomes destructive" to the happiness of the people, "it is their right to alter or to abolish it. Our first duty is, to carry out and maintain the constitutional rights of each portion of the Union; our next duty is, to examine into and remove all just cause of complaint. The most humble citizen is entitled to a patient hearing in this body.

Now, Sir, for a moment, let us look into this address, and ascertain why dissatisfaction exists among our southern friends.

The general cause of complaint is, that this National Government has failed to secure and encourage oppression; that under its administration men are rending the chains that have bound them for ages; that they are rising from a state of degradation, and resuming the rights with which God endowed them.

We of the free States regard this as the best of all possible arguments in favor of the Union. We look upon it as carrying into practice the very objects for which it was formed. These gentlemen, however, evidently think it was formed, not for the purpose of encouraging liberty, but to uphold slavery. Thus I am again brought to this point of divergence, mentioned at the commencement of my remarks. Southern men holding this doctrine shape their legislation to the support of slavery, believing that the legitimate object of our association; while we of the North direct our efforts to the promotion of freedom, believing that to be the design for which our government was instituted. Thus we start in different directions, and while we travel, we shall of course increase the distance between us.

This address will serve in a great degree to inform the country of the true issues between the advocates of slavery and those who are laboring to promote the cause of human rights. We hope that southern men will no longer deal in vague generalities. We rejoice to see them in this address come down to distinct specifications. This enables us to meet them understandingly, and to compare our views on specific points.

They first complain, that we lend them no aid in the arrest of their *fugitive* slaves. They evidently think that by the terms of our compact we are bound to aid the slave-holder in arresting the bondman who flees from oppression. On this point we are not left without definite information of the intention of those who framed the Constitution.

When Mr. Butler, of South Carolina, moved, in the Convention that framed the Constitution, an amendment making it the duty of the free States to arrest and deliver up fugitive slaves in the same manner that we are bound to arrest and deliver up fugitives from crime, Mr. Willson, of Pennsylvania, objected that such a provision would involve the people of the free States in the *expense* of arresting such fugitive slaves; and the motion was withdrawn.

Mr. Madison, in his history of the formation of the Constitution, gives us this information. South Carolina did not then hold the doctrine now maintained by her most distinguished statesmen. Such claim was then spurned by northern men, and was abandoned by those of the South. Our obligations are embraced in the following clause of the second section of the fourth article:

> "No person held to service or labor in one State, and fleeing into another, shall, in consequence of any law or regulation therein, be discharged from such service or labor; but shall be delivered up on claim of the party to whom such service or labor may be due."

These are our stipulations. We are to pass no law, make no regulation by which the person escaping shall be discharged. Our duty thus far is negative. We are *not* to act; we are to refrain from all action, to leave master and slave to themselves.

The latter part of the clause says, "he shall be delivered up on claim of the person to whom such service or labor may be due." How delivered up? This question is distinctly answered by the Supreme Court of the United States, in the case of Prigg *v.* The Commonwealth of Pennsylvania. They say he is to be delivered up in the same manner that we deliver up our friends to the civil officer in our own State. We are bound to permit the master to take him wherever he finds him. We must not secrete him from the master. We must not defend him against the master; nor are we to rescue him from the master's custody after he shall have taken him. This is the way in which he is to be delivered up, according to the high tribunal which is authorized to give construction to the Constitution; and it is worthy of remark that a majority of the Court making this decision were slave-holders. They have determined our duties; I believe them in strict accordance with the intentions of those who framed the Constitution. These slave-holding judges do not pretend that this government, or the people of the free States, are bound to encourage or sustain slavery; on the contrary, they solemnly declare that our whole duty is to abstain from secreting, defending, or rescuing the slave. These obligations we observe to the very letter. They may have been violated by individuals. I have heard and read of cases where citizens of my own State have been convicted of violating these stipulations, and have suffered the legal penalties attached to such violation.

It is proper, on such occasions as the present, that we should speak with perfect frankness. I therefore remark, that our people consider these obligations as restraining the exercise of our moral duties. They therefore very properly refuse to go farther than is required by the Constitution. Their sympathies are with the slave, — such is the ordained law of the human intellect. We cannot suppress the feelings of our nature; we cannot look with indifference upon the panting fugitive as he flies from bondage; we will not do it. We receive him into our houses, we feed and clothe him, and treat him as a *man*. We inform him, teach him his rights, and point him to that immortality that awaits him. Sir, our people know their constitutional obligations on this subject. It is useless to say to them that it is their duty to assume the character of bloodhounds, and give chase to him who is fleeing from a land of chains and tears. No, Sir, they have neither sympathy nor respect for the slave-catcher. We look upon him as a moral pestilence, a legalized pirate; we will not admit him to our dwellings; we drive him from our premises; we regard him as unworthy to associate with any portion of our race.

I understood the gentleman from Indiana, (Mr. Thompson,) and the gentleman from Pennsylvania, (Mr. Brown,) and my

29 *

colleague (Mr. Taylor) to say, that in their districts the master who pursues his slave is treated with hospitality and respect. They further said their people aided the master in tracking out the trembling object of his pursuit. It is due to candor that I should assure southern gentlemen, that no such beings reside in my district. They would find no associates there. In the language of that eminent patriot, Mr. Gerry, he hold that "we have nothing to do with slavery in the States; but we will be careful to lend it no sanction." We rejoice to see our fellow men who have been subjected to all that is wrong and barbarous and cruel, breathing the air of freedom, and wending their way to a land of safety. Nor will we interpose the slightest obstacle to their escape; but we will lend them all the aid in our power, without violating the Constitution or laws of the land.

This address further complains that the people of the North discuss the subject of slavery; that debating clubs examine into its demerits; and that members on this floor denounce it as wrong, as destructive to the best interests of mankind; and that the newspaper press is left untrammeled by a censorship.

This feeling did not exist when the framers of the Constitution solemnly declared, "that Congress shall make no law abridging the freedom of speech or of the press." The founders of our government had no idea of rendering the press subservient to slavery. Deeming it one of the bulwarks of liberty, they placed its freedom beyond the power of Congress. They had no thoughts of sealing the lips of freemen, or of members of Congress, in order to uphold and continue the slavery of the South.

Yet it is a lamentable truth, that for a time these rights were surrendered, ingloriously surrendered by northern timidity. Yes, in servile obedience to slave-holding dictation, for a time we established a vitiated state of public sentiment throughout the whole North. Fifteen years since, it was regarded as disreputable to discuss the demerits of slavery in our social circles. Our pulpits were silent in regard to the most heaven-daring crimes when connected with southern oppression. Our presses dared not speak the language of freedom; and here, in this hall, a tyranny more absolute and unrelenting than exists in any deliberative body in the civilized world, held undisputed sway. I speak with some feeling on this subject. I witnessed that tyranny; Sir, I *felt* it. For years I sat here under the inexorable rule of the slave power; reproached, assailed, insulted, and driven from my seat, because I insisted upon my right, as an American statesman, to speak the sincere convictions of my heart.

But, Sir, after years of toil, of solicitude, and of responsibility, we have regained the freedom of speech. Do not gentlemen know that we found our right to speak our thoughts both here and elsewhere upon the Constitution, upon the very rock of our political salvation? Do they desire again to seal our lips? Do they complain that truth spoken here excites their slaves to strive for freedom? I rejoice to hear such tidings. Would that I were able, from this forum, to make every bondman in the nation hear me. I would teach them their rights, and if truth could instantly effect it, I would, before I resume my seat, strike the chains from every slave in the wide universe.

I am perfectly aware that these gentlemen are correct, when they assure the country that these discussions are constantly weakening and relaxing the cords by which the slaves are bound. I rejoice at it. Truth is doing its perfect work. Justice is beginning to assert her rights. The voice of humanity is listened to. Our press of the North is beginning to speak out. The people talk of slavery as they do of other great iniquities. Truth and righteousness are now preached from our pulpits. While Turks and Tartars denounce the sins of slavery, shall Americans keep silence? While the followers of Mohammed are purifying themselves from its crimes, shall Christians uphold and encourage its God-provoking iniquities? Here, in this city, in every street, we meet our brother man, borne down, trampled upon, and held in the most abhorrent degradation. From the windows of this hall, we witness the barracoons, those legalized hells, established by our laws, and now sustained by this body. And shall we keep silence? We possess the moral and constitutional right to speak and print whatever shall conduce to the elevation of our race. Duty to our fellow men, and obedience to God, require the exercise of those rights. They will never be surrendered.

Those gentlemen also complain that we regard slavery as sinful and wicked. I presume at this day it would be superfluous to argue that any act or institution which detracts from the happiness of mankind, or inflicts misery and suffering upon any portion of our race, except as a punishment for crimes, is opposed to the design of our Creator, and in violation of his law. I believe this may be regarded as an admitted principle. How is it with slavery? How does the civilized world regard it? How have we as a nation regarded it? When, in 1804, the semi-barbarians of Tripoli seized and enslaved our people, did we not regard it as sinful?

By the most accurate data we can obtain, the number of human lives sacrificed upon the sugar, cotton, and rice plantations of the South, amounts annually to more than twenty thousand. These murders are effected by driving the slaves so hard as to render their average existence upon those plantations from five to seven years. And will southern gentlemen assert that this worse than savage barbarity is innocent? Does our religion teach this bloody code? Sir, happy would those slaves feel if they could escape from professed Christians, whose hands are dripping with human gore, to the protection of the most unrelenting despotisms of the Old World; or, could they even fall into the hands of the savage Arabs of Morocco, they would regard it as an unspeakable improvement of their condition. Look at the victims of our domestic slave-trade! Mark the agony, the horror, the transports of grief which they suffer! Listen to their sighs, their groans, and wailings! Do you believe that a holy, pure, and righteous God, approves the infliction of such suffering? Sir, these gentlemen are correct, when they assert that we regard slavery as a *sin*. We look upon it not only as wicked and sinful, but as compounded of the worst of crimes. It *robs* men of their labor; it *steals* from them their domestic and intellectual enjoyments; it *degrades, brutalizes, and murders them.* For my own part, I can conceive of no greater crime than that of slavery. It is on that account that the Christian world are opposed to it.

Another and principal cause of complaint set forth in this address, is the expected exclusion of slavery from our newly acquired territory. In establishing a government there, we have an object by which we are guided. What is it? The answer is given in the American Declaration of Independence: "Governments are instituted among men to secure the enjoyment of life and liberty." Northern men are now ready and willing to form such a government in California; but our southern friends insist that a government shall be established there by which a portion of the people may be robbed of those rights, may be brutalized, disrobed of their humanity. We reply, that such an act would be vitally opposed to the objects for which our Union was formed, at war with the principles of justice, of humanity, and the Constitution. This subject, however, has been so fully argued by others, as well as by myself, on former occasions, that I will not detain the committee longer upon it. I will merely add, that the people of the North have examined and considered this subject, and, I think, have made up their judgments in regard to it. Their motto is, "*No slave territory, — no more slave States.*"

I again remark, that this address in its general aspect, and in each and every particular, is founded upon the erroneous assumption that this government is bound to regard slavery with favor, and to uphold and encourage it; while we of the North hold that the ultimate design of our Constitution is unyielding hostility to slavery, and every species of oppression.

It is this error into which southern men have so generally fallen, that leads us to differ in relation to the abolition of slavery in this district. By our law of 1801, we took possession of this territory, and extended over it the laws of Maryland. In that act we declared that the laws of that State then in operation here, *should remain and continue in force.* Among those laws was the entire slave code of that State. This we adopted with the others as laws of the district. By this enactment, they became "*acts of Congress.*" They are to this *day* sustained and made law by this act of 1801. It is, therefore, solely by virtue of this act of 1801, that slavery exists in this district. It is that which sustains the slave-trade. By force of this Congressional enactment, men are bought and sold, women are made the subjects of traffic, and a commerce in children is carried on within this territory, under the jurisdiction of this Government.

Now, Sir, all that the advocates of freedom ask, is the repeal of that law of 1801. Let that be repealed, and the chains will instantly fall from every slave in the district. This is the doctrine which, for ten years, we have constantly held forth in this hall. We insist that our power to repeal this law of our own enacting is clear and indisputable. I have never been able to find any member of this body willing to deny this position. Yet we sit here and listen to long and eloquent speeches, denouncing us for attempting to interfere with the rights of slave property here. We have heard a most ingenious argument from the gentleman who has just taken his seat, (Mr. Crisfield,) urging that we have not the constitutional power to abolish either slavery or the slave-trade in this district. I had hoped that he would have met this position. While listening to his speech, I greatly desired to ask him whether he denied the power of Congress to repeal its own law to which I have referred. He, however, refused to be interrupted. I see the gentleman is now in his seat. I feel desirous of knowing whether he and I differ on this subject; and in order to determine that question, I respectfully ask him, whether he denies the power of Congress to repeal that law of 1801, to which I have referred? And I tender him the floor to answer that interrogatory.

Mr. Crisfield said he had not been paying particular attention to what the gentleman from Ohio (Mr. Giddings) was saying. But he had refused to be interrogated, and should refuse answering any questions.

Mr. GIDDINGS. Yes, Mr. Chairman, that is probably a more convenient mode for gentlemen to get along with this subject. Evasion, Sir, is their only mode of escape. I call on the House and the country to witness, that I desire to meet this question openly and candidly. At the very opening of my remarks, I tendered the floor to any gentleman who deemed me in error, for the purpose of setting me right. I regard it as a favor to me, and an act of friendship in any gentleman who will propound to me questions for the purpose of eliciting truth. That, Sir, is the very object for which I speak. Now, if the gentleman admits our power to repeal our own laws, then there would be no issue between us in regard to our constitutional authority.

The gentleman, and his colleague (Mr. McLane) who spoke the other day, insist that we ought not to abolish slavery here, until Maryland abolishes it in that State. Slavery, as I have already shown, exists by virtue of our own laws. Its existence has no more connection with slavery in Maryland, than it has with that institution in Algiers. We, Sir, the people of Ohio, — of all the free States, — uphold and sustain slavery in this district. Its wrongs, its outrages, its crimes, and its guilt rest on us. To God and to mankind we are responsible. Yet we are told that we must continue involved in all these enormities until the people of Maryland shall awake to the turpitude of slavery. The guilt of sustaining the crimes of that institution, sits heavy upon the consciences of our people. They are deeply anxious to be relieved from it.

Again, Sir, the slave-trade carried on here, forms a part of the institution itself. But the gentleman from Maryland denies that the slave-trade exists in this district, or that slave prisons are to be found in this city, or that persons are brought here from Maryland for sale. Why, Sir, this very day I was applied to for counsel in a case where three persons, said to be legally entitled to their freedom, were brought from Maryland, and during yesterday were sold and taken to Alexandria. At the last session, I was called on for counsel in a case where a large family was brought from that State and sold South, where, if living, they are now dragging out a miserable existence. But the gentleman denies that there are slave prisons in this city. If he will go to either of these front windows, and cast his eye down Maryland avenue as far as Seventh street, he will see a large brick building, standing back from both streets, its out-buildings surrounded by a high brick wall. Sir, I hesitate not to say, that if he will ask any colored person in the city of ten years of age, they will tell him "*that is a slave pen.*" I have visited it. I went there to redeem my fellow man with "sordid dust," from the grasp of the soul-driver. On my right, sits my friend from Pennsylvania, (Mr. McIlvaine,) who accompanied me. I leave it for that gentleman to give a full description of the scene which we witnessed on that occasion. I have no language adequate to that purpose. The man whom we redeemed was there some six or seven days. He assured us that every night during his stay, slaves were brought in from the country and confined in that receptacle of suffering humanity.

When gentlemen deny the existence of the slave-trade here, do they intend to charge falsehood upon the venerable Justice Cranch, and ten hundred and sixty-three other respectable citizens of this district, who have assured us that this traffic, with all its horrors and attendant crimes, is continually carried on in this city? There is their petition praying us to deliver them from those painful exhibitions of this slave-trade which your law has authorized. Yet gentlemen say there is no traffic carried on here. Will they deny that in April last, Hope H. Slatter, a noted dealer in slaves, marched fifty-two men, women, and children, victims of this commerce, from the jail in this city, through Pennsylvania avenue, to the railroad depôt, thence to Baltimore, for the southern market, where they now pine in bondage? No man will deny these specific facts. They are known to the whole country.

The gentleman from Indiana (Mr. Thompson) said that he had seen nothing of this slave-trade, and sneeringly remarked that "gentlemen who had *looked for it may have seen it.*" Sir, I receive his taunts with all humility. I am one of those who feel it my duty to look around me, and learn the effect of the laws which we enact. I have attended the sale of slaves at auction in this city for this express purpose. I have witnessed the chained coffle as they passed by the very walls of the building in which we are now sitting; where the star-spangled banner which floats over us, threw its shadow in bitter irony upon those victims of your barbarous law, which we now uphold and sustain.

Now, Sir, I repeat, that this government was not formed for the purpose of thus robbing men of their rights, — of degrading and brutalizing them. It was not for such purpose that our fathers of the revolution toiled and bled. They struggled to establish a government that should suppress outrages and crimes like these.

But it is said that this slave-trade causes no suffering; that it produces no distress. There is no doubt that great pains are taken to prevent the promulgation of facts which illustrate the barbarous character of this traffic. Generally, the slaves of the district are sold when they are unconscious of the fact. They are sent by their masters to some place agreed upon with the purchaser; there they are seized, gagged, and instantly taken to the slave-pen, and few, if any, spectators witness the horrid process. Those purchased out of the city, are brought here in the night, and are taken away during the hours of darkness. This caution has increased as the public attention has been turned to the subject, until now but few of its enormities are witnessed by the public.

On a former occasion, I stated that some years since, a man of this city, more white than black, having a wife and several children, was informed by his owner that she had sold him to one of those dealers in our common humanity who hover around this city. The man, in a transport of despair, attempted to cut his throat. He was seized, and the wound was dressed; but no sooner was he released from the grasp of those who held him, than he ran to the bridge over the canal on Seventh street, and threw himself into its turbid waters. In death he sought relief from the barbarity inflicted upon him by your laws. If the gentleman from Indiana wishes to know more of this transaction, I refer him to the then representative from the city of Boston, who saw the body taken from its watery grave the next morning. Nor is it unusual for the victims of this commerce to seek relief in death from those sufferings to which your laws subject them.

At a more recent period, I was told of a young woman who attempted in the day time to escape from the establishment situated on Maryland avenue, to which I have referred. She was making her way back to her home in Virginia, and while on the bridge over the Potomac, was pursued. Those who sought to arrest her gave the alarm to some men who were coming from the other side of the river. She halted, looked forward, then behind her. She saw that escape was impossible. But one appeal was left; that was to her final Judge. She threw herself from the bridge; the waters closed over her body; her spirit ascended to the "Judge of all the earth." Believe you, Sir, that He will hold us guiltless of her blood? Is there no responsibility resting on us, who now maintain these barbarous laws?

A few members are exerting all their efforts to relieve the people of the free States from the stain of such infamy, but all our labors are baffled by those who show themselves anxious to continue these outrages upon humanity. I feel constrained to speak frankly on this subject, to point the people to existing facts.

Sir, the Speaker of this House is a distinguished friend of the incoming Executive. He was an advocate of General Taylor's nomination, many months prior to the occurrence of that event. He arranges the committees who hold jurisdiction of this slave-trade. A majority of those committees are the avowed friends of General Taylor. The petitions of many thousands of our northern people, praying to be released from the guilt of supporting this infamous traffic, are sent to those committees, and are by them buried in silence. We can extort no report upon them. Without such report, the friends of humanity can do nothing. There stand the committees, placed by the Speaker between us and the slave-dealers, upholding the law, and encouraging the crimes to which I have referred.*

Mr. Evans, of Maryland, (interrupting Mr. Giddings,) said that he understood the gentleman from Ohio to say that the Speaker placed an undue proportion of southern men on those committees, while the facts were that a majority of each committee were from the North.

Mr. Giddings resumed. I had not charged the Speaker with placing a majority of southern men on those committees. I said they were so arranged by the Speaker, that all efforts to obtain a report from them upon the petitions referred to their consideration, had proved fruitless. They will neither report in favor of continuing the sale of slaves in this district, nor will they report in favor of abolishing it.

Mr. Edwards said, they had reported a bill on that subject.

Mr. Giddings (resuming) remarked, that they had reported a bill to prohibit bringing slaves from the surrounding country to this market; but they had left the people of the district (those entitled to our protection) to be bought and sold, at the option of those who claimed to own them.† After all the demonstrations of popular feeling, and after the reiterated expression of the sentiments of members in this hall, those committees still persist in sustaining the slave merchants while they pursue their hated vocation. I would not be uncharitable; but it is my duty to let the people understand facts. No man has a right to complain when his official acts are placed fairly before the public. I will not prejudge General Taylor. I wish merely to call public attention to the course which his leading friends pursue on this floor. They are generally loud in their protestations of devotion to the cause of humanity. Yet no man can doubt that had they failed to exert themselves

---

* Mr. Winthrop of Massachusetts was then Speaker.

† This bill passed in 1850, and it was heralded through the pro-slavery press with exultation that the slave-trade in the District of Columbia was abolished. But sales of slaves are now (1853) published in the leading newspapers of Washington city, and sales of human beings are actually made there at public auction.

to reconsider the resolution of my friend from New York, (Mr. Gott,) this slave-trade would, ere now, have been abolished. At the time that resolution was adopted, a distinguished friend of the incoming Executive, said to be a candidate for the office of Secretary of the Treasury, (Mr. Smith of Connecticut,) positively fled the hall in apparent dismay. Another gentleman from Indiana, said to be a candidate for a cabinet appointment, (Mr. C. B. Smith,) I believe, failed to vote, though he remained in the hall; and other lesser lights from the North, who are looking for minor offices, voted against the resolution. But it was adopted. And we looked upon the slave-trade as abolished.

It is said that the slave-dealers commenced closing up their business, and the slave mother, pressing her child more closely to her bosom, breathed her silent gratitude to God for the prospect that she would soon cease to tremble at the thought that the soul-driver would tear from her the object of her tenderest affections. But, gentlemen, leading friends of the incoming administration, appeared anxious to reconsider the vote adopting the resolution. The gentleman from Indiana (Mr. C. B. Smith) said he was desirous to reconsider it, as he wanted "some *practical* legislation." What could have been more practical than its entire and instantaneous abolition, I have yet to learn. But both the gentlemen to whom I have just referred, and other northern members, said to be candidates for executive appointments, voted to reconsider the resolution; and their efforts prevailed. The resolution was reconsidered, and now stands on your calendar, never again to be taken up.

The slave-trade is revived; the dealers in humanity have made new investments; more men have been purchased, more women have been collected, and an increased number of children obtained for the southern market; and here ends the gentleman's "*practical* legislation." Sir, I am sick at heart, my soul is nauseated with these deceptions, evasions, and never-ending tergiversations. I tried to draw from the gentleman from Indiana (Mr. Caleb B. Smith) an express avowal of his own wishes. I respectfully asked him, in the presence of the

House, whether he desired to continue slavery in this district? But I could not learn. He answered that his opinions were well *known*. Now, Sir, they may have been known to himself and to his more intimate friends; but I did not know, and could not learn. He refused to inform me; but he sneeringly said, that "when he submitted the question to the people of this district, *he would not allow negroes to vote.*"

I believe that gentleman was born and educated in a State where negroes vote, where the equality of *all men* is recognized. He may now revile the sublime truths, the maintenance of which constitutes the true glory of that "old Bay State" which gave him birth; he may despise the doctrines which gave unfading lustre to the names of Hancock and of Adams; he may pander for the slave-holders; but time will demonstrate to him that the people do not regard that course as the evidence of patriotism.

Thus, Sir, are slavery and the slave-trade in this district upheld and protected by leading friends of General Taylor. In calling attention to these facts, I shall do no injustice to any man or any party. We shall soon see farther developments. Will General Taylor, with these facts before him and known to the country, select his officers from among those who now exert their official influence to protect this slave-trade, to sustain crimes which strike us with horror? If he does, such indications will be regarded as establishing the character of his administration. Those members who believe that the powers of this government ought to be exerted to rob men of their inalienable rights, will sustain him; and he will be opposed by those who think such powers should be exerted to secure those rights and to elevate our race.*

I am fully aware that a great effort is making to divert public attention from this issue, and to revive old party divisions. But I am of opinion that the experience of the present session

* Mr. Smith and eleven other members who voted to reconsider the resolution to abolish the slave-trade in the District of Columbia, were appointed to high and profitable offices; but it is believed that not a member who voted against such reconsideration received any favor from the Executive.

has fully demonstrated the perfect hopelessness of that attempt. A portion of both the old parties will, under all circumstances, sustain the doctrine that we are bound to support this system of southern oppression; while a large portion of both parties will oppose it with all the power and influence which they possess.

I need say nothing of the importance of this transcendent question. It is the same issue which led our fathers to the battle-fields of the Revolution. They intended to separate our country from the advocates of oppression; from the influence of those who used civil power to deprive men of their just rights. But the spirit of oppression had taken deep root upon this American soil. It was suffered to remain; and, at the formation of the Constitution, it retained possession of the slave States as the only field of its operations. It is ever aggressive. It now demands aid of this government to extend its sphere, and to maintain its ascendancy in this district and upon the high seas. The freemen of the North are now called upon to participate in its crimes and share its disgrace. Shall we comply? That is the question. Shall we assist in subverting the fundamental doctrines of our government? Are the principles of freedom which we have so long cherished now to be basely surrendered?

The manifestations of popular sentiment exhibited at Buffalo in August last, seconded by three hundred thousand free electors in November, and responded to by the legislature of nearly every free State, sustained by a hundred presses, now give an emphatic answer.

Tell me not of the whig party, or of the democratic party, while their hands are dripping with the blood of innocent victims daily hurried to their final account by the barbarity of those laws which they support. Whether those crimes be protected by whig or by democratic votes, I will not participate in the turpitude.

The time has arrived when parties must separate on this absorbing question. Those who support outrage and crime will be politically opposed by those who adhere to the "self-evident truth" of man's equality. On those truths we base our action. Those who are not with us are against us. There can be no neutrals. Every man is in favor of this slave-trade and its attendant crimes, or he is against it. Those with whom I act are opposed to every man and every party who upholds oppression.

We shall put forth our utmost endeavors to strike the chains of bondage from the limbs of mankind, wherever this government has power to legislate. "Free soil, free men, and free speech," is our motto. If General Taylor and his friends unite with us, we shall rejoice to act with them. They may have the offices; we want them not. We desire to extend liberty to the down-trodden, to raise up the bowed-down, to exalt our race. To this object our energies will be directed. And if General Taylor's administration shall be devoted to riveting the chains of servitude upon our fellow man, to the degradation of any portion of our race, then, Sir, we shall be opposed to him. I make these remarks that our position may be distinctly understood.

There is one point on which some gentlemen appear to deceive themselves. They urge the passage of a bill to organize our Mexican territory, in order to silence the agitation in regard to slavery. They should be undeceived. They should distinctly understand that, while the people of the free States are involved in the support of slavery in this district, or of the coastwise slave-trade; while Congress lends its powers and influence to rob a portion of the people of their inalienable rights, northern philanthropy and northern patriotism will make their voices heard in this hall. Nor will they be silenced until this district is rendered *free*, until the nation's flag shall cease to float over cargoes of slaves, and the territories of the United States shall be exempt from the curse of oppression. We wish to deceive no one. We desire all to understand our position. We base our efforts distinctly upon the letter and the spirit of the Constitution. Separation of the Federal Government and the people of the free States from all participation in the support of slavery, constitutes our object. Nor shall we relax our exertions while a slave shall be held as such under the laws of Congress.

But myself and political friends are charged with "agitation." What is intended by this language I do not precisely understand. No man accuses us of bringing irrelevant or improper subjects into discussion, or that we speak upon them at improper times; nor do they charge us with misrepresentation or erroneous statements. If they intend by this language to say that we speak truth without disguise, that we do not attempt to suppress facts, then, Sir, I admit the correctness of their assertion. They do not deny our doctrines. No man, either North or South, will rise here and take issue on any principle embraced in our political creed. I repeat, that I am wholly incapable of understanding the import of this charge of *agitation* made against the free soil members of this House.

Gentlemen have constantly asserted that northern members were invading the rights of the South. The gentleman from Indiana, (Mr. Thompson,) and the gentleman from Pennsylvania, (Mr. Brown,) and my colleague, (Mr. Taylor,) were all understood as imputing to us efforts to interfere with southern rights. For years I have listened to such charges. They seem to be stereotyped. For years I have called on gentlemen to come down from these *general* denunciations, and specify *an instance* in which any proposition was ever made in this body to invade the rights of the South. I have constantly called on them to state *who* made such proposition; to give us the name. When was such proposition made? What was the proposition? To all these questions a respectful silence is the only answer which I have ever been able to obtain.

But gentlemen find fault with northern democrats for voting with us. One gentleman charged them with having changed their course of action on the subject of slavery. And who has not changed on this subject? I well recollect that my late venerable and lamented friend (Mr. Adams) interested me greatly when describing this change in his own mind. We have all changed. But it is said that the democrats are not sincere in their professions. Of that I can only judge by their acts. The voice of inspiration has taught us to show our faith by our works. If men will speak, and act, and vote right, I will leave the examination of their hearts to "Him who searcheth the heart." But those gentlemen who make this complaint will neither speak, nor act, nor vote in favor of freedom; yet they complain of the motives of others. "O! consistency, thou art a jewel." I am constrained to regard these gentlemen as sincere, when voting against *freedom*, precisely as I feel bound to believe those sincere who vote against *slavery*.

During the discussions of this body, those with whom I act have been reproached for having supported for President a man who, in former times, was opposed to the abolition of slavery in this district. Sir, the charge is true. Mr. Van Buren, in 1837, like all our public men of both parties at that time, was undoubtedly opposed to the abolition of slavery in this district. The subject had undergone no investigation by them. They had not looked into it. Even John Quincy Adams, the distinguished friend of humanity, was then opposed to that measure. The gentlemen who now assail us not only supported the same doctrines at that time, but they now sustain both slavery and the slave-trade in this city, and assail all who attempt to abolish them. The difference between these gentlemen and Mr. Van Buren is this: he now avows our doctrines; they adhere to the slave-trade, with all its turpitude; and they supported a man for President who made no professions on the subject, but who is a slave-holder, and whose interest and associations are all in favor of that institution.

It is also true that Mr. Van Buren, while President, followed the example of General Jackson, in lending the influence of his office to sustain the coastwise slave-trade. In this he complied with the avowed opinion of the Senate. That august body adopted resolutions, as late as 1840, unanimously declaring it to be the duty of this government to protect those who were engaged in that detestable traffic. Neither whig nor democrat then denied the correctness of that doctrine. No man who now denounces Mr. Van Buren, *then* even objected to his policy. Indeed, when I alone, and single-handed, denied its correctness, not one of them stood by me or sustained me in that denial. But the Convention at Buffalo which nominated Mr. Van Buren, declared it the duty of this government, "to relieve itself from all support of slavery and the slave-trade." In answer to this doctrine, Mr. Van Buren replied, that "it breathes the right spirit;" and he pledged himself to its support. Before Heaven I believe the doctrine to be right. I had no doubt of his sincerity, and I advocated his election cheerfully and cordially. Sir, I would rather have been the author of that letter than to enjoy all the honors that he has ever gained in discharging the duties of President.

Several gentlemen have inquired, rather vauntingly, what we have effected by our labors in the cause of humanity? They will find a very satisfactory answer to this interrogatory in the address of the southern members to which I have called attention.

When I first took my seat in this hall, the petitions of our people asking to be relieved from the burden, the guilt, and disgrace of supporting the slave-trade, were not received, nor were they permitted to be read; but they were treated with the most marked contempt. I found here that distinguished statesman whom history will describe as the great champion of popular rights, (Mr. J. Q. Adams;) he was laboring to regain the right of petition. His zeal and devotion to that cause were unbounded. His spirit was undaunted, and his energy never relaxed. Who that was then here has forgotten his herculean labors? No difficulties embarrassed, no dangers deterred him. His determination of purpose appeared to be more and more developed as opposition increased. We saw him arraigned at your bar, like a base felon, for no other charge than that of sustaining the right of the people; and as the dark storm of human passions gathered thick, and the tempest raged, and the waves of vituperation and calumny rolled and dashed in wild confusion around him, he stood calm and unmoved in his purpose as the adamantine rock. Who has forgotten the boundless resources of his intellect, or his unrivalled eloquence, or his terrible invective? They were all called forth and exerted in favor of the right of petition. I rejoice that he lived to witness the consummation of his labors. He has now gone to his rest, but the affections of a nation cluster around his memory.

At my first entrance to this hall, no member was allowed to speak irreverently of the slave-trade, or of slavery. A more unrelenting tyranny never existed in a Turkish divan, than reigned here. The gentleman who now fills the Presidential chair then presided over our deliberations, and most effectually did he exercise his authority for the suppression of truth and of liberty. For years my lips were hermetically sealed on the subject of humanity. Often have I listened for hours to language insulting to myself, to my constituents, and to the people of the free States, without the liberty of saying a word in vindication of those whom I represented, or of expressing in any degree the indignant emotions which prompted the utterance of salutary truth. Often have I seen the venerable and world-honored member from Massachusetts (Mr. J. Q. Adams) peremptorily ordered to his seat when he dared even to allude to the slave-trade, or to the slavery which was sustained in this district by laws of our own enactment. But how changed the scene! I can scarcely realize that this is the hall in which I have witnessed the display of deadly weapons, exhibited for the purpose of intimidating northern members to keep silence in regard to the crimes and disgrace of slavery. Here, Sir, in this body has been displayed, in the most striking manner, the power of truth. *The freedom of speech has been regained.*

We now give free utterance to the emotions of the soul in behalf of suffering humanity. We have regained and now enjoy an equality of privileges with southern members. This important reformation has been brought about by toil, and labor, and suffering which never will and never can be appreciated by any person who has not shared in them. It is, however, due to truth that I should say, northern servility, manifested through a venal press, and exhibited to this body in speeches, in a variety of ways, has presented even greater obstacles to the progress of truth than all the opposition of southern men.

Another evidence of the progress of the great reformation now going on is to be found in the action of the Executive. In 1832, a slave-ship, (the Comet,) laden with slaves, sailed from this district for New Orleans, and was wrecked on one of the British West India Islands. When the slaves reached British soil they became instantly free, and each went in pursuit of his own fortune. The slave-dealers demanded that the British authorities should arrest and return them to their owners, but they spurned the degrading proposition. The slave merchants, thus failing in their speculations, returned to this city, and demanded that the character and influence of the nation should be prostituted to aid them in obtaining a compensation for their loss from the government of England. And strange to say, the President, instead of recommending to Congress the passage of laws to punish with death the crimes of which they had been guilty, sent orders to our minister at the Court of St. James to demand, in the name of this government, indemnity for the loss of those slaves. The orders of the President were obeyed.

Our minister, (Mr. Stevenson,) however, still further disgraced the government. In order to obtain pecuniary indemnity for crimes of the deepest dye, he had recourse to misrepresentation — to flagrant falsehood. I invite the friends of that gentleman to call me to an account for what I am saying; to demand explanation before this body and the country, for the charge I make against him. He, however, deceived the British ministers, and obtained the money. The people of Great Britain have paid these slave merchants for the commission of crimes more aggravated than that of murder or of piracy. Other slave-ships were wrecked, and their cargoes obtained freedom in the same manner, and compensation was demanded, and in once instance obtained; in others it was refused. The South became clamorous. The Senate passed resolutions unanimously declaring that it was the duty of this government to support this coastwise slave-trade. A report from the Committee on Foreign Relations in this body was made, hinting at war in case indemnity was withheld from these slave-dealers; and speeches were made, even by northern members, which indicated a willingness to see our country involved in a war to support this infamous traffic.

The case of the Creole is fresh in the recollections of all who hear me. On board that ship the slaves, conscious of the rights with which God had endowed them, and true to the noblest impulses of our nature, asserted and maintained in practice the doctrines of our revolutionary fathers. They regained their freedom by their own physical strength. They then navigated the ship to the island of New Providence, and each sought his own happiness. At that time a whig administration controlled the government. Mr. Van Buren, now so much denounced for his favor to the slave power, had retired to Lindenwold. The Executive sent immediate orders to our minister at London to demand compensation of the English government for the loss of these slave merchants who had been unable to control their human cargo.

Sir, I then saw the party with whom I had always acted about to commit itself and the government to the support of a detestable commerce in mankind. I saw the Constitution violated, by a prostitution of our national influence to support a traffic detested by men, and cursed of Heaven; a traffic abhorrent to every feeling of our nature, and at war with every principle of Christianity. I had sworn at your altar faithfully to support that Constitution. I saw no way but to express my views, humble and unpretending as they were. I did so in a series of resolutions, denying the right of this government thus to involve the people of the free States in the expense, disgrace, and crimes of the slave-trade. The effect of that movement upon myself was unimportant—of that I do not speak; but the effect which it exerted upon the government should be known and understood by all. It called public attention to the subject. The press of the North spoke forth the sentiments of the North. Leading men and statesmen denounced the practice of involving the people of the free States in the support of crimes at the contemplation of which humanity shudders.

In view of these demonstrations, a slave-holding Executive hesitated in his course, doubted, and ceased to follow a practice which for years had disgraced the nation. I speak from contemporaneous history. I refer to the first volume of "Wheeler's Political and Biographical History," a work compiled with great labor and ability, and which may be consulted even by statesmen with profit. The author, speaking of the effect of that movement, says that he "has been unable to learn that the demand of this government for the loss of slaves was ever renewed." I have other evidence, satisfactory to myself, that the demand was never pressed afterwards.

Thus, Sir, the Executive has been driven from a position at war with our national honor, with justice, with humanity, and with the Constitution.

When asked what we had effected by our efforts, I answer, that in Congress we have regained the right of petition and the freedom of debate. We have relieved the government from the ostensible support of the coastwise slave-trade. We have called the attention of statesmen and jurists to the investigation of those rights which northern freemen hold under the federal compact. We have rendered northern servility unpopular. Where now are those timid, faltering statesmen of the North who filled these seats ten years since? During the short period of my service in this body, I have seen whole generations, as it were, appear here, avow their detestation of those who maintained the rights of our people and of humanity, meekly bow to the dictates of the slave power, and then depart to that political "bourn from which no traveller returns." Where are now those northern members who, only seven years since, voted to censure me for merely asserting the rights of my constituents to be exempt from the crimes attendant upon the coastwise slave-trade? Why, Sir, three or four of them yet remain, the "spared monuments" of the people's mercy; but I believe not one of them has been reëlected to meet me here in December next. A few days will separate us probably forever. Towards them I feel no unkindness; and I now refer to the fact as showing the progress of that revolution which is going forward.

Look at the other end of the capitol, and you will find unmistakable evidences of the change now going on in the popular mind. Read the proceedings of our State Legislatures. In Ohio, at one vote, they have erased from our statutes the whole code of black laws which have disgraced the State for nearly half a century. In Pennsylvania, they have gone even farther in the cause of justice and freedom; they have very properly rendered it penal for the citizens or officers of that State to aid or assist the slave-catcher in seizing upon the victims of his unrighteous oppression, as they fly from bondage. New York, too, that "Empire State," is assuming a position on this subject worthy of herself.

Of other States I need not speak. The effects of our labors are seen and felt in every free State — in every county, town, and school district of the free States. They are visible in our social circles, in our pulpits, in our literary publications, our newspapers, our debating clubs, our political discussions, and in all departments of society. The foundations of the mighty deep of popular sentiment are broken up. Political parties are disorganized, and party attachments are disregarded.

These are some of the effects of that moral and political revolution now going forward in this nation. I trust it will continue to progress, until this government and the people of the free States shall be fully redeemed and purified from the contagion of slavery and all manner of oppression, and the Constitution and the rights of humanity shall be fully vindicated.

SPEAKER OF THE HOUSE OF REPRESENTATIVES.*

HIS POWERS—DICTATES THE BUSINESS OF THAT BODY—THE MANNER OF HIS ELECTION IN EIGHTEEN HUNDRED AND FORTY-NINE—THE FORMER SPEAKER—HIS CHANGE OF POSITION—HIS SUPPORT OF THE MEXICAN WAR—OF SLAVERY IN THE TERRITORIES—OF THE SLAVE-TRADE IN THE DISTRICT OF COLUMBIA—REJECTED BY THE ADVOCATES OF LIBERTY—THE WHIG PARTY—THEIR CHANGE IN RELATION TO THE SLAVE-TRADE—THOSE WHO THUS CHANGED, SUBSEQUENTLY APPOINTED TO OFFICE—COURSE OF THE FREE DEMOCRACY VINDICATED.

[At the assembling of Congress in 1849, the free democracy held the balance of power. Neither whigs nor democrats could elect a Speaker without their aid. The contest was continued for three weeks, with unusual excitement. The free democrats stood firm; they proclaimed their determination to vote for no candidate who would not pledge himself to use his influence for freedom in the territories, and against the slave-trade in the District of Columbia. The whigs endeavored to make the country believe their candidate was in favor of that policy. He had presided over the former Congress, and had so arranged the committees as to maintain the slave-trade in the District of Columbia, and to prevent any report in favor of excluding slavery from the territories, until ordered so to do by the House. With these facts before them, the free democracy would not support him. The whigs, however, with the aid of a portion of the democrats, adopted a resolution giving the election to the candidate having the highest number of votes, instead of electing him by a majority of the votes given. Mr. Cobb of Georgia, a slave-holder, was elected; and the free soilers were assailed by the northern whig press, and charged with electing Mr. Cobb, instead of Mr. Winthrop, who they alleged was in favor of excluding slavery from our territories, and opposed to the slave-trade. To vindicate himself and friends against these charges, Mr. Giddings made the following speech.]

MR. SPEAKER,—The appointment of all committees of this body, is confided to its presiding officer. He assigns to each

---

* Speech on the Rules of the House. Delivered December 27, 1849.

committee, such members as will speak his views, and carry out his policy, which may generally be regarded as the views and the policy of the party electing him. His powers for the time being, are, perhaps, greater than those of any other officer of the government. He holds a position in which he wields far more influence upon the legislation of Congress, than the President of the United States.

The recent contest for that office, has been one of great interest here and throughout the country. A slave-holder has been elected, and it has been with no small degree of astonishment, that I have seen through most of the northern whig papers the announcement, that I and my political friends have effected his elevation by our votes.

Sir, I desire to say to this body and to the country, that the present speaker holds his office as the legitimate effect of the plurality rule, for which nearly every whig voted; and they must have done so with the full knowledge that such would be the result. They doubtless intended, by the adoption of that rule, to drive the advocates of liberty back to their former party attachments. This they had no right to expect. The free democracy is not made of such pliant materials; but had they separated, and each gone to his former party, the present speaker would have been elected by a majority of four votes. One hundred and sixteen members had been elected by the democrats, or by aid of democratic votes, and one hundred and fourteen only by whigs, or by aid of whig votes, and two of them were absent. With these facts before us, no one can doubt the effect of the plurality vote, adopted almost exclusively by whig votes.

Mr. White. Was there any other way to organize the House?

Mr. Giddings. There was. If the question of freedom in the territories had been regarded by the whigs as an object, they might at any time have elected a democrat favorable to that policy. They could have elected the gentleman over the way, (Mr. Strong,) who is said also to be in favor of river and harbor improvements, and a protective tariff, or they might have elected my friend from New York, (Mr. Preston King,) or my friend from Pennsylvania, (Mr. Wilmot,) or my colleague from the Huron district, (Mr. Root). Had the whigs voted for any one of those gentlemen, they could have elected him at any ballot. Free soilers had intended to be liberal and just. They had voted for my whig friend from Pennsylvania, (Mr. Thaddeus Stevens,) a man recommended as a whig, but one who had no hesitation in avowing his attachment to freedom. Had the whig party voted for him, he might have been elected at any time. In short, Sir, had the whigs united on any man who was unconditionally committed to the cause of free soil and of humanity, even if a whig, he would have been elected. They were informed of these facts by free soilers, at different times during the ballotings; but they adhered pertinaciously to their caucus nominee. They appeared determined to stand or fall with him. They would go for no other candidate. Indeed, it appeared to me that they intended to elect him, or a slave-holding democrat.

All were conscious that the free soil vote would be given for any candidate of either party who stood publicly pledged to the Wilmot proviso, so soon as their vote would effect his election. I could, therefore, see no other object in a proposition to unite whigs and democrats on some new plan for electing a Speaker, than to avoid the election of a man committed to freedom in the territories. This conviction was so strongly impressed on my own mind, that I called the attention of the House to it on the morning of the 20th instant, as plainly as I could under the gag resolution then in force, by the interrogatories propounded to a gentleman from Massachusetts, (Mr. Ashmun).

But the vote of a plurality of this body would, under the Constitution, confer no right whatever to the office of Speaker. This was well understood by the House. The vote merely operated as a nomination, while the election was made by adopting the resolution of the gentleman from North Carolina, (Mr. Stanley). That resolution reads as follows:

"*Resolved*, That the Hon. Howell Cobb, a Representative from the State of Georgia *be*, and he *is* hereby declared duly elected Speaker of this House for the thirty-first Congress."

This resolution gave him the office, constituted him Speaker. Without it, he would have had no claim to the Speakership. This was adopted, and the Speaker elected by the united vote of nearly the entire whig and democratic parties, and was clearly a part of the original agreement by which the plurality rule was adopted. The whig press now turn round and charge free soilers with electing the present Speaker.

Mr. SCHENCK inquired if Mr. Giddings had not an opportunity of choosing between the present Speaker and a whig committed to the proviso?

Mr. GIDDINGS. Certainly; I did so when I voted for the gentleman from Pennsylvania, (Mr. Stevens).

Mr. SCHENCK inquired if his colleague did not have the opportunity of choosing between the whig nominee and the gentleman elected?

Mr. GIDDINGS. I regret that my colleague has pressed that question upon me. I had not intended to make any personal allusions to the honorable gentleman who filled the Speaker's chair during the last Congress, (Mr. Winthrop). It is known to the House and to the country, that on the assembling of the last Congress, two honorable gentleman, who had acted with the whig party, together with myself, refused to vote for the gentleman at that time nominated by the whigs. A learned and honorable gentleman from Massachusetts, (Mr. Palfrey,) with my entire approbation, propounded to the candidate interrogatories as to the manner in which he would, if elected, constitute certain committees to whom petitions in regard to the slave-trade and slavery in this district, are, by the rules of the House, committed. The gentleman refused to inform us; but referred to his past acts and votes, from which we were to judge of his future course. These were not satisfactory, however, and we refused to vote for him. My colleague now inquires, if I did not know that that same gentleman was in favor of the proviso? I answer, I do not know any such thing, — how could I know it? He refused to declare his sentiments. Why did he withhold them from the public? Every man is aware that he did so in order to obtain votes from members who would not sustain him if his opinions were known. While I felt no disposition to defraud others, I had no desire to be made a dupe myself. I therefore could not vote for him. His public acts do not show him in favor of the proviso. The Committee on Territories selected by him, refused to report a bill excluding slavery from California until peremptorily ordered by the House.

Mr. Rockwell asked if the gentleman intended to say that the Committee on Territories refused to report such a bill?

Mr. Giddings. I will say they *neglected* to report such a bill. Probably that term is more appropriate than to say they *refused* to report it.

The Committee on the District of Columbia, during the late Congress, appeared to have been arranged in such manner as studiously to protect that infamous commerce in human flesh now carried on in this city. That committee had before them thousands of petitions from the North, praying the abolition of the slave-trade carried on here. They had witnessed the heart-rending scenes which transpired on our principal avenue in May, 1848, when that slave-dealer, Hope H. Slatter, with his mournful procession of fifty-two fathers and mothers and children marched through that court street of our city, on their way to graves in the far South. I cannot say that the then Speaker, and the committees which he had arranged, were personally present and witnessed that worse than barbarian spectacle. But if they were not eye witnesses of that revolting scene, they knew all the facts, and understood its true character. Yet not all these considerations, aided by the voice of northern philanthropy, enforced by thousands of petitions, could extort from these committees a report against the slave-trade, or even a reproof of that traffic.

But it may be urged that the Speaker was ignorant of the views of the gentlemen whom he had placed on these committees. Did he mistake the character of those whom he placed on committees which exerted a political influence? Not at all. The character of every anti-slavery man in this body was as well known, as was that of whigs or of democrats. But surely no excuse of this kind could possibly apply to him at the second session, when he again arranged those committees. He then certainly knew the character of every member. Their sentiments were on record, and he could not have mistaken the views of any one. Nearly all of the same members were a second time placed on these committees; and the slave-trade was again upheld and protected by them. The petitions of the whole North were again suppressed; and there those committees stood between us and those who deal in human flesh,—who commit crimes at which humanity shudders. Those crimes were protected; and those who perpetrated them were encouraged by committees placed there by a Speaker elected by a party with whom I had once felt proud to act.

Now, Sir, the same gentleman was at this session again presented as a candidate, and free soilers were asked to vote for him,—to sanction the arrangement of those committees, and to approve the slave-trade, with its Heaven-daring iniquities. We were called on to choose between him and the gentleman who now occupies the chair. God forbid that I should choose between them! I speak with proper respect for both those gentlemen; they look upon these things in a different light. I speak of the character in which the slave-trade presents itself to my view. I do not believe that a member on this floor, or a person in the whole country, has for a moment believed that I could be made to vote for either of those gentlemen,—that I could be constrained by any circumstance to lend the sanction of my vote to any one who exerts his official influence to maintain this execrable commerce in human flesh. Yet one thing is certain, the present Speaker can do no worse than the last; he *may* do better.

I regret, Sir, that my colleague felt it his duty to press me into this explanation, which I was desirous of avoiding. I now speak to the country. The people of my district understand this matter. These things were all pressed against me pending my last election. An appeal was then made to my constituents. I was charged with refusing my support to the gentleman from Massachusetts. I left the district early in the canvass, and did not return until after the election. The hunker whigs and hunker democrats united for the purpose of defeating me. But my constituents approved my course; they sent me back by a majority of some thousands, with the expectation that I would maintain my position. To them and to the country I stood pledged to vote for no man to the office of Speaker who lends his influence to support the slave-trade.

[Mr. Winthrop, Mr. Rockwell, and Mr. Schenck followed Mr. Giddings, in opposition to the views he had expressed.]

Mr. Giddings having again obtained the floor, said that no gentleman regretted the present discussion more than himself; and the House would bear him witness that he had been forced into it. I came here, said he, intending to discharge my duties in a quiet, unpretending manner; but when I saw myself assailed through the leading Taylor papers of the North, I felt it a duty to say a few words in vindication of my own course. On this floor I have been assailed, because I dared to vote for such man to the office of Speaker as my judgment and my conscience dictated. In short, it has come to this, that gentlemen in this hall undertake to say who I shall vote *for*, and who I shall vote *against*.

Now, I was sent here to act according to the dictates of my own judgment. I came here with no expectation or intention to look to any man, or to any number of men, for instruction as to the candidate for whom I should cast my vote. While I was previously on the floor, I stated some of the reasons why I refused to vote for the gentleman from Massachusetts, (Mr. Winthrop). This was done in the most general terms possible, in order to avoid a conflict with that gentleman. But he, in reply, has seen fit to refer back to the commencement of the last Congress, and to allude to further objections which I made to him as a candidate for Speaker at that time. The gentleman having referred to my published vindication, with some warmth of feeling pronounced a statement which I then made to be *false*. The language is rather unusual for this hall. It was used under very evident excitement. But it is my duty to reply to it dispassionately. Sir, during the Presidential campaign of 1844, the whole whig party denounced and execrated the Mexican war. None did this with more zeal or more sincerity than myself. The gentleman from Massachusetts also denounced it. I supposed him and other whigs to be sincere and honest in their denunciations; but when the question came before us in 1846, that gentleman changed his position and voted for the war.

Mr. WINTHROP. Does the gentleman say that I voted for the war?

Mr. GIDDINGS. I intend to say that the gentleman did vote for the war, — for the bill declaring war. It was this change of position on that momentous question which constituted one of my objections to him as Speaker in 1847.

Mr. WINTHROP. I deny that I ever changed my position.

Mr. GIDDINGS. This constituted but *one* of my objections. At that time, as at the recent election, I felt bound to obey the dictates of my own judgment, and voted for another gentleman. For thus daring to think for myself, for not permitting a whig caucus to think for me, to dictate my course of action, I was denounced by the Taylor papers of that day as an apostate from the whig party. The papers most warmly in support of the gentleman from Massachusetts were loudest in their attacks on me. I thought proper to publish a vindication of my vote. In it I stated distinctly the change of that gentleman's position in regard to the war, as one of the objections which I had to his election. It was this tergiversation to which I stood opposed.

In writing out my vindication, I stated the fact that he had voted for the war, and in a whig caucus had proposed that the party should vote for it. The fact that he thus voted is placed upon the Journal of the House. No effort can change, no time can erase it. There it stands, and there it will remain forever, conclusive and indubitable proof of the gentleman's change of position. It was the most solemn evidence that he approved the war. In his subsequent administration, he arranged the committees so as to continue the war; so as to recommend appropriations to carry forward the work of devastation and bloodshed, instead of withdrawing the army and doing justice to Mexico. Neither he nor his friends ever have, or ever will deny these solemn truths which appear on record. But, admitting all these, he attempts to evade their force by saying that, although he voted for the war, he did not recommend in caucus that others should vote for it. He thus attempts to leave the substance, for the purpose of contending about the shadow. If it were right for him to vote for the war, it could not have been wrong for him to advise others to do so; yet this collateral fact is not a matter of record. I stated it from positive knowledge, from what I knew. He denies it, and says it is *false*. He may, and undoubtedly has forgotten it. The Honorable E. D. Culver, in a letter published at the time, relates all the facts to which I alluded in my vindication. Yet he does not hesitate at this time to pronounce the statements of myself and of Mr. Culver both *false*.

But this point on which he attempts to make up an issue, is merely collateral to the important fact that he changed his position in relation to the war. I repeat, that fact is indisputable; it is on record. To that record the country will hold the gentleman. He cannot escape through an immaterial issue. No chicanery of special pleading can relieve him from the charge of voting for the war, and of sustaining it, after he and his party had denounced and execrated it. But, Sir, I had no intention of referring to this matter. The gentleman has dragged me into this part of the debate, and I am constrained to meet him. It gives me no pleasure thus to refer to his past political course. My objections rested in my own breast, and would never have appeared before the public, but for the attacks made upon me by him and his friends.

The gentlemen says that the member from Tennessee (Mr. Johnson) has assailed him because he was opposed to the interests of slavery, and that he will leave that gentleman's speech and mine to answer each other. Unfortunately for the gentleman from Massachusetts, the gentleman from Tennessee said nothing opposed to what I have advanced; nor have I said any thing opposed to what he has asserted. His charges stand independent of mine, and mine have no relation to his. How, then, they are to answer each other appears not very obvious to my comprehension.

The gentleman from Massachusetts says that the Committee on the District of Columbia reported a bill to abolish the slave-trade in this district. The assertion is not sustained by the record. No such bill was reported. The bill to which I presume the gentleman refers, is entitled "A bill to prohibit the introducing of slaves within the District of Columbia as merchandise, or for sale or hire." It does not even allude to the slave-trade carried on within this district. It has no reference to your slave-auctions; to your slave-prisons; to your slave-dealers; to the transportation of the slaves of this district to southern graves.

Sir, the history of that bill was this. After the resolution of the gentleman from New York (Mr. Gott) was defeated, there was some excitement here and in the country as to the manner in which the slave-trade had been upheld. The friends of the administration appeared to feel the pressure of public sentiment. The Common Council of this city adopted resolutions desiring Congress to pass a law prohibiting the bringing of slaves to this district for sale. This was presented to the House, and referred to the Committee on the District of Columbia. They reported such a bill on the 31st January. It merely prohibited the bringing of slaves from the surrounding country to this city for sale or hire. Those slaves could be sold at any other place. It simply refused to their owners the benefit of this market. All within the district were left as they had been, — subject to be sold and carried South. Had the bill passed, it would not have prevented the sale of a single slave, either here or elsewhere. It was a "device," a "get off," an apology for doing nothing. Nor did the fraud end there. The committee who reported, did not attempt to pass it. They reported it to the House. That was the last that was heard from it. It went to the tomb of the Capulets. To me (and I think to all reflecting men) the transaction bears upon its face conclusive evidence of an intention to deceive the public. I felt some degree of surprise and astonishment at hearing it referred to as a bill to abolish the slave-trade now carried on here. It contains no allusion to it. The assertion that the committee reported such bill is entirely unfounded.

The gentleman from Massachusetts, on my left, (Mr. Rockwell,) thinks I was not authorized to impute neglect to the Committee on Territories, in reporting a bill for organizing a territorial government in California. Our treaty with Mexico, by which that territory was obtained, bears date on the 2d February, 1848. It stipulated, on the part of this government, for the protection of the people of the territory ceded, and their admission to all the rights of citizens of the United States. It was officially proclaimed on the 4th July, 1848. From that moment delay could not be justified. I can find no excuse for the committee's neglecting to report a bill another week. The gentleman, in his speech, referred only to the last session. He attempted no excuse for the delay from the 4th of July up to the 14th of August, when Congress adjourned.

Here, Sir, was ample time to have reported and passed a bill organizing governments in California and in New Mexico. But no movement on the subject took place in that committee, nor am I aware that any other reason for such inaction has ever been assigned, except that a southern candidate for President had been nominated, and that the party had adopted the policy of inaction and delay on all matters touching slavery. I therefore appeal to the good sense of the House and of the country whether I was not fully justified in imputing neglect to that committee.

When we reassembled in December, the public mind had become dissatisfied with the silence of this body in regard to those territories. It is quite certain that the public regarded the delay as unreasonable. Notwithstanding the delay at the former session, the same committee were reappointed on the 7th December, instead of the 10th, as the gentleman represented.

After this reappointment six days more elapsed, when my colleague introduced his resolution, peremptorily ordering the committee to report such bill. It was reported on the 20th; but was suffered to take its place on the calendar of business. No attempt was put forth to make it the special order for a day certain. There, Sir, it lay until the 15th January, when the gentleman from Massachusetts, (Mr. Rockwell,) not the chairman of the committee, moved to make it the special order for the 22d of that month. When this latter day arrived, it was again postponed, on motion of a southern member, until the 30th, and finally it passed the House on the 27th February, and was thus sent to the Senate four days before the close of Congress. The question of neglect, I submit to the consideration of all candid men. It may not attach to the gentleman on my right, (Mr. Rockwell,) but it must attach to the majority of the committee. Now, Sir, after the long delay of this committee to move on the question during the first session of the late Congress, at a time when the public mind had become excited by this extraordinary delay, it would appear that the Speaker might have found members here, who, if placed on the committee, would have acted promptly and efficiently. If he had been anxious for the success of the measure, would he not have placed the power to act in the hands of men who were ready to exert themselves in favor of it?

I will now reply to some of the remarks of my colleague (Mr. Schenck). That gentleman, in his defence of the whig candidate for Speaker, was pleased to say, that the gentleman who filled the Speaker's chair in the last Congress (Mr. Winthrop) placed on the Committee upon the District of Columbia five members from the free, and four from the slave States. Now my colleague should understand that I have not objected to the *location* of any man. A slave-holder in Ohio is just as exceptionable as he would be, if he were from a slave State. Six members of that committee were supposed to be slave-holders, although two of them (Mr. Edwards of Ohio, and Mr. Ficklin of Illinois) resided in free States. Our objections are to the sentiments, to the principles, the doctrines, of those who composed that committee.

My colleague says the gentleman from Massachusetts had, some years since, offered the proviso excluding slavery as an amendment to the Oregon bill. That is quite true. But men change their opinions. I ask my colleague and the country, why did the gentleman hesitate to avow his adherence to that proviso? If he really held to it and intended to carry it out, why has he refused to say so at this session? — why refuse to say so now? The very fact that he remains silent on the subject — that he refuses to avow his sentiments, satisfies me that I ought not to have voted for him.*

My colleague has misrepresented me in saying that I demanded that the House of Representatives should come to *me*, or not be organized. I, in common with all free soilers, have asked them to support certain great and important principles. We demanded that they should recognize the "self-evident truths" on which this government was founded. We desired the House to acknowledge the fundamental axiom "that governments are constituted for the purpose of securing all men in the enjoyment of their inalienable rights." The free soil party stand on this doctrine. From it I trust in God they will never depart. I hope and believe they will never vote for any man who refuses to acknowledge these fundamental, these essential elements of our Government. I take this opportunity of saying to my colleague, that while the whig party denies these doctrines, or refuses to recognize them, I cannot and will not support it.

My colleague has represented my objections to the gentleman from Massachusetts as based solely on his opposition to the Wilmot proviso. I surely had given him no cause for such an assertion. My objections were based upon the whole polit-

* When the question of adopting the proviso came before the House, subsequently to the delivery of this speech, Mr. Winthrop left the hall, and thereby evaded voting upon it.

ical character of that gentleman. I refer to his celebrated toast at Faneuil Hall on the 4th July, 1845, in favor of Texas; I refer to his motion at a whig convention in Massachusetts, in 1847, to lay on the table the resolution of his late colleague, (Mr. Palfrey,) pledging the whigs of that State to oppose any candidate for the presidency who was in favor of extending slavery; to the various demonstrations of his party; to the remarks of his colleague, (who, I presume, spoke his sentiments,) at the whig caucus in this city, on the Saturday evening previous to the present session, "that the Wilmot proviso constituted no part of the whig policy."

Mr. ASHMUN. To whom does the gentleman allude?

Mr. GIDDINGS. To the gentleman now addressing me.

Mr. ASHMUN. I did not use such language.

Mr. GIDDINGS. Gentlemen have all seen the remarks to which I refer. I believe he said that the whigs of Massachusetts, or the people of Massachusetts, made no such test.

I have already mentioned the change of that gentleman's position in relation to the Mexican war, and to the arrangement of the Committees on the Judiciary, the District of Columbia, and the Territories. I go farther. I object to that gentleman on account of his having sustained for President a man whose education, interest, associations, and prejudices are opposed to freedom. The effect of the election of General Taylor upon the whig party has been most marked. My colleague has referred to the candidate of that party for Speaker, and says he would support any whig who had been regularly nominated by them. I could not go so far. While that party adhered to the fundamental principles of human liberty, it was my pride and my pleasure to act with it. It gives me no satisfaction to expose their abandonment of former doctrines. But my colleague has referred to the party in a manner which leaves me no choice. I will refer to one instance, as illustrating the change of position by the whig party of the North.

On the 21st December, 1847, I myself introduced to this body a petition from the people of this district, praying the abolition of the slave-trade, and moved its reference to the

Committee on the District of Columbia, with instructions to report a bill in accordance with the prayer of the petition. A motion was made to lay my proposition on the table. The object of the motion appeared to be to silence all agitation on the subject. The whig party of the North voted against the motion, without a single exception. The vote was such as did them credit. It was such as I expected from them. Now mark the change! Precisely one year subsequently, that is, on the 21st December, 1848, my friend from New York, on my right, (Mr. Gott,) introduced his resolution instructing the same committee to report a bill for the same purpose. Gentlemen then voted agreeably to the righteous impulses of their hearts. There was no time for party drill, or to bring the power of party discipline to bear upon members. The resolution was carried by a majority of eleven votes. A motion was made, however, to reconsider the vote adopting the resolution. This motion came up six days subsequently. A motion was then made to lay the proposition to reconsider on the table. On this vote the friends of humanity rallied, as they thought it the most favorable point on which to concentrate their whole power. If that motion had been carried, it would have left the resolution in full force, and a bill for abolishing that "execrable commerce" would have come fairly before us. We therefore believed that every member whose heart beat for freedom, who really abhorred the traffic in men, would vote with us on that occasion.

But, Sir, to our disappointment and dismay, twenty-six northern whigs voted against laying the proposition to reconsider on the table; thereby lending their influence in favor of that disgraceful traffic in mankind. Thus, Sir, in the short space of one year and six days, a majority of the northern whigs then voting, faced to the right about, changed their position, and lent their influence to sustain the slave-trade. Why this change of front? this undignified tergiversation? Because General Taylor had been elected President. He was a slaveholder, and depended on the slave-trade to supply his plantations with laborers. To condemn that traffic would be to condemn him; to uphold that commerce would be to propitiate his favor.

And now, Mr. Speaker, a word in your ear. My colleague, who has just addressed us with so much eloquence, who has referred to my humble self with so much severity, (Mr. Schenck,) was one who thus suddenly turned a political somerset in favor of the slave-trade.

Mr. SCHENCK (interposing) said he was absent when the resolution was adopted. That when the vote was taken upon laying the proposition to reconsider on the table, he opposed it, as he was desirous of striking out the preamble which was offensive to the South.

Mr. GIDDINGS resumed. My colleague says he was opposed to the preamble; that it was offensive to the South. Was there any thing in it that was not strictly true? I hope he does not regard truth as offensive! That preamble is before me. Its language is as follows:

> "Whereas the traffic now prosecuted in this metropolis of the republic in human beings, as chattels, is contrary to natural justice and to the fundamental principles of our political system, and is notoriously a reproach to our country throughout Christendom, and a serious hindrance to the progress of republican liberty among the nations of the earth."

To language thus true, thus appropriate, my colleague objects. Why so? On what are his objections founded? Is not the slave-trade "opposed to natural justice?" Is it not unjust to sell a man, — to degrade and brutalize him, — to tear his children from him, and sell them like brutes, — to dispose of his wife at auction? Was my colleague afraid to speak these solemn truths in the face of the South? Again; is not this commerce in our own species "opposed to the fundamental principles of our political system?"

Our government is based upon the self-evident truth, "that all men are created equal, and are endowed with the inalienable right to life and liberty." Now, Sir, to deny the equality of man's political rights, — to rob a portion of the people of their liberty, — to sell them like oxen in the market place, — to make merchandise of them, — is most obviously opposed to the spirit of our institutions. Again, Sir; is not this slave-trade a "reproach to our country?" Does my colleague doubt it? I am sure he does not. We, as a nation, have set the seal of our own condemnation upon it. We regard the slave-dealer who pursues his vocation on the eastern shore of the Atlantic as a *pirate*. Our laws pronounce him such. When taken, he is regarded as an outlaw, unfit to associate longer with our race. We hang him without mercy, and doom his memory to execration. Yet he is far less guilty than he who follows the same vocation in this city. And was my colleague afraid to utter such palpable truths, lest southern slave-dealers should be offended? He would hang one man for dealing in slaves, but would be cautious and delicate in the language he uses towards another.

Why, Sir, if there be a crime in the universe for which I would hang men, it is that of dealing in mankind, — of making merchandise of human flesh. He who deals in slaves here, is far more guilty than he who follows that business in Africa. His victims are more enlightened, and suffer far more than the victims of the African slave-trade. But, Sir, did southern gentlemen object to this language? From whence arose my colleague's paternal love of these slave-dealers? Were southern members here incapable of taking care of the rights of the South? I have usually found them quite willing not only to take care of themselves, but they are generally disposed to take care of the North also. This, Sir, is going a great way to find an excuse for upholding this slave-trade. My colleague out-Herod's Herod. Yet such excuses have passed current for forty years.

Mr. VINTON interposed. He said when the resolution of the gentleman from New York (Mr. Gott) was offered, the previous question had been called. His colleague (Mr. Giddings) had voted for the previous question, by which a motion to strike out the preamble was cut off. He had himself voted to reconsider, in order to strike out the preamble.

Mr. GIDDINGS resumed. I am aware, said he, that my colleague last up, not only voted to reconsider the adoption of the resolution, but he also voted against laying the proposition to reconsider on the table. The journal also shows that my colleague moved to postpone the consideration of the subject for two weeks. He, too, it seems, was desirous of using language of delicacy in reference to crimes the most Heaven-daring that ever marked the depravity of mankind. Sir, I repeat, why did not my able and respected colleagues leave these objections to be made by slave-holders? Why were they so fastidious as to the delicacy of language towards those who deal in the bones and muscle, the blood and sinews of their fellow men?

When I was interrupted by my colleague, (Mr. Schenck,) I was speaking of the change of the whig party after the nomination and election of General Taylor. I had spoken of the manner in which the resolution of the gentleman from New York (Mr. Gott) was reconsidered. It was then placed on the list of resolutions, where it could never more be heard from. That was the last of it. Thus, Sir, by sheer management, the subject was given the "*go-by.*" It was thus put at rest, and the slave-trade was upheld and sustained. More men were purchased, more women were obtained, and more children collected for the southern market. It was the first instance on the records of the nation in which the whigs of the North had showed themselves more servile defenders of the slave-trade than the northern democrats. But the truth should be spoken though the heavens fall. While twenty-six northern whigs thus lent their influence in favor of the slave-trade, only *twenty-three* northern democrats united with them in that unenviable exercise of political power.

But, Sir, I am constrained to look still farther into the policy of the whig party, as connected with this slave-trade. I will not say that gentlemen voted to uphold that traffic under the promise or expectation of reward; I have not the record evidence on which to base the assertion. Yet one of those gentlemen who voted thus to protect the slave-trade (Mr. Smith of Connecticut) received the offer of a seat in the Cabinet, but for some reason did not accept it; another (Mr. Preston of Virginia) is now a Cabinet officer; another, (Mr. Collamer of

Vermont,) who did not vote at that time either for or against the slave-trade, also holds a seat in the Executive Cabinet; another (Mr. Barringer of North Carolina) represents this nation at the court of Madrid; another (Mr. Marsh of Vermont) is our minister to the Grand Sultan of Turkey; another (Mr. Caleb B. Smith of Indiana) is commissioner of Mexican Claims; another (Mr. Alexander Irvin) is marshal of the western district of Pennsylvania; another (Mr. Edwards of Ohio) is a general superintendent or examiner of hospitals in the United States; and the son-in-law of another, (Mr. Vinton of Ohio,) is chief clerk in the Department of the Interior.*

I repeat, that I cannot say that these offices were conferred as rewards for the votes given on the occasion referred to; but it is a remarkable coincidence that not one of those gentlemen who opposed the slave-trade on that important vote has, so far as my information extends, received any favor whatever from the Executive. Had the same thing occurred under a democratic administration, I should at once have characterized it as "a bargain and sale;" and I think every whig would have sustained me in the charge. Yet now I am told that I ought to have voted for the gentleman from Massachusetts, for the reason that he belonged to the "*whig party*."

Names, Sir, have little weight with me. Why, Sir, is it less wicked, less criminal for the whig party to sustain the slave-trade than it is for the democratic party? One thing stands recorded upon the history of the past two years; the slave-trade has been sustained, protected, and upheld in this district during that period, while the whigs held a majority in this hall. Sir, all our movements to put it down have been baffled and defeated. All attempts to relieve our fellow men here from crimes at which humanity revolts have been thwarted. These facts stand written, as it were, in characters of "lurid light" upon our country's history. They are known and read of all

* Mr. Schenck was, soon after the delivery of this speech, appointed minister to Brazil.

men. Yet, Sir, I am told that free soilers, — men who hate oppression and detest crime, — are bound to come up to the aid of those who sustain these transcendent iniquities.

Most of the old members will recollect a colored man who for some years waited in the refectory below us. On the week previous to our assembling here, as report says, he became alarmed at the idea of being sold South, and attempted to make his escape. The bloodhounds were soon upon his track. He was captured, and as he looked with certainty upon the fate that awaited him, he drew a knife from his pocket and cut his own throat, in the presence of his captors. He, Sir, appealed directly to the God of justice against this traffic, which for the last two years has been upheld by the whig party of this House. These suicides are common. Even mothers have been known to murder their own children, to save them from the tortures of this traffic. The blood of these people stains our garments. It is dripping from our hands. Yet we fear to speak forth the language of truth. We vote against resolutions for preventing these crimes, unless they are couched in delicate language. Yea, we are told that we must choose between men who carefully arrange the committees of this body so as to protect these crimes. I deny that such obligation rests on us. I mean no injustice to any gentleman, when I assure you, that I would be as willing to go down to the corner of Seventh street and Delaware avenue, and select the slave-dealer who presides over that piratical establishment for a Speaker of this body, as I would vote for any man who sustains him in his hated vocation. I care not whether he be called a whig or democrat. Others no doubt view the subject differently.

By reading the remarks of Mr. Phillips of Boston, my colleague has attempted to show that free soilers are in favor of a dissolution of the Union. He seems to have brought the paper containing these remarks to the House, ready folded and marked for the occasion; from which I judge that these attacks were preconcerted, conned beforehand, and manufactured to order. My colleague could not have been ignorant that Mr. Phillips, as well as himself, is opposed entirely to the free soil party; I thought it uncandid, therefore, in him, to represent that gentleman as a free soiler. Such insincerity detracts from the force of my colleague's remarks. He would never have had recourse to misrepresentation, while he could find truth to sustain his purposes. But he intimates that there is danger of dissolution of the Union, from the steady firmness with which free soilers press their principles. This has been the stereotyped argument for thirty years. It is a species of mock-thunder, too well understood to effect any harm. It has ceased to frighten the nervous misses at our boarding schools. It has become the jest of our school boys.

Sir, does my colleague meet us on our principles and say that we are wrong? Not at all. He even professes to outdo us in the support of our doctrines; to go beyond us in the maintenance of our principles; then he turns suddenly round in the same speech, and tells us that we shall produce a dissolution of the Union. Would he urge us to surrender our rights and the rights of humanity, — permit the Constitution to be trampled upon, its essential elements subverted, in order to prevent southern slave-holders from seceding from the Union? He will not do that. His patriotism, his independence will revolt at such a proposition. Does he not know that a dissolution of the Union would be the death of slavery? Why, Sir, every intelligent man must be aware, that when northern freemen cease to uphold that institution, its death will be inevitable. Southern men understand this subject; they will be the last to seek a dissolution of our Federal Union. When I see the condemned culprit standing upon the gallows, with the rope about his neck and fastened over his head, coolly kick from under him the platform on which he stands, and thus sever his union with the world in which he has lived, with the atmosphere which he has breathed, I may then be made to believe that southern men will dissolve their connection with the northern States.

My colleague has commented with some freedom on the vote which I and some of my friends gave for the gentleman from

Indiana, (Mr. Brown). I heard this lecture, I trust, with becoming meekness. "To his own master," each of us "must stand or fall." Yet I am quite willing that my colleague should show to me this kind of paternal supervision. Free soilers, Sir, were determined to vote for no man who would so arrange the committees of this House as to sustain the slave-trade. When the gentleman from Indiana became a prominent candidate, my friend from Pennsylvania (Mr. Wilmot) propounded to him interrogatories on this subject. The gentleman from Indiana answered promptly and distinctly. He did not hesitate to place his solemn pledge to freedom on record, so that the whole world might see and read it. On the faith of that pledge, I voted for him cheerfully. I had no fears that he would violate it; I had no suspicion that he would prove recreant to his faith, thus solemnly plighted. How was it with my colleague? Did he vote for a candidate thus pledged? No, Sir. He had no such assurance on which to rely. But intimations are bandied through the public press, that the gentleman from Indiana would not have redeemed his pledge.

Gentlemen have no right to assume that such violation would have followed his election. We were told that he served a long time as Secretary of the State which he in part represents. He served here in the twenty-eighth Congress. He was an Assistant Postmaster-General during the administration of Mr. Polk, and has been again returned to Congress by a constituency and from a State devoted to the Wilmot proviso. And were we to distrust the solemn word of such a man? Sir, when those southern gentlemen abandoned him, they did so because they feared that he would prove true to freedom. They who had the slave interest in their keeping, believed that he would not answer their purpose, and they changed their votes to defeat his election. Will my colleague say that their fears were unfounded? that they, as well as the free soilers, were mistaken?

But my colleague says the gentleman from Indiana voted against the proviso in the twenty-eighth Congress. This is true; and so did others who now vote for it. Men change in these days. I have already shown how twenty-six northern whigs wheeled entirely round in the short space of one year and six days. They changed from the support of human rights to the opposite side of that question; whereas the gentleman from Indiana, in the space of four years, changed the other way. He once opposed the proviso; he is now pledged to sustain it.

But my colleague says a man must be judged by his past life. I have shown that the candidate for whom he voted, lent his official influence to sustain the slave-trade. If my colleague judges that gentleman by his past life, he must himself be in favor of that measure. Sir, you may search the journals of this body, but you can never find a vote of the gentleman from Indiana so exceptionable, so hostile to freedom, so opposed to humanity, as that given by those twenty-six whigs to whom I have referred.

Sir, let me know that a man is right *now*, and I will forgive and overlook his past life. Had the gentleman from Massachusetts at this session, publicly avowed his adherence to the proviso, I should have voted for him with great pleasure. I could at once have forgiven and forgotten the past. That cannot be recalled; its errors only can be avoided in future. All history and all experience show the absolute necessity of taking men as they *now are*, instead of what they have been. Paul was converted suddenly. Nor was he afraid or ashamed to avow his change from evil to that which was right and just.

And, Sir, on this subject of slavery we have all been silent and supine, while slavery was subverting our interests and our constitutional rights. If, therefore, the lovers of freedom were to adopt my colleague's rule of judging men by their past conduct on these questions, we should condemn all; for all have sinned in this respect. My colleague, and his associates, and their candidate, as well as myself, would all be found wanting, if weighed in such a balance.

But my colleague objects to any man who gives evidence of a change of mind in regard to slavery. I object to any one who refuses such evidence. It is said that the gentleman from

Indiana pledged himself also to southern gentlemen. If such were the fact, it was entirely unknown to free soilers. It is certain that he *refused* any written pledge to them. They wrote him, requesting a pledge in writing. He refused to give it. So did the candidate of my colleague, when addressed in that way. If the objection applies to one, it is equally applicable to the other. Sir, it was wrong in both. They should have spoken freely when called on. But free soilers knew nothing of such refusal by the gentleman from Indiana.

Again; it is said by southern members, that the gentleman from Indiana (Mr. Brown) pointed them to his past votes and acts for evidence as to his future course. This was precisely what I objected to on the part of the whig candidate. He pointed northern men to his past acts for proof of his future course, refusing to express his present views. In that way, were both wrong. The one deceived the *North*, the other deceived the *South*. The very object of a candidate's withholding his views, is to deceive some of those whose votes he expects to receive.

There sits the gentleman from Alabama, (Mr. Alston); he is sincerely of the opinion, that it is unconstitutional for Congress to exclude slavery from our newly acquired territory. He would not dare vote for a man who is known to be in favor of such a measure. Here is my colleague who has just addressed us; he holds that it is unconstitutional to permit slavery to exist in those territories; nor would he support a man who entertains the opposite opinion. Yet, Sir, we saw these gentlemen sit here day after day, voting for the same candidate. Each of them, doubtless, thought he was overreaching the other. Each believed the other to be the dupe. Each had been referred to the past acts and votes of their candidates. Those acts and votes satisfied both; they read to suit each; and each entered upon the balloting with the positive knowledge that either himself or the other must eventually be deceived, if they elected their candidate. It was a mutual attempt at fraud, — a political lottery, — a gambling transaction. Free soilers enter into no such game of chance. They will not unite in that political play of "blind man's buff."

But, Sir, from the commencement of the contest for Speaker, free soilers at all times stood ready to aid in electing the candidate of either party, if such candidate publicly adhered to the Wilmot proviso. This intention was made known, probably, to every member of this body. The gentleman from Indiana, as already stated, boldly and unreservedly avowed his adherence to that measure. I had not any doubt as to his sincerity. With these views, I felt constrained, as an honest man, as an independent member of this body, to vote for him. With that belief I could not have conscientiously done otherwise.

But my colleague appears to regard an avowal of sentiments as dishonorable. On this point, he will permit me to differ from him. I regard the withholding of a candidate's views as positively dishonest, and therefore dishonorable. Such I know to be the prevailing sentiment of northern Ohio.

For years it has been the practice in this hall for the Speaker so to arrange the committees having charge of all petitions relating to slavery, as to suppress them in the several committees to which they are referred. Members here from the North present these petitions; they are respectfully referred; they there remain forever unheard of afterwards. The representative, if called on for information, replies that he presented the petition; that it was referred; "but that the committee had neglected their duty in not reporting upon it." The constituent denounces the committee as recreant to freedom; but regards his representative as a faithful public servant.

Sir, he is not aware that his representative deceives him; that he has been defrauded by the very man whom he praises. The constituent is unconscious that his representative voted for the Speaker, with the full knowledge and perfect expectation that he would place on those committees a certain class of members for the very purpose of suppressing these petitions. He is ignorant of the fact that their suppression is as really and substantially the *act of his representative*, as though such representative had burned the petition with his own hands. This fraud upon the public mind should be exposed. The people of the North should understand it. When, two years since, I was assailed for refusing to vote for the gentleman from Massachusetts, and published my vindication, I said to the people of my district, in the most emphatic language I could command, that their petitions in regard to this slave-trade would be suppressed by the committees which the Speaker had appointed. I foretold the fraud about to be practised upon them. What was then prophecy, has now become history. During the two years of his administration, not one of the many thousand petitions against the slave-trade, sent to those committees, has since been heard from.

For two years, Sir, the people of the North have been defrauded, deceived, and imposed upon by the whigs of this House. The Constitution of our country has been violated and trampled under foot; and the voice of northern philanthropy has been stifled by the votes of northern whigs. Free soilers were lately called on to become parties to this deception; to approve this fraud; to unite in these violations of the Constitution, by suppressing the right of petition, and to vote for the candidate who has thus contributed his official influence to consummate these infringements upon northern honor and northern rights. I regret that the duty of making these exposures has devolved on the humble individual who addresses you. I wish the task had fallen upon some one more able to do justice to the righteous cause we advocate. I feel, deeply feel, the manner in which these recorded facts involve the official conduct of gentlemen here. It is true that the country has a right to know them. Their suppression by me, would involve a dereliction of duty on my part; yet, Sir, I feel an extreme reluctance in publishing to the world matters thus involving the official acts of my fellow members. I certainly should not have done so at the present time, except for the attacks made upon me. I am assailed because I will not unite in these deceptions, these frauds, these violations of the Constitution, by which oppression and the slave-trade are upheld and maintained.

Sir, I regard governments as constituted for the high and holy purpose of securing the people in the enjoyment of "*life, liberty, and happiness.*" These undying truths were proclaimed by our patriot fathers; they were placed on record by them. They, Sir, were not ashamed nor afraid to avow them. I most solemnly, most devoutly, cherish and support them. Nor will I at any time sustain for the office of Speaker of this body, any man who disbelieves these fundamental truths, or who hesitates to avow them.

CALIFORNIA.*

HER RIGHT OF ADMISSION TO THE UNION — COMPLAINTS OF SLAVE-HOLDERS — THEIR CHARACTER — CHARACTER OF OUR GOVERNMENT — ITS OBJECTS DEFINED — SLAVERY IN FACT, AND IN LAW — MANNER OF ITS EXISTENCE — HISTORY OF ITS EXCLUSION FROM OUR TERRITORIES — FROM THE HIGH SEAS — ARGUMENTS EXAMINED — DOCTRINE OF LEAVING IT TO EXIST IN TERRITORIES REFUTED.

[Every reader is aware that the object of the leading advocates for annexing Texas, and obtaining Mexican territory, was to extend and perpetuate slavery. But when the treaty of peace had been formed, and California came to frame her Constitution, she rejected the policy of holding slaves. Her Constitution was, however, transmitted to the House of Representatives for its action upon the application of California for admission to the Union as a State. The southern members opposed its admission; and, on that occasion, Mr. Toombs, of Georgia, made a speech, in which he declared this to be a "slave-holding government," and that the "people of the free States were bound to protect the master in his dominion over his slaves with their blood," and that the "United States were bound to sustain slavery wherever our flag may float." In answer to these positions, Mr. Giddings delivered the following speech.]

Mr. Chairman, — The people of California have formed and adopted a Constitution. Her representatives are here awaiting admission to this Union as one of our sister States. I desire to act upon this application without delay. Southern gentlemen, however, object to her admission, on account of that clause in her Constitution which excludes slavery from her territory.

The advocates of liberty rejoice at this exhibition of human-

* Speech on the President's Message communicating the Constitution of California. Delivered in Committee of the whole House on the state of the Union.

ity by their brethren of that new sovereignty. Southern men, however, complain that Congress is encroaching upon their rights. Yet no one has condescended to point us to any right or interest in particular which he regards as encroached upon; their complaints are general, without specification.

The gentleman from Georgia (Mr. Toombs) assumed a bold and manly position, saying, in explicit language, "this is a pro-slavery government." The expression would indicate that he regards the object, the ulterior design of its formation, to be the maintenance of slavery; that it was "constituted not to secure liberty," but to perpetuate slavery. This is an important discovery; and, if correct, should be understood by the people. He even went farther, and declared that "we are bound to maintain the dominion of the slave-holder over his slaves with our blood, and to carry slavery wherever our flag floats, and we have jurisdiction." If this be so, if northern freemen are bound to shed their blood, in order that the southern slave-holder may hold his minions in subjection, that he may scourge them, degrade and brutalize them, our mission is certainly not enviable. The obligation of northern men to die in defence of slavery must of course arise from the Constitution. And if the framers of that instrument intended thus to dishonor the freemen of the North, our curses, our heaviest execrations should rest upon their memories; and the sooner such a constitution were discarded, and such a union were rent asunder, the better. There is, however, no compromise consistent with honor and with duty. I discard all compromises, and reject all offers to compromise. I came here to enforce, to carry out the provisions of the Constitution; not to compromise, nor to surrender, the rights secured to us by that instrument.

I regard the constitutional obligations of this government towards the institution of slavery as too obvious to be misunderstood by statesmen. The line of demarcation which separates the people of the free States from the support of slavery has been so plainly drawn, that it would seem no intelligent, unprejudiced mind could mistake it. It is, however, true that obscurity is thrown upon the subject by the ingenuity and the sophistry of those who profess to reason upon it.

Much has been said about slavery being the "creature of municipal law." Men in both political parties now urge that "slavery cannot exist, unless sustained by *municipal law.*" They say that this is the doctrine of jurists; that the most profound judges have so decided. Others deny this doctrine. Now, what is the fact? History shows us that it was introduced into Virginia, and existed there for years before there was any municipal regulation concerning it.

We know from history that it existed in each of the slave States of this Union long prior to the enactment of any laws on the subject. It found its way into Oregon, into California, Deseret, and New Mexico, without any law. It has been sustained in all those States and Territories, not by municipal law, but by the superior physical and intellectual power of the white over the colored people. This was slavery in *fact*, but not in *law*. For instance, — slavery continued in Ohio, even against the provisions of our Constitution, and in violation of all our laws, as late as the year 1840. It exists in Illinois to this day. Slaves are there bought and sold, not merely *without* law, but *against* law.

But as the attention of the people becomes awakened to this subject, as information is promulgated, they enforce the laws, and slavery disappears at once; or when those held as slaves become informed of their rights, and demand their liberty in a court of justice, the judge finds no law by which one man holds another in subjection. He calls on the claimant to show his authority, but no such authority is known to the law. The judge says "slavery is the creature of municipal law," without which it cannot be sustained in a court of justice. He means by this that no *legal* slavery can exist without such law. While he and all others know that men are in *fact* held in bondage against law; that they are sold and transferred from owner to owner, for the reason that the laws are not enforced.

In a state of nature, the rights of all men are equal; but the superior intellectual and physical power of one man is often exerted to subject others to his will. In that state, however, each possesses the right of self-defence. Not so in slave States. There the right of the slave to protect his liberty or his life is taken away by the laws of such State. For instance,—if a slave in Virginia lifts his hand against his master in self-defence, the master may at once slay him with impunity. But this right of the master depends on the law of that State; and the moment the master goes beyond the jurisdiction of that State this right ceases. Let him bring his slave to Ohio, and the moment they stand on our soil, under the jurisdiction of our laws, the slave becomes a *man*, possessing the equal rights and powers and privileges with the master. Such is the case whenever they go beyond the jurisdiction of Virginia into free territory.

These principles have often been advanced. They were familiar to our fathers. They had been declared by the courts of Great Britain, prior to our Revolution. Slavery, at that time was regarded as wrong, and the people of nearly every province were anxious to rid themselves of it.

My colleague (Mr. Campbell) has shown, in an able manner, that the objects of the people of the South, before and at the commencement of the Revolution, was the entire abolition of slavery and of all slave laws. These objects were proclaimed in language most direct and appropriate, in 1776, when entering upon the war of the Revolution. After the close of that memorable struggle, the Confederated Congress, in 1783, sent out an address to the people of the United States, penned by Mr. Madison, in which they say, "Let it be remembered, finally, that it has been the pride and the boast of America that the rights for which she contended *were the rights of human nature.*" These were the sentiments and feelings then prevalent in all or nearly all the States.

Our western territory was held by individual States; Virginia exercising jurisdiction over the greatest portion, and slavery actually existing upon it. She transferred her jurisdiction to the United States, and her laws ceasing to operate therein, slavery of course ceased. And the ordinance of 1787 prohibited it from being again established there. The Convention to frame our Constitution was then in session. They desired also to make the high seas free so far as American ships were concerned. Accordingly the States surrendered their jurisdiction over commerce and navigation to this government. We have enacted no law authorizing slavery there; our flag floats proudly free upon that great highway of nations, giving practical contradiction to the doctrine of the gentleman from Georgia. He says we "are bound to carry slavery wherever our flag floats." Washington and his associates, Jefferson, Madison, Adams, Monroe, Jackson, and their associates repudiated that doctrine; and, I trust, it will ever be repudiated by this government.

The gentleman cites the privilege granted in the Constitution for the States to import slaves until 1808, as an evidence that we "are bound to carry slavery wherever our flag floats." So far from agreeing with the gentleman on this point, this provision constitutes in my mind an irrefutable contradiction of his doctrine. The stipulation that Congress should not prohibit the importation of slaves until 1808, carried conviction to the whole people that it would be prohibited at that time. So far from its being evidence of our obligation to protect it, it furnished conclusive proof that we would prohibit it. And in accordance with that general, that universal expectation, it was prohibited by act of Congress passed in December, 1807; and never, to my knowledge, has any statesman doubted the justice or constitutionality of that act until this day. The gentleman's reference to this provision of the Constitution, shows the monstrosity of his argument.

The gentleman also cites that clause in the Constitution which provides for the recapture of fugitive slaves as a further evidence of our obligation to protect the master. I have on a former occasion shown, that our duties under that provision are simply non-interference; to leave the master and slave to themselves; we are not bound to protect the master against his slave; that, if the slave in defending his liberty slays his master, we do not punish him. I will not, therefore, enter upon that argument.

He also insists, that slaves are property. But, on a recent occasion, I called attention to the fact, that slaves are referred to in the Constitution solely as *persons*, and not as *property;* that we so regard them. And so fully has this view of the subject been established, that I will not detain the Committee by any further reply on that point.

The next compromise of the Constitution to which the gentleman from Georgia (Mr. Toombs) refers, is that of the slave representation, as provided in the third clause, second section, of the first article of the Constitution. In regard to this article, it would appear that no difference of opinion could possibly exist. There can be no doubt that it was intended to give the slave States an advantage over the free States. The slaves are not represented in this hall, nor can we legislate for their benefit; but the slave-holders have a representation here, in proportion to the number of slaves they hold in bondage, counting five slaves equal to three freemen. For more than sixty years the slave States have enjoyed this privilege. No man has ever denied it to be their right under the Constitution. But it is equally plain, that this clause was intended to give no farther privilege. It alludes to no other subject, and cannot be construed to give any other powers. The gentleman (Mr. Toombs) referred to it to show that this is a slave-holding government; that we are bound to maintain the master's power over his slave with our blood; and to carry slavery wherever our flag floats. But the way and manner he brings this clause to sustain his positions, he has failed to show us. I repeat, that the whole object and intention of this clause has been thus far observed and carried out. South Carolina has now three representatives on this floor more than she would be entitled to according to the number of her freemen; and twenty members from the slave States are admitted here solely by virtue of this superior advantage which the slave States possess over the people of the North.

It gives to the South an influence over our rights and interests, not according to their love of freedom, but proportioned to their disregard of liberty. The holder of five slaves exerts an influence in this hall and in the Federal Government equal to four citizens of the free States; and the owner of a thousand slaves possesses political powers equal to six hundred citizens of the North.

I know of nothing more humiliating to the pride and dignity of our people than this inequality of our political influence. We are placed in a political position between the supercilious master, and his crouching menial; superior to the one, and inferior to the other. It was a compromise of northern honor; it gave a bounty to oppression; bestowed privileges upon those who disregard "self-evident truth," and trample upon the inalienable rights of man; it has taught northern men to regard slave-holders as politically entitled to superior consideration; it has taught us subjection to slave-holding dictation; yet, degrading as this provision is, we have observed it strictly; we have submitted to it, and I trust in God we shall stop at that point, and not degrade ourselves farther by going beyond the Constitution to retain a system of oppression which we abhor and detest. I can see no legitimate reason urged by the gentleman why we should go beyond the Constitution, and compromise the rights secured to ourselves and to humanity by its adoption.

In order to establish the duty of this government to sustain slavery, we are referred to the obligation imposed upon us to "protect each of the States from invasion, and against domestic violence."

This provision extends to the free, as well as to the slave States. History informs us, that the rebellion in Massachusetts was the occasion of its adoption. Mr. Madison informs us, that members from the slave States assured the Convention that they neither needed nor required any provision of the kind. But no man can mistake the object and design of this section. We are bound to protect every State from invasion. This protection is thrown around the *State*, including all the people therein; the righteous and the wicked, the bond and the free, the black and the white, the hardened assassin and the innocent child, are all protected against the foreign enemy.

And you may allege that this clause was adopted to protect pirates and murderers, with the same propriety that you can assert it to have been adopted to protect slave-holders, or any other men of a particular character.

The same reasoning applies to the suppression of domestic violence. We are bound to protect the whole people of the State against domestic violence. We do not institute an inquiry as to the character of the people! We do not ask whether they are slaves or masters, white or black, righteous or wicked. The insurgents are shot down by our troops, without inquiring who they are! The master found in arms is shot down precisely as the slave, and the insurgent slave is butchered with just as little ceremony as the insurgent master. Indeed, we know of no distinctions in such case. Our troops have nothing to do with *slavery;* their duty is to quell the violence. That done, every slave in the State may walk off to Canada, in full view of our army, and they possess neither the right nor the constitutional power to interfere.

But in case of invasion or of insurrection, the power of the government in repelling the one, or suppressing the other, is unlimited by the Constitution. The whole physical power of the nation may then be brought into action for that purpose, and if deemed necessary by the Executive, who is the commander of the army and navy, he may liberate every slave in such State for the purpose of saving the people or of restoring peace. This is a power, however, lying behind the Constitution, based upon the right of self-defence, upon the duty of preserving the government, and existing only in time of foreign or of civil war.

It is constantly asserted that, by adopting the Wilmot proviso, we shall "exclude the people of the South from emigrating to those territories with their property." We are charged with attempting to create "distinctions between the people of the free and those of the slave States." These arguments are unfounded. The exclusion of slavery is for the express purpose of permitting all men, of every State and nation and kindred and tongue and people under heaven, to go there "upon terms of perfect equality." We propose to give to *all* the same protection, the same security to life, liberty, and property; to admit of no distinctions except those of moral worth. It is this "equality of political rights" to which southern men *object*, and not to the want of it. Their excitement arises from the fact, that we recognise *no* distinction, that we will permit no man to hold the body of another at his disposal, to deprive him of liberty, to beat and scourge, to degrade and brutalize him. Such are our objects, and such are the objections to them. If, Sir, we permit slavery to establish itself in these territories, we shall show ourselves unequal to the discharge of our duties as statesmen, and insensible to our obligations as Christians; we shall deserve, and must receive the censure, the condemnation, of the civilized world.

It is not my purpose on this point to travel over ground already occupied. The moral turpitude of permitting slavery and slave markets to be established on territory hitherto consecrated to freedom, has been ably examined by other gentlemen. There is, however, an abstraction, first advanced within the last two years, but now advocated by individuals of both political parties, denying our right to prohibit slavery in those vast regions. I believe the devotees of this new theory admit that, owning the lands, and holding the sovereignty of those territories in our own hands, we may prohibit the robbing a man of his money, his watch, or his horse; but if the robber goes farther, and commits the greatest of all possible crimes, by robbing his fellow man of his wife and children, of his liberty, his intellectual enjoyments, his future hopes — of himself — such robbery must be permitted, and we have no right to prohibit it.

I stated that this theory was *novel*. It has certainly been discovered since 1776. Then our fathers declared "that governments were constituted for the very purpose of securing the people in the enjoyment of life and liberty." Now it is said that, in establishing government over our conquered territory, we must leave the question of liberty out of view, to be determined by the *people* of that country. Who do gentlemen mean by the *people*? Do they include all persons who now live in

New Mexico, or who shall hereafter go there? Do they intend that each human being shall have a voice and a vote on this question of his own liberty? Will they, by legislative enactment, secure the right of such vote to every man? No, Sir; such is not the intention of gentlemen who use this language. They intend that one portion of the people shall determine whether they will rob another portion of their liberty, and hold them as *property*. Such is the effect of this policy; yet gentlemen are unwilling to come out before the country, and avow this intention in undisguised language.

Again; it is urged that slavery cannot exist there. In the opening of my remarks, I showed that it has existed in Oregon and California; that it now exists in Deseret; and, if we can credit accounts apparently correct, it has existed in New Mexico. In my opinion, the mines of New Mexico will furnish as profitable employment for slaves as can be found upon the face of the earth; that, if permitted, those mines will be filled with a dense slave population. And such we know to be the opinion of slave-holders generally; and they are competent judges. I regard these arguments merely as apologies for leaving the question precisely as slave-holders desire it to be left. Time will not permit me to examine these points farther.

These questions have no reference to the admission of California. Gentlemen seek to turn attention from the subject before us, under pretence that slavery has not received such support from this government as it ought. They know, however, that the territory was obtained without our consent, and against our will. The day after war against Mexico was declared, I foretold to the slave-holders the very state of facts which now exist. I then gave them to understand that Mexicans would be no friends to slavery, and that any State we should obtain from Mexico would be *free*. Slave-holders now complain; but the difficulty has been brought upon themselves by their attempts to strengthen slavery. California must, and will be admitted.

We wish all to understand distinctly and fully our views and ulterior designs. We intend to limit and confine slavery to its present bounds; to repeal all acts of Congress which sustain that institution; and totally to separate the people of the free States and the Federal Government from all responsibility of sustaining slavery or the slave-trade; to restore the government to the position relative to that institution in which it was placed by the Constitution. We then hope to direct its energies and the influence of the nation in favor of justice, of truth, of liberty, and of humanity.

I am aware of the efforts now making to arrange and to compromise these questions; to quiet this agitation; to roll back the tide of popular feeling now manifested, not only in our free States, but in Europe and throughout the civilized world. Sir, feeble and impotent are the powers of Congress, when brought in conflict with that rising voice of the people, now heard in every quarter of our nation. Can we, by legislation, take from twenty millions of freemen their consciences, their thoughts, their judgment? Can we prohibit their investigations of truth? This struggle has been going on for centuries. Men may denounce it, but it will go forward. Reforms in all ages, and in all nations, have been denounced. Oppression, guilt, and crime always seek silence and darkness; but as intelligence increases, and becomes more and more generally diffused, abuses will be corrected, and the work of reformation will proceed.

For the last twelve years I have watched the progress of this great political revolution. Its advance has been regular, constant, and uninterrupted. I have seen the influence of the Executive, of Congress, of the public press generally, and of politicians, put forth to retard its progress, but they have not even checked its onward course.

The arrogance of the slave power has been beaten back; the spirit of northern servility has been rebuked and brought into contempt; the freedom of debate has been regained; the advocates of truth and justice have increased, and are already seizing upon the strongholds of oppression. In our State Legislatures, the language of freedom and of truth finds abun-

34 *

dant utterance. With the most unshaken confidence, in the assurance of unwavering faith, I expect, at no distant day, to see this government and the people of the free States redeemed and purified from the guilt and the crime of slavery.

NEW MEXICO.*

ITS ANCIENT BOUNDARIES — ITS GOVERNMENT — ITS CONQUEST — OUR DUTY TO ITS PEOPLE — CLAIMS OF TEXAS — PAYMENT OF MONEY TO TEXAS — ITS OBJECT — AGITATION — LAWS OF PROGRESS — THEY CANNOT BE RESISTED — DISSOLUTION OF THE UNION RIDICULED — NORTHERN SERVILITY REPROVED.

[Perhaps no greater fraud was ever perpetrated upon an intelligent people than that by which ten millions dollars was taken mostly from the laborers of the free States, and paid over to Texas. Some advocates of the measure pretended it was to be done as a compensation for the claims which Texas had to New Mexico. Others, however, admitted it to be paid to prevent Texas from dissolving the Union. But the most potent cause was probably the distribution of Texas scrip among influential men. Three millions dollars were said to have been held by officers of government, agents, and members of Congress. The passage of the bill above-mentioned raised the value of this scrip at least fifty cents on the dollar, and hundreds of splendid fortunes were supposed to have been realized for services rendered in obtaining the passage of said bill. While it was under consideration, Mr. Giddings delivered the following speech.]

Mr. Chairman, — I should do injustice to my own feelings were I to withhold an expression of my views upon this subject, of establishing the boundaries of Texas, and paying to her ten millions dollars from the public treasury.

To the great joy of the northern people generally, as well as to a portion of those residing in the slave States, the "compromise bill" has been defeated in the Senate. But, while the public are rejoicing over that fortunate termination of eight

* Speech on the bill to establish the boundaries of New Mexico and Texas. Delivered in Committee of the whole House on the state of the Union, August 13, 1850.

months' labor of that body, they have suddenly sent us this bill containing the most exceptionable features of that compromise. In fact, the bill now on your table is more objectionable in its provisions than the compromise itself. Senators who voted for striking these provisions from the "omnibus bill," have turned round and voted for them in the bill before us. And we are now told that they are to be carried through this body by "whig votes." This rumor, I hope, may prove unfounded; time will soon disclose its truth, or its falsehood.

I, Sir, am entirely opposed to the bill, or rather to its two principal features, to wit, that which gives to Texas some forty thousand square miles of territory within the ancient boundaries of New Mexico, and that which provides for the payment to Texas of ten millions of dollars from our treasury. My objections to each of these provisions are inseparable. On a former occasion, I fully examined the boundaries of Texas.* I do not hesitate to say, that no man here or elsewhere, who professes ordinary intelligence on that subject, believes Texas to have any right whatever within the ancient bounds of New Mexico.

Mr. Polk, in his annual message of 1846, declares that "New Mexico, with its capital, Santa Fé, had been captured by our arms." He, Sir, regarded New Mexico as an unit, a State with its *capital;* as conquered from the enemy; not as belonging to Texas. The absurd thought of its being a portion of Texas had not entered the Executive mind. But we are now told that it belonged to Texas after she declared it so in 1836. It is certain that Mr. Polk did not regard it such. He did not enforce Texian laws; nor did he pay any regard whatever to Texian authority. No, Sir; he established a military code of laws. The system bore no similitude to that of Texas. It was the code of New Mexico. Under it, claims were litigated; criminals were tried, convicted, and executed. To this day those laws are in force. They have been maintained and executed throughout New Mexico. This was done

* Vide Speech on President's Message of 1846.

by a democratic administration. We are now called on, under a *whig* administration, to surrender up a portion of this territory, and to purchase the remainder at ten millions dollars. *Will we do it?* After giving Texas one half, we are called on to pay her for the other a greater sum than *the whole of Texas and New Mexico are both worth.* And this, we are told, is to be done by aid of "whig votes." I hope, for the honor of the whig party, that these intimations are unfounded.

Why, Sir, to this hour, no northern whig ever admitted that Texas possessed a shadow of claim to any portion of this territory. Indeed those northern whigs who now urge the passage of this bill do not pretend that Texas has any right or title to any portion of New Mexico. All northern members of that party, both in and out of Congress, wholly and totally deny such right. The only reason assigned for thus delivering up this free territory to the curse of slavery, is to pacify Texas, and appease the slave power; to quiet their clamor; to induce Texas to abstain from dissolving the Union; to purchase clemency and mercy at her hands. Let those northern members vote for that measure whose spirit and feelings are so abject, so servile, as to permit them; but surely no independent statesman will do it.

Again, Mr. Chairman, if this territory belongs to Texas, let her have it. I would not keep it from her. If it be a portion of New Mexico, it belongs to us, and none but a craven heart would surrender it. Yet, Sir, we are told that it is to be done by *whig votes.* Let the degrading act be consummated; let northern honor be surrendered; but let those who do it place their names upon record; let this act go to the country; let the North know *who* it is that betrays her interests, and the interests of humanity.

You, Mr. Chairman, belong to one section of our Union — I to another. Whatever belongs to you under the Constitution, I am willing you should enjoy; whatever belongs to the people of the North, shall never be surrendered by my vote, or with my consent. I repudiate and detest the policy of surrendering up a portion of our rights, in order to purchase a recognition of other interests. Such policy belongs not to independent freemen.

But, Sir, the worst feature of this bill is that which proposes to purchase of Texas this territory which already belongs to us; which was first conquered, and then purchased from Mexico. This ten millions of money is to be drawn from the pockets of our people and handed over to Texas; not because she has any shadow of title to this territory; not for any property or jurisdiction she possesses there — no such thing is urged by northern men. Why, then, shall we pay her that vast amount? The only answer is, we must do it "*to save the Union!*" To buy of Texas the privilege of continuing this government! To induce her to remain with us, and not to sever the tender and interesting relations existing between her and the other States. Why, Sir, they were brought into connection with us for the purpose of making northern freemen sustain her slavery; and now we are to be taxed ten millions dollars for the privilege of supporting this vilest system of oppression that ever disgraced civilized man.

Mr. Howard said, that Texas did not seek annexation to the United States; nor does she ask compensation for the territory; nor was he certain that she would take it.

Mr. Giddings. It cannot have escaped the recollection of any member, that Texas, in 1837, sent her agent here to solicit annexation to our Union!

Mr. Howard. But she withdrew it.

Mr. Giddings. And waited until she could induce our "chargé d'affairés," Mr. Murphy, to recommend her annexation to this Union. And as to accepting the money, I wish she might reject the offer, if tendered. But during the whole session has she not, by her agent, like the daughters of the horse-leech, cried give, give, give? Her Senators voted for this bill to tax the people of the free States to the very modest amount of ten millions of dollars, and to give it over to the holders of Texas scrip. Had not those Senators voted for the bill, it would have been defeated. But, Sir, who is Texas, that she should make such demands of this government? How came she to be a member of this confederacy? The treaty-making power, the only constitutional tribunal capable of admitting her as a member of this confederacy, rejected the application. She then "climbed up some other way." She consented to come in by joint resolution, which, as the present Secretary of State then showed, was entirely unconstitutional, *null* and *void*. The resolutions may be repealed to-morrow, or at any moment when a majority of the two Houses shall think best. That would leave Texas as we found her. She now holds no constitutional position here; nor have her Representatives any more right under the Constitution to hold seats in this hall, than have the subjects of the Grand Sultan, or of the Emperor of Russia. Yet she attempts to lay the nation under contribution for her aggrandizement. If she were to ask for ten or fifteen millions as a consideration for leaving us — for going out of the Union — for ceasing to trouble us, I might, perhaps, vote for it. But I will never consent to give her the first dime to retain her in the Union.

Sir, can we, can our constituents forget the consequences of her annexation? the long, bloody, piratical war in which it involved us? the hundred and fifty millions dollars debt which she entailed upon us? the thirty thousand valuable lives she cost us? And shall we now crown this series of outrages upon the free States, by paying her ten millions of dollars for thus bringing upon us the curse and crimes of such a war, — and of slavery?

Mr. Howard. Why does the gentleman seek to send an army to Texas, if we do not belong to the Union?

Mr. Giddings. I never thought of sending an army to Texas. I abhor offensive wars; and if Texas please to go out of the Union, she shall never be called to an account for it by force of arms, if my vote or influence can prevent it. But I believe in the right and duty of self-defence, and I would bring the whole military force of the nation to the defence of New Mexico, if necessary to preserve her boundaries, and to protect her people; and I would welcome every hostile Texian who comes there with arms in his hands, to a "hospitable grave." While I say this, I repeat that I would oppose the march of an army to Texas, or to any other State who may secede from the Union. I would not seek to *compel* them to remain with us by force of arms. I do not believe in a government of bayonets and of gunpowder, at this age of the world.

The people and each State must govern themselves; or if they see fit to leave the Union, I would say, "Go in peace, *and may the blessing of God rest upon you.*" I would neither shoot them, nor cut their throats for thinking they can do better out of the Union than in it. But when they shall once have left the Union, I will never consent to their return, until they shall become so far civilized and christianized as to purify themselves from slavery. These are my views in regard to attempting to hold States in this Union by fear of the sword. Our Union cannot be preserved in that way. It must be sustained by making it the dispenser of constitutional justice to all the States, the instrument for maintaining the rights of all.

Sir, the payment of this ten millions of dollars constituted the most objectionable feature of the "omnibus bill." It is designed to raise Texas scrip from fifteen cents upon the dollar to "par value;" to make every dollar of Texas scrip worth six and a half; to make splendid fortunes in a short time; to rob the people, the laboring men of the nation, of this vast sum, and place it in the hands of "stock-jobbers" and "gamblers in Texas scrip."

And this is said to be *whig policy,*—the policy of the new administration! Such is the language of the President's organ of this morning. I hope it is not the case. I am unwilling to believe it. This policy is a strong and direct appeal to those members, if any, who are interested in Texian stocks. If I knew it were true that one or two million dollars was owned by individuals on this floor, I should regard the fate of the bill as settled; but it would not be in order, under parliamentary rules, to suppose such a fact to exist. I therefore would not insinuate it; yet should the bill pass, I shall ever believe that considerations, unseen by the public eye, have co-operated with Executive influence to produce that result. I do not believe the President's favor sufficient, at this time, to secure the support of a majority of the House for such an object.

Sir, certain Senators in the other end of the capitol, have for months been endeavoring to convince the people of the necessity of passing the "omnibus bill," as it is called. No arguments could be raised in favor of that measure, for it was not founded on reason. One consideration alone was pressed upon the public mind. The cry was raised that "*the Union was in danger!*" The newspapers here responded, "*the Union is in danger!!*" The country press repeated the alarm. The cry was caught up and echoed by every timid, faltering poltroon of the North. Petitions to "*save the Union*" were circulated. Public meetings were held in our commercial cities where Texas scrip was mostly influential, and resolutions were adopted "*to save the Union.*" Fourth of July orations were delivered, and theological pamphlets were published, and morning prayers were put up in this hall to "*save the Union.*" The supplications were not that we "*may legislate in righteousness,*" deal out justice and mercy to those who are oppressed and degraded by our laws. These were regarded as objects of trifling importance, when compared with the pending danger that *Texas would dissolve the Union.* Indeed, they are never mentioned by our chaplain.

Sir, I am nauseated, sickened at this moral and political effeminacy; this downright cowardice. It is unworthy of American statesmen. Our constituents sent us here to maintain and defend their rights; not to surrender them; not to make ourselves and our people tributary to Texas. In electing us, they had no expectation that we would turn upon them and violently thrust our hands into their pockets and take therefrom ten millions of dollars, and hand it over to the slaveholders of Texas, for territory which belongs to us, and to which Texas never had any title whatever.

Sir, gentlemen here may say what they please; the people have no fears of a dissolution of the Union. They understand this kind of gasconade. The cry of "dissolution" has been the dernier resort of southern men for fifty years, whenever they desired to frighten doughfaces into a compliance with their measures. It may alarm gentlemen here; but I do not think you can find in northern Ohio an equal number of nervous old women or of love-sick girls, who could be moved by it.

Again, it is said that we must stop this agitation in relation to slavery! The people see us here passing laws to enslave our fellow men; to sell women in open market; to create a traffic in the bodies of children. They know this to be opposed to the self-evident truth that "all men are created equal," "that governments are constituted to sustain that equality of rights;" and they converse on the subject, examine the reasons on which such traffic is based, and vote for men who will oppose such barbarous practices. This is called *agitation;* and gentlemen here talk of suppressing it by passing such laws as that on your table. This is the manner in which we are to stop the progress of truth; to seal the lips of philanthropists; and to silence the voice of humanity. Yes, Sir; it is gravely proposed that we should set bounds to the human intellect, and to limit political investigations by statute laws.

Sir, the great founder of our holy religion, when he proclaimed the Heaven-born truths of his Gospel, was denounced as an "*agitator*." He was arrested, condemned, and executed for asserting truths which the Scribes and Pharisees were too stupid to comprehend. It was done to stop *agitation;* but truth, emanating from "the Holy One," has extended, spread, and progressed, and will "go on conquering and to conquer," in spite of all the political Scribes and Pharisees in Congress, and the quaking and trembling of doughfaces here and elsewhere.

This progress in morals and in political intelligence, is in strict accordance with the law of our being, and cannot be prevented. The idea of setting bounds to the human intellect, of circumscribing it by statute law, is preposterous. Why not limit the arts and sciences by conservative legislation, as well as moral and political progress? Why not follow the example of those who attempted to stop the agitation of Galileo, when he proclaimed the truth of our solar system, and the laws by which the planets are retained in their orbits? He caused great agitation, and was excommunicated for his *infidelity*, in thus daring to proclaim truths which the *conservatives* of that age were too ignorant to comprehend. It required two hundred and fifty years for the stupid clergy of that day, to understand the truths for which he had been expelled from their Christian fellowship. How long it will require certain theological professors of the present day, to comprehend the "self-evident truths" of man's equality, is not yet determined. Or how long it will require our political doctors to comprehend the very obvious fact that an educated and reflecting people *will think and act for themselves*, is yet to be ascertained.

But, if we are to have conservative legislation, let us tear down the telegraphic wires, break up our galvanic batteries, and imprison Morse, and stop all agitation upon the subject of your "magnetic railroads of thought." Lay up your steamboats, place fetters upon your locomotives, convert your railroads into cultivated fields, and erase the name of Fulton from our history. Go down to yonder Institute; drive Page from his laboratory, break in pieces his galvanic engines, and unchain the imprisoned lightning which is there pent up; then pass an act of Congress prohibiting all further agitation on these subjects, and thus carry out your conservative principles, of which some men are continually boasting.

Sir, this, above all others, is an age of progress. Look at the peasantry of Europe. They are struggling against oppression. Ground down by the iron heel of despotism for centuries, they are rising in their might, and teaching tyrants to understand the power that dwells with the people. While these political revolutions were convulsing kingdoms, overturning thrones,—while crowns were tossed about like the baubles of children,—Le Verrier, alone in his study, was agitating a question of science. By a course of observations and mathematical calculations, he demonstrated the existence of another planet; far, far away in unlimited space, infinitely beyond the utmost bounds to which even the thoughts of former astronomers had extended. So, Sir, the philosophical statesmen of our own land, reasoning from past observations, and drawing reasonable deductions for the future, see clearly in the distance the star of freedom, shining and glittering in refulgent splendor, far beyond those regions of thought within which the mind of our political savans are accustomed to revolve. Those savans and political doctors will talk of "conservatism," and of "quieting agitation." They are behind the age in which they live; and there they will probably remain.

I know it is said that we must quiet these agitations before Congress will act upon a tariff, and other old party issues. Let me assure gentlemen that revolutions never go backward. It is too late in the day to make intelligent men believe that you have any very pure regard for the laboring men of New England, while you sustain laws here to sell the laboring men and women of this district, like brutes in the market; that you have any real intention to pass laws for the relief of the laboring men of the North, while you keep in force laws for carrying on a coastwise commerce in the bodies of southern laborers. Such pretences are shallow, and no intelligent man will regard them as sincere.

But I ask gentlemen if they really feel capable of convincing the people of the North that it is our duty to give Texas a large portion of New Mexico, and then pay her ten millions of dollars for taking it? Let gentlemen go to the dairymen, the farmers and mechanics of northern Ohio, — and nine out of every ten are as correct judges as we are of the boundaries of New Mexico, and of the propriety of maintaining them, as well as of admitting California and New Mexico when they present their constitutions. They will judge for themselves, too, when we take from their pockets ten millions of dollars for Texas. I should like to hear gentlemen who now advocate this bill, undertake to make those farmers and mechanics believe that it is their duty to contribute a portion of the substance, accumulated by their toil, to make up this tribute to Texas. I imagine they would find the task a difficult one.

Sir, if you wish to *create* agitation among them, *pass this bill!* Take from their hard earnings this ten millions of money and pay it over to Texas, and I will promise you agitation, *increased agitation*. Let northern men vote thus to render their constituents tributary to Texas, and such representatives will find agitation at home; agitation that, like Banquo's ghost, will not "down at their bidding."

For seven months, we have been debating the admission of California. Her senators and representatives have been waiting here, respectfully asking admission, to which there is no real objection. But that subject has been delayed, postponed, and put off, from time to time, without any earthly excuse. Northern whigs and northern democrats were not prepared to act upon this matter. They desired to wait for the Senate to act upon it. It has been in vain that we have called on them, and solicited and importuned them to act on this plainest of all questions ever presented to this body. Well, Sir, the bills admitting California have been laid aside in both Houses, and this bill to give Texas a State carved from New Mexico, and to tax our people to supply the coffers of Texas, is on your table; and the very men who have urged further delay in regard to California, after the bill had been discussed for seven months, now turn round and are willing to pass this most objectionable measure without discussion. These sudden changes of position appear unaccountable to those who are not initiated into such political mysteries. Why is this delay of one measure, and this hot haste to dispose of another? Why, Sir, there is but one answer,—the slave power commands; and northern servility obeys.

We are told that the President is anxious for the settlement of these questions, and his late message shows such to be the case. To this message I will now ask a moment's attention.

So far as it treats of our rights to the entire territory of New Mexico, and the duties of the Executive to protect and defend the people and territory until Congress shall dispose of the subject, its doctrine is sound and its argument conclusive. To this extent I believe the people of the free States, including all political parties, will sustain and uphold the doctrines of the message; and they will stand ready at all times to aid and assist the President, in carrying them into effect.

Sir, I take this opportunity to declare, that neither myself, nor the political friends with whom I act, are disposed to make war on any man or any party. We are contending for what we deem great and paramount principles; and so far as the President and his party shall carry out our doctrines, we shall rejoice to act with him; and whenever he or his party departs from the essential doctrines on which our government rests, or adopts a policy opposed to justice, or to the rights of the people, we shall freely express our disapprobation and make known our objections. We shall expose his errors with the same freedom that we sustain him when right. I therefore repeat, and I take pleasure in saying, that to the extent before stated, the message is right and satisfactory, and will be supported.

But when the President goes on to describe the dangers arising to our Union from the blustering of Texas, and more than intimates the propriety of our paying Texas for a portion of New Mexico, merely to purchase her silence, and to hire her not to intimidate us, I feel constrained to say that I regard such intimations as unworthy of his high station. It is undignified, and bespeaks a timidity unbecoming the Chief Magistrate of a mighty nation. No man can mistake the President's anxiety for the safety of the Union, which none ought for a moment to regard as endangered; and his anxiety also to make peace with Texas, without very particular regard to the terms on which it shall be obtained, is too apparent to be misunderstood.

Every attentive reader of the message must be satisfied that it begins with General Taylor's policy, and ends with that of the Secretary of State. It begins boldly, but ends pusillanimously. It commences by a fair maintenance of our rights, and closes by advising us to purchase safety of Texas. It opens by informing Texas that she must submit to constitutional authority, and concludes by intimating that she shall be well paid if she will abide in the Union with us.

The message was most evidently intended to facilitate the

passage of the bills to which I had referred. Indeed, the *National Intelligencer*, the organ of the President, comes out this morning giving a programme of our action upon these measures. It not only informs its readers that these objectionable bills are to pass this body, but it descends to the detail, and gives us distinctly to understand that they are to be acted upon "in the order in which the Senate sends them to us." It gives us the assurance that this bill giving up a portion of New Mexico to Texas, and paying her ten millions to take it, is in perfect accordance with the Executive views. We are also told that we are to have no farther delay, that the session ought to be brought to a close, and that these bills must not detain Congress at this season of the year.

Why, Sir, these admonitions, coming from such a quarter, are surely worthy of consideration. I have this morning heard it suggested that the whole thing was arranged and agreed upon before the "compromise bill" was defeated in the Senate. That leading members, at both ends of the capitol, concluded to force these bills through this body under the screw of the previous question, without discussing or amending them. And this, I understand, is to be effected by "whig votes." I shall await these movements with great interest. To this day, as I have remarked, the entire whig party of the North has at all times and under all circumstances denied that Texas possesses *title* to any portion of Mexico. I am unwilling to believe they will now throw a political somerset, and admit that she has title there, and vote for paying her ten millions of dollars for it; "but we shall see what we shall see."

Representatives here have learned that there is a power not *behind*, but *above* the throne — one that will command obedience even from the President himself. When General Taylor first ascended the presidential chair, he was anxious for the establishment of civil governments in California and New Mexico. All will recollect his anxiety to save the people there from the government of the bowie-knife and pistol.

Sir, a few free soilers, aided by whigs and democrats, resisted the establishment of such governments unless slavery were excluded. The *indignant frowns* of the President were threatened to be poured out upon the free soil party, if they again opposed that measure. These threats had no effect. Free soilers and the people stood firm. General Taylor saw the course of public sentiment and wisely changed his policy, and himself opposed the establishment of civil governments in our territories, to which the whole whig party responded, Amen. General Taylor now sleeps with his fathers. "Peace to his ashes."

But a generation of whigs has now risen up, who seem not to have known General Taylor, or his policy, who now turn their backs upon his plan, and vote for civil governments in Utah and New Mexico without any exclusion of slavery. Well, Mr. Chairman, it is the duty of the soldier to face to the right, or to the left, or to *right about*, according to the word of the drill-sergeant. We shall soon have the opportunity of witnessing the manner in which these subsidized troops obey the word, and how many whigs will now "take their turn upon the springboard," and give us specimens of "ground and lofty tumbling."

This, Sir, was the principal object for which I rose. I wished to call the attention of the House and of the country to the alacrity with which members here change their position, and vote in direct opposition to their former professions. Why, Sir, it is known to the whole country, that two years since the entire whig party North, stood pledged to the establishment of governments in our territories, *with the proviso excluding slavery*. I think on various occasions every northern whig member voted for it. The proviso or no proviso, was the issue in all the northern States in the presidential canvass of 1848. On this issue General Taylor was elected, and General Cass was defeated. When General Taylor avowed his doctrine of non-action, the whigs changed their position and sustained that policy. Now, Sir, we are told they are to take one step more. They must go for territorial governments in Utah and New Mexico, without the proviso. This, we are told, is the plan agreed upon — one which is warmly advocated by the organs of the party here. This will bring them, as a party, entirely round into the loco-foco doctrines of General Cass in 1848.

These measures — that is, the establishment of civil government in Utah and New Mexico; the establishment of the boundary line between Texas and New Mexico; and, to crown all, a bill for compelling northern freemen to become the catch-poles of southern slave-holders, were all suggested by the present Secretary of State, some five months since, while a member of the Senate. They were then regarded as odious by nine-tenths of the entire whig party North. They were then looked upon with disgust, and their author with general disfavor. He is now at the head of the Cabinet. All his measures, odious as they are, are now pressed upon Congress, sustained by the executive organ, and said to be a part of the Executive policy. I hope it is not so; I am unwilling to believe it; yet when I look back to the avowals of the Secretary of State while in the Senate, and bear in mind that he was selected to the premiership while openly advocating these measures — when I see them sustained by his leading and confidential friends in this hall, and in the other end of the capitol, and by leading whig papers, I am unable to resist the conviction that the President favors them. I am conscious that he cannot do it from a love of slavery. His message unfolds the secretly operating cause. It is the fear of domestic violence, of civil war with Texas.

Southern gasconade has excited alarm in older men than the President. It has been the usual weapon with which to assail the North for the last fifty years. I think the time has arrived when it should be regarded by the President, and by Congress. If Texas and other southern States have determined to secede from the Union, the paying of ten millions of dollars will satisfy them only for the moment; other and more extravagant demands will soon be made. Indeed we know, that most of the southern malecontents make the rejection of California the test of abiding in the Union. They assure us that the Union shall be dissolved, if California be admitted. To yield to these demands, is to admit that we have no government, nor an association that is competent to exercise the functions of a government. And this vast sum which we are to pay Texas, is to reward her for abiding in the Union. No northern man pretends the money is to be paid for any other purpose. Those who advocate its payment, all admit it is to "buy our peace" with her. If she remain with us, she will do so for hire — for a compensation paid by northern men.

Sir, I have no language to express the feelings which this proposition creates in my own mind. Those who wield the government of Texas, must have great contempt for her people, or they would not for a moment attempt to sell her allegiance in this manner. And we, Sir, must hold them as exceedingly degraded, or we would not attempt to purchase their fidelity by dollars and cents.

Of what possible benefit can Texas be to this Union? Since she professed to belong to it, we have been at constant and heavy expense to protect her against the miserable hordes of savages who infest her borders. For the transportation of her mails, the people of our free States pay a heavy sum yearly; and the keeping up of custom-houses requires a large annual appropriation beyond all the revenue they collect. We are constrained to pay our judges, marshals, and district attorneys for that State, in order to maintain a judiciary there. In short, under ordinary circumstance, every laborer of the North pays from his earnings an annual contribution to maintain the government of Texas. We all know these facts; and from the nature of her soil and population, she will probably continue to be an expense to us for the next half century. And now we are called on to pay her ten millions dollars for the privilege of continuing this yearly burden upon our people. Why, Sir, this was all foreseen at the time of her annexation, and the policy of forming a union with her was based upon the expectation that "it would extend and perpetuate slavery." If, therefore, we pay this money, it must be paid for that purpose. This truth should be distinctly understood by every northern man.

Before I conclude, it is due to myself, and to the political friends with whom I act, that I should say, we have done all in our power to avoid the present aspect of this question. It was our wish to have disposed of the California bill at an early day, and in the ordinary course of legislation. We foresaw the difficulties now before us, and endeavored to avoid them. But gentlemen now in favor of this measure were anxious to delay final action in regard to the admission of California. That important measure, in regard to which our duties were so plain, has been put off, and delayed in every possible manner.

We are urged to await the action of the Senate, to see what they would do in regard to it. Well, Sir, counsels other than ours have prevailed. We have awaited the action of the Senate; they have sent us a bill establishing a civil government in Utah, and this bill to establish the boundaries of Texas and New Mexico. These, in the order of business, now precede the bill admitting California—we must act on them first. And we are told plainly that if we pass these bills, we may then take up and pass that admitting California. But we are also assured, that if we reject these bills, "California shall not be admitted;" that southern gentlemen will, by a factious course here, defeat all attempts to legislate on that subject; in other words, we must pass this bill giving to Texas money to pay her debt, *or our government is to be brought to an end.* We are to legislate under this kind of duress.

Sir, I stand here as a free man, the representative of freemen. Thank God, I represent no slaves. I feel conscious that I could offer my constituency no greater insult than to vote for this bill—*I shall not do it.* If the stability of our Union were to depend on the passage of that bill, I would spurn it with indignation. Never, Sir, under any combination of influences, of interests, or of political considerations, will I consent to the passage of any law taxing the people of Ohio to pay the debts of Texas.

ANNUAL MESSAGE OF THE PRESIDENT.*

DECLARATION OF HIS PRESENT POSITION — HIS FORMER DOCTRINES — HIS CHANGE OF PRINCIPLES — HIS VIOLATIONS OF WHIG PRINCIPLES — HIS DEVOTION TO SLAVERY — HIS FRIENDSHIP FOR THE "FUGITIVE LAW" — THE CHARACTER OF THAT LAW — ITS BARBARITY EXPOSED — ITS UNCONSTITUTIONALITY — FEELING OF THE NORTHERN PEOPLE.

[During the Presidential campaign of 1848, the advocates of freedom were urged to support the whig candidates, for the reason that Mr. Fillmore was an avowed supporter of liberty. It was also understood, that General Taylor had taken position, with his cabinet, against the organization of territorial governments in Utah and New Mexico; and in favor of admitting them as States so soon as they should form State Constitutions, and ask admission to the Union. Upon the death of General Taylor, this policy was entirely changed. Mr. Webster, while in the Senate, on the 7th March, had laid down the programme of "compromise measures," which for their servility to southern dictation were condemned by most northern men. This speech of Mr. Webster was a very clear indication of his hostility to General Taylor's policy. When Mr. Fillmore assumed the Executive duties, after the death of the President, he called Mr. Webster to the office of Secretary of State, and in that capacity he was regarded as giving dictation to the policy of the administration, and as principal author of the message under consideration, when the following speech was delivered.]

Mr. Chairman, — The President's message is now before us, and I avail myself of a long established custom to express my views in relation to the doctrines and policy avowed by the Executive. For the frankness with which the President declares his positions upon the interesting questions which

* Speech on the annual Message of the President, of December, 1850. Delivered in Committee of whole House on the State of the Union, December 9, 1850.

now agitate the public mind, I tender him my thanks. It was due to himself, to his political friends, and to the country, that his views on these questions should be distinctly set forth; that the nation should understand whether he is *for* or *against* this fugitive law, now so odious throughout the free States.

I approve the doctrine which the President lays down respecting the exercise of his veto power. I regard it as the doctrine of the Constitution. It is true, however, that it overthrows and wholly discards the avowed policy of the party which elected him. The party declared its doctrine to be, that the veto power should never be exercised, except when the bill presented for the President's approval was *clearly unconstitutional.*

This doctrine the President repudiates, and goes as far in the support of that prerogative as Jackson, or Tyler, or Polk. I approve this independence, this casting aside the trammels of party. I am now curious to see how many of those friends will turn round and go with the President in this change of doctrine.

But, by looking at the latter part of the message, it becomes evident that the President intends the country shall understand that he will veto any bill for the repeal of the fugitive law. To do that, while holding to the doctrines on which he was elected, would have been palpably inconsistent. In order, therefore, to make a show of consistency, he must first repudiate this important doctrine of his party. As to the morality of this deception, I forbear to make any remarks.

The boldness with which the President avows his friendship to the fugitive law, is not only commendable, but should entitle him to the thanks of the whole North as well as of the whole South.

When the vote was taken upon that bill, there was found north of Mason and Dixon's line only *three whigs* in this body who possessed the moral courage to meet the odium of voting for its passage. From the day of that vote until the reading of this message, the whig press of the North, with nearly unanimous voice, repeated and reiterated this fact, in order to exonerate their party from the odium of that measure, and to place the responsibility of its enactments upon their political opponents. The message meets and exposes this unmanly subterfuge, and boldly defies the odium attached to this measure. A short time will determine how many northern whigs will now face about at the bidding of the Executive, and share with him the unenviable fame of sustaining and continuing an enactment which is a libel upon all that is called *law*. These *changes*, Sir, may prove inconvenient to the younger members of the party, — to those who have had but little experience; but to those who have been accustomed to follow the leaders of that party, these political somersets must have become familiar.

Most of our whig editors of the North have assured their readers that the feelings and conscience and judgment of the President were opposed to this fugitive law. This message will teach them that he thinks his own thoughts, and speaks his own wishes, and acts upon his own judgment; and that it is for them to turn round and swallow their words, and go in for a continuance of this law which they have so loudly denounced, or they will be read out of the party.

Sir, had the President avowed his desire for the passage of this law, prior to his election in 1848, how many votes, think you, he would have received in the free States? I imagine they would have been few. At that time he was represented as a friend of freedom, a supporter of northern rights, and devoted to the cause of humanity. Upon these principles he was sustained in the North. But no sooner were the clods adjusted upon the grave of his predecessor, than we were informed that he had abandoned every doctrine in relation to slavery which his party had maintained pending his election. He adopted the entire programme of measures announced in the Senate by the present Secretary of State on the 7th of March last. His influence was exerted for the delivery of some fifty thousand square miles of free territory to Texas and to slavery, — to pay Texas ten millions dollars, to hire her to abstain from driving the army from our western territory, and from dissolving the Union. He was in favor of the passage of laws to organize governments in our territories, without excluding slavery; and he was in favor of this fugitive law.

No man had ever come into the Presidential chair, who so unceremoniously cast aside and repudiated the important pledges of his friends and his party. No public man of high standing, from the free States, has so suddenly and so boldly abjured the cause of freedom, and, before the world, pledged fealty to the slave power, saving and excepting his Secretary of State, whose counsels he appears to have adopted.

But this boldness, this manly frankness with which the President announces his change of position, and tacitly calls upon his former friends to follow him, may teach us the propriety of hereafter understanding the principles of our presidential candidates *before* we vote for them, rather than undergo the mortification of those party changes and countermarchings. The public will watch with much interest to see how many of his party friends will change their position, in order to stand with him in favor of this fugitive law and of slavery.

The President informs us that the Constitution has made it his duty to "take care that the laws be faithfully executed." All are aware that such is made his duty. But how has he performed it? He has seen the mails violated in South Carolina and other States, robbed of newspapers which do not suit the taste of their people, and the laws of Congress held in contempt and trampled upon. This is done by his own officers, who hold their appointments at his will; but, Sir, has he ousted such men from office? We have yet to learn that he has even reproved them, much less has he hinted at these things in this message. He sees the free colored citizens of New England, and, indeed, of nearly all the free States, seized, imprisoned, and sold into bondage by southern men. He is aware that hundreds, and, perhaps, thousands of free born northern citizens now pine in southern chains; he witnesses this transcendent outrage upon the laws, upon the Constitution, and upon humanity, in perfect silence; he does not even hint at their existence. He has seen the agents of Massachusetts driven by mob violence from South Carolina and Louisiana, when sent there to sustain the legal rights of the citizens of that State now held in slavery. He knew that no northern State nor individual could rescue those citizens from the chains of servitude. Upon outrages more aggravated than any that have ever occurred under this government, he makes no comment.

Sir, the House and the country must see that the only sympathy exhibited in the message is for *slavery ;* he has none for freedom. He recommends us not to repeal the fugitive law, but recommends no law to sustain the liberties of our own people, or to redeem those freemen who mourn in southern bondage ; still he assures us that, "in our domestic policy, the Constitution shall be his guide," and that "he regards all its provisions as equally binding." That this declaration is entirely erroneous, is too obvious to require further exposure.

Mr. Chairman, our opposition to the fugitive law is based upon the soundest principles of ethics and of law, as well as the dictates of the common sense of mankind. While the southern men are thus seizing northern freemen, enslaving and brutalizing them, they turn round and call on us to leave our employments, give chase, arrest, and return their fugitive slaves. While violating our national compact in its most vital features, they ask us not merely to observe and keep our stipulations, but to go far beyond our covenants to uphold their slavery.

Now, Sir, these southern men have no claim whatever on us to observe the compact, while they disregard and trample upon it. Such are the dictates of law, and of justice, and the teachings of common sense. A compliance with such demand would constitute us the mere subsidiaries, the appendages of southern slavery. This feeling has thus far been suppressed by our intelligent people, hoping that Congress would relieve them from the position in which they have long been placed. If this fugitive law be kept in force, and Congress shall exert its power and influence to degrade our people, I, Sir, will not predict the consequences. They may be read in our past history. One thing may be regarded as admitted truth, — while northern freemen are held in southern chains, the people of the free States will not arrest, nor return fugitive slaves. I speak for no other portion of the country. But the South and the North, the East and the West, may understand, that, while the inhabitants of our State shall be held in slavery, (and there are many there,) few, *very few*, slaves will return to bondage from that section of country where I reside.

Sir, suppose a man born among us, educated in our schools, baptized in our churches, professing our religion, but who has been seized and held in southern slavery, should make his escape, and revisit the scenes of his birth and childhood; but, while quietly and peaceably among us, the baying of human bloodhounds should be heard upon his track, and the whole army of slave-catchers, including certain high dignitaries who procured the passage of the fugitive law, should be seen coming in hot pursuit, with handcuffs and chains and fetters prepared and clanking in their hands; do you, Sir, think they would take him, and fetter him, in the presence of our people, and drag him back to a land of sighs and tears? Sir, if the President, or members of this body, or that class of clergymen who are preaching that obedience to this law is a religious duty, believe this can be done, they had better study the character of our population more thoroughly.

Under that law, such cases may frequently occur; and whether there be a neighborhood north of Mason and Dixon's line, where such a freemen can be taken back to a land of whips and chains, I leave for others to judge; I will not argue the point.

But the President is not satisfied with quoting the words of the Constitution; he closes the paragraph with the following sentence:

> "You, gentlemen, and the country, may be assured, that to the utmost of my ability, and to the extent of the power vested in me, I shall at all times, and in all places, take care that the laws be faithfully executed."

This language is understood by the House and by the country. No one can mistake its import. It is the language of menace, — of *intimidation*. He distinctly avows that, "*to the extent of the power vested in him, he will see*" this infamous law executed. The power of the army and the navy is vested in the President. This power he assures us, will be used to shoot down northern freemen, if necessary to enforce this law. This attempt at menace is unworthy of the President. It is unbecoming his station. I feel pained while contemplating the position in which the President has thus placed himself. No language could have been more destructive to his influence. This taunting menace should never have been addressed to freemen; to men who understand the Constitution, and know their rights. I have shown some reasons why our people of northern Ohio will *not obey that law.* The President may speak to them of the "*power vested in him;*" of the army and navy; and he may tell them that he will use the whole military power of the nation at all *times,* and in all *places,* to enforce this detestable law; but, Sir, they will hurl back defiance both at him and his army. He may send his troops, — his Swiss guards of slavery; he may put all the machines of human butchery in operation; he may drench our free land with blood; he may entitle himself to the appellation of a second "*Haynau;*" but he will *never compel them to obey that law.* They will govern themselves; they will obey every constitutional enactment; but they will discard and repudiate this fugitive bill. I speak what I feel before God and man. I speak what every enlightened statesman must feel and admit, when I say that no free, enlightened, and independent people ever was, or ever will be, governed by the bayonet and the sword. No, Sir. I will say to the President with all kindness, but with unhesitating confidence, our people will never be compelled by the bayonet or the cannon, or in any other manner, to lend any aid or assistance in executing that infamous law; *nor will they obey it.*

The President should have learned ere this, that public sentiment, with an enlightened and patriotic people, is stronger than armies or navies; that he himself is but the creature of the people's will, — their servant, — elected to execute their purposes. In the enactment of this law, their feelings were not consulted, their honor was disregarded, and their wishes were treated with scorn. Sir, a large portion of the northern people were not represented in this body at the passage of that law. Their servants fled from this hall, and left the interests, the rights, and the honor of their constituents to be disposed of by slave-holders and their obsequious allies. This law "was conceived in sin," and literally "brought forth in iniquity." It is due to our southern friends that we should inform them distinctly that the law *cannot* and *will not* be enforced. Our people, Sir, know what constitutes law. This enactment I call a law merely for convenience, because our language furnishes no proper term in which to characterize it. It has the *form*, but is entirely destitute of the spirit, — the essence of law. It *commands* the perpetration of crimes, which no human enactment can justify. In passing it, Congress overstepped the limits of civil government, and attempted to usurp powers which belong only to God. In this attempt to involve our people in crimes forbidden by inspiration, by every impulse of humanity, and to command one portion of the people to wage a war upon another, Congress was guilty of tyranny unexampled.

This enactment is beyond the power, outside the duties of human government; it imposes no obligation to commit the crimes it commands, it can justify no one for committing them. For this reason, the people *will not obey it*. Nor is this doctrine new, either in theory or in practice. In every State of the Union, statutes have been enacted which never have been, and never could be enforced. They are so opposed to the public sense of justice and propriety, that they remain a dead letter from the day of their enactment. Congress has enacted many such laws, which no President ever could or ever will enforce. This fugitive law must be repealed, or, if it remain unrepealed, it will remain a dead letter. Of the fifteen thousand fugitives in the free States, probably not ten have been returned to bondage, and I doubt whether ten more will be returned under it.

When Mr. Jefferson came into power, he found men imprisoned under the sedition law, which he deemed unconstitutional. He did not hesitate to pardon them. They had been deprived of their liberty without constitutional authority. But Mr.

Fillmore pledges himself to exert his power to punish every man who assists his fellow man to regain his liberty. Such, Sir, is the difference between Mr. Jefferson and Mr. Fillmore.

Mr. Chairman, I now wish to call the attention of the House to the assertion of an important principle, in which I most heartily concur. The President says:

> "Every citizen who truly loves the Constitution, and desires the continuance of its existence and its blessings, will resolutely and firmly resist any interference in those domestic affairs, which the Constitution has clearly and unequivocally left to the exclusive authority of the States."

And why did the President seek to interfere with slavery? Why not let the slave States take care of their own institutions? Why did he urge the passage of this fugitive law? Why attempt to make the people of the free States interfere to catch southern negroes? Why prostitute his official power and the power of the government to such degrading purposes?

If there be any one feature of the Constitution, which the whole history of its adoption has made plain, it is that slavery is a *State institution, over which Congress has no control,*— with which this Federal Government *has no legitimate powers to interfere.* We, Sir, of the North, will not be constrained, even by your fugitive law, to interfere with it. The slavery of Virginia belongs to her. If she possess the power and the disposition to uphold it, we cannot put it down or abolish it. If she sees fit to abolish it, we have no power to interfere to sustain it.

I have often defined the views of anti-slavery men, and of free soilers, on this subject; others have often done it; yet we are misapprehended and constantly misrepresented. That clause of the message now under consideration, was intended to impute to us a purpose, a desire, to interfere with southern slavery. That idea, false and unfounded, has been asserted and reiterated for years. The President should have been better informed. For the hundredth time I repeat, that Congress, nor this Federal Government, have any more power to interfere with the slavery of the southern States than they have with the serfdom of Russia. The slave States hold their "peculiar institution" as independently of this government, as Russia holds her serfs. Again, Sir, this government possesses no more right to involve the people of the North in the support of southern slavery, than it has to involve us in the support of Russian serfdom. Congress possesses no more power nor right to make us the catchers of southern slaves, than of Russian serfs.

These were the views and feelings of those who framed the Constitution. They never dreamed of making us the catchpoles for southern slave-hunters.

In the Convention which framed the Constitution, Governeur Morris said that "he never would concur in upholding domestic slavery." So say I, and so say our people of the North. We never will concur in upholding that institution. Mr. Morris added, "it is a nefarious institution. It was the curse of Heaven upon the States in which it existed."

So we say. It is a curse upon those States; but the curse is *theirs*, not ours, and we will not share in it. Your fugitive law shall not compel us to share in it. Our fathers would not consent to be involved in its crimes; we will not.

Mr. Gerry of Massachusetts said, "while we have nothing to do with slavery in the States, we should be careful to lend no sanction to it." Sir, we will lend no sanction to it, nor shall your fugitive law compel us to sanction it. Mr. Dickinson "thought it a proper subject for the general government to interfere with, as it affected our national happiness." But southern members resisted this proposition. They would give to the Federal Government no powers to interfere with slavery for any purpose.

But I desire to come more directly to the clause relating to fugitive slaves. When the committee reported the draft of a Constitution, it contained the clause for the arrest and return of fugitives from justice, as it now stands. They were to be delivered up by the Executive of the State to which they should flee; and this was to be done, also, at the expense of such State. While this report was under consideration, Messrs. Butler and Pinckney of South Carolina moved to amend it, so as to "require fugitives, slaves, and servants to be delivered up like criminals."

Mr. Wilson of Pennsylvania said, "this would oblige the Executive to do it at the *public expense*."

Mr. Sherman of Connecticut "saw no more propriety in the public seizing and surrendering a fugitive slave or servant, *than a horse*." And on these suggestions, Mr. Butler withdrew his proposition. These facts were recorded by Mr. Madison; and no stronger evidence could have been left of the intention of the framers of the Constitution to save the freemen of the North from all expense, and guilt, and disgrace, of arresting fugitive slaves. The clause for the return of fugitive slaves, as it now stands, was subsequently adopted, with the concurrence of Mr. Wilson and of Mr. Sherman. It provides that the State to which the slave flees shall not, by any law or regulation, *release him from labor*. "Non-interference" between the master and slave, was their intention, their ulterior design. The last member of the sentence says of the slave, he "shall be delivered up on claim of the person to whom such service or labor may be due."

This language has been understood by some as rendering action necessary on the part of the people of the State to which the slave may have fled. This construction is opposed to the whole spirit of the Constitution. Every reader will see at once that such obligation is not imposed upon the Governor, nor upon the people of the State, nor upon any individual. The Supreme Court has given a construction to this language which is in accordance with the intention and object of the framers of the Constitution. We are to deliver up the fugitive slave, as we deliver up our friends to the civil officer. We are bound to permit the master to arrest and carry back the slave, in the same manner that we permit the civil officer to seize our friends, under process, and take them to prison.

And such was the law of 1793. It followed the Constitution. It saved the master from interruption, while pursuing his slave. It provided fines and penalties against any person who, disobeying the constitutional compact, should secrete or defend or rescue the slave. There the law of 1793 stopped. It went no farther. It gave the master no process under the seal of your courts, by which to arrest his slave. It commanded no officer of this government to aid the master in making such arrest. No powers of this government were prostituted to such degrading purposes. "Non-interference" between the master and slave was the rule by which that whole law was framed. And it is to the honor of the Supreme Court that, in their construction of the Constitution and of the law, they have carried out this view. They have adopted the very idea of Mr. Wilson and Mr. Sherman. They declare the right of the master to recapture his slave to be the same as his right to take his property which strays into a free State. They construe our duties to *deliver up* the fugitive slave, to be the same as to deliver up the stray horse. If the horse or the slave come among us, we permit the owner or master to take him. But in neither case can the owner or master call on us to catch the slave or the horse.

Neither the law of 1793, nor the Constitution, contemplated the organization of northern freemen into a constabulary force for catching negroes. Nor did it give the master a guard and assistance to carry back his slave at the *expense of the nation.* Such provisions could never have been approved by Washington, who signed the law of 1793, nor by his associates who had aided in framing the Constitution, and who also voted for that law. They understood their constitutional duties.

The extent of our powers consists in prohibiting the people from interfering between the master and slave. And this fugitive law is unconstitutional to the full extent to which it attempts to exert its powers in aid of slavery. The appointment of officers, making it their duty to issue process, to pursue the slave, to arrest, to carry him back, and the paying expenses from the treasury, are all unconstitutional acts. They, Sir, interfere with slavery, and are repugnant to the whole spirit of the Constitution. The President, in the quotation I have made, unintentionally condemns these acts. I condemn them, the country condemns them, humanity condemns them.

All who read this message must see that the only interference with slavery which the President professes to deprecate, is that which tends to *loosen* the chains of bondage; he appears to have no objection to that interference which rivets them closer. Could he have believed that the intelligent freemen of the North would fail to detect the palpable contradiction between that portion of the message which deprecates interference with slavery, and that which urges the continuance of this law, which was enacted for the very purpose of interfering in support of that institution?

Could any interference have been more direct and palpable than that which makes it the duty of the deputy-marshal or commissioner, under a heavy penalty, to exert his utmost powers to arrest the fugitive? Which gives him authority to call the whole power of the State to assist him? Which "commands all good citizens to aid and assist in the prompt" arrest and return of the trembling slave? This interference the President approves. It rivets tighter the chains of bondage, while we are all aware that he disapproved our efforts to exclude slavery from the free territory of New Mexico.

But this law goes farther; it not only attempts to strike down God's law, which commands us "to feed the hungry," but it attempts to convert every freeman of the North into a savage. If a fugitive from oppression reaches my door amid the ragings of the storm, half clad, and benumbed with cold, fainting and weary, sick and in distress, and asks to warm himself by my fire, this law interferes, and forbids me, under heavy pains and penalties, to comply with his request. If I obey the law, I must drive him from my door, to perish with hunger and cold. If I receive him to my habitation, warm him by my fire, — if I feed him, and give him drink, and restore him, so that he pursues his journey and escapes, I am subjected, under this law, to a fine of one thousand dollars and to six months' imprisonment. This law the President *approves*, and advises us to *continue it in force.* This practice he sustains, and asks us to uphold. I reply, in his own language: "Every citizen who truly loves the Constitution, will resolutely and firmly resist" the interference which this law enjoins.

Sir, our people will continue to feed the hungry, to clothe the naked, to visit the sick, and to relieve the oppressed; and no interference of this fugitive law will prevent this compliance with the dictates of our religion, with that law which came from God himself, and which no enactment of slaveholders and doughfaces can repeal or nullify. I speak for no one but myself and constituents; others will choose whether to obey God or the oppressors of mankind; but as for us, we will obey that higher law of kindness, benevolence, and humanity, which was implanted in the breast of every human being, and written upon the hearts and consciences of mankind, by the finger of our Creator.

Mr. Chairman, the doctrine of "non-interference with slavery," laid down by the President, is at war with every provision of this fugitive law. If we maintain that doctrine, this law must remain a dead letter upon our statute book. He who sustains this doctrine must disobey the law; for the Constitution and this law are antagonisms — at war with each other. If we adhere to one, we must discard the other. My constituents will maintain the Constitution, while they will hold this law in contempt. Sir, from the adoption of the Constitution until 1841, never was this doctrine of "non-interference between master and slave" denied by the Executive. At that time, the present Secretary of State, in a correspondence with our Minister at London, substantially avowed it to be the duty of this government to protect southern slave-dealers while pursuing their vocation. This doctrine, coming from a Massachusetts man, inspired his successor (Mr. Upshur) to maintain the same principles, while advocating the annexation of Texas in 1843. Up to 1841, I repeat, that "non-interference between master and slave" was the doctrine of the North and of the South, of whigs and of democrats.

It is true that our slave-holding Presidents at times lent their powers *silently* to uphold slavery; but no officer of government ever *avowed* it to be the duty of Congress, or the Executive, thus to interfere, until the present Secretary of State put forth that construction in 1841. I repeat that, from the day of adopting the Constitution until 1841, the doctrine of "non-interference with slavery in the States" was never denied, to my knowledge, by any public man of this nation; and no member of this body ever attempted to overthrow it by argument, until the last session of Congress. To the gentleman from Georgia, (Mr. Toombs,) not now in his seat, belongs the honor of being the member of this House who boldly and publicly demanded that the powers and energies of this government should be prostituted to the support of slavery. The President and his Cabinet may adopt this new theory — but the people of the North will repudiate it.

The message further says, "the law is the only sure protection of the weak, and the only efficient restraint upon the strong." This, Sir, is said with direct reference to this fugitive slave law, to induce the people to execute it. It would seem that the President intended to see how far he could impose upon the intelligence of the public. Sir, what protection does this law lend to the poor, weak, oppressed, degraded slave, whose flesh has often quivered under the lash of his inhuman owner, whose youth has been spent in labor for another, whose intellect has been nearly blotted out? When he seeks an asylum in a land of freedom, this worse than barbarous law sends the officers of government to chase him down — to carry him back to chains and suffering. The people are constrained to become his pursuers. Famishing and fainting, he drags his weary limbs forward, while the whole power of the government under the President's command, the army and navy, and all the freemen of the land, are on his track, to scourge him back to bondage. And this law, the President tells us, is the only sure protection to that miserable slave. Does the President intend to insult our intelligence? Or did he mean to insert in this grave document a satire upon this barbarous enactment?

Sir, there is not a man in this body, there is not an intelligent man in the free States but knows, if he delivers a fugitive into the custody of his pursuers, that he will be carried back and sold to the far South; and, ordinarily, his life will be sacrificed in five years, if employed on the sugar plantations, and in seven years on the cotton plantations. The men of the North look upon this as murder, and would almost as soon turn out and cut the throat of the defenceless negro as to send him back to be scourged to death. As soon would they do this as comply with a law which violates every principle of humanity, and consigns the fugitive to a lingering death by a slow torture of five or seven years. The common law holds him who aids in a murder, as guilty as he who strikes the knife to the heart of the victim. Under our law, a man is hanged, if he fails to prevent a murder, when it is plainly within his power to do so. Such a man is held guilty of the act, and he is hanged accordingly.

And will any one suppose that he who assists in arresting and sending a fugitive slave to torture and death, will be less guilty than he under whose lash the victim expires?

Sir, I have compared this capture of a fugitive to a common murder. In doing that I do injustice to the common murderer. To capture a slave, and send him to the South to die under a torture of five years, is far more criminal than ordinary murder, inasmuch as it adds the guilt of torture to the crime of murder.

Sir, we will not commit this crime. Let me say to the President, no power of government can compel us to involve ourselves in such guilt. No! The freemen of Ohio will never turn out to chase the panting fugitive; they will never be metamorphosed into bloodhounds, to track him to his hiding-place, and seize and drag him out, and deliver him to his tormentors. They may be shot down; the cannon and bayonet and sword may do their work upon them; they may drown the fugitives in the blood of freemen; but never will freemen stoop to the degradation of catching slaves.

Let no man tell me there is no higher law than this fugitive bill. We feel there is a law of right, a law of justice, of freedom, implanted in the breast of every intelligent human being, that bids him look with scorn upon this miscalled law.

Sir, I was about to make some comparisons, but, perhaps, they may be regarded as indelicate. I, however, shall not hesitate to speak truth. During last summer, two distinguished gentlemen of the same name occupied much of the public attention. One was said to have committed murder, and the other to have procured the passage of this law. One was hanged for his crime; the other, for his efforts, was taken to the Executive cabinet. One destroyed the life of an individual, the other contributed his influence for the passage of this law, which, if executed, must consign hundreds, perhaps thousands, to premature graves. I, Sir, cannot speak for others; but, for myself, I would rather meet my final Judge with the guilt of him who has gone to his last account resting upon my soul, than that of him who sits in yonder Cabinet. Sir, do you, or does any one, conceive that it is less criminal to take the life of one of those fugitives than it would be to slay any other individual? Is not he who gives his voice and influence from yonder Cabinet, for the murder of those people, as guilty as he would be to lend his voice and influence for the murder of others? Shall men in high stations, from ambitious, from corrupt motives, lend themselves to the degradation, the destruction of hundreds, nay, thousands of human beings, and yet be shielded from animadversion by their political position? Has it come to this, that place and power are to be regarded as exempting their occupants from moral guilt, from responsibility, both here and hereafter?

An idea appears to exist in some minds, that obedience to an act of Congress, however criminal that act may be, cannot involve the person who thus obeys the law in any *moral* guilt. In other words, they appear to think that, if under this fugitive law they drive the famishing slave from their doors to perish with cold and hunger, or if they seize him, place the fetters upon his limbs, and drag him to bondage to be massacred under the lash, to be murdered by slow torture, they will, when called to their final account, plead this enactment in bar of *Omnipotent Justice.*

That kind of theology I leave to those teachers who preach sermons and write pamphlets and newspaper essays in defence of this law; to those divines who hold that *we*, the *members of Congress,* possess the power to step between God and our fellow creatures, and authorize them to disregard His command, and to commit crimes at which all the feelings of our nature revolt. Such teachings may have been received as orthodox in the *ninth,* but they will be rejected in the *nineteenth* century.

Why, Sir, no man, not even the slave-holders, will deny to the fugitive the same natural and inalienable right to his liberty that either of us possess; that it is his duty to maintain and defend that right whenever it shall be in his power to do so; that it is his duty to escape if he can; that if, while making his way to a land of freedom, the master interpose, and he has no other possible way of escape than to slay his master, he is bound by every obligation to himself and his offspring to resort to that extremity. He has no right tamely to surrender up the liberty with which God has endowed him, and to consign his offspring in all coming time to degrading servitude. Our people so advise the fugitives; and the fugitives are generally armed, and prepared to receive their pursuers; and I am informed that one of them, when hard pressed recently, shot one of those human bloodhounds dead, and wounded another, and then went on his way. Sir, we all feel that he did right; that we would have done the same thing had we been in his situation.

Some months since there were said to be *fifteen thousand* fugitives from labor within the free States, including men, women, and children; many of them were born and educated among us. These men, with their wives and their little ones, were in the enjoyment of domestic life. Most of them had acquired, or were in the way of obtaining, sufficient real and personal property to insure them the necessaries, and even many of the luxuries of life. They were educating their children, and becoming intelligent and useful members of community. Many of them belonged to our various churches, and maintained an orderly and Christian deportment.

Against these inoffensive people, the President and Congress have waged a barbarous and unrelenting war. We have required our officers and the freemen of the North, when called on, to seize them; to drag them from their firesides, their homes, their friends, their schools and churches, their lands, and their flocks and herds; to separate husbands and wives, parents and children, and consign them indiscriminately to all the horrors of slavery and of the slave-trade. I hesitate not to say, that, for its barbarity, that law is unequalled in the history of civilized legislation. Is there a reflecting man who will pretend that this barbarous enactment imposes upon those people any moral duty to obey it? Will preachers of righteousness tell them to submit, to let the slave-dealer rivet the chains upon the father, tear the mother from her children, and doom her to a life of wretchedness? Will such preachers advise the daughter *peacefully* to surrender herself into the hands of slave-hunters, and submit to a life of pollution and shame? And will such men be called promoters of *holiness and purity*? I trust there are few such teachers in this American land. Sir, all good men must detest this law. God has no attribute which will permit him to look upon it, except with abhorrence.

Yet the President assures us that it ought not to be repealed; that it should be kept in force; that these outrages should and ought to continue; that he regards this law as a *final* settlement of the slave question; and that it is wrong farther to agitate the subject. Vain advice. Agitation will never cease until the law ceases. While such crimes are authorized by statute, the American people will not keep silence.

The President, referring to the bill surrendering to Texas and to slavery fifty thousand square miles of free territory, and paying her ten millions of dollars, and that allowing slavery to be extended over New Mexico and Utah, and to this fugitive law, says:

"I believed those measures to have been *necessary*, and required by the circumstances and condition of the country."

I rejoice, Mr. Chairman, that he has boldly avowed this fact. Nearly the whole North believed that he was in heart and conscience opposed to this bill. Almost every whig press in the North said plainly, that the President did not favor this bill, but that he was coerced; that he signed it by compulsion; that it was the whig doctrine concerning the veto that compelled him to sign it. The President's views are now before the country, and he avows his position. He places himself upon this law; and here I wish to say to the House, that we all know where the President is. *He is in favor of continuing this law;* he not only places himself there, but his administration and his party must stand or fall by this law. I rejoice at it! They must sink or swim, live or die, stand or fall, with this enactment.

There is no lingering doubt, no difficulty, no obscurity, resting on the party which supports this administration. All the whigs throughout the country, (and I speak it with some degree of feeling, for I once had the pleasure of acting with them, when they had principles; then we avowed and acted upon the doctrines I have stated to-day) — all the whigs throughout the country must now feel that their unity is gone. They see that the party has departed from its doctrines and principles, and has descended, step by step, from its former position, until the remnant has literally become a slave-catching party.

The President informs us that these measures "were adopted in a spirit of conciliation, and for the purpose of conciliation." "I believe," says he, "that a great majority of our fellow citizens sympathize in that spirit and that purpose, and in the main approve it." Sir, where does the President find this evidence of approval in the popular mind? Does he draw his conclusions from the result of the elections in Delaware, New Jersey, or Ohio?

That third State of the Union has separated itself forever from all men and all parties who would involve our people in the support of slavery, or degrade them by sustaining your fugitive law. Does the President find consolation in the voice of the "Peninsular State," as lately expressed through the ballot box? Or can he take pleasure in referring to the election in Wisconsin, or when he examines the result of those measures in his own State? Or has the demonstrations in Massachusetts inspired him with confidence that the popular mind is in favor of this law?

Methinks that as he looks over the newly made graves of his political friends, and counts their number, and reflects upon that political cholera which has cut down so many of his supporters and advocates of this law, he might have doubted its popularity. Many gentlemen in this hall, who so boldly stood forth in the pride of their political manhood a few months since, and voted for these measures, are now doomed to a speedy departure, and the places that now know them shall know them (politically) *no more.* To those gentlemen, the language of the President can bring but poor consolation.

The public meetings of the people of all parties throughout the free States, the spirited resolutions which they have sent forth, are but feeble manifestations of the popular mind. Throughout the North, where free schools have been encouraged, where newspapers circulate, and intelligence is disseminated, there public sentiment is loud in condemnation of this law. This feeling is increasing and extending, and rolling forward, and gaining strength and impetus, and will continue to do so, until that law shall be repealed, and numbered among the things that were.

Sir, if the President will look at the statute lately enacted by the whigs of Vermont, he will be able clearly to read the "handwriting upon the wall." The people have weighed this law in the balance, and it is found wanting.

Near the close of his message the President says:

> "I cannot doubt that the American people, bound together by kindred blood and common traditions, still cherish a paramount regard for the Union of their fathers; and that they are ready to rebuke any attempt to violate its integrity, to disturb the compromises on which it is based, or to resist the laws which have been enacted under its authority."

As to the "Union of *our fathers,*" I venerate it. There is something pleasing and solemn in the recollection of that

Union, — in the history of its formation, and the difficulties and dangers which surrounded it. But it is now nearly half a century since that Union ceased to exist. The prospect of commercial advantages induced us to abandon it, and form a new one with Louisiana. Then, Sir, we again abandoned it, and took Florida to our embrace. Then, to extend and perpetuate slavery, we abandoned that Union, and brought in slave-holding Texas, assuming her war, and carrying devastation, rapine, and bloodshed to the heart of Mexico. And, to cap the climax, you have passed this fugitive law, and made the citizens of Ohio, and of all the free States, the catchpolls to Texian slave-hunters.

It is not to be disguised, that the people of the free States feel less attachment to Texas than they did to the old thirteen States. We are not bound to them by common traditions. The Mexicans, and Spaniards, and other foreigners of that State, shared not in the toils nor the dangers of our revolution, nor in those of our second war of Independence. The arrogant and supercilious manner in which Texas threatened to drive our army from New Mexico, and to dissolve the Union, has not served to strengthen the cords of affection which should have bound us together.

But neither the President, nor any other person, will charge the North with disloyalty to the Union. But that portion of the sentence just quoted, which refers to the "attempts to disturb its compromises," was intended to refer to those political friends with whom I act.

Sir, those compromises referred to by the President, left us entirely free from the support of slavery. By the passage of this fugitive law, those compromises have been disturbed, and the people of the North involved in the degradation and guilt of sustaining slavery; and, Sir, in the language of the President, "they are ready to rebuke" those who have thus disturbed the compromises, — and they will rebuke them. Our people, too, will resist, by every constitutional means, the execution of that law.

This practice of attempting to sanctify every enormity in

legislation by referring to the "*Union of our fathers*," has become very common among a certain class of politicians; but I did not expect to meet with it in the message of the President. It does not comport with the dignity of such a paper. It is almost as much out of place as it would be to appeal to the loyalty which our fathers anciently bore to the British crown. The Union of our fathers was adopted as the best means of preserving the liberties, and promoting the happiness of the people. It was abandoned for the same purpose. Even our Union with Texas was framed for that avowed object. A majority of Congress thought and believed that it would increase the wealth and the happiness of the people. For the same purpose we waged a war with Mexico, and conquered another vast territory, and brought another State into the Union. The Union now existing will be retained so long as the great mass of the people shall regard it as conducive to their interests and happiness. Yet, whenever they shall be convinced that it subserves the cause of oppression, that it has become an instrument for degrading themselves, another revolution will take place, and they will lay it aside, as our fathers did their union with England. They feel as the patriots of that day felt, that "whenever any form of government shall fail to sustain the self-evident truth that *all men were created equal, and are entitled to the enjoyment of life and liberty*," it is the right of the people to lay it aside, and to "adopt a new form of government, basing its action upon such principles as shall best promote their interests and happiness."

But this cry of "danger to the Union" is becoming understood by the people. "To save the Union," we annexed Texas; "to save the Union," we paid her ten millions of dollars; "to save the Union," fifty thousand square miles of territory which had been consecrated to freedom by Mexico, and conquered by our arms, were delivered over to Texas and to slavery; "to save the Union," the people of the free States have been compelled to become slave-catchers; and we are now told that, "to save the Union," this infamous law must be kept in force; "to save the Union," we must drive the famishing, weary fugitive from our doors, or seize him and send him back to his prisonhouse of bondage.

Sir, it has come to this: the cry of "danger to the Union" is now resorted to, for the purpose of justifying every outrage upon the people of the North, which the slave power demands. Under this cry, meetings are called in your commercial cities, and resolutions adopted to "*suppress agitation among the people.*" And the Secretary of State and distinguished Senators, write letters "*to save the Union.*" Dinners are eaten, and wine drunk, and speeches made, "*to save the Union.*" For the same purpose, the Secretary of State votes against the candidate of his own party, and a distinguished Senator from a western State threatens to leave the whigs, with whom he has acted from early life.

Sir, this clause of the message has reference to that new party which is already in process of formation, and which is to be based upon the doctrines of this message, — upon the policy of continuing in force this fugitive law, — the laws that sustain the slave-trade upon our southern coast and in this district, — and of opposing all efforts to exclude slavery from our territories, and from the District of Columbia. In short, Sir, this new party is to oppose all attempts to separate the people of the free States and this government from the support of that institution.

I, Sir, rejoice at the prospect of seeing every public man, and every elector of the nation, take his position either for freedom or for slavery. The President has come out boldly and manfully on the side of oppression, in favor of compelling the people of the North to become the catchers of southern slaves. He calls on his friends to take position with him. They will do so. We shall soon have but two political parties. One will contend for the emancipation of the free States and this government from the control of the slave power; to restore vitality to the Constitution; to give that instrument effect; to maintain the rights of all the States under it; to secure all men under our exclusive jurisdiction in the enjoyment of life, liberty, and happiness. With Mr. Morris, and those who assisted in framing the Constitution, that party "*never will concur in upholding domestic slavery.*" With Mr. Gerry, "while they have nothing to do with it in the States, *they will lend no sanction to it.*" With Mr. Sherman, they "*can see no more propriety in seizing and surrendering a fugitive slave than a horse.*"

With these framers of the Constitution, the party of freedom will stand. These principles they will maintain and carry out; they will separate and purify themselves from the sin and the shame of slavery; they will redeem this government from its support; they will leave it within the States where it exists. The judgment and conscience of the people are with us; they know our doctrines to be correct. The popular heart beats for freedom. Party prejudices are giving way. Truth is doing its legitimate work. A great political revolution is going forward. No partizan influence can stay its progress. The history of the last few months and years, must bear to every reflecting mind, a consciousness that the principles of justice, of righteousness, of humanity must triumph. The moral sentiment of the nation demands the repeal of those acts of Congress which authorize and enjoin the commission of crimes. *They will be repealed*, and the government will be redeemed from its present position; and its laws and influence will be exerted for the benefit, for the elevation of man.

AGITATION OF THE SLAVE QUESTION.*

BUSINESS OF THE HOUSE NEGLECTED UNDER PRETENCE OF AVOIDING AGITATION—AGITATION PRECIPITATED UPON THAT BODY AT IMPROPER PERIODS—AGITATION BY THE SECRETARY OF STATE AND HIS FRIENDS—THE PRESIDENT'S PROCLAMATION—HIS POWERS DEFINED—HIS AUTHORITY OVER THE HOUSE DENIED—INDEPENDENCE OF REPRESENTATIVES VINDICATED—INDELICACY OF MR. CLAY EXPOSED—HIS DICTATION SPURNED—HIS ATTACK UPON THE NEGROES OF BOSTON REPROVED—THEIR RIGHTS DEFENDED—MR. CLAY'S ASSAULT UPON MR. THOMPSON CONDEMNED—ATTACKS OF MEMBERS UPON MR. ALLEN MET, AND INVESTIGATION CHALLENGED.

[Our treaty of peace with Mexico, bound the United States to pay to that government fifteen millions dollars, in four instalments. One of them became due in May, 1852. The transmission of nearly four millions dollars to Mexico, was regarded as a matter of great speculation, as bills on the United States are usually sold in the city of Mexico for about twelve per cent. premium. Different bankers therefore were desirous of obtaining the contract. Mr. Clayton, Secretary of State under General Taylor, refused to make arrangements for transmitting these funds, as he regarded it the appropriate duty of the Secretary of the Treasury. General Taylor died in July, and soon after Mr. Fillmore assumed the duties of President. His Secretary of State, Mr. Webster, immediately on entering upon his duties, made a contract with certain bankers in New York, Boston, and Washington, in connection with the Barings of England, to pay this money to the Mexican government, without giving notice of such intention, although the Rothschilds and other bankers were desirous of competing for the contract, and notwithstanding nearly two years were to elapse before the money would become due. On the 25th February, 1851, a bill came up for consideration in the House of Representatives, making appropriation of the money to pay this instalment, and directing the Secretary of State to make the proper arrangements for paying it to the Mexican gov-

* Speech on the bill making appropriations for the Army. Delivered in Committee of the whole House on the state of the Union, February 26, 1851.

ernment. Mr. Allen, of Massachusetts, objected to imposing that duty upon the Secretary of State, who he thought was too much indebted to the bankers and brokers of Wall street, New York, and of State street, Boston, to perform this duty without bringing upon himself suspicions of pecuniary obligation and favoritism. He stated that he had good reason to believe the Secretary of State had received forty-five thousand dollars, raised by voluntary subscription, at the very time of making the arrangement to which allusion has been made. That he understood this amount was raised as a fund to compensate Mr. Webster for going into the office of Secretary of State. He stated his desire to bring before the House the evidence that would establish these facts, and demanded the appointment of a committee for that purpose.

This proposition called forth an excited debate, which continued through that evening, and a portion of the next day. The friends of Mr. Webster assailed Mr. Allen with great bitterness, and extended their assaults to his political friends. The bill was passed, however, and the army bill was taken up. But these attacks upon the free democracy continued, and late in the evening of the 26th, Mr. Levin, of Pennsylvania, not only assailed the free democracy generally, but Mr. Giddings in particular. Up to that time, no free democrat, except Mr. Allen, had spoken. But this speech of Mr. Levin called from Mr. Giddings the following answer.]

Mr. Chairman, — Last evening a proposition was before us, directing the Secretary of State to make arrangements for transmitting to Mexico the money soon to become due from us to that government. The amount was great, and would enable the Secretary to give fortunes to his friends, by preferring them to other bankers who were anxious to do the business. My friend from Massachusetts (Mr. Allen) was opposed to placing this money in the hands of the Secretary of State, and frankly stated his objections. This gave offence to certain friends of that officer. They bitterly assailed the gentleman who thus spoke his honest convictions; these assaults were continued through the evening of yesterday, and during the most of this day.

During the present evening, these assaults have been extended to my humble self, and to all opponents of the fugitive slave law; and I have risen to call the attention of the House and of the country to the fact, that this agitation of the slave question did not commence with the friends of liberty. It comes from an entirely different quarter. It comes from the Administration party, — from the particular friends of the Secretary of State, (Mr. Webster,) who has said so much, and written so many letters, to "*put down agitation.*" Well, Sir, if he really desires to effect that object, let him put down his "Union meetings," suppress his "Union letters," silence his "hunker papers," quiet his "silver gray" friends. Let him go to the Senate chamber, and soothe the agitated elements there; let him quiet that body; then let him come to this hall, and persuade his friends here to attend to the business of the nation, to pass our appropriation bills, and to abstain from assailing their fellow members; from threatening the people with an army to be used in cutting the throats of all who refuse, at the bidding of the President and of your fugitive law, to chase down the flying bondman, as he hurries to a land of freedom.

Sir, when I came here this evening, I had no intention of occupying the floor for a single moment. I came with the intention to hurry through this bill as rapidly as it could be done, and thereby hasten the necessary legislation, which remains to be perfected before we separate. I was asked and requested to speak on the subject of this fugitive law. I replied that I could not; I had made no preparation, and was unwilling, at this late hour of the session, to draw down upon myself the unkind feelings which would be excited against me, if I were now to speak on that subject, at an hour when every member ought to be impatient for the passage of the bills necessary to carry on the government.

History will record the events of the present session, and will point unerringly to those who have endeavored to suppress *legitimate* discussion at the proper time, and who now interpose such speeches as we listened to last evening and to-day, — at a moment so unsuited to a calm and dispassionate examination of the effects of this fugitive law. What are the facts? Why, Sir, on the first day of the session the President sent us his annual message. It contained a full development of his policy, and was therefore important to the country. It had ever been the practice to discuss the annual message fully in Committee of the Whole, at an early period of the session, when we have little else to attend to. Our fathers deemed this practice not merely right, but expedient and important, in order that the country should fully comprehend the policy which was to guide the administration.

In accordance with this long established usage, on the 9th of December, while in Committee of the Whole, I ventured to express my views upon the message. Before my brief hour was out, I saw around me a score of members with anxious countenances, awaiting the precise moment that my time would expire; and no sooner had the chairman's mallet touched the sounding-board than a scorce of voices demanded the floor; and a motion was made for the committee to rise, for the reason that we had just commenced on the short session of Congress, and had so much important business to transact, that it became us to *labor*, and not to spend time in *discussions*. A resolution terminating the debate *in five minutes* was instantly adopted; and throughout the whole country I was denounced for thus *delaying the business of Congress*. On Thursday following we adjourned over until Monday, and although we could spare but *precisely one hour and five minutes* to discuss the President's message, I believe we have found it perfectly convenient to spend at least *twelve days in doing nothing*, and, at least, during fifty other days our sessions have not, I think, averaged more than two and a half hours in length.

Nor is this all; the general appropriation bills which usually call out political discussion, were not reported until the tenth of the present month, and the first, I believe, was called up for action on Saturday last, there being at that time but eight legislative days of the session remaining. Sir, I cannot say that this delay was brought about for the purpose of sealing the lips of the minority here; of that the country must judge. This army bill and the fortification bill and the navy bill might as well have been called up sixty days since as at this hour.

The States have not been called for resolutions, under the rules of the House, during the entire session, and no opportunity has been afforded the opponents of the fugitive slave law to present a bill for its repeal, or obtain a vote on that subject.

Thus, Sir, have the lips of the free soilers been sealed in relation to the fugitive law, during the entire session, except the humble speech of my own, made, as before stated, on the 9th of December. So fully have my political friends appreciated these facts, that not one of them has attempted to speak on the fugitive law, although I know that many of them have been anxious to occupy a brief hour on that subject.

While the river and harbor bill was under consideration, the gentleman from North Carolina, (Mr. Clingman,) and my colleague, (Mr. Taylor,) both interposed speeches on the fugitive law. Free soilers might have done so, but they appreciated the impropriety of thrusting this question before the House on that occasion; and up to this time we have been compelled by this parliamentary legerdemain to sit in mute silence on this important subject.

In the other end of the capitol, the friends of the Secretary of State have been engaged, day after day, in exciting debates to "put down agitation." I feel constrained to call attention to the debates in that body, before I proceed to the examination of the subject which has called out these attacks upon my friend from Massachusetts (Mr. Allen).

Sir, parliamentary rules, as well as common courtesy, forbid all direct allusion to the remarks of gentlemen made in one branch of Congress by members of the other. But, Sir, the manner in which certain senators have lately extended their supervision over members of this House, demand at my hands a passing notice.

On Friday last, a distinguished senator from Kentucky, (Mr. Clay,) while speaking of the President's late proclamation, and the negroes of Boston, is reported to have said:

"The proclamation is not aimed solely at the miserable negroes, stimulated, no doubt, by those outside of the court house, who laid all the plans, and some of whom — one at least — was at the door beckoning to the negroes to come in — not a negro — I beg pardon, a white negro — standing at the door beckoning to the negroes to come in. Does not everybody know that it is not the work of those miserable wretches, who are without the knowledge and without a perfect consciousness of what became them, or what was their duty? They are urged on and stimulated by speeches, some of which are made on this floor and in the House of Representatives, and by prints which are scattered broadcast throughout the whole country."

This attack upon the intelligence of the negroes of Boston, I think, is in bad taste. Among them is a lawyer of respectable standing, with whom I am acquainted. A large portion of them are men of character. They know their rights. They understand and appreciate the barbarous character of this law. They possessed philanthropy and manhood enough to rescue their brother from the jaws of the Executive bloodhounds who had fastened upon him. For that act I honor and approve them. Their names are worthy of standing upon our country's history, with those patriots who used Boston harbor as a tea-kettle in 1775; those who resisted the stamp-act and the tax on tea.

Mr. MASON interrupted Mr. Giddings, and inquired whether Mr. G. approved the mob in Boston?

Mr. GIDDINGS resumed. That contest, Mr. Chairman, is entirely between the administration and its officers on one side, and the negroes of Boston on the other. With that I will not interfere. All I have to say is, "give them a clear field and a fair fight." The senator speaks of them as "miserable wretches, without knowledge and without a consciousness of what was their duty." Let their action vindicate them from these aspersions.

Mr. MASON wished to know if Mr. Giddings approved of the conduct of those white men who were engaged in the mob?

Mr. GIDDINGS. I have yet to learn that any white man was concerned in it. It was solely the work of the negroes; they managed their own movements, guided their own action, defeated the execution of the fugitive law, and fairly outmanaged the slave-catchers. I ask pardon of the negroes for thus connecting them with a class degraded so far below them. But the gentleman wants an explicit and more particular avowal of my sentiments. I then say to him, that I would not advise forcible resistance to this law; neither would I advise against it. I would leave the colored people to act according to the dictates of circumstances and of their own judgments. They ought not to resist when there is no prospect of success. In this instance they rescued their brother from chains, torture, suffering, and death, to which this infamous law and the slave-catchers would have assigned him. Were I a colored man, as I am a white man, I would not hesitate to slay any slave-catcher who should attempt to lay hands on my person to enslave me. Nor would I stop to inquire whether such person were commissioned by the President to seize and manacle me, to rob me of that right to liberty with which God has endowed all men. I repeat what I said in December: "When human governments overstep the bounds of their constitutional powers, in order to rob men of life or liberty, their enactments are void; they impart no authority to any human being to perpetrate the crime." No, Sir; neither the President's commission, nor your detestable law, imparts any moral right to your slave-catching marshals to commit murder or piracy, or crimes far transcending them in turpitude.

But I have been led by the gentleman's questions, from the remarks of the senator which I had brought to the notice of the House. Alluding to the negroes, he says "they are urged and stimulated by speeches, some of which are made on this floor and in the House of Representatives." Well, Sir, thanks be to God and to the founders of our republic, I stand here a freeman, the representative of freemen, speaking the convictions of my own judgment, avowing my own sentiments, acknowledging responsibility only to God and my country, holding in contempt the frowns of any individual who would control my political actions. Will that senator undertake to say *when* I shall speak, and *what* I shall say? But the senator goes further, and says:

> "The proclamation, then, has higher and greater aims. It aims at the maintenance of the law; it aims at putting down all those who would put down the law and the Constitution, be they black or white."

Well, Sir, if the President has *aimed* his proclamation at gentlemen on this floor, it will prove like the poet's gun:

> "Deep charged, and ill *aimed* at duck or plover,
> Bears wide, but *kicks the owner over.*"

Sir, do I not stand as independent in this hall as the President in the White House? — as far above his reach as he is above mine? — with the same right to *aim* a proclamation at him that he has to *aim* one at me? Every man who has examined the first principles of our government must be conscious that it is based upon this perfect independence which the members of this body hold, and the perfect official equality which exists between the members of its various departments. I possess the same power to hold the President amenable for his opinions or acts that he has to *aim* his proclamations at me.

But the senator says, "it aims at putting down all those who would put down this law." Sir, I hold my commission here from one hundred thousand intelligent, independent freemen. I came not here by the President's appointment, nor by the recommendation of the senator from Kentucky. I hold my seat at the will of the people of my district. I am merely their agent, to maintain their interests and protect their rights. They have placed me in public life; *they, and they alone, can put me down.* Neither they nor myself are accustomed to language of this character. It smacks too much of the plantation. It strikes harshly on the ears of freedom, yet it may be very proper when addressed to slaves; but it is unsuited to a northern latitude.

I would put down this law by every constitutional means. I would hold it up to the public gaze in all its revolting turpitude. I would point every Christian and every philanthropist to its barbarous character.

Mr. McKissock (in his seat). Would you put down the Constitution also?

Mr. Giddings. I cherish and maintain the Constitution, and will vindicate it against this law, *here and elsewhere*, by the wayside and by the fireside, in public and in private. Any man who sustains this law *puts down the Constitution*. Its enactment was treason to our constitutional compact. It strikes at the rights of the people. It attempts to constrain them to violate their moral duties, their solemn obligations to their fellow man, against the dictates of their own judgment and their duties to the laws of their States.

The Constitution has placed under the control of the Federal Executive the marshals, deputy-marshals, and federal officers. These he can command. They are subject to our control. We can also authorize the appointment of a constabulary force, and place it under the President's direction, if we deem it necessary. We can authorize him to employ the army, the navy, and the militia *when in actual service.* But, Sir, neither Congress nor the President can command the officers or the citizens of any State, unless while serving as militia. He has no more power over them than he has over the people or officers of Canada. They may, and always will aid in the execution of all constitutional and just laws. But the act is *voluntary.* The President cannot *command* their assistance.

The people of Boston did not see fit to interfere between the administration and the "negroes" of that city. In the name of humanity I thank them for it, and assure them and the country that those whom I represent never will interfere in such case. The citizen who would do so, would be driven from decent society in northern Ohio. It is here, on this point, that I take issue with the supporters of this law. That portion which commands me to assist in catching slaves, is a flagrant usurpation of power, unauthorized by the Constitution. My constituents hold that portion of the law in detestation. They spurn and abhor it. I say, as I have often said, "my constituents will not help you catch your slaves." They will feed the hungry, clothe the naked, and direct the wanderer on his way, and use every peaceful means to assist him to regain his God-given rights. If you pursue your slave there, they will let you catch him, if *you can.* If he defends himself against you, they will rejoice. If you press him so hard that he is constrained actually to slay you in self-defence, why, Sir, they will look on and submit with *proper resignation.* In such cases they will carry out their *peace* principles by abstaining from all interference. The President may "aim his proclamation at them." The distinguished senator may make speeches *at* them; but they will not be likely to heed either. They look neither to the Senate, nor to the White House, for instruction respecting their constitutional rights or duties. They have studied them in a different school.

But, while referring to the senator's speech, I cannot pass over his allusion to a distinguished member of the British Parliament; an orator and philanthropist, whose labors in the cause of humanity in Europe, in India, and in America, are known to every intelligent reader of our public journals. I quote the senator's words:

> "Sir, look at the manner in which a foreign hireling has been introduced into this country, in order to propagate his opinions and doctrines with regard to the subversion of one of the institutions of this country. I allude to a man who is said to be a member of the British Parliament, by the name of Thompson. He has been received, not in one place only in Massachusetts, but in various places, and the police on one occasion assembled to protect him, when they had not the heart to assemble around a court of justice to maintain the laws of their country."

This is empty declamation. He attacks none of Mr. Thompson's doctrines, nor does he attempt to meet his arguments. I have read some of that gentleman's speeches, and so far as I have become acquainted with his doctrines, I assure you the senator will never take issue upon his facts, nor attempt to overthrow his principles. But, Sir, this is the only mode in which the supporters of this fugitive law meet us. When we state our arguments, they will assail us with personalities and declamation, in order to divert the public mind from the questions in issue. Sir, look over the whole debate in Congress for the year past, and you will find this system of evasion and personal detraction almost uniformly adopted by the supporters of that law. This new and improved system of tactics was carried out here during the debate of yesterday and to-day, of which I will speak hereafter.

The object of the senator's personal attack is a most sincere and eloquent advocate of the rights of humanity. He may have errors. I know not that I agree with him on all points; but I do say that if the senator had pointed us to any erroneous doctrine of Mr. Thompson, instead of this personal abuse, he would have entitled himself to greater respect.

Sir, I object to this undignified treatment of a distinguished member of a foreign government by an American senator. It does no honor to the body in which that speech was made. But the senator scolds the people of Massachusetts for assembling to hear Mr. Thompson, when they would not aid in catching slaves. Who authorized the senator to read political or moral lectures to the people of Massachusetts? Was he not told a year since that they would not catch slaves? He then insisted that they would. He now finds that his prophecy was fallacious, and he evinces his vexation at the disappointment, by lecturing the people of the Old Bay State whom they shall hear, and to whom they shall not listen.

Why, Sir, the senator goes far beyond the old "alien and sedition laws." Have not the people a right to hear whom they please? May not even "error of opinion be tolerated, while truth is left free to combat it?" This fear of trusting the people to discuss any truth, moral, political, or religious, is opposed to the intelligence of the age, the whole theory of our government! This is literally a government of *the people.* They are our *sovereigns,* we their *servants.* Shall the servant dictate to his master what he shall discuss? What code of political faith he shall adopt? This distrust of the intelligence of the people, of their ability for self-government, constitutes "*political infidelity.*" No man who maintains it, can hold fellowship with the political church to which I belong.

I now return to the subject which called forth the speech of the gentleman who has just taken his seat, (Mr. Levin).

As I have already stated, our free soil friends have been denied any opportunity to test the sense of this House upon a bill to repeal the fugitive law. No time has been afforded them to speak a single hour on that subject since the 9th of December, without violating all rules of propriety, thereby incurring the displeasure of our fellow members.

Last evening, in the course of legitimate remark upon a subject before the House, my friend from Massachusetts (Mr. Allen) opposed the placing of a vast amount of the public treasure at the disposal of the present Secretary of State. He clearly and explicitly stated his reasons; in calm and unimpassioned language declared the convictions resting upon his own mind. The facts which he stated had previously reached the ears of several members of this body. They came to us from respectable sources. Of their existence, I entertained no doubt. The gentleman (Mr. Allen) was full and explicit in his statements. No one doubted his convictions of the perfect accuracy of what he stated. The substance consists in the charge, that prior to entering upon his official duties, the present Secretary of State informed his friends in Boston, that he must have a pecuniary consideration to induce him to take office; that merchants of New York raised for him twenty-five thousand dollars, and those of Boston nineteen thousand dollars, being more than twice the amount to which he will be entitled for his services from the public treasury, if he serves three years.

To this charge, the gentleman's colleague replied. I expected to hear him ask the House to suspend its opinion until the Secretary of State could be consulted; or that he would promptly ask an investigation of the subject on behalf of that high functionary. But he did neither. Following out that general system of tactics to which I have already referred, he commenced a personal assault upon his colleague, for presuming to call public attention to the subject. Both gentlemen were heard again this morning. The particular friend of the Secretary (Mr. Ashmun) came up to the point, and *denied* the statements of his colleague, and pronounced them *unfounded in the aggregate and in detail.* For this he declared that he had authority, which is understood to have been furnished in writing by the Secretary himself. On the other hand, the gentleman from the Worcester district, Massachusetts, (Mr. Allen,) avowed himself ready and able to prove his statements, if the House would appoint a committee for that purpose.

To me it seemed that but one course remained, either for the friends or for the opponents of the Secretary of State. That was to appoint a committee, and ascertain the *facts.* Yet the gentleman who has particular charge of the Secretary's reputation, (Mr. Ashmun,) expressed no desire whatever to demonstrate the Secretary's innocence by proof. On the contrary, he appeared anxious to assail his colleague (Mr. Allen) with gross personalities.

Now, Sir, far be it from me to defend the gentleman from the Worcester district, (Mr. Allen). In the first place, his character needs no defence; and, in the second place, he is abundantly able to take care of his own reputation, if permitted to speak for himself. But there are cormorants in this body, greedy for executive favors, who, with the rapacity of the vulture, pounce upon every member who has the independence to think his own thoughts, or speak his own words. This whole flock of unclean birds have been hovering around my friend, (Mr. Allen,) striking at him with their talons; and each endeavoring to propitiate Executive favor by exhibiting their hostility towards a man who dares stand up here and maintain the truth. Every candidate for a foreign mission, or a "chargé d'affaires," or consul, thinks to secure his object by assailing my friend, (Mr. Allen).

Mr. Levin. Those offices do not spring from the people, and I expect no other than those which the people confer.

Mr. Giddings. All offices spring from the people, and I am sure the gentleman will take any he can get.

No sooner had the gentleman from the Springfield district, Massachusetts, (Mr. Ashmun,) closed his remarks, than the reverend gentleman from Alabama, (Mr. Hilliard,) with sacerdotal dignity, demanded a hearing. The gentleman from Massachusetts (Mr. Allen) had made no allusion to him, either directly or indirectly; nor is it possible for me to comprehend how my friend (Mr. Allen) should have incurred the severe displeasure of the clerical gentleman. Soon as the gentleman rose, he commenced a high wrought eulogy of the Secretary of State. He was ignorant of the facts, and had not the conscience to deny the statements which so deeply implicated that functionary; but he appeared anxious, by the most fulsome laudation, to secure his favor. Instead of advising the House to examine the matter, and to wipe from that officer all stain and reproach, he appeared desirous to cover all these suspected iniquities with a coating of obsequious flattery, "*thickly laid on.*" His eulogistic praise was eloquent. I heard it with interest, and could almost unite in the desire of a distinguished statesman, and wish that we might enjoy "stated preaching" of that kind every evening, *provided it were true;* but when he came to the *application* of his discourse, and assailed my friend from Massachusetts, (Mr. Allen,) for daring to put forth statements which at that time no one denied, I began to doubt his logic, and his policy.

Sir, instead of these extravagant laudations of the Secretary of State, and these attacks upon my friend, (Mr. Allen,) why did he not demand an *investigation?* Why not ascertain the truth of this matter? Why not inform the country? If the Secretary be innocent, he is most unfortunate in the selection of his friends here. I would save him from such friends. Were I acting as the friend of the Secretary, I would demand an investigation; I would know the truth of these charges; I would inform the country of the facts. It strikes me that the professed principles of the gentleman, (Mr. Hilliard,) should have taught him that *truth* is more important to the Secretary of State at this time than declamation and bombast. If the statements of the gentleman from Massachusetts (Mr. Allen) shall be sustained by proof, the gentleman from Alabama (Mr. Hilliard) will find himself in a very awkward position. He will then be constrained to recall all he has uttered.

Next came the gentleman from Delaware, (Mr. Houston,) who, at the close of a short speech, took occasion to express his belief that the statements of the gentleman from Massachusetts (Mr. Allen) were unfounded calumnies. Well, Sir, if they be such, it becomes that gentleman and the House to demonstrate that fact; to let the country know that a member of this body from the old Bay State has wantonly, and without cause, preferred charges against the Secretary of State. The gentleman from Massachusetts (Mr. Allen) demands the scrutiny. His friends demand it. Such investigation must implicate the Secretary of State, or subject my friend (Mr. Allen) to the imputation expressed by the gentleman from Delaware.

Here, then, comes the test. Who seeks, and who avoids investigation? And I say to the House that the friends of the gentleman from Massachusetts (Mr. Allen) will do all they can to obtain it. If they can get a resolution for that purpose before the House, they will press it to a vote. They will not hesitate to move such resolution, if they can obtain the floor. Then, Sir, will come the test.

I am aware that the friends of the Secretary are already endeavoring to find a way for retreat; some difficult passage through which to escape. It has been intimated that, if true, the charges do not amount to bribery. In fact, it is said that they carry with them no moral turpitude. If true, why has his colleague (Mr. Ashmun) denied them? Why has the Secretary authorized such denial? These are important questions. If the facts stated by my friend (Mr. Allen) do not impeach the honor nor the integrity of the Secretary of State, why is that member so bitterly assailed for making statements that are harmless? Sir, I call the attention of this House and the country to these contradictions and inconsistencies on the part of those who attempt, by raising a cloud of dust in this hall, to cover the retreat of the Secretary of State.

But, Sir, I pass on to the transactions of this evening. Soon after our meeting, I moved to strike from the army bill then before us, the appropriation of fifty-six thousand dollars for enlisting new recruits for the service. I was anxious to explain my own views in regard to the amendment, but such was the pressure of business upon us, that I could not justify myself in occupying even three minutes of our time. Yet the gentleman from Pennsylvania (Mr. Levin) rose, and under these circumstances addressed the House at length in favor of maintaining a standing army, and assailing free soilers generally, and the gentleman from Massachusetts (Mr. Allen) and myself in particular.

Following the programme laid down by the leaders of the administration, he was careful not to deny the charges, but rather admitted them to be true, but assailed the gentleman from Massachusetts (Mr. Allen) for uttering them.

Mr. LEVIN. I reiterate that if the facts were *fairly* stated, they do not reflect upon the Secretary of State. My remarks were based upon the supposition that Mr. Webster had received aid from his friends.

Mr. GIDDINGS. Surely the gentleman would not have supposed a *falsehood.* But suppose he disbelieved the statement. Still he evidently intended to preserve a place for retreat, by an argument intended to show that the charges, if true, do not impeach the honor of the Secretary. The gentleman from Pennsylvania is a lawyer. He has heard the indictment in this case, and in the ancient language of judicial proceedings, I demand of him to plead either "*guilty*" or "*not guilty.*" That is the question in which the people are interested. The farmers and laborers of the great West desire to know the *facts.* They will wish to understand, in plain and explicit language, whether the Secretary of State assumed upon himself that office under the assurance, the expectation of receiving some forty or fifty thousand dollars of the merchants and bankers of New York and Boston. Let them once possess the facts, and they will not ask the gentleman nor myself to make an argument on the subject. They will form their own opinions and act upon the dictates of their own judgment.

The gentleman (Mr. Levin) urged the maintenance of the army. He declared, if there ever was a time when the army ought to be kept up, it is important at this juncture; and referred to the charges now made against the Secretary of State as the occasion for supporting the army. Well, Sir, he desires an army to put down the freedom of debate in this hall. He very significantly pointed at my humble self, and spoke of the doctrines which I advocate, — doctrines avowed by Jefferson and Hancock, and a mighty host of patriots and statesmen who have gone before us. These doctrines consist of "*self-evident truths.*" He desires an army to put them down, to prevent the promulgation of principles held sacred by our fathers, to stop discussion, "*to put down agitation.*"

Mr. LEVIN. I confess that I am an agitator. What storms

are to the atmosphere, — what tempests to the ocean, — the agitator is to the political world. He puts its particles into motion, he produces an excitement which carries off the corruptions and scum that have been accumulating for years. I am an agitator for good, but not for evil, — to protect, but not to destroy.

Mr. Giddings. Well, Sir, we are all conscious that *much scum* has been thrown off here within the last twenty-four hours. But to proceed with my remarks. The gentleman thinks an army should be maintained for another purpose, — to compel the people to carry out this fugitive law; a law enacted by a minority of the Senate and of the House; a law enacted by slave-holders and a few of their northern allies, while the mass of the northern members fled from the Senate chamber and from this body; a law which is odious to all the free States, which commands the people to leave their firesides and work-shops to aid in seeking out the hunted fugitive. The people refuse to perform that detestable service, and we are to maintain an army to cut their throats for such refusal. We, the servants of the people, want an army to butcher our masters, because they will not obey this odious law! In fact, this is substantially the doctrine of the President's late message.

Mr. Levin. Let the country remember that the gentleman boldly proclaims that no man is bound to obey the laws unless he approves of their justice, and that each individual is invested with the power of judicial construction! A solecism like this applies the axe to the very root of our government.

Mr. Giddings. Sir, that man has lived to little purpose who, at the age of forty, does not know that a standing army, in time of peace, is the bane of free governments. It is the instrument of tyrants and usurpers. For what purpose would the President now use the army, except to enforce this odious law; to subject the people of the North to the slave power; to shoot them down if they refuse to violate their own sympathies and God's commands? I would say to gentlemen, here and elsewhere, that the advocates of freedom are not to be intimidated. They know their power; it is the power of truth.

They see it operating upon the popular mind. The great heart of this mighty nation beats in unison with our doctrines. This feeling is increasing and extending into every vein and artery of society. Its power at this moment holds in check the legislatures of four sovereign States of this Union, neither of which is able to elect senators to Congress who oppose the truth we preach. Our progress is onward. Neither threats of using the army, nor the army itself can retard the rapid advance of truth.

No cry of "danger to the Union" can alarm the people, or frighten them into obedience to this law. This "*ignis fatuus*" of *dissolution* has for more than a year constituted the entire capital on which certain political leaders have traded. A greater *humbug* was never conceived or brought forth. The gigantic intellect of the Secretary of State, aided by the political experience of certain distinguished senators and politicians, could alone have given birth to this "*splendid failure*," which, if put forth by men in the more humble walks of life, would have entitled them to lodgings in some lunatic asylum. There is but one mitigating consideration connected with it; that is the *consistency* with which the President and his cabinet are striving to keep up the deception. The late proclamation against the negroes of Boston, constitutes a burlesque upon civil governments which is strictly in keeping with "Union meetings" and the cry of "danger to the Union," put forth in this House, in the Senate, and by the Executive.

The history of the times will show these things in their true light, and place these disunion panics among the most extraordinary *inventions* of any age. The authors should at once obtain patents both here and in Europe. Sir, I have been betrayed into a much longer speech than I intended. I now come to the present position of the subject which has brought upon my friend from Massachusetts such an avalanche of denunciation. That gentleman made statements of facts. If true, the country is entitled to know them. They are important. The Secretary of State exerts great influence in the government. He is in truth regarded as the "master-spirit which guides the ship of State." If he took that station as the employee of merchants, brokers, and bankers of New York and Boston; if they bestowed upon him forty or fifty thousand dollars to induce him to go into the cabinet, it follows as an irresistible conclusion that he is now acting as *their agent*, and not as the agent of the people generally. The facts stated by the gentleman from Massachusetts, (Mr. Allen,) will explain the efforts of this Secretary in favor of "Union meetings;" the letters he has written in favor of the "fugitive law;" the energy he has exerted to suppress the freedom of speech, under pretence of "putting down agitation;" the speeches he has made; the dinners he has eaten, and the wine he has drunk, "*to save the Union.*" Forty-five thousand dollars constitute a fair price for all these labors to protect the commerce of those cities, with the slave States, from interruption.

Sir, it is a law of mind that we should sustain the interests of those from whom we receive our bread; that we should consult the welfare of those on whom we are dependent. The merchants and bankers of Wall street and of State street never did, and never will give their money in such profusion, without expecting a "*quid pro quo.*" If they have bestowed forty thousand dollars on the Secretary of State, they expect his services in return. They expect him to consult their interest. *He will do it.* Their interest is opposed to that of the laborer, the farmer, the mechanic. They want your splendid lines of mail steamers, your powerful navy, your numerous army; all of which are opposed to the interests of the great body of the people.

Sir, the people have a right to understand these facts. It was due to them that the truth should be placed before the country. It is due to the honorable Secretary that he should have an opportunity to vindicate himself from these imputations. The gentleman from Massachusetts (Mr. Allen) acted no less in accordance with his duty to the Secretary of State than with that which was due to his constituents and the country, in calling attention to this subject. His statements were not lightly made, without consideration. He frankly pledged himself to prove them, if an opportunity shall be afforded. That opportunity can be given at any moment that the Secretary shall desire. He, an officer of government, can demand an investigation as a matter of *privilege*. Will he do it? His friends control the business of the House; they can move an investigation at any time. Will they do it? If they do not, others will see it performed, if they possess the power.

Mr. Chairman, when an innocent man is charged with impropriety, his first wish and desire is to demonstrate to the whole world the falsehood, the injustice of the charge. A late cabinet officer, (Mr. Crawford,) when thus charged at the last session of Congress, did not hesitate for a moment. He sent his demand here for an investigation; we acknowledged his right to it, and appointed a committee. I speak with some experience. At our last session I was myself charged, through the public press, with facts which, if they had existed, should have excluded me from a seat in this hall. I did not wait to cast imputations upon my accuser; such a policy did not enter my mind. I did not wait an hour, but demanded an investigation by this body. I was conscious that a demonstration of my own innocence would constitute a conviction of my accuser. And I would say to the friends of the Secretary of State, that, if he be as pure as they represent him, they need not waste time in attacking my friend (Mr. Allen). Call for a committee. Let the facts be known; and if the Secretary be free from these charges, the development of that innocence will save them the trouble of assaulting the gentleman who has called our attention to the subject.

It has been objected that we have not time to make the investigation before our adjournment. It is true we have not time to bring witnesses from Boston or New York; still, if I am rightly informed, members on this floor can state facts which, if published to the country, would throw light on this transaction. I have good reason to believe gentlemen here could give us much information. Indeed, rumor would lead us to suppose there were members of this body whose pockets were lighter in consequence of the facts stated by the gentleman from Massachusetts, (Mr. Allen). It is also said that other testimony may be obtained, without going beyond the limits of this city. Indeed, it is said, that a gentleman who paid over a part of the money is now among us.

Again, the committee would at once hear the whole story of the Secretary himself. He would have the benefit of vindicating himself in an honorable and legitimate manner before the whole country.

Now, if that functionary and his friends refuse to avail themselves of this opportunity of vindicating his innocence, what will the people think? What will every reflecting person think of such a policy, so incompatible with his innocence?

Under such circumstances, we see his friends denying the accuracy of the statements against him, but refusing to demonstrate his innocence in a manner which must silence all his opponents. And then they turn round and assail the gentleman who stated the facts, and stigmatize him as a *calumniator*.

I would say to those gentlemen, that, should they succeed in rendering the character of my friend as unworthy as his colleague represented it; should they put him down, and destroy his fair fame, it will in no degree relieve the Secretary of State. *Truth* is unchanging, *eternal*, and is the same, whether uttered by a fiend or an angel of light! The voice that pronounces truth, neither changes nor modifies its essence. It is one of the attributes of the "*Eternal Mind*," and is as unchangeable as "*Deity himself*." If that truth be unfavorable to the Secretary of State, no subterfuge, no attacks upon others, nor vilification of those who bring forward these charges, can impair its effects upon him. If the truth be favorable to his innocence, the sooner it shall be understood, the better for him and for the country.

Under the circumstances which surround this question, I give it as the conviction of my own mind, that, if neither the Secretary nor his friends ask an investigation; if they suffer this session of Congress to close, without giving him an opportunity to manifest his innocence — such conduct will constitute in the public mind satisfactory evidence of the accuracy of the statements made by the gentleman from Massachusetts, (Mr. Allen).

The people have a high and important interest in this subject. They have a right to understand the facts. As one of their representatives, I respectfully call on the Secretary of State for his own version of this matter, through a committee of this House, before our session closes. I respectfully ask his friends on this floor to aid us in constituting such a committee; and let us have such facts as they may obtain before this Congress shall dissolve. Sir, let these imputations of venality be removed from the Executive cabinet; let it be purified, not merely from this charge, but from the suspicion of corruption.

THE COMPROMISE MEASURES.*

THE ACTS OF CONGRESS WHICH CONSTITUTE THEM — WHIGS AND DEMOCRATS COMMITTED TO THEIR SUPPORT — THE CHARACTER OF THOSE LAWS — THE CRIME OF SUSTAINING THEM — PROSPECTIVE INCREASE OF SLAVES — CORRESPONDING INCREASE OF EXPENSE IN SUPPORTING THAT INSTITUTION — THE PEOPLE OF THE FREE STATES OUGHT NOT TO BE INVOLVED IN THIS CRIME OR EXPENSE — THEY WILL SEPARATE THEMSELVES FROM THEM.

[On the day of the meeting of Congress, in December, 1851, the whigs met in caucus, and resolved to sustain the "compromise measures." The democrats met also, and laid similar resolutions on the table. At twelve o'clock, the members of all parties met in the hall of representatives to organize. But before a vote was taken for Speaker, a discussion arose upon the subject of slavery. This agitation for suppressing agitation, continued at almost every meeting of the House until the 16th of March. Up to that time, no free soiler had mingled in those debates. On that day, Mr. Hillyer of Georgia, while speaking on the subject, referred distinctly to Mr. Giddings, and assured him that, notwithstanding all the efforts of the anti-slavery men, negroes bore as high a price at the South as they had done at any previous time. Mr. Giddings then obtained the floor to reply, and delivered the following speech.]

MR. CHAIRMAN, — The discussion of these questions, touching slavery, are precipitated upon us at most unpropitious periods. Indeed, it appears difficult for us to extricate ourselves from those exciting subjects which it has been the object of the administration to keep out of view. Thus far, the agitation has been kept up and continued solely by those who denounce agitation. From the commencement of our session, I have en-

* Speech on the Deficiency Bill. Delivered in Committee of the whole House on the state of the Union, March 16, 1852.

deavored, so far as able, to guide the business of this body in the regular and appropriate channels marked out by our predecessors in the earlier and better days of the republic. I endeavored, by the small influence which I could command, to take up the President's message in the first months of the session. On examining that document, all parties could have brought forward their views. Each member would then have had an appropriate opportunity to define his position on the slave question. It would have been discussed; and, when discussed, it would have been laid aside, and we should now have been engaged in the legitimate subject before us; but a different policy has prevailed. The friends of slavery, while professing to do all in their power to silence agitation, are constantly agitating in order to put down agitation. The gentleman from Georgia, (Mr. Hillyer,) who has just taken his seat, professing a horror at agitation, could not resist the temptation to boast of the high price of human flesh in his State, notwithstanding the efforts of our philanthropists in favor of civilization and humanity.

Now, Sir, I will say to him, that I regretted that declaration. This does not appear to be the appropriate place for the expression of such barbarous ideas. It would have been better fitted to the quarter-deck of an African slaver, or to the barracoons of the African coast, than to this forum. But, Sir, I love to see men express the honest emotions of their hearts. The time and place are matters of taste rather than of principle. But while the slave-holders and their allies are deprecating all agitation, they are constantly discussing the subject themselves.

Sir, on the morning of the first day of the present session, one of the great political parties of this body, in caucus assembled, resolved to sustain the compromise measures of the late Congress. The other, assembled in like manner, laid similar resolutions on the table. The support of these measures became a subject of agitation and discussion, before we had proceeded so far as even to ballot for a Speaker; and few days have since passed, in which a portion of the time has not been occupied by such agitation.

The compromise, I understand, to consist of a series of laws enacted by the late Congress, consisting, first, of the law which admits California as a State. The object of that bill being accomplished, no attempt to disturb it will of course be made. Secondly, that which defines the boundaries of Texas. This, too, has accomplished its object, and is therefore settled, and no longer a subject of controversy. Those establishing governments in our territories, that excluding the slave-breeders of Maryland and Virginia from the markets of this district, and that for the recapture of fugitive slaves, are in operation, — subject, like other statutes, to modification or repeal. But it is said, that all questions of slavery were settled by the passage of these laws; that they are to operate as a final *quietus* of the whole slavery agitation.

These ideas were not advanced in this body at the time those bills were passed. Indeed, if my recollection be correct, there was no discussion upon the passage of the fugitive law, or the laws establishing governments in Utah and New Mexico. They were passed under the previous question, without examination. Few members of that Congress, I think, entertained the absurd notion that their action would impose any obligation upon those who should succeed them. I must judge of my own duties, and so must other gentlemen; and the corruptions or follies of the past Congress can never excuse me for violating justice and propriety. Few members from the free States who voted for these measures have survived the storm of popular indignation, brought upon themselves by the passage of those laws. Their successors were sent here for the very purpose of repealing these enactments; and I am of opinion that it will require strong argument to convince them that the reprehensible conduct of their predecessors is to control and govern this Congress.

I am aware that men in high official stations have announced to the country that the slave questions are settled, — that all agitation has ceased. But what are the facts? We see and know that discussion has increased and extended more rapidly since the enactment of those laws than at any former period,

Our elections are very generally made to depend on the slave question. It has placed new and able members in the Senate, and it has driven others into retirement. It has occasioned great changes in this body. Where now are the northern members who advocated these compromise measures? Gone, Sir, most of them to that land of political forgetfulness from which they will never return. What questions entered into the late contest in New Hampshire? What were the issues in Massachusetts at her late autumnal election? What has occasioned the political revolution in Ohio? These elections turned upon the question of slavery. And while on this point, I would ask what has blasted and withered the last political hopes of the present Secretary of State? Every man knows that it is this very question of slavery. While he has been writing letters and making speeches to demonstrate that the slave agitation had ceased, it was operating in the popular mind, was silently stealing his political breath, and has now pronounced the sentence of death to his political hopes. In most of our elections for State and county officers, it is rapidly becoming the principal disturbing element. The people in some portions of the country will not confide in those who are the advocates of freedom, in other parts they will confide in no other.

The institution of slavery has increased its victims, in sixty years, from six hundred thousand to *three millions.*

The slave States, early finding themselves unable to hold their bondmen in subjection, called on the Federal Government to assist them in recovering their fugitives from the Indians. Without discussion, or, so far as we know, without objection, the Executive power effected a treaty providing for the return of fugitive slaves to their masters. This constituted a precedent. Another similar treaty followed. The Indians failed to live up to their stipulations. The sending of their fellow men back to chains and bondage was a barbarity at which they revolted. At length the first Seminole war ensued. Then the second. And untold millions of the people's money was squandered in returning them to bondage.

Slavery and the slave-trade, in this district, was established early in the present century; and in a few years thereafter, Congress established the coastwise slave-trade. As the institution increased, more slave territory was demanded. Louisiana was purchased; then Florida. Texas was annexed. War with Mexico followed, and vast territory was acquired. Three millions slaves could not be held in bondage by the power of the slave States. We were called on to permit the institution to be extended into our territories, — we did so; to give free territory to Texas, — and we did it; to pay her for territory which our arms had conquered, — and we did it; to take upon the nation the burden of capturing and returning fugitive slaves; to appoint officers or slave-catchers in all parts of the free States; to subject the citizens of the North to the expenses and disgrace of chasing down the hunted fugitive, as he flies from a land of chains and sighs and tears. The people of the free States have witnessed these things. They know them to be unconstitutional — violations of their rights — inhuman and barbarous. They, of course, understand that the remedy is with themselves, and they are endeavoring to cast these burdens from them. *And they will do it.*

Looking forward, as all reflecting men must, we see that in sixty years more we shall have twenty millions slaves in the United States, — a greater number than our present white population. Now, Sir, if this Federal Government is to take upon itself the burden and expense of holding that vast number of human beings in bondage; if we are to appoint officers to catch all who shall hereafter attempt to regain their freedom, and to pay the expenses of returning them to bondage; if we are to provide territory for them, and to maintain slave markets for such a population, we shall, at no distant day, find ourselves involved in business which may well occupy our whole time.

For three years past, this body has done very little except to legislate for slavery. But what else can it do, when that institution shall be three times as great as it now is? Sir, this agitation will increase as slavery increases, unless this government shall respect the constitutional rights of the free States, and relieve them from the burdens, the disgrace, and the crimes of that institution.

I have so often discussed the constitutional rights of the several States respecting slavery, that I now feel no disposition to repeat the doctrines on which I base my political action; but I may be permitted to say, that Congress has no more right to bestow its energies for the support of the slavery of the South, than it has to sustain their banks, their railroads, or their system of apprenticeship, or the laws of those States respecting minors, or those which regulate the rights of husband and wife. Slavery, with all these subjects, are matters which each State must regulate for itself, and with which this government has no right to interfere, and with which we cannot interfere, except at the expense of the constitutional rights of the North.

To this view of our constitutional obligations, both the great political parties of the nation are committed. I need only quote the resolution of this House in December, 1838, which is in the following words:

> "That this government is a government of limited powers, and that, by the Constitution of the United States, Congress has no jurisdiction whatever over the institution of slavery in the several States of this Confederacy."

This resolution was introduced by a distinguished democratic member, and was sustained by a vote of one hundred and ninety-eight yeas to six nays; nearly every member of both parties voting for it. The Baltimore platform contains resolutions substantially embracing this doctrine; and now the entire democratic party of the nation stands pledged before the world to maintain this important right of the people of each State, to hold just such an attitude, in regard to slavery, as to them shall appear just and reasonable. Such, too, were the positions of the whig party, up to the passage of the compromise measures, to which I have referred. Indeed, the whigs were more strongly committed to this policy than were the democrats. The *free* democracy at Buffalo adopted this great leading principle of State rights, as the basis of their organization. But the distinction which marked that party as separate from both the others was, and still is, a determination to bring into practice this important doctrine, upon the maintenance of which the liberty and the rights of the people depend; while both the other parties have, practically, deserted their professed and avowed principles.

To the maintenance of the compromise measures as a *final settlement* of the slave question, the President, in his message, exhorts the people to adhere. The whig and the democratic parties are each striving to go beyond the other in their devotion to this plan for silencing all further agitation of the questions of liberty and slavery. The whigs, at the commencement of this Congress, apparently got the start of their competitors *in servility.* They passed resolutions, pledging their party to the support of the compromise. And here, in this hall, certain leading members publicly boasted of the fact, before we had even commenced the election of our officers. I do not say that the whole whig party were present at the caucus, but the act has gone forth as the act of the party. Those individuals who were present, evidently thought that servility to the slave power was the only means of securing political success. But we are given to understand, by leading democrats and by the press of that party, that their national convention will do that which their congressional caucus refused to do, by passing resolutions pledging their party and their candidate to maintain the compromise measures. On the other hand, we are now told that the whigs will play dark; that they will make no avowal of principles, but will select as their standard-bearer a gentleman of acknowledged military renown; will spike his cannon, take the flints from their own muskets, and go forth to the conflict without music, wrapt in the silence of a funeral.

And now, Mr. Chairman, the question comes home to every elector of this nation; to every man, woman, and child, whether bond or free. *What will be the effect of maintaining the compromise?* What the effect of silencing further agitation of the slave question? These are important inquiries, which, as yet, have never been answered; nor have they been discussed in this body.

The first consequence resulting from the support of the compromise, will be to *maintain slavery and the slave-trade in this district.*

As observed on a former occasion, in 1801 Congress passed a law, by which the institution of slavery in this district, with its attendant commerce in human flesh, was continued and established under congressional enactment. That law remains in force to this day. Here, Sir, under our own observation, within our own jurisdiction, by virtue of our own laws, man is degraded, robbed of his intellectual enjoyments, kept in deplorable ignorance, and disrobed of his manhood. By virtue of those laws, he is transformed into a chattel, brutalized, and sold like swine. Here, Sir, men and women are bred for market. Beings in human shape follow the business of rearing boys and girls for sale; and by that business sustain themselves and families, and accumulate wealth.

To sustain the compromise is to sustain this revolting practice, — to give these slave-breeders license and encouragement to pursue an occupation abhorrent to every feeling of Christianity and of decency. Yet, Sir, the whig members of this body, on the first day of our session, resolved, distinctly and emphatically, to support this practice, which is spurned and held in disgust by Mohammedan governments. I wish to be understood, and therefore repeat, that the support of the compromise measures is identified with and inseparable from the support of slave-breeding and slave-dealing, now carried on in this district. To sustain the compromise is to sustain these practices. To prohibit the slave-trade here, would violate this pretended compromise.

It is required, I understand, of each of the democratic candidates for President, that he shall sustain the compromise, and thereby lend his whole official influence to uphold and encourage the breeding and sale of slaves in this district. Unless pledged to this, he cannot receive the support of that party; while the whig candidate is to say nothing about it, to express no opinion in regard to it, to stand neutral upon the subject.* To stand neutral, to do nothing, is to lend an influence in favor of this growing human flesh for the purposes of sale. This traffic in the bodies of females depends on the voice of Congress. If we say stop, it ceases forever; if we are silent, it continues. To remain supinely silent, is to continue it.

Now, I do not think there is a member on this floor from a free State, who dare speak out boldly and say to this House and to the country that he is in favor of this breeding of mankind for the shambles; that he approves of this traffic in God's image. If any member from the free States should do it, I think it would seal his political fate. Yet gentlemen do not hesitate to rise here and declare their intention to support the compromise, thereby lending their entire influence to sustain this business of breeding human cattle for the market. I respectfully ask the gentleman from New York, (Mr. Brooks,) who first publicly swore allegiance to this compromise, whether he is in favor of sustaining this traffic in human flesh? I desire to understand the position of gentlemen, and hope they will stand up manfully and avow their doctrine and their policy. I therefore respectfully ask the gentleman to say what he will do in regard to this slave-trade? Will he vote to continue or to abolish it? I await his answer.

[Mr. Giddings having made a pause, and Mr. Brooks making no answer, Mr. G. proceeded.]

Inasmuch as that gentleman remains silent, I respectfully ask any other northern man who sustains the compromise, to say whether he is willing to sustain this traffic in human flesh? I repeat, that I understand the compromise to embrace this slave-trade; that if we sustain the compromise, we must sustain this traffic. And I desire to see gentlemen stand up, like honest, honorable men, like the representatives of freemen, and avow their sentiments; and if there be a northern member

* This policy was changed at the Baltimore convention of 1852, and the whig platform there adopted, pledged its party to the support of the compromise measures.

who will avow himself in favor of this traffic, in the face of this House and of the country, I desire to hear him, and I await a response.

[No member answering, Mr. Giddings resumed.]

Inasmuch as I have been addressing whigs more particularly, I will also inquire of gentlemen on the other side of the House on this point. I noticed the letter of the gentleman from New Hampshire (Mr. Hibbard) to his constituents, alluded to by the gentleman who preceded me. I understand that he considered himself pledged to support the compromise. I should like to know whether he will sustain the slave-trade in this district?

Mr. Hibbard. I voted for the bill of the last Congress abolishing the slave-trade in the District of Columbia. That vote explains my views on that subject. If the gentleman wishes to know whether I would vote for a bill abolishing slavery in the district, or the trade between the people of the district, I answer that I should vote against it. I am opposed to the further agitation of the subject.

Mr. Giddings. I thank the gentleman for his frankness. I understand him, and the country understands him. I was mistaken in supposing there was no man from a free State who would sustain this commerce in the bodies of women and children. But I like to see a man bold, even in his iniquities. I have more respect for the gentleman who thus says what he will do, than I have for members who refuse to speak, but cast their votes and exert their influence to maintain this slave-trade. I presume the gentleman honestly represents the views of his people, that they approve of this breeding of men and women for market.

But the compromise embraces also the slave-trade upon our southern coast. All are aware that, by the ninth section of the act of 1807, slave-dealers are authorized to carry (under certain regulations) slaves from one port of the United States to another, under the flag of our Union. Men, women, and children are purchased in this district, and in the northern slave States, and placed on board these slave-ships and carried to the torture and premature deaths, which, it is well known, await them upon the cotton and sugar plantations. There they are murdered under a slow torture by the lash of inhuman overseers. It is estimated that twenty thousand human victims are thus annually sacrificed to southern barbarity. The blood of those victims rests upon the members of this body.

We have the power to stop this flood of human gore. But, while these victims toil in chains, and sigh and weep under the tortures to which our law consigns them, members here refuse to examine this subject, refuse to permit the introduction of a bill to repeal this law; but they stand here and exert their utmost powers to revive, to galvanize into life, the old party issues on which they have heretofore contended. They endeavor to close their eyes to notorious facts, and soothe their consciences by occupying their own attention, and that of others, upon the miserable party conflicts, which have no higher motive or aim than to secure the spoils of office to one or the other political party. I judge not for others, but so far as I am myself concerned, I should feel far less guilt were I to strike a stiletto to the heart of a single victim, than I should to exert my influence to sustain that slave-trade, or than I should were I to sit here in silence and permit that infamous traffic to continue without uttering my solemn protest against it.

It is frequently the case, that men and women, apparently doomed to the tortures of the far South by this trade, commit suicide rather than meet its horrors. All will recollect the story of the father, mother, and children confined in a slave prison in a neighboring State, destined to the southern market. The parents, having deliberated upon their situation, and that of their children, took the lives of their offspring, and then sought death by their own hands. Do not we who sit in this hall, and by our silence and inaction continue this slave-trade, share in the guilt of those dark and damning iniquities? Does not the blood of those victims stain our garments? And, when we appear at the bar of final retribution, shall we plead this compromise as a justification for crimes which would strike terror to a savage heart?

I am aware that some of my colleagues have pledged themselves to sustain these compromise measures, thereby upholding this slave-trade. Now, Sir, I wish to inquire of those gentlemen whether they are willing to rise on this floor, and say frankly to the people of our State that they are in favor of supporting this slave-trade? I desire a full and fair understanding on this subject. I wish to understand the position of the whig party of my own State. Will they sustain this coastwise slave-trade, or will they not? or are they to play dark and keep silent? I mean no disrespect to my colleagues of either party. I am solicitous that the people of Ohio should understand how each of their representatives stands on these questions.

The people of the North have been deceived long enough by politicians, who proclaim their intention to sustain the compromise, without descending to particulars and explaining what they mean by such support. Indeed, gentlemen dare not avow their intention to sustain the slave-trade in this district, upon our southern coast, and in our territories, and to maintain the infamous fugitive slave law. It was a truism uttered by my Lord Coke, when he said, "fraud lurketh in generalities." This general expression in favor of sustaining the compromise, embraces all these iniquities; and when a man, either here or elsewhere, avows himself in favor of the compromise measures, he, in substance and fact, avows himself in favor of breeding men and women for market in this district and in our territories, and of prostituting our flag to the protection of a commerce in human flesh. I would be as willing to traffic in God's image, as I would to sustain the owner of yonder slave prison in his accursed vocation, by upholding the law which authorizes him to pursue it. I would as soon vote for Williams, the slave-dealer and owner of yonder barracoon, to the office of President, as I would for any man who sustains him in his execrable commerce. Yet, Sir, strange as it may seem, your presidential candidates of the democratic party appear to think they will have no chance of success, unless they patronize those worse than savage practices, while the whig candidate is to keep silence in regard to them.

But the compromise was intended also to, and, if observed, must, forever, close all hope of excluding slavery or the slave-trade from our territories. On this point, there is no longer uncertainty. The official returns from Utah show that slavery exists there. Servile politicians can no longer deny the fact. The honorable Secretary of State, I think, will not repeat that gigantic falsehood which he put forth in the Senate on the 7th of March, 1850, when he asserted that slavery was "excluded from that country by the laws of God." Indeed, at the time when that attempt to deceive the people of the North was made, it was known here and throughout the country that slavery existed in Utah. The fact had been published some two months previously in most of our leading newspapers; and if the author of that declaration was ignorant of the fact, I think he was the only member of Congress uninformed on that point. Slavery also exists in New Mexico, as we have seen by the public press.

Now if the compromise be sustained, then are these territories to be delivered over to the curse of slavery. The soil which, under Mexican law, had been consecrated to freedom, is now, under American law, to be cursed with the most degrading oppression that exists upon earth; and slave markets are to be established, and men bought and sold, and women made the subjects of purchase and sale, on territory conquered by our arms. To vote for presidential candidates who uphold the compromise, is to vote for slavery, for the slave-trade, with its attendant crimes, to continue in those territories.

Mr. Chairman, when I hear members on this floor rise and proclaim their intention to support the compromise, I understand them to say emphatically, that they have made up their minds to support slavery in this district and in the territories; and to maintain the slave-trade, with all its crimes and guilt, here, and in the territories, and on our southern coast. If gentlemen mean any thing by their declarations, they mean this. When they say the slave question is settled, they intend to be understood by southern men as giving their influence in favor of maintaining slavery and the slave-trade, wherever they now exist under the laws of the Federal Government. I desire the people of the North to understand them. I rose to speak for this purpose. I ever have been, am now, and trust I ever shall be, hostile to political deception and double-dealing. I desire to see gentlemen openly maintain their opinions at home and in this hall. I have no respect for that man who will hold one set of doctrines before the people, and then lend his influence to overthrow them here. The people have no respect for such men; nor do I believe that such men have respect for themselves.

Mr. Chairman, who that held a seat in this hall, during the last and present Congress, could listen to the gentleman from Massachusetts, (Mr. Rantoul,) who spoke so frankly and so ably a few days since, and help comparing that speech with the conduct of a certain honorable member from the same State, (Mr. Winthrop,) who, in the last Congress, fled from the hall in dismay, rather than to give a vote on a pending question, lest that vote would show his constituents and the country his position on the subject of slavery. I care nothing for political names. The people will look at the *man*, and compare him with the *servile*. All men, of whatever party, must approve the course of him who frankly avows his sentiments; and all must pity him who has not the moral courage to give a vote where slavery is involved.

Sir, I would commend to our whig friends the example of the gentleman from the old Bay State, who recently spoke so boldly on this question. I greatly desire to see gentlemen on this side of the hall speak as boldly as he did. I know there are some who hold the same sentiments. I hope they will not hesitate to express them. And I also desire to see all who hold that it is our duty to maintain the compromise, to lend our influence to the support of slavery and of the slave-trade, come forth, and say so manfully, as becomes those who represent an enlightened people. This expression of our honest sentiments is due to the people; it is due to ourselves. We have been pained at exhibitions of tergiversations here; at the exposure of gentlemen who hold to manly sentiments of freedom at home, and when they once get here, turn round and swear allegiance to slavery. There is no excuse for this deception. If our constituents desire us to act for slavery, let us do it openly and boldly. If they wish us to maintain the cause of freedom, let us do it manfully, or resign our seats in this body; but let us not deceive those who honor us with their confidence.

Again, Sir, by maintaining the compromise, we shall uphold the fugitive law, with all its infamous and unconstitutional provisions. The constitutional provisions, in regard to fugitives from labor, have been so often argued by me, that I will not, on the present occasion, repeat my views. I will only say, that a proposition to involve the people of the free States in the expense and disgrace of arresting and imprisoning fugitive slaves, was offered to the Convention that framed the Constitution; that the proposal was objected to; and so strong were the objections, that the member who offered it withdrew it, not daring to take a vote of the Convention. We are all aware that on that occasion no member expressed the opinion that the people of the free States were bound by that instrument, or by any moral or political principle, to participate in the expense or the disgrace of capturing fugitive slaves. We know, historically, that it was the intention of the framers of that instrument to do no more than to secure to the master the same right to pursue and capture his slave in a free State, that he possessed to pursue and capture his horse or mule. We are not to obstruct the master in reclaiming him. This was the view expressed by the Supreme Court, in the case of Prigg *v.* the Commonwealth of Pennsylvania.

This is perfectly consistent with the views of the gentleman from Massachusetts, (Mr. Rantoul,) who, I think, has taken the ground entertained at the time the Constitution was adopted by the people in their several State conventions. But, for the sake of the argument, I will go beyond him, and admit that Congress possesses the right to legislate so far as to secure the owner in the exercise of this right; that we may, by legislation, punish any person who interferes with that privilege, either by making such interference penal, or giving a compensation to the owner. This was the view evidently entertained by the Congress of 1793. They endeavored to effect this object; but there they stopped. They made no attempt to involve this government or the people of the free States in the burdens, expense, and disgrace of catching and sending the trembling fugitive back to bondage.

Here, Sir, at this precise point, I take issue upon the constitutionality of that portion of the law of 1850, which imposes upon this government the burden, expense, and disgrace of chasing down the flying bondman, and sending him back in chains.

Those portions of the law which authorize and require the appointment of officers to grant process for the arrest of slaves; that part which makes it the duty of judges to grant such process; that part which directs marshals and deputy-marshals to arrest the slave; which authorizes them to call on the people to assist in that piratical work; which renders it penal for a man to feed a famishing or starving fugitive, by which he shall be strengthened and enabled to pursue his flight; which involves the people of the free States in the expense of sending the fugitive back, — these provisions are each of them unconstitutional, unjust, abhorrent to the principles and the feelings of the people of the North, inhuman and barbarous.

Mr. Chairman, it has pleased certain gentlemen, on various occasions, to allude to myself and my political friends, as *opposed* to the Constitution. They will not meet our arguments on this point. They recoil from legitimate debate, and seek to misrepresent us by general charges, carefully avoiding every specific point. I now repeat, that, to the full extent to which the law of 1850 involves this government, its officers, and the people of the free States in the burden, the expense, and disgrace of recapturing and returning fugitive slaves, it is *unconstitutional.*

And, Sir, I here desire to understand if there be a member from Ohio, or from any free State east of it, who denies this position? Is there one who holds that his constituents and himself are bound to participate in the expense and crime of chasing slaves? If so, I desire that he will announce the fact. I long to find one such public man; and if there be one here, I wish he would avow it.

No, Mr. Speaker, I blush for my country, when her representatives take shelter behind unmeaning generalities, and refuse to avow their honest sentiments.

If gentlemen intend to support the compromise, they must of course intend to chase down the trembling female, as she flees from the inhumanity of a worse than savage oppressor. And, in the opinion of some men, no candidate is fit for President or other office, unless he is willing thus to degrade himself in view of those who respect the dignity of our race.

Mr. Chairman, we are under neither moral nor political obligations to legislate on the subject. We may leave it as it is, and wash our hands of all its guilt, if we choose.

Mr. Chairman, for sixty years this construction of the Constitution has been acknowledged and observed. During that period, no statesman advanced the revolting doctrine of subjecting the laboring men of the North to the disgrace of catching slaves. The history of our government shows this fact, and coming ages will read it. This law, which takes from the laboring men of the North a portion of their earnings, to pay for catching and returning fugitive slaves, is a thousand times more repugnant to their feelings than was the stamp act, or the tax on tea. Under this law, they are involved in supporting an institution which they detest; compelled to contribute to the commission of crimes abhorrent to humanity. This oppression, this violation of conscience and of their constitutional rights, this tyranny they feel and deprecate. It is impossible that an intelligent, a patriotic people, can long be subjected to such violations of their rights and the rights of humanity.

The conscience of the nation cannot be long separated from its government. It will be in vain for navy-yard chaplains to deliver lectures, and write essays, to convince our people that it is their duty to uphold the slave-trade and the fugitive law. It will be in vain for "ministers of the lower law," to preach up the duty of Christians to commit crimes against God and humanity, at the contemplation of which our very natures revolt. The voice of reason and of conscience will find utterance. The escape of Shadrach at Boston, the just and holy manifestation of the popular mind at Syracuse, the merited death of Gorsuch at Christiana, should teach the advocates of the fugitive law, and of the compromise, that the "higher law" of our natures, dictated by God, and imprinted upon the hearts of a Christian people, will eventually set these barbarous enactments at defiance. The shooting slaves in the mountains of Pennsylvania, the inhuman murder of a fugitive in Indiana, as stated in the public papers, could not fail to be followed by the resistance to which I have referred.

The slaves, as already stated, are to increase; the number of fugitives will of course increase more rapidly. Our railroads, steamboats, and the vast increase of intercommunication between our free and slave States, cannot fail to carry knowledge and intelligence to the whole colored population, North and South. With them there must be hostility and hatred towards their oppressors, whether they be slave-holders, or the allies of slavery. It is a law of the human mind. All honest men must unite in the acknowledgment of their rights. It is our duty to carry intelligence to every being who bears the image of our Creator. Thousands of agencies are at work, bearing information to the oppressed and down-trodden of our land.

By an inscrutable law which pervades the moral world, our very efforts to sustain slavery are converted into the means of its overthrow. The slave-trade in this district is upheld for the purpose of sustaining slavery in our southern States. But where is the reflecting man, who does not see that every slave sold from this city carries with him intelligence of his rights, and becomes a missionary of freedom when transferred South? Why, Sir, in that mournful procession of fifty-two victims of this infamous commerce, taken from this city in 1848, was an individual of unusual intellect. His name was Edmondson. He called on me at different times to aid him in raising money to redeem his sisters. They were, however, sold, and subsequently repurchased by some benevolent people at the East, and are now free. I am told that his whole family were endowed with intellects of the highest order. He was himself, so far as propriety of language, gentlemanly deportment, and intelligence are concerned, not the inferior of gentlemen here, or of the President of the United States. But he was a victim to this slave-trade; and unless he now sleeps in a servile grave, he is preparing the minds of southern slaves for that work which lies before them; a work which, if not accomplished by the voice of truth and justice, will be perfected in blood. That, too, is the case with every fugitive slave who is returned to bondage. The whole northern slave population are becoming intelligent. They read, or hear read, the discussions of our northern press. They learn what is said in this hall. The remarks I am now making will reach the ears of many thousands who are borne down by oppression. To them I say, "All men are created equal;" "you are endowed by your Creator with an inalienable right to liberty;" and I add the words of one of Virginia's noblest sons, "*give me liberty, or give me death.*"

Mr. Chairman, the day of redemption for this people *must come.* No human power can prevent it. All reason, philosophy, and history demonstrate the approach of that day. Look at the British West Indies. There the Africans for centuries labored under the scourge; they clanked their chains; they toiled and wept under the hand of oppression. But they increased in numbers, as do the slaves of our southern States. Their oppressors became enervated by indolence and luxury, while the slaves increased in numbers, in knowledge, and in power, precisely as do the slaves of this land, sarcastically called a land of *freedom.* They became an expense to their government, as do ours. That expense increased, as ours does, until the government had no other course than to purchase them and set them free. The same result is intended by those who now advocate the compromise, which is nothing more nor less than an attempt to throw the burden of abolishing slavery upon this federal government.

41 *

As was well remarked by the gentleman from Massachusetts, (Mr. Rantoul,) it is a *federal* measure, a centralizing measure, calculated to concentrate power in this government, and to destroy the influence of the States. The plan has often been hinted, and this day it is more than hinted, in the leading organ of the administration of this city. This grand scheme will subject the nation to a debt of one billion two hundred million dollars, — a debt one-third greater than that of England, — a debt that to an indefinite period will weigh down the laboring men of this nation, cripple our energies, and bring upon us the oppression, the suffering, which now render the English peasantry the subjects of pity throughout the civilized world. The compromise is but the incipient step to this final consummation. If we are now willing to subject the funds of the nation to sustain this institution, — if we silently submit to this compromise, I assert, without hesitation, that a proposition to relieve ourselves from this burden, by the purchase of the slaves of the nation, will be made at no distant day. I therefore say to the laboring men of the North of all parties, your constitutional rights, your liberties, are in danger. To pay one billion two hundred million dollars would, however, be far less degrading to the northern character than this fugitive law.

While the old party issues have been fading away, the great and overshadowing questions of humanity have been increasing, strengthening, and extending throughout the nation. Justice to the enslaved has entered into all our moral and political controversies. It is discussed in our social circles, our political conventions, and our pulpits. It occupies the attention of our State legislatures and of Congress. Europe sympathizes with us in this great work. The question of man's right to his life and liberty, now occupies the attention of the civilized world. It has thrown Europe into commotion. Her people, her statesmen, are discussing it. It has taken an undying grasp upon the conscience, the judgment of this people. The agitation will go on, until this government shall be redeemed and regenerated from oppression, until the stain of slavery shall be wiped from our national escutcheon.

Let me assure gentlemen that a noble band of patriots, of philanthropists, are now laboring to bring about this "consummation so devoutly to be wished." Upon the broad basis of truth, of justice, of equal rights, of the brotherhood of man and of nations, we have taken our stand. Our numbers are increasing. The effects of our labors are becoming manifest. Our cause is advancing. Our moral and political influence is extending, and our final triumph is certain. We have no hostility to any party. Our contest is waged against oppression in all its forms, — against tyranny and usurpation. Nor will we cease our warfare, until victory, rendered glorious by results that will reach forward to man's remotest existence, shall crown our toils ——

[Here the hammer fell.]

THE BALTIMORE PLATFORMS.*

THEY NOW CONSTITUTE THE POLITICAL CREED OF THEIR PARTIES — THEY AGREE IN PRINCIPLE — NO ISSUE BETWEEN THEM — BOTH THOSE PARTIES ARE COMMITTED TO SUPPORT THE COMPROMISE MEASURES — TO SUPPRESS DISCUSSION — THEIR COMBINED INFLUENCE DEFIED — AGITATION WILL CONTINUE — IT IS AN ELEMENT IN ALL REFORMS — REASONS WHY WHIGS AND DEMOCRATS WISH TO SUPPRESS IT — ITS EFFECT ON PUBLIC MEN — ON PUBLIC MEASURES — THE ORGANIZATION OF THE FREE DEMOCRACY VINDICATED.

[At the Democratic National Convention of 1852, that party resolved to sustain the compromise measures, and to resist all attempts to renew agitation on the slave question. Many of the northern whigs professed opposition to those measures, and declared that their party would not follow the lead of the democrats. They insisted that the free democracy ought to vote with them. Many of the free democracy appeared to waver in their faith, and proposed a union with the whigs; while a portion of the free democratic press appeared to be undecided.

When the Whig Convention assembled, however, that party took position nearly upon the same principles. Many leading friends of liberty appeared to despond; it was a time of darkness and trial to the advocates of humanity; and the author of these speeches felt greatly oppressed by the discouraging circumstances around him; but availed himself of the earliest opportunity, after the close of the whig national convention, to deliver the following speech.]

MR. CHAIRMAN, — The two great political parties of the nation have held their conventions. From all parts of these United States delegates have assembled, deliberated upon their platform of principles, avowed their doctrines, nominated their candidates for President and Vice-President, and now have

---

* Speech on the bill to supply deficiency of appropriations. Delivered in Committee of the whole House on the state of the Union, June 23, 1852.

entered upon the presidential campaign. Preparatory to this state of things many speeches were made here, to which the free democrats, the advocates of liberty, listened with commendable attention. And now I rise to occupy a brief hour in vindicating the position of the party to which I am attached. Often, during the last six months, the question has been propounded to me, whether we should vote for the candidates of the whig or the democratic party? This question, so far as I am concerned, will probably be answered satisfactorily before I take my seat.

It is not my purpose to examine very critically the principles of those parties. It may be sufficient for me to remark, that they agree as to the policy which ought to control our government. The democrats first avowed their doctrines. Their confession of political faith having been two weeks before the public, and being read and duly considered before the assembling of the Whig Convention, that body took issue upon none of the doctrines avowed, nor upon the policy maintained by the democrats.

I notice in some papers that much is said in relation to "internal improvements." The democrats say, "the Constitution does not confer upon the General Government power to commence and carry on a system of internal improvements." Do the whigs take issue on this general and unmeaning assertion? Not at all. They answer, "the Constitution vests in Congress power to open and improve harbors, remove obstructions in navigable rivers, &c., said improvements being in every instance national and general in their character." Now, Sir, no democrat ever did, or ever will, deny this doctrine. So, too, the democrats make assertions about "fostering one branch of industry to the detriment of another;" and the whigs refuse the issue thus tendered, but, in answer, assert doctrines which no democrat denies. The democrats attempt to galvanize into existence the obsolete idea of a national bank, to which the whigs make no reply, admitting by their silence the democratic faith. Neither advances a principle which is denied by the other; they stand on the record in perfect harmony. And no other contest exists than a strife for office, for place, and power; for the spoils, the loaves and fishes.

This is the first time, for many years, that these parties have each put forth an avowal of their doctrines. In the change of times, and the ordinary course of events, they now find themselves in perfect harmony with each other. The day of their contention and disagreement has passed away. The issues which once really existed between them have become obsolete, or surrendered. Their usefulness is at an end, and their history will soon be written. The increase of intelligence, the improvements of the age, demand new organizations and new parties. For years, the old parties have intermingled constantly, and no influence has been able to keep them separate. Here, and throughout the country, some whigs act with the democratic party, and some democrats act with the whig party. For the last four years, there has been no matter of legislation before this body, on which the members have arrayed themselves according to their party character. On every question, a portion of whigs have acted with the democrats, and a portion of democrats have acted with the whigs. Indeed, Sir, those who have watched the proceedings here for the past few years, could not fail to see that slavery constitutes the only question of interest before us.

Notwithstanding the whigs and democrats are acting in perfect harmony with each other, they have united in tendering to the friends of liberty important issues. One of those issues is so extraordinary, that it demands my first attention. The proposition is to stifle all further examination of chattel slavery, and is expressed by the democrats in the following language:

> "*Resolved*, That the democratic party will resist all attempts at renewing, in Congress or out of it, the agitation of the slavery question, under whatever shape or color the attempt may be made."

The whigs resolved, —

> "That . . . we will discountenance all efforts to continue or renew such agitation, whenever, wherever, and however made."

We, Sir, the free democracy, will agitate the subject of slavery, and its correlative, freedom. Here, Sir, is an issue formed between us. I, Sir, am about to agitate this question. I intend to speak plainly of slavery, of its most revolting features. I will endeavor to use no offensive language, but I will talk of the practice followed by men in this district, of purchasing slave women, and then selling their own children into bondage. Now when I do this, the democrats are bound to *resist*, and the whigs to *discountenance*, my efforts. In order that we may start with a perfect understanding of this conflict, I desire to learn the manner in which the democrats will manifest their *resistance*. I am now agitating this subject, and what will you do about it?

Now I hope gentlemen will not feel any particular delicacy in showing their resistance. Do not be alarmed; just stand up here, and now, before the country; show your resistance. Be not afraid, gentlemen; I am less than the stripling of Israel, who went forth to meet Goliath. You stand pledged to *resist* God's truth, — to silence the tongues of freemen. I meet you, and hurl defiance at you and your infamous attempts to stifle the freedom of speech. And now, who speaks for the carrying out of this resolution?

Mr. Chairman, we may "call spirits from the vasty deep," but they will not come.

I repeat to the democrats, — I want to know what you are going to do? You are pledged to *resist*.

The whigs, in their convention, also resolved that they "will discountenance all efforts to continue or renew such agitation, *whenever*, *wherever*, and *however* the attempt may be made." The language of this resolution differs from that of the democracy, but its spirit and object are the same. They intend to suppress the freedom of speech, here and among the people. On this point, the two great parties of the nation have cordially united. A coalition for a more odious purpose could not have been formed. Duty to myself, to this body, and the country, demands an exposure of this conspiracy against the Constitution, against the rights of members here, against the people.

Mr. Chairman, is it contemplated to silence the popular voice in this hall? If that be not the case, these resolutions mean nothing. They are mere "*brutum fulmen*," made for show, to frighten men of weak nerves. They may do very well among doughfaces; but when those parties attempt to frighten free soilers, they should better understand the character of their opponents.

The Constitution has provided "that Congress shall pass no law abridging the freedom of speech." That Constitution we have sworn to support, and by the blood of our ancestors we will maintain it. Slave-holders and doughfaces, whigs and democrats, may combine to trample that sacred instrument under their feet, by suppressing the freedom of speech; but, Sir, they have not the moral, nor the political power, to effect that object.

Agitation or discussion is not only to be put down here, but among the people; they are to have no more anti-slavery meetings; no more free soil conventions; no more sermons in favor of God's law; no more prayers to heaven for the oppressed of our land; the declaration of independence is to be burned; our printing establishments broken up, and our social circles are to speak no more of the rights of all men to enjoy life and liberty. A new political police is to be established, and the American people placed under slave-holding surveillance. Our literary writers are to be driven into exile. But I am paying undeserved attention to these base, these puerile attempts to stifle discussion on the subject of humanity. I hold these resolutions in unutterable contempt. I trample them under my feet.

And here I will leave this ridiculous attempt to ape the despotisms of Europe, by stifling discussion upon the absorbing question of liberty.

I will now proceed to examine the reasons why these resolutions were adopted.

Why should these parties, in their national conventions, take Congress, the Constitution, and people, under their control, and command universal silence upon certain measures? Evidently because investigation and discussion would endanger the future success of their organizations. The very proposition shows that they have no confidence in the people. The man or party who strives to silence discussion, to shut out truth, admits that he is in error. No man or party who feels that he is *right*, hesitates to let the whole truth be known. He feels that he will be vindicated by the development of truth, and his honor will be sustained.

But why should the whigs and democrats unite to keep the truth from the public eye, in regard to the compromise measures ? Why, Sir, the first of those measures was, that establishing territorial government in Utah, admitting slavery and the slave-trade to be established there, on soil consecrated to freedom by Mexican laws. I well know the people were told that slavery could not go there, as it was excluded by the laws of God. Well, Sir, official documents now show that assertion to have been a gigantic falsehood. The census returns show that slavery exists there ; that man is there held in bondage, lashed into subjection by his fellow man ; women are sold like swine in the market, and children made subjects of barter.

Now, Sir, we free democrats insist that slavery and the slave-trade should be excluded from that territory. The motto of our party is, "no slave territory." We do not believe it right thus to deal in God's image. But this law, which permits these outrages, the whigs and democrats say, is a *final* settlement, that these practices may continue in all coming time. But they dare not go before the people admitting this truth; nor dare they deny these facts. To avoid this unpleasant question, they resolve to *resist* every attempt to speak or write upon it. Their only way of escaping from popular odium is to keep truth from the people. Now, Sir, does any democrat or any whig believe that free soilers will vote for any candidate pledged to sustain those revolting practices ? If any one who ever held a place in the free democracy shall cast such a vote, it will be some other man than myself.

Again, Mr. Chairman, the last Congress provided by the law aforesaid, that one or more States may be admitted from said territory, with or without slavery. They were unwilling that the members of the next or any future Congress should judge for themselves, whenever Utah shall ask admission into the Union; and they have made this foolish attempt to dictate the action of this body in future ages. The provision is, that an indefinite number of slave States may be admitted. Of course their political power, under the Constitution, will be in proportion to their slaves. The man in Utah, who buys a slave woman, and raises four bastard children, and holds them as *property*, wields as much political power in that State, as *four* of those educated and intelligent democrats who sit before me add to the political influence of a free State.

Now, Sir, we, the free democracy, are unqualifiedly opposed to this insult to northern dignity. We do not believe that the man who thus sets at defiance God's law, and tramples upon decency, is any better than an educated, intelligent, virtuous freeman of the North. But whigs and democrats say that this disgraceful inequality of political power shall be allowed to the people of Utah, and be maintained. They know that public indignation would be kindled against every man who would thus degrade the people of the North. Our freemen would hurl from place and power such men, if the facts were known to them. They therefore seek to smother the truth; to keep the people in ignorance; and resolve to *resist* agitation, to *discountenance* discussion. They pledge their candidates to carry out this disgraceful combination against liberty and the rights and honor of the free States, and then turn round and ask honest men, those who possess self-respect, to vote for their own disgrace. Sir, free soilers, men of intelligence, will not thus stultify themselves.

The same law, or a law with similar provisions, was enacted in relation to New Mexico. The people of that territory may, if they please, enter into this speculation in human flesh. They may curse that land with bondage also. Whigs and democrats say that this law shall be a *final* settlement of that subject; that slavery and the slave-trade shall not be excluded; and the democrats are to *resist*, and the whigs are to *discountenance*, all discussion in relation to it.

One or more slave States are to be admitted from New Mexico, upon the same terms of degrading inequality to the free States, as those from Utah, and northern men are to submit without discussion. Agitation would, in the words of the whig resolution, endanger the peace of the whig party. They, therefore, deprecate agitation. Well, Sir, the proper meaning of the verb "to deprecate" is to "pray against;" and the whigs will therefore pray against agitation, as it will endanger their peace. Such prayers would simply be "*an abomination;*" they would do no other hurt. And as for the peace of the whig party, I should far rather see it endangered than to see one child sold from its parents, or one woman flogged, or one man degraded.

The motto of free soilers is, "*no more slave States.*" This is our unyielding, determined position. We wage an exterminating warfare against every party, which would extend the curse of human servitude, or increase the slave power in any degree. The democratic party and the whig party unite in the extension of slavery and of the slave power, and then ask the friends of liberty to vote with them! *I shall not do it.*

Another measure of the last Congress was a law entitled "an act *to abolish the slave-trade in the District of Columbia.*" A flagrant falsehood was sent to the people in this title; for the law itself does not profess to abolish the slave-trade in this district, and only excludes from this market the slave-breeders of Maryland and Virginia, leaving the sale of men, women, and children to continue here. And this commerce in the image of God is to go on and continue forever. The whigs say it shall not be disturbed, and the democrats say they too will protect it. These parties have taken position between us and the slave-dealers, and say we shall not discuss the morality of their vocation; that we shall not agitate the cause of freedom.

You, Sir, lately saw an advertisement in the leading whig paper of this district, in these words: "*For sale, a handsome and accomplished lady's maid, aged just sixteen years.*" Except in this city and New Zealand, I do not think any government within the bounds of civilization, would have permitted such an outrage upon decency. I speak of New Zealand, without intending any disrespect to the people of that island by comparing their habits with ours. They buy men and women for food only. The object is far more honorable and Christian-like than that for which the young women of this city are advertised and sold.

Mr. Chairman, General Scott and General Pierce are both pledged to maintain this traffic in the bodies of women, and the advocates of liberty are asked to aid in electing them. Sir, let those parties revel in such moral and political wickedness; let them pledge themselves and their candidates to perpetrate crimes thus revolting to humanity? but I beseech them not to insult honest men, philanthropists, and Christians, by asking them to participate in such transcendent iniquity.

Another of the compromise measures is the fugitive slave law. Of the character of this law, I have spoken on former occasions. Of its unconstitutionality, I think no unprejudiced mind can doubt, who listened to the speech of the gentleman from Massachusetts, (Mr. Rantoul). Of the crimes committed under this law; of the enormities of sending free men into slavery, under color of this law; of the barbarous and savage character of the agents selected by this administration to carry it out, I have no time to speak. I noticed in the address of a clergyman, lately delivered before the Home Missionary Society, a statement that the reverend speaker was in the central parts of Russia during the last summer; that an intelligent nobleman taunted him with the character of this fugitive law, saying: "You can find nothing in the legal code of Russia, nor in the decrees of her emperors, equal to that barbarous law."

No, Sir; I do not believe that any despot of Russia, or of Austria, was ever guilty of putting forth so barbarous a law; yet the democratic party and the whig party tell us that this law shall remain as a *final* settlement of this subject. The whig party, it is true, reserve to themselves the right of making it more barbarous. But it is to remain a law and continue in force while time shall last. Yes, when the "archangel shall descend from heaven with a rainbow upon his head, and placing one foot upon the earth and the other upon the sea, shall swear by Him who liveth forever and ever, that *time shall be no longer*," the dread summons shall find the people of Philadelphia, New York, and Boston, upon the "*qui vive*," hunting for slave mothers, who have fled from all else they hold dear in life, in order to enjoy liberty. The whigs and democrats will be found supporting this law; and when they shall close their eyes upon terrestrial objects, they will be listening to the baying of bloodhounds, the clanking of chains, shrieks of slaves, and the roar of muskets; while the dying groans of slave-catchers, and their wounded associates, the bloodhounds; the last death-sighs of murdered fugitives will all rise from this earth, and mingle with the archangel's voice, as he shall summon us all to the bar of final retribution. I would speak of the future with solemnity; but if men are to carry with them into the coming world their leading traits of character, as some hold, it would seem that their residence in the spirit land will be made vocal with the sighs, and groans, and shrieks of associated beings.

But both parties and their candidates are pledged to maintain this infamous law. And they will "*resist*" and "*discountenance*" all agitation in regard to it, "in Congress or out of it." The policy of silencing discussion upon it must be apparent to every man. The slave-holders demanded the passage of this law, northern doughfaces submitted; some voted for it; others fled the hall. They then knew it would be death to the measure, and political obliteration to themselves, to discuss it; and therefore voted against its discussion, against all agitation, and a *minority* of this body actually passed it under the previous question; and now whigs and democrats say it never shall be discussed. That when our people of the North see a fellow being seized, chained, dragged into slavery, and sold and flogged, they shall say nothing about it, here or elsewhere. That they shall look upon the murdered corpses of fugitives shot down by the agents of government, and may moan over their barbarity, but they must not discuss, they must not agitate the repeal of this law. Well, Sir, I assure them the people will discuss these things.

But it is said, through the whig press, that we cannot repeal this law. I saw this morning an article, in some respects an able article, denouncing this law, in a whig paper, professedly anti-slavery. The editor, however, admitted that the law would not be repealed, perhaps, for twenty years. Sir, the admission shows the author to be unconscious of the people's power.

It is this miserable, cowardly submission to the slave interest, which has degraded northern men. Let the people send to this body forty members whose hearts are devoted to freedom, who have confidence in the power of truth, and this law will be repealed in six weeks. It will be swept from our statute book, and curses deep and loud will rest upon its authors.

The editor to whom I alluded, proposes that we shall contribute from the national funds to pay for fugitives. I could have forgiven the editor for almost any other political offence. What, Sir! are we, the descendants of the Pilgrims, of those who bled at Bunker's Hill, and on every battle field of the Revolution, rather than pay a paltry tax on tea and on stamped paper, are we supinely to become tributary to southern task-masters? When the barbarians of Algiers seized and enslaved our people, we sent an armed force there and slew them, holding them unworthy of a place upon God's footstool. No, Sir; by all the hallowed associations which cluster around the memory of English and American patriots, I avow that I would sooner see every slave-holder of the nation hanged, than to witness the subjugation of northern freemen to such a humiliating condition.

Sir, when it comes to that, I, for one, shall be prepared for the *dernier* resort, — an appeal to the God of battles. I am a man of peace, but am no non-resistant; and I would sooner have the ashes of my hearth slaked in my own blood, and the blood of my children, than submit to such degradation. And here I will take occasion to say, that if this law continues to be enforced, civil war is inevitable. The people will not submit to it. Why, Sir, civil war already exists. At Christiana, civil war, with all the circumstances of force, under color of law — resistance in defence of natural right — bloodshed and death took place. In my own State, a similar transaction occurred; and I assure gentlemen that other instances will occur, if attempts be made to enforce that law. In my own district are many fugitives who have informed their masters where they may be found. These men have become desperate. They desire to see the slave-catchers. They pant for an opportunity to make their oppressors "bite the dust." Sir, send on your commissioners and deputy-marshals and bloodhounds, and I assure you that a civil war will soon be in active progress.

Gentlemen talk of enforcing this law. *It cannot be done.* The people have already passed sentence upon it and upon its authors; and that sentence will be speedily executed. Nor can you stop agitation in regard to it.

Agitation, discussion, and examination are the agents, the instruments, for carrying forward all reforms. The Saviour of man spoke truths boldly. They fell harshly upon the ears of scribes, pharisees, and hypocrites. They denounced him as an agitator; seized, tried, condemned, and crucified him as an agitator. From that day to the present, every man who has boldly avowed truths unwelcome to the ears of despots, tyrants, and the oppressors of our race, have been denounced as agitators. Jefferson, in the Declaration of American Independence; Samuel Adams, in the Continental Congress; Washington, on the battle field, were "distinguished agitators;" John Quincy Adams, while in this hall, for years maintained and defended, with inimitable powers, the right of petition, and was denounced throughout the country as an agitator. He was arraigned at the bar of this House, and tried as an agitator. Every member of this body who defends the rights of the people, is denounced as an agitator. To me, these epithets have lost their terrors.

For hundreds and for thousands of years the instruction and elevation of mankind have been carried forward by agitation. By means of it, tyrants and despots have been driven from power, and popular rights have been extorted from barbarous rulers. Without agitation, no people ever gained their rights, or retained them, after they had been extorted from their oppressors. Now, suddenly, to prevent the progress of liberty, whigs and democrats unite to suppress this element in all reforms. They declare that discussion shall cease, and the slave-trade and slavery shall continue forever, and the fugitive law shall be rendered perpetual.

Mr. Chairman, well do I recollect the evening after these laws had been passed. I then viewed them in all their horrors. I saw the degradation to which the people of the free States were subjected, — the crimes which we had authorized. My heart sunk within me, as I contemplated the public men who had aimed this blow at liberty.

Sir, on yonder avenue I heard the songs of drunken revelry and the insane shout; bonfires lighted up the heavens, and the thunder of cannon told the immoderate joy of slave-holders, slave-breeders, doughfaces, and dealers in human flesh. Their gratitude naturally flowed out to those most instrumental in the passage of these laws, to which I have alluded, called the compromise and fugitive law. In the fulness of their hearts and stomachs, they repaired to the dwelling of the Secretary of State, and called on him for a speech. He readily complied, commencing his congratulations by saying, "Now is the winter of our discontent made glorious summer." He then informed the motley crew around him that this question of slavery was settled, and that they were no more to be troubled with agitation.

Sir, from that day up to the close of the Baltimore Convention, he wrote letters and made speeches declaring and avowing that agitation had ceased; assuring the country in substance that the slave-trade in this district and in our territories would go on undisturbed. That oppression here and in the territories now had nothing to fear. The whole energies of the government were put forth to enforce the fugitive law; but they generally proved abortive. Every possible exertion was made in Boston and Philadelphia to convict those charged with obstructing its execution; but all failed. The blood of Gorsuch, a piratical slave-catcher, who fell at Christiana, is unavenged, in spite of the public treasure and Executive influence put forth to obtain a conviction of those who righteously slew him. The patriots who assisted Shadrach to escape the fangs of the Boston bloodhounds, yet laugh to scorn your infamous law. At Syracuse, at Rochester, and a hundred other places, the friends of liberty rejoice at the impotency of this law, although it has thus far been backed up by Executive power. These defeats of the Executive, and of this enactment, libellously called a *law*, have resulted from *agitation ;* and well may slave-catchers and doughfaces now seek to stifle discussion, to silence the people.

Sir, while these things were going forward, the Secretary of State was looking for, and expecting a return for the services he had rendered the slave power. The presidential chair and White House was looked to as the reward for his treason to God and humanity. But there again agitation had done its work. All reflecting men knew that he could receive in the whole Union scarcely twenty electoral votes. And when the Baltimore Convention passed upon his claims, not a southern vote was cast for him. Chagrined, mortified, and discontented, he will soon retire, and history will record the *truth* concerning him and us. But, Sir, I will not aggravate the chills of political death, nor call to mind the sins which must "sit heavy on his soul," when a darker night shall close around him.

Agitation has brought to the scaffold another conspicuous victim. The President of these United States lent his whole influence to the promotion of those compromise measures to which I have alluded. His devotion to the slave power has been openly and boldly avowed. Steadily and basely has he prostituted the influence and power of his office to the purpose of supporting slavery, oppression, and crime. At the Baltimore Convention, the slave-holders, I believe, were unanimously in his favor. But northern delegates dared not support him. Agitation had informed the people of his having deserted their cause, and gone over to the enemies of freedom. The popular voice of the North had pronounced his doom; he was cast aside; the political grave yawns for him; and on the 3d of March he will be laid in it. Were I to write the epitaphs of these men, I would inscribe upon their tombs, "killed by agitation." Think you not that these men and their party have cause for their hostility to discussion — to the dissemination of truth?

The democrats, also, have cause for opposing agitation. Their ablest, their most experienced statesmen, have fallen victims to it. General Cass, the man who of all their candidates was best qualified for the presidency, in an evil hour signed a letter pledging himself to these compromise measures. It proved his political death-warrant. When, too late, he found that the people of the North would sustain no man who had thus pledged his influence to measures which the popular voice has condemned as *barbarous*, as disgraceful to our nation. At the Baltimore Convention his friends bore him to his political grave; and

> "Not a drum was heard, nor a funeral note,"

as they quietly deposited his remains in their final resting-place; Such, too, was the fate of Pennsylvania's favorite statesman. He had long been anxious to serve the slave interest. He pledged himself in the most unqualified manner to maintain these laws as a perpetual settlement of the slave question. But he, too, was cast aside at an advanced age, when he can look for no further preferment. *These men all died of "eating southern dirt."*

Circumstances appear to render it indelicate for me to speak of other candidates of the democratic party. Yet I would remind them all of the fate which must await those public men who prove false to liberty and humanity.* I assure them and the country that agitation will continue and increase until the people of the free States shall be relieved from all participation in the disgrace and crimes of slavery.

But this opposition to freedom, so dominant in the whig and democratic parties, led to the organization of the friends of liberty into a separate political party in 1848. The extraordinary circumstances which then surrounded the advocates of

---

* Senators Houston and Douglas, who had been candidates for nomination, were present, listening to this speech.

freedom, called together a mighty host. On the memorable ninth of August of that year, fifty thousand freemen met in solemn convocation. There were men of distinction, men of intellect, statesmen, and philanthropists. They were conscious of the responsibility resting upon them. In framing a confession of their political faith, they laid its foundations upon the enduring, eternal principles of justice. The equal right of all men to enjoy life, liberty, and happiness, constitutes the basis of our creed; and the next article asserts "that governments are constituted among men to *secure these rights*." All our action under the Constitution should be to protect the life and liberty of every human being within our exclusive jurisdiction. That our legislative powers in this district, on the high seas, in our territories, should be exerted to secure every being who bears God's image, in his right to life and liberty, instead of establishing and sustaining oppression and slavery. Here, Sir, at this point, an issue between us and the other parties, deep and broad, is presented. And from this position the friends of humanity will never depart.

It is an important fact, that neither the whig nor the democratic party profess to pay any respect or attention to moral principles in their legislation. By their practice they deny the responsibility of human action, so far as politics are concerned. They hold that members of this body may pass laws which deprive our fellow men of life or liberty, and that those who enact such laws are not morally guilty of enslaving or murdering their fellow men. We, Sir, hold that those who enacted the fugitive slave law are as guilty in the sight of God and good men, as they would be were they themselves to seize a white man, place irons upon his limbs, and send him to slavery without law. In such crimes, we, the advocates of freedom, will not participate. One of our resolutions adopted at Buffalo was in these words:

"*Resolved*, That it is the duty of the Federal Government to relieve itself from all responsibility for the existence or continuance of slavery, wherever it possesses constitutional authority to legislate on that subject."

This resolution is in direct and unqualified conflict with the entire policy of the whig and democratic parties relative to slavery. It is in conflict with the platforms of those parties, to which I have called attention. Basing our whole political action upon the plainest principles of justice, liberty, and humanity, we challenge examination, discussion, *agitation*. We seek to cover up nothing, to keep nothing from the popular ear. The more you examine and discuss our doctrines and policy, the better are we pleased.

We, Sir, would drive the slave question from discussion in this hall. It never had a constitutional existence here. Separate this government from all interference with slavery; let the federal power wash its hands of that institution; let us purify ourselves from its contagion; leave it with the States, which alone have the power to sustain it, — then, Sir, will agitation cease in regard to it here; then we shall have nothing to do with it, our time will no more be occupied with it; and, like a band of freemen we can meet here, legislate for freedom, for the prosperity, the improvement of mankind, for the elevation of our race.

Mr. Chairman, I have served in this hall some fifteen years. During that period, I think at least two-thirds of the time of this body has been occupied by the subject of slavery, and other matters connected with that institution. For the last three years, we can scarcely be said to have done anything else but discuss and legislate for slavery. This, Sir, is all wrong. Slavery is a local institution, existing only in a portion of the States. The attempt to nationalize it, is unwarranted and unconstitutional. To do this, is now the object of both the whig and democratic parties. Against these attempts, we, the free democracy, wage unceasing, undying, unyielding hostility. This war we shall never give up. We shall never lay aside our arms until victory shall crown our efforts, — until this government shall be redeemed and disenthralled from the foul stain of chattel slavery. Against oppression, in all its forms, and in all places, we have sworn eternal hostility. Our sympathy for suffering humanity is broad as creation, reaching to all climes, and embracing all who bear the image of our Creator. To persecuted Hungary we tender the assurance that "we feel for those in bonds as bound with them." On this subject, the democrats have spoken oracularly.

The whigs talk about "entangling alliances, and standing on foreign soil;" but they dare not take distinct issue on the propriety of exerting our moral power, our political influence, to maintain the law of nations. Substantially, both whigs and democrats are opposed to us on this subject. They would permit Russia or Austria to swallow up Hungary, without any protest or expression of our disapprobation. We sympathize with the oppressed of all nations; and we, the free democracy, literally constitute the party of progress. At Buffalo, we adopted the policy of "*cheap postage for the people;*" and inscribed it upon our banner, and unfurled it to the breeze. We foresaw the advantages of increasing the facilities of communication among the masses, and determined to confer upon our country these benefits, while whigs and democrats were too timid to take a position either for or against it.

I am aware that we are often charged with being men of one idea, — indeed, we are sometimes called the *party* of one idea, — and I refer to these facts to vindicate ourselves from that charge. We dared go where neither of those parties were willing to follow us, nor to oppose us; and in less than three years the correctness of our position has been acknowledged before the country.

"Lands for the poor, homes for the destitute," free of expense to all who will immigrate to the West, was another article in our political creed. To this policy, neither the whig nor democratic party dared express their consent; nor dared they oppose it. At this session, a bill carrying out our views on this subject, passed this body by a vote of nearly two to one. The Senate will doubtless comply with the popular will of the nation, by passing this measure of benevolence, which will cause thousands of hearts to swell with gratitude and joy. Sir, the free democracy believe that governments were constituted to protect, elevate, and render our race, our whole race, more happy. That it is our duty as statesmen, as philanthropists, as

Christians, so far as we have constitutional power, "to raise up the bowed down," "to exalt the humble," "to inform the ignorant," "to comfort the distressed," and increase the prosperity and happiness of all who come within the sphere of our political, our moral, or our religious influence. Of course, we are hostile to those compromise measures which the whigs and democrats are pledged to sustain.

In 1848, nearly three hundred thousand freemen cast their votes for our presidential candidate. Since that period, our moral and political power has greatly increased. Probably one third of the members on this floor are indebted to men who sympathize with us for their seats, and many were elected solely and entirely upon our principles. Three members of the Senate were elected as free democrats, while others are partially indebted to the votes of the free democracy. In several State legislatures we hold the balance of power; but this is but little evidence of the rapidity with which our principles are extending. Our progress is marked by the change of feeling towards our doctrines in both the other parties; their hostility is diminishing daily; they are becoming acquainted with our views, and, of course, respect our motives. In all elections now, throughout most of the free States, candidates are selected whose doctrines and principles are not obnoxious to us. The cloud which, in 1848, was like unto a man's hand in size, has now overspread the whole North, and will soon extend over the nation, and finally over the world. But it is said that those friends in the State of New York, who came from the democratic party, have returned to it. I deeply feel and deplore this fact. I loved and honored them, — I still respect them; but I must say that, in my judgment, they have erred in departing from us. I, however, will not judge them; to their own masters they stand or fall. Had they continued with us, there is, in my opinion, no doubt that we should, in November next, have effected the election of a President favorable to our views. That they are friends of liberty, I know; that they will sustain the doctrines laid down in the democratic confession of faith, or vote for Pierce and King under the circumstances attending their nomination, I do not believe. The members of our party, generally, entered upon an organization with a deep feeling and conviction that such an organization was necessary. Time and experience has confirmed us in that opinion. I have stated the basis of our doctrines; they are permanent, *eternal* as God himself. While standing on those principles, *we cannot be wrong.* The political and moral regeneration of our country, the entire reformation of this government from its practice of sustaining oppression, slavery, and crime, is our object. To effect this great and holy purpose, must require time and perseverance. In what I have said and done on these questions, I have but reflected the sentiments and feelings of those I represent, — indeed, among them are many, very many, "older and *better* soldiers" than myself. That people, Sir, will stand firmly, steadfast, and immovable, upon the doctrines and the organization which they have adopted.

I am aware of the arguments so often used to persuade free soilers to vote for this or that man, for this or that party, in order to gain some supposed temporary advantage. But, Sir, we organized for the maintenance of doctrines important not merely to the people of a township, a county, or a State, but to *man* wherever he is found, — important not merely to-day, at this election, or next year, but *in all coming time.* Can we leave such a position, to unite with either of the other parties, in order to elect this or that man to office, while he stands pledged to maintain slavery and the slave-trade in this district and in our territories, — to continue the infamous fugitive law, — to uphold and support all these measures as a *final* settlement of the subjects to which they refer, and to discountenance all examination, discussion, or agitation, as to the propriety of these measures? Sir, were we to unite with either party to elect a President thus pledged, we should lose our own self-respect, — we should lose the respect and confidence of the world. Politically, Sir, we are "a city set upon an hill, which cannot be hid." Throughout the country, our influence is felt. In this hall we wield a moral power far beyond our numbers. Let no man charge me with indelicacy when I assert, that the free soilers of this body exert all the influence to which their numbers entitle them. Whigs and democrats have confidence that we shall in all cases be guided by judgment, by reason and justice, and not by the paltry considerations of *party*.

The effect has been most salutary. Ten years since, no man here dared separate from his party. No matter what was the subject, or his own judgment, every member was compelled to fall into line and vote with his party leaders. Free soilers have set an example here of independence. The commencement of our trials on this subject was severe. We were frowned upon, vilified, and denounced; but, thank God, we had the firmness to bide our time, and now for years many whigs and democrats have followed our example, and dared to vote as their judgments and consciences dictated. In short, Sir, here party lines upon most subjects of legislation have become obliterated. This of itself constitutes a great reform.

At Baltimore, a portion of the whig party contended manfully against committing themselves to the outrages and crimes of the fugitive law and compromise measures. In that respect, they did more than the democrats. My sympathies, and the sympathies of our party, and of all good men were with them.

And had the anti-slavery whigs in this House and the Senate, promptly and energetically met the supercilious pretensions of the slave power with decision and firmness, I have little doubt they would have inspired a feeling at Baltimore which would have repudiated a platform that has stamped indelible disgrace upon their party. In this hall, the democrats have sustained the constitutional rights of the free States more ably and faithfully than the whigs have during the present session.

But I am aware that a strong effort is making to induce our free democracy to sustain the whig candidate at the coming election. With the gentleman nominated, I have long been acquainted. To him nor to the democratic nominee have I any personal objection; but, if elected, he is pledged to maintain the outrages, the revolting crimes, pertaining to the compromise measures and fugitive slave law, to which I have called attention, — to render them perpetual, so far as he may be able, — to prevent all discussion relating to them. To vote for him is to vote for this policy, — to identify ourselves in favor of the avowed doctrines which he is pledged to support, — to give proof by our votes that we approve the platform on which he stands. But, Sir, why vote for Scott in preference to Pierce?

The doctrines of the whig party, as I have shown, pledge them and their candidate to maintain slavery; the breeding of slaves for market; the sale of women in this district and in the territories; to uphold the fugitive law in all coming time; to admit as many slave States as shall apply from New Mexico and Utah, and to silence discussion on all these subjects. This is as far, I think, as human depravity can go. If the democratic party has dived deeper into moral and political putridity, some archangel fallen must have penned their confession of faith. If there be such a distinction, it can only be discovered by a refinement of casuistry too intricate for honest minds to exert. Sir, suppose there were a shade of distinction in the depths of depravity to which these parties have descended, does it become *men*, — *free* men, — men of moral principle, of political integrity, — to be straining their visions and using intellectual microscopes to discover that shade of moral darkness? No, Sir; let every man who feels that he has a country to save, a character to sustain, — that he owes a duty to mankind and to God, — come forward at once, and wage a bold and exterminating war against these doctrines, so abhorrent to freedom and humanity.

But it is said that the democratic party, if defeated again by the anti-slavery sentiment, as they were in 1848, will disband, and the masses will then unite with us in support of justice, truth, and liberty. The defeat of the democratic party might disband them, and it might not. There is no certainty on that point. If we were to unite with the whigs, we might, or we might not, defeat the democrats. If we were to try the experiment and fail, whigs and democrats would despise us. We should despise ourselves. If we should succeed, we should become identified with the whig party, and swallowed up by it. In every aspect in which I can view such a policy, we must lose the moral power which we possess. Standing upon elevated principles, — professing, avowing, and proclaiming the political gospel which we present to the people, — we cannot descend to mingle in such a contest without a sacrifice of that moral and political influence which now commands the respect of all honest men and of our own consciences.

Mr. Chairman, I know not the course which the people whom I represent will pursue. From the past only, can I judge of their future action. A residence of half a century among them has given me some knowledge of their character. Their past action on this subject is "known and read of all men."

That people do their own thinking and their own voting. They know their rights, and will maintain them, so far as moral and political action on their part will do it. They are at all times prepared to discharge their duty. Sir, in 1848, there was more political effort made to induce our friends there to vote for the present Executive, than was ever put forth on any other occasion. Distinguished gentlemen from other States, of great ability, and of anti-slavery sentiments, were imported, to show us the propriety of voting for men who feared to speak in favor of free principles. But those efforts failed, and few men can now be found who will admit that they ever cast a vote for the present Executive — a man who has prostituted the power of his office to the support of slavery and crime. Now they are to be called on to vote for men openly pledged and committed to the work of eternizing slavery and the slave-trade, and the fugitive law. I will leave the free democracy of the Reserve to speak for themselves. They have always done that.

Sir, we are in the midst of a revolution. The two great parties are striving to convert this free government into a slaveholding, a slave-breeding republic. Those powers which were delegated to secure liberty, are now exerted to overthrow freedom and the Constitution. It becomes every patriot, every lover of freedom, every Christian, every man, to stand forth in defence of popular rights, in defence of the rights of the free States, of the institutions under which we live, in defence of our national character.

Sir, I am getting old, — the infirmities of age are coming upon me. I must soon leave the scenes with which I am surrounded. It is uncertain whether I shall again address this body; but one thing I ask, — that friends and foes, here and elsewhere, in this and in coming time, shall understand that, whether in public or in private, by the wayside or the fireside, in life or in death, I oppose, denounce, and repudiate, the efforts now put forth to involve the people of the free States in the support of slavery, of the slave-trade, and their attendant crimes.

www.ingramcontent.com/pod-product-compliance
Lightning Source LLC
LaVergne TN
LVHW021309110826
845150LV00003B/535

* 9 7 8 1 4 2 5 5 5 8 7 8 9 *